Other books by Gail Burkett

Gifts from the Elders: Girls' Path to Womanhood (2004)

Girls' Ceremonies of Nine Passages, Kindle Edition (2013)

Soul Stories: Nine Passages of Initiation (2015)

A guide to celebrate life
purr-fect
Gail Burkett

The Life Spiral

NINE PASSAGES
for Women and Girls
Ceremonies and Stories of Transformation

Gail Burkett, PhD, author

Janis Monaco Clark, editor

Laura Wahl, designer

TURTLE
MOON
PUBLISHING

Editor Extraordinaire: Janis Monaco Clark
Genius Book Design & Illustrations: Laura Wahl
Illustration credit: Laura Wahl
Photos credit: Kay Walker, Mason White, Gail Burkett, Arianna Husband, Judith Lay.
The Life Spiral illustration: Jean Herzel

Burkett, Gail

Nine Passages for Women and Girls: Ceremonies and Stories of Transformation
(2016) 978-0-9913590-2- 8

Boxed set

Nine Passages for Women and Girls
Ceremonies and Stories of Transformation

Children [Birth, Middle Child, First Blood]
Adolescents [First Blood, First Flight, Womanhood Bloom]
Adults [Womanhood Bloom, Deepening Womanhood, Elder Encore]
Elders [Elder Encore, Spiritual Elder, Death]

Categories: Rites of Passage, Women's Studies, Ritual, Mentoring, Developmental Psychology, Transformation, Women's Spirituality, Child Development, Anthropology

Dedication

Seriously, this book is dedicated to Mentors.

All Mentors.

Mentoring is the way forward and the change we need to see.

To help me understand something more about myself,

I am grateful to the Mentor Spirit I received from these glorious teachers:

Sharon Sweet, Rick Medrick, Susan Morgan, and Joe Meeker,

I thank you.

Honoring Recent Teachers

Clarissa Pinkola Estés said in her wonderful audio, *How to be an Elder,*

"We all know how to do Rites of Passage, it comes from inherent knowledge of ritual."

In *The Water of Life: Initiation and the Tempering of the Soul,* Michael Meade said,

"Initiation involves an increase in knowledge, especially self-knowledge, as well as a loss of innocence."

Expressed so well in this excerpt offered by **Bill Plotkin** in *Nature & the Human Soul: Cultivating Wholeness and Community in a Fragmented World* © 2008

"A rite of Passage, after all — even the most effective and brilliantly designed ceremony — rarely causes a shift from one distinct stage of life to the next. Much more often rites of Passage only confirm or celebrate a life transition that has already (although recently) been achieved by the individual, accomplished through years of steady developmental progress.

What happens between life Passages is considerably more important to the process of maturation than are the Passages themselves (and their associated rites). The primary work of maturing takes place gradually every day as we apply ourselves to the developmental tasks of our current life stage. Children and adolescents need help with these tasks — help from mature adults. And that's precisely where we are failing our youth."

Helen M. Luke found her way into my heart from one of the women journeying through *Soul Stories.* I am grateful for this gift from Laurie Evans and the gift of Helen Luke's wisdom.

"Each of us, as we journey through life, has the opportunity to find and to give his or her unique gift. Whether this gift is quiet or small in the eyes of the world does not matter at all, not at all; it is through the finding and the giving that we may come to know the joy that lies at the center of both the dark times and the light."

CONTENTS

Invitation

A little prayer: Please guide me most benevolent spirit world, angels and help-er-beings. Please guide me animal, plant, bird, and fish kingdoms. Celebrating your wild heritage, I offer my gratitude for sightings, visitations, and the blessing of your company seen through tracks and signs. Please guide me friends, relations, and family, I owe my life and breath to you. I give thanks for all life not mentioned, seen and unseen, the standing and fallen trees, the mycelium running between as the virtual support systems of our Great Mother Earth. I feel the blessed support from our Moon and Sun.

Rites of Passage or Passage Rituals, what does this mean? A natural intersection where an internal biological clock meets a spiritual longing, this is often the case. After one round of seasons, everything feels different. With a language that is slowly returning to the culture, welcome each biological change and make a ceremony that marks your maturity; release old patterns of behavior so that new ones may find room to grow. Ultimately, Passage ceremonies celebrate accumulated change and growth. By marking the expansion of your body, mind, and spirit, personal evolution of your inner Genius is sparked to seek more of life—experiences, curiosities, and spiritual answers. A Rites of Passage ceremony is the springboard for a new quest on a timeline marked by your Soul. See the glossary, here.[1]

For the longest time, I held this question: How can we bring Rites of

Passage back to the culture? It seems like such a simple question: Nothing is further from the truth, except there is hope.

The language has disappeared, so that is a big consideration. Fluency will take some time. Biological changes common to all people offer an entrance, these doorways belong to everyone. I love to focus a light on the generations who missed Passage Rituals, parents and grandparents: Through some catalyst of change, we did transform, we did have a personal experience with initiation. Generally, no one witnessed our change so no one else benefited and very often the catalyst came without invitation and we would not wish a repeat. Often ritual was completely missing. Rites of Passage ceremonies smooths out all this roughness and makes change a welcome event.

There is a way to harmonize with the Soul who guides us, by seeking change consciously, by listening for our original instructions, and by meeting a transformation with a ritual. This is the way of change. When we face the inevitably of change, cross a Threshold, and greet the tender new stage of life, change will feel harmonious. When we accept that maturity is desirable, it can happen by honoring our stories and by releasing our attachment to the past. With the Spiral of Life metaphor, we can know ourselves better and create a clearer vision for the journey ahead. When Passage Rituals are shared inter-generationally, the bridge rises naturally between the generations. I feel like a pioneering girl and woman and an Elder simultaneously.

The Life Spiral

Before we can talk about the Rites for each Passage, we must find our place. I am in the small space between Elder Encore and Spiritual Elder, a place of growth and excitement, a place of mystery and hope. I have carefully danced myself through a review of all of my stages which I personally consider an Elder's initiation; I unearthed the catalysts of change that created each Threshold and how new challenges were metaphorically represented by cobblestones.

I invite you to gaze into this Spiral and find yourself; find the members of your clan. I invite you to become innovative with me. There are stories to be told and ceremonies to be made.[2]

As I was taught about Rites of Passage, through academic circles, a framework was provided which includes hearing a call from one's Soul, separating from one's ordinary life, facing and crossing a Threshold to wander alone in the wilderness in a seeking manner, and returning to a community ceremony of welcome and integration.[3] What I call a portal is a liminal space of mystery, often created by ritual ceremony, a blended space for mind, body, and Soul to discover a new agreement. In cosmic terms, this may take a year, in women's terms, 13 Moons.

I am one of many now lifting up Rites of Passage for the culture because it's needed. I bow to the many others, gathered under one umbrella called Youth Passageways, all those bright thinkers with strong hearts are bringing Passage ceremonies to young people. This large group serves as the answer to my original question.[4]

Nine Passages is a book of stories with nine initiation ceremonies, including Birth and Death. It's a book of mentoring and offers many tools for moving a body with its Soul through natural biological changes. Each of the nine stages of development creates a seismic change longing to be noticed. Initiations are Soul-work that assists one's body coming more and more into consciousness of itself, Passage by Passage. Initiation ceremonies evolve the sense of self for all who attend and all who pay attention. This is a movement for Evolutionaries ™.

Those who feel open to biological maturity as their birthright will resonate as kindred spirits. Anyone seeking personal evolution will resonate and will relish finding doorways. These women will not hesitate. Many Mothers will resonate with Rites of Passage offering the gift of maturity to their offspring even if they did not receive such celebrations. Perhaps out of a deeper knowing than even gentle kindness, seekers and Mothers will open this door for others.

Having enough research in me to satisfy me, I wish to show respect to the Medicine Wheel for bringing me through the past two decades. These ancient teachings have never remained buried for long, in fact, Earth Mother presenting her seasons in harmony with the Sun helps the Wheel remain eternal.

My muse has been nourished by an unimaginably long lineage of Grandmother Spirits who have watched over this work. Those nearlings woke me before dawn thousands of mornings to prepare me for the day when I could finally write this introduction.

With curiosity and readiness, with a global view and pregnant with these teachings, I have lived the challenge of personal development and of Passage ceremonies. Response to the urge to personally grow and evolve rises with each person's longing for fulfillment. I denied hearing the call until the pain was unbearable. Then, one dawn a decade after my Womanhood Bloom, a long line of elk walked past my bedroom window. The events that followed that miracle woke me up. Along such a circuitous route, I have learned to observe a reverence for our Great Mother, sweet Earth listens and holds and encourages. My preparation to create and now offer this work has come through long talks with my Council of Elders, women who have stepped up to offer their piece for this puzzle. Every Soul like the one who lives and breathes inside of you, holds the whole of this developmental span of life. Your inner circle is your tribe and your Village. Allow ceremony to join you together, with your soul, like a sacred marriage.

Mothers continue to give birth to both sexes of babies and in equal numbers. I do not plan a gender translation for this book at this time, but the biological changes may be interpreted. I grew from a baby girl into a big girl and finally a woman becoming and suddenly an Elder. It is a natural occurring phenomenon that I would write a book for women and our girls.

Best wishes on raising your children and raising yourselves.

First of Summer 2016, this comes with love, Gail Burkett

NOTES FOR INVITATION

1   Glossary for the Language of Passages:

Rites of Passage is time away from normal or mundane life, a time to be with spirit and Soul, listening for new instructions. In this liminal time, an altered state of being brings about true change.

An internal biological clock bundles an accumulation of life experiences which encourages a Threshold to appear. Allow resistance to fall away. Threshold is the moment, often an actual doorway, where you agree that change is unavoidable and desirable.

Spiritual longing is individually interpreted and usually most pronounced in silence.

Often an initiate needs 13 Moons to feel a new normal. This allows for comparison of old and new and for integration. After one round of seasons, everything feels different. Because we are women, change comes with our Moon cycles.

Biological changes occur under the science of ontology, unique to each person. Many psychologists use a 7 year mark, but ontology is not so rigid; e.g., my First Blood came at 13.5 and my Last Blood happened at 45.5.

Ceremony may be the trickiest of these terms, but gather a circle of friends (because they benefit), light candles on an altar, include meaningful symbolic treasures, sing songs, speak from your heart: What is inviting change, how do you feel, what do you hope for? You may be surprised to hear what you have to share; others in the circle may find their own longing to mark change.

Maturity is the most tested of any cultural measurement. Arrested development is extensive because communities have lost the habit of noticing and applauding growth and change.

Soul and quest, these terms are related and come with adolescent longings. If life is as luscious as your dreams, those longings turn into Adult and then Elder desires without ceasing.

2   If you have never experienced Rites of Passage for yourself, a great journey of a year may seem alluring. I wrote *Soul Stories: Nine Passages of Initiation* as an invitation for women over 30, often over 60, to find their change agents and experience a celebration of the many changes throughout their lives. I wish to honor Elders, circles of Elders, who will flourish with ceremonies in their years ahead.

3   Those early teachers included Arnold van Gennep whose *Rites of Passage* (1960) was posthumously published after his anthropological discoveries and treatise in 1905; Joseph Campbell's major works inspired the anthology *A Hero's Journey*, (2014, 3rd Edition); Mircea Eliade, *Rites and Symbols of Initiation: The Mysteries of Birth and Rebirth* (1994); Michael Meade, *The Water of Life: Initiation and the Tempering of the Soul;* Martin Prechtel, *Long Life, Honey in the Heart* (2004), and one I have yet to study deeply, Bill Plotkin. These men all stand out as too important to not mention.

4   I am very pleased to stand with others who wish to uplift Rites of Passage ceremonies. Youth Passageways (.org) follows good council. So many spiritual rituals have elongated from Indigenous threads. Many of those did not lay down their threads as my Ancestors did; Indigenous Peoples are the original teachers and are being well respected by the efforts of this umbrella organization.

BIRTH PASSAGE

THE INTENTION:
CREATING AND ASSEMBLING THE VILLAGE

I am singing a new lullaby, Welcome! Welcome! A Soul has arrived from her long journey, from his long journey. I clasp my hands together to feel the deep wonder of it all and celebrate this moment with Mother and Father. No greater magic exists on Earth than Birth. To the Great Creator and to the Source energy many call God and Goddess, may we bow our heads to feel the connection that binds us together as humans, the mystery we ponder when we take a few moments in prayer. I give thanks to be upright, to bear witness, to offer my love where it may be a salve, a welcome, or returned in joy.

Dear Mothers, Grandmothers, Aunties, and Mentors:

Every single child born to this world comes as a mystic to reweave the Village. This potential lives in each adult from our birth, the hope to reweave the Village. I see a local, slumbering capacity to fulfill our Soul's purpose as part of a greater awakening flowing like an underground river just beneath the surface of our culture. This is a fascinating time to be alive to welcome these new little mystics and further awaken to ourselves.

I write to encourage you. I wish to teach rather than preach, so please interpret my intentions with your heart as big as mine. As an Elder, now, a tiny bit of wisdom is beginning to emerge. I have been studying ceremony and connection for twenty years and feel the various ways that hearts come together in harmony. Connection holds a charge, do you feel it? Always an opportunity to reach across generations, look for the connections between hearts and even to Divine Love and the spirit world. Little children are the most sensitive beings on the planet. To become more upright as people, this word, connection, needs to become one of our core responsibilities. Connection is what I do when I take excursions out on the land. I connect to Nature, I feel the intuitive messages come through my heart. Feel connection, feel your strong love, allow solemn rituals to shape you; this is what the beautiful child in your arms most needs and deserves.

Last year when I sat very still and quieted my monkey mind, I noticed Souls for girl and boy babies coming out of the Cosmos and into the astral layers above the Earth. My relations seven generations back, the Ancestors, also noticed the numerous Souls headed my way. I attended to this wonder-rush with daily prayers while each little babe was still in the womb.

What I know for sure, the birth of a little baby returns people to our most natural condition of wonder and awe, which feels like spirituality. If women and men designated as relatives, blood and adopted, are awake enough to encourage these tiny children, to coach them through teething and crawling, through walking and talking, to invite their natural Genius to emerge, this generation can and will change the world. We know enough to raise these babes as the mystics they are at birth.

Prayers Made Visible for Babies in the Womb

Looking up as they traveled through the etheric dimension, I made prayers visible for these wee womb-mates. At the Baby's Rock Garden, I often used their name and shouted, "Welcome!" over and over. As each one came nearer, their Soul began to attach to Earth and to the very moment of birth. By attending to one Soul and then the next with messages of 'welcome baby,' I began to change. Musing about the arriving Souls, I came to understand Birth to be the most dramatic of the Nine Passages; people in our Villages need to come in-close to celebrate.

Once I began welcoming this new generation, I found no way to stop. It was far too rewarding. With my own Greats- and Grands and my parents looking over my shoulder from beyond, we all welcomed this 7th Generation together.

The women who carried these babies created personal and varied womb experiences. Some Mothers-to-be worked a regular job right up to delivery, others did not. A few Mothers were quite sick while others remained vitally well. My expectant Mothers represented this cross section. I began to examine the prenatal days as one of the growth stages, susceptible to environmental influences of all varieties. Thankfully, for all new Mothers, a tremendous amount of factual information is available for all their questions: The range of searches covers books, periodicals, and an entire online universe of mommy-blogs, social media, and neo-natal research. New Mothers-to-be: Begin at your local library, talk to experienced Moms, widen your search to make it relevant and current.

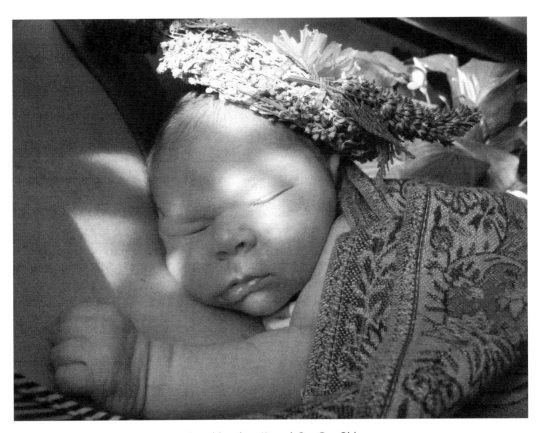

Granddaughter Kestrel, One Day Old

While a baby is developing, especially the second half of the nine-month womb term, the barrier of stretched skin to baby's newly forming senses is exquisitely designed for the babe to feel, hear, taste, and almost touch everything on the outside. Certainly when Mother places her palm anywhere around the womb-bowl where baby grows inside, baby can feel the delicacy of Mother's touch through the layers of skin. Baby can hear music, conversations, bird-song, and raised voices. This makes the baby's womb-world a receptive environment for wonderment and imprinting. All of this happens while the baby's Soul hovers nearby in the treetops and examines the story already running in the parents' lives.

All of my post-doctoral life has been devoted to coming-of-age and womanhood ceremonies.[1] Truth reveals—never have I been invited to be near a baby's birth. Imagine my delight when one tiny piece of all this watching and welcoming changed that for me.

The pain of birth is meant to be forgotten, it's meant to highlight the bond between Souls. What begins with labor pains and ends when the umbilical cord is cut is beyond miraculous. Every baby's story is unique as every Mother-Father story is unique. These are moments to tie up into personal story form, where Mother is heroine to herself, baby is the star-child and Father is best supporting actor. Baby will want to hear this story again and again. Embellish and polish, please; the rest of the Village wants to hear too!

Birthed and suckling, a newly born baby girl lies quietly, eyes closed, nestled in her Mother's arms. This scene repeats hourly for days on end, as feeding and mutual adoration create a bond between Mother and daughter. Take just a moment to consider the miracle of this babe who just moved from her watery-wet world out into an airy-dry world; for months she breathed with a cord, now she breathes God's air, every breath a breath of God. Each time I think of that first breath, I move easily to a state of unknowing the full measure of this wonder.

Body chemistry and psychology blend hormones, emotions, breast feeding, partnership qualities together with the new presence of baby for a unique state of mind known to experienced Mothers as mommy-brain. This new and confusing state can last for six months or more and is different for every woman. In addition to the relief of childbirth, emotional experiences are big, huge actually, and range from excitement and joy to anxiety, control issues, sleep deprivation, and fear. There is more, words do not express the continuous connection Mothers feel with this new life: It is all consuming.

While in this adoration interval, resting after birthing, creativity has been spent and Mother attends to the moment. No one can imagine this new baby's whole, creative life or the gifts that might have come with her Soul. Enjoy the moments, little Mother. There will be time later to consider the Soul and her Genius. Tend to those poopy diapers and rest. Light a candle and feel the calm of breath and the great joy of community. Men and women alike feel profoundly invested in celebrating this birth because Village life pulls from the ancient pool of ancestral memory, yours, mine, and ours together. We deeply feel all the generations drawing in. As time and nourishment will change this new wee Soul from baby to toddler to girl, parents and relations find themselves dazzled by the awe in these strong connections.

Throughout each child's early adventures, opportunities will rise to heal parenting wounds, to cast off "the spell of fathers and the curse of mothers."[2] New parents have this psychological and emotional work to do, to heal themselves, to discover their fractures and awaken to their own wholeness. A Genius-mystic lies in their arms and must not be crushed.

A long line of dreams unfold a woman's life journey to create her birth-scene; she uses her majestic creativity to blend visions and ideas from a wide assortment of relations. Over the next months, time after time, memories that tug on Mother will bring smiles and tears. Simultaneous healing occurs deep inside many wounded places, all the times where this new Mother felt a need unmet, a want unfulfilled. Miraculous as spirit, healing pours out of her like a salve for herself and her baby so the generations draw closer.

Baby's Soul Coalesces

WELCOMING BABY

At the time of Birth a welcoming ceremony to invite this Soul to remain here on Earth might be a dusting of cornmeal, like stardust, on her forehead. Bathe her feet in water to offer something familiar to welcome and invite her to stay. The glow of candlelight offers ambience. Almost any song, bird song, rattle-song, or a lullaby will harmonize with candle-lit wet feet. Beware of ceremonies that contain little or no humor, this little doll was delivered through hard labor and needs to hear laughter.

New Mothers believe they are ready for the baby when it finally emerges. In reality, every new Soul who arrives brings surprise. This is the presence of Soul, the part of a being that teases and holds dreams and offers complicated hidden purposes. We can hardly even speak about the reality that a Genius has just arrived. Holding another human in love and safety for an entire life-span seems too daunting, so we joke about 18 years of devotion. We remind each other the baby chose this scenario. We know nothing about how far back or how far into the future her choice might actually stretch.

We cannot know the age of the Soul who just arrived. We can't know in a scientific sense about reincarnation that may reach 100 or 10,000 years back, but we can open our minds to possibilities and be watchful. In the whole Universe, perhaps Earthlings are the only ones who count years. Wonderments, such as time and reincarnation, are barely spoken beyond the new arrival's "Old Soul" look. Still when our hearts are teased open the unknowable strikes us silent. Living in a scientific age which requires proof, many people feel uncomfortable talking about Souls coming to Earth in successive lifetimes, because everyone experiences the great forgetting. We simply know a mystic has arrived. Because we cannot know the specifics of the life journey that her birth initiated, the Genius-mystic must be honored for every possibility, every potential. Every time Grandmother or Auntie holds this babe, welcoming passes between our hearts, and we watch for gifts to emerge.

Every day as the child grows, any information and experience that touches passion will switch on remembering. Passion is our greatest clue, flying from one discovery to another. One of the driving forces of a little growing being is the searching, seeking, and finding purpose that will satisfy the urgent energy of the Soul. Even though it's wonderfully fun for adults to guess a child's destiny, most children exhibit early signs of their gifts.

Being open, we begin to query in ways that are not scientific, but befitting the mystic. Can we observe the hints about who just arrived? When I heard mythologist Michael Meade tell the story of Poder, I realized that science has nearly washed away mysticism and spirituality. The Mayan story of Poder is an old story of a midwife who received and safeguarded the boy-baby's gifts until the age of claiming. We who welcome a baby with all her gifts and blessings, may return to this mystical state in ourselves and remain open to all that is invisible. Can we be mirrors for children who begin to seek answers about Ancestors, origins, where they come from, and why they came?

I like to observe the positions of each planet at the moment of birth and use numerology for her given name and birthdate. I will take my clues wherever I can find them rather than wait 30 years for manifestation. These oracles, the I Ching and Tarot also, have much deeper roots than this age of pure science and proof. Using oracles with an open and curious heart may expand and enlighten our wonderment about the mystic in our midst and return each one of us to the realm of spirituality. Because I have felt a deeply personal resonance, I pray for openness to discover more about the Soul who recently arrived.

When life is steeped in ceremony from Birth, that foundation will sustain a reverence for all mystery as consciousness grows throughout life. Pull in your ceremonialists to help open and discover a sacred way to welcome baby. Do what comes through your imagination, it will be absolutely correct. Who knows how the Ancestors transmit your heritage. Follow intuitive threads, do not hesitate, and celebrate!

Like everyone, this baby's gifts will arise when she learns with all of her heart and mind to listen to her Soul. Each child will crawl, walk, and dance through thousands of days, giving to self and to others in her unique rhythm.

Each Soul attracts a unique bundle of lessons to be learned, some will be about resistance, some about acceptance. Every single lesson delivers a challenge instigated by her Soul. That mysterious part of each child, Soul, will use the fire of curiosity to clear the way through dreams and passions enough for motivation and action. Mother's molding begins to shape a self. Mother is especially influential through Early Childhood and through the Middle Childhood years, and the phenomenally valuable imprints before and just after age nine.

Forming a Village around each child causes everyone to look inward. Mothers and Fathers have sacred work to journey through any ceremonies they may have missed to update their own development. I feel a ceremony wrap around each chapter of my development story and feel grateful I have discovered the catalysts for change that initiated each new stage. This introspection has shown me how Rites of Passage weave continuously throughout life. Ceremonies bring the Village together to wrap a bundle of changes.

Fulfill your longing to belong to the Village, begin with your newborn babe. Life lived a sacred way with ritual offers something special, something less tangible and more satisfying so each person feels like a mystic and a Genius. I have learned this needs only deep quiet and attention. Attending to our Soul's urgent messages, we learn to care for our Souls and reconnect to the reasons we ask why!

Each new parent needs to focus one part of their fully capable brain on inner-personal growth and private memories. If there were things, events, raw emotions or triggers left over from a childhood long past, those need to be coaxed to the surface and examined. This is a wonderful process to do with a fully functioning adult brain. Doing this work prepares each parent for an adulthood or middle adult ceremony of their own, but do not rush this process. Reach for the manual, the guide I wrote called *Soul Stories*[3] for assistance. Take the time to cull through the memories, to journal and art which past memories need adult kindness.

The dance is this—awaken, heal, do ceremony, and repeat.

THE STORY: GRANDMOTHER'S GLORY

This story-of-the-day includes the voices of turtle and otter, dragon and cougar, dog and eagle, horse and honey bee. These voices and many others gathered around a sacred fire in a great November snowstorm.

In so many ways, wee Souls make relations. My baby-relations came through sister's son's wife or husband's nephews' wives or adopted initiate-daughters. I love all the different ways we can become related. Tribes weave together in one twist and then another until the bond grows strong. Relations are simple sometimes, as in a straight lineage, but even then, the bond must be nurtured. Other times, like this story, unlikely threads found their way into my heart and I found myself woven inside.

Babies' little bodies gestated in wombs all across the land and spanned every season as 2013 melted into 2014. Three babies were born to nieces and five babies came to women who had been with me in initiation ceremonies. Babies are teaching me about the global culture; they continue to come to my adopted relations all around the planet. As surely as the Sun rises, I become related to anyone who stands in ceremony with me. Welcoming these babies helped me feel the Grandma energy; five births happened before our home baby arrived. My sweet neighbor and adopted daughter, Cassie was pregnant through summer and fall and extremely pregnant for most of the winter.

Cassie's baby has come near enough for me to touch and see and tell her whole story, the story of Kestrel. On the coldest day in February, the Moon crossed into Taurus high up in the dawn sky and showed regally as a half white orb beyond the tops of grand firs; it was then that Kestrel was born. I give great thanks for this babe and all her womb-mates who are still arriving to bring their gifts to the Earth. I hurried across the barnyard to welcome Kestrel and placed a smudge of ceremonial cornmeal on her Third Eye, so she would know welcome. This single word of love communicates belonging and comfort; we all want to feel welcome and at home. Love has many expressions. The day Kestrel began her life, her parents' story was blossoming love and the great adventure of two lives twining. Kestrel became a major milestone in my life because I adopted her as my granddaughter.

In Hood River, Oregon, Kestrel's womb-mate, Amelina, was born four days later under a Cancer Moon. These girls will have ceremony in their lives and this Grandma's welcome.

Kestrel's beautiful Momma Cassie knew a ceremony would reveal itself at the right time. I wanted to connect the Blessing Way Ceremony offered by the Village Aunties; Mother Cassie also wanted a ceremony when she and baby would stand together as two whole Souls and Father Graham's arms could surround them both. Winter turned into spring and nobody could imagine a ceremony for Kestrel's first three months when she was the tiniest babe in arms.

Fully blooming springtime provided opportunity for parents to venture out across the landscape and consider all the imprints this child could absorb. My eyes spied stroller, sling, backpack as Mother and child or Father and child began exploring the natural world together. My digital album is filled with hundreds of photos; this is how Grandmothers behave in every corner of the world. When Comfrey burst forth in bloom, big furry bumble bees occupied Kestrel for a long time. That imprint is desirable, so are my visions of Graham standing in the fast moving current of Grouse Creek so Kestrel would grow to know water. At dawn, they were out in the ice-snow at the end of spring so Kestrel could learn about crisp air and ambient light.

To millions of grandparents everywhere, the mystery most apparent is the presence of Soul and the invisible gifts of potential each Soul carries from the stars. Grandmothers and Grandfathers have the advantage of this vision; like the acorn that sprouts, roots, and grows from one tree ring to another into a mighty and powerful oak, which spans generations. Every important imprint attaches to invisible neurons to help your baby's Soul remember herself. In the philosophy of spirit-moves-through-all-things, the bees and the water create connections inside baby's body and brain that will link back to this time when she was a wee babe in your arms.

As my Elder-self began to grow this Grandmother persona, I noticed that Kestrel taught me something very valuable. When summer turned to early autumn, she revealed personality traits like laughing out loud and reaching for me, melting away the crusty part of any day. As I watched her Genius, seeing places where a glimmer of her gifts began to emerge, I could see that she was growing into her skin. Just when she turned nine months, her strong determined personality became more insistent; Kestrel expressed her desire to be involved, to explore, and to learn on her own terms. Her hands made connections to everything. She engaged most objects with her mouth, taste was her main connection to the world. I peered into and saw her eyes making important connections to her neocortex. We were amazed at how Kestrel thirsted for everything. Finding space to talk about these growth phenomena while we played with her, we agreed that her Soul had fully arrived. Kestrel would soon leave her tiny infant self behind and walk in the world; the right time for ceremony grew near.

All through her infancy, she has been very funny, making people laugh. She insists we accept her invitation to play. When she hears me laugh out loud, she does too, almost like a call and response, we are laughing together. Kestrel quickly learned about the powerful tool in her eyes; being preverbal, she expresses her wants through her eyes and her reach. The expression of "I need" or "I want" with no words, began to shape her personhood and complex interactions began to develop. Mother Cassie taught her the meaning of 'ouch' and 'sit down' so smoothly, hearing quickly became a tool. Kestrel moved gracefully to this level of awareness where every one of her five senses engaged; that was the sign we needed. By this time, nine months out of the womb, Kestrel's Soul had fully arrived. Cassie called for a Second-Nine-Month's Ceremony to celebrate this first level of growing into a whole human.

Life expresses through us in colorful threads of people and events that we may use to weave our personal tapestries into stories. One strong thread we could see and feel with our hearts came from the dear friends and kindred spirits who lived in Oregon, a mere seven hour drive away. This thread began with

Cassie who met Kathryn and they became friends. Talking as friends do, they discovered they were both pregnant at the same time. The Soul-directed life of their babies meant these girls connected in the stars to be womb-mates for life.

In the summer season, Kathryn, Shane, and their baby Amelena had found me on the rocky bar listening to the wind and the water and playing with river stones. When all my senses are receptive, serendipity sings a clear Soul message. Shane engaged me to think about all the heart rocks I was finding: Were they gifts from some First Peoples of long ago? Why were there so many? While we examined big heart stones, I gathered their story pieces. These two baby girls, Kestrel and Lena, were born four days apart with very different birth stories. I knew these girls would walk into their woman-life as kindred spirits. Our ceremony plans wrapped like a lasso around Kathryn and her clan, we wanted to share the experience of this ceremony. We would make it happen for both babies, a double Second-Nine-Month Ceremony. The Village formed around Kestrel and Lena to add a new dimension in our tapestry.

Similar, but different, the High Mass Baptism in a cathedral for my Grand-niece Sloan was an outstanding ceremony full of drama and meaning. Many of my closest relatives were present and felt the long lineage of ceremony and deep blessing in our own Souls. I was struck by how the rituals had been practiced millions of times over the past millenniums.

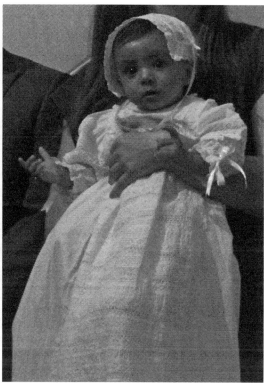

Birth and Baptism

AT HOME

Two Moms, Cassie and Kathryn, created an Earth-based ceremony around a central fire for Kestrel and Amelena. This welcoming and blessing ritual had also been practiced millions of times, but perhaps it was handed down rather than written down. We all declared our intention to hold our Circle around the fire, no matter the weather.

All the parts and pieces, logistics, altar pieces, people in the Village, even relations who could not come, appeared before us as a mosaic and fell into place when we spoke about them. Email and text, so well embedded in our cultural toolkit, connected us rather quickly like a shuttle weaving back and forth. Cassie was the communication queen for a month. At the very mention of ceremony, Cassie's mother Sue came for a long visit. I love this response the most. If I could have only one response to ceremony, hers is the highest: How can I help? I feel very grateful for Grandma Sue because I relaxed about all the details and so did Cassie. A program outline formed to guide this Birth Passage ceremony marking the second nine months as Soul-arrival time.

I credit remote Elders for inspiration—Angeles Arrien, Michael Meade, Clarissa Pinkola Estés—who have plumbed the depths of initiation and ritual to explain our world; and Jon Young who has taught thousands about Nature connection.[4] We bow to the great initiator of change, our own Souls. Academia has made human development a very deep and complicated discipline without ever mentioning Soul: This will always be true. We love that there is so much to know, especially the combined threads of Anthropology, Psychology, Child Development, Human Ecology, Brain Science, and the transpersonal extensions of these disciplines. No one can know it all. We can, however, be vigilant and interpret the Soul expression in those we love, including ourselves, and remain curious. We live in a time when our Souls emerge as the lead teachers. Mothers, Fathers, babies, hovering Grandmas, and every loving Village member, we are only required to slow down, watch, listen, and share stories.

Sacred Relations

When the car arrived filled with kindred spirits from Hood River, everyone stepped into the flow and all our plans began to feel Divine. From my Elder sanctuary, I came across the barnyard feeling excited and grateful the weather had offered a window of safety for this family. Maybe the best way to *be* with nine-month-old babies is on the floor, to join them in their world. The scene was hilarious, actually, with half of the adults rolling around on the floor giving focused attention to both curious, exploring infants. We observe a developmental edge in these babies who pull themselves up by the pant-legs of adults or by the furniture and let go. This ceremony would honor their similar and different birth-to-nine-month stories held by the parents, and celebrate the completion of the Soul's arrival for Kestrel and Lena.

The following ceremony day morning, I woke very early and watched the darkest outline of dawn reveal the Grand Firs and bare Cottonwood trees in relief against clouds. For our 11 a.m. gathering time, a crowd formed around the much needed fire to focus our attention. These babies had evoked deep emotional responses in each person around the Circle. Snow began to fall, lightly then heavily just as Grandma Sue provided a beautiful welcoming with words that centered our attention.

Sue invited everyone to give their burdens to the fire during this ceremony. Through the lineages of every person's Ancestors, the fire connected us to those guardian spirits. Making eye contact across this fire space, strangers became friends and we all melted together as relations. With clear intentions of our whole hearts, we formed a Village around Kestrel and Lena. Everyone had a story of connection to the parents and to the babes; threads of memory-moments rose in our hearts and we wove a strong new story tapestry of a Passage ceremony for two babies.

Ceremonial Smudge

Wrapped inside our winter coats, our pounding hearts held this wonder of high honor for two tiny Souls. Ceremony causes new relationships to form, everyone's heart to open, and ripples to spread, connecting other relations and other ceremonies. I can still see and feel us standing together in awe, getting covered in a heavy wet snow. No one in our culture is an expert in Rites of Passage, but everyone's heart really poured into this ceremony for Kestrel and Lena. A humble medicine man whose gifts derived from an old lineage in Peru, a relation to Lena who came from Hood River, stepped forward to smudge and bless each person. Dave cast a magic spell of quiet and respect as he invited the Ancestors to come to our ceremony while he fanned the wood-smoke over us, smudging the protective "holy wood" Palo Santo, to bring us good fortune.

Lena's mother Kathryn offered a song-sheet to soak up the snowflakes and sing along, *I hear the voice of the Grandmothers calling*.[5] I thought about the women who taught me that song and sent them love. Cassie spoke a prayer of Thanksgiving for the spirit of the land and the company of her creatures. Kestrel's Aunt Debra offered her original Grandmother Song, which I cherish.

Uncle Daniel enlivened us with a call and response song of respect for the energies alive in the natural world. I led a ritual to invite the guardian ancestors of the seven directions and added my welcome to the very long line of Ancestors who watch over us.

From Joanna Macy, the Elder who created the *Council of all Beings* ceremony,[6] we borrowed inspiration to bring blessings to these two babes. I felt grateful to borrow the muse of Joanna, who has led thousands of *All Beings* ceremonies to honor and to bring awareness to the animals who share Earth with us. For babies to feel most welcome on Earth, animals are essential companions. I pulled out a wadded wet paper and began with this quote from Thomas Berry:[7]

> *"We all possess a 'shamanic personality,' which can understand and speak for other beings. This personality is essential to our survival. It frees us from our self-centered culture-nature and dispels the trance of industrial civilization. The life-giving powers shaping creation from the beginning of time are still present within us, accessible through our imagination. All that is required is clear intention; it is like opening a door in the mind and walking through. It's an act of humility and generosity."*

Four-legged critters, winged ones and all the sacred Others in the bioregion will be companions to entertain and educate these babes about the mystique of the natural world. Everyone standing around the sacred fire melted into an animal voice bringing a blessing for these baby girls of the Earth.

On land or water, Turtle dwells in two worlds, moves slowly and close to the Earth. She carries the powerful symbol of being buried as an egg, she is born of the Earth: Indigenous peoples say she is the symbol for Mother Earth. Turtle, ancient as the dinosaurs, displays a shell design of 13 Moons for girls to remember. Offering this blessing to sleeping babies, the Souls of Kestrel and Lena felt Turtle enliven their inner mystic self to receive all the blessings that followed.

Blessings from voices around the sacred fire offered potent words from

Others: Beaver offered the blessing of using teamwork to act on dreams; Otter offered feminine playfulness and intuitive Earth wisdom; and Dove offered peace blessings.

Energies shifted as the natural world stepped out of the fire and blessings gathered a life-force. Earthworm brought transforming blessings by attending to the precious soil and Deer and Elk people brought deep listening and double-love. The fierce nature of Song Sparrow blessed the babes with protection, which powerfully echoed through a second Otter, more protective, and not as playful as the first Otter. Two Horses, both real and fantastical, reared blessings on the babies with companionship and created an arena for the parents' blessings.

Draco offered the mystery of star-spirits and delivered Dragon blessings for the future. Feeling powerful, Cougar delivered focus and graceful dancing through life. There was a mention of Owl with the blessing of divine love coming from Dog. The Eagle's blessing offered patience and the majesty of living in the Now with the help of keen sight.

The second Horse came from dreamtime to offer a blessing of clairvoyant listening with the splendor of power and presence. Buzzing with so many blessings already, two Honeybees offered blessings of abundance and dedication for life, diligence and preparedness, and finally receiving joy for true work.

Others, present on an invisible outer ring of energy, also delivered blessings of unique diversity: Momma Moose and her yearling visit often and so do the less visible ones, Wolf, Raccoon, Dragonfly, Snake, Skunk, Salmon, Woodpecker, Grouse and many more bird species. Every bioregion is this rich and potent with animals' blessings left in every track and sign. I give thanks for this knowledge.

Womb-mates: Kestrel 4 Days Older than Amalena

WRAPPING THIS BUNDLE

These babies are now the leading edge of an energetic cultural shift to lift up Rites of Passage. I feel strongly that ceremony is for the Village as much as each child. Elders about to become Grandmothers for the first or the twelfth time can give the breath of life to this idea so that it may spiral all the way up through the generations. Elders who themselves were born as mystics also require acknowledgment with a sacred fire after one full initiation year.

Receiving Blessing: Kestrel's Mother Cassie

When she stands in ceremony with her Village, Mother begins to see clearly the Soul of her own creation. She is the one who says yes and makes lists, invitations, decides on the flow of events, and how to offer food to complete the celebration. Inside the Soul are multiple gifts, first to bring warmth and laughter, and later to shine as an evolving human remembering her purpose for coming to Earth.

So many blessings flow from this one Birth Passage, an emergence for Mother as much as for Baby. I have been gifted with the sight of two women receiving blessings for their babies while, for themselves, the sacred fire revealed the truth of Self returning strong and free. Cassie and Kathryn began to feel a rebirth of their Woman/Soul which peeked out of the nurturing/nursing Mother/Self. While one foot will remain steadfast and diligent, the other foot will prepare to step forward.

Everyone who dined on the gift of food offered in gratitude from these two Mothers, Cassie and Kathryn, realized the Second-Nine-Month Ceremony out of the womb was perfectly Soul-full.

My winter prayer shelters the star-seed of this Passage story and prepares to reach out to others. I pray that the Souls of all babies come to feel welcome. Each old Soul comes because the Earth and all of her inhabitants are in need of new gifts.

Lena's Mother Kathryn

Lena's Father Shane

Kestrel's Father Graham

GIFTS FROM THE ELDERS: BIRTH PASSAGE

As a babe in the womb, while our Soul is traveling from the stars, we are in the mystic-making part of the human journey; look forward to the exact moment of meeting our Soul incarnate. "From stardust" is a less than scientific answer: Mothers came along eons before scientists; ask any one of them where babies come from. Egg and sperm are cultural and biological answers, what is the spiritual answer?

Womb-time reflection serves to connect your Soul with your baby's Soul from tiny origins. Perhaps her Soul brings essences from past lives, one of the next Passages may reveal more. With candlelight, celebrate that your spirit and your baby's have a Soul essence, a harmony. You chose one another for this Earth journey. Your arms are filled with this teensy little being who knows but will need to remember that the two of you are destined to become mystics together from the lessons you learn, day by day.

Soul waits in the nearby treetops, double checking the choice of you as her parent, smiling about the landscape and the lay lines of the Earth for her birthplace. The alignment of the planets and the position of the Moon for the very moment of birth, your baby's Soul chose all the proper channels of support for her life-long journey.

Consider this Soul, who came in **from the stars** to meet biology happening in your Mother's womb. Yes, otherworldly. A stretch in beliefs, perhaps, still a phenomenally new way to think about what makes you, and your wee babe unique and magical beings.

We cannot know the age of the Soul who just arrived. We cannot know in a scientific sense about reincarnation which may reach 100 to 10,000 years back, but we can open our minds to possibilities and be watchful.

Do you know your **Ancestors?**
Does your family have birth stories? Do you know yours?

Mothers, Grandmothers, Aunties, perform a **welcoming ceremony** for your newborn with candlelight and music, sprinkle cornmeal. Invite the new babe to stay. Sing a lullaby of welcome, welcome!

Can you observe hints about the new Soul who has just arrived?
Will you observe the positions of the planets at the moment of Birth?

Promise to tell her **Birth story** at all of her birthdays so that at her Middle Child Ceremony, your daughter will tell it with you.

NOTES FOR THE BIRTH PASSAGE

1   *Gifts from the Elders: Girls' Path to Womanhood* (2004), still available on Amazon, was my first published effort for Mothers of girls, sourced from my research findings about Rites of Passage as my doctoral dissertation (published in June 2000). The pre-adolescent girl became my most loved specialty for a decade; as the girls grew, I found I also loved teen girls.

2   Michael Meade spoke these words, "the spell of fathers and the curse of mothers" in a long workshop about initiation, October 2013. He creates an atmosphere of mythology where truths emerge, often starkly. Ringing in these intriguing mythic tongue twists, there is often a hidden truth about personal relations. Truth is intimate to healing family dynamics and dysfunctions. How they ring for each person will be completely unique, but worth contemplating. Meade published the story about a child's gifts, a Mayan story about a boy-child called Poder in *Fate and Destiny: The Two Agreements of the Soul* (2012).

3   Mothers and Grandmothers may experience a guided initiation for themselves through *Soul Stories: Nine Passages of Initiation* (2015). Initiation in this culture is on a threshold of becoming mainstream, each person who takes a Passage journey steps us closer. I believe when Elders experience Rites of Passage, their Villages will begin to heal. The Spiral represents all nine Passages from Birth to Death.

4   These early influences, Angeles Arrien, Clarissa Pinkola Estés, and Michael Meade taught me so much about initiation and ritual. They each can be found through easy searches on the Internet. Jon Young, the father of the Nature Connection movement, received the gift of bird and animal language as a young boy and has spent his whole life developing this Nature Connection legacy for our post-modern world. He teaches how to be deeply engaged with all of the inner workings of Village life.

5   Voice of the Grandmothers is one of the Earth Chants shared widely in Women's Circles. It goes this way: I hear the voice of my grandmothers calling me | I hear the voice of my grandmother's song | They say wake up wake up, they say wake up wake up | Listen Listen | Listen Listen ... It can be sourced here https://tribesofcreation.wordpress.com/2010/01/02/the-voice-of-the-grand-mothers/

6   I called on my original ceremony teacher, Joanna Macy, an Elder creative who, in language original to Deep Ecology, offered the Council of All Beings ceremonies around the world. Her website is equally wide and deep, every one of her teachings is profound. http://www.joannamacy.net/

7   Thomas Berry wrote *The Dream of the Earth* (1988) as a spiritual activist for the Earth, I pay homage to his beautiful words.

MIDDLE CHILD RITES

THE INTENTION:
MAKING ALL RITES POSSIBLE

I stand before the great unseen powers with a gift in my hands, feeling its nature, sacred and powerful. This is my root prayer for women and girls: Great Mystery, I ask for Divine guidance to bring initiations to all peoples in ways of old made new. Each Rite of Passage pulls a little more Genius into being, a little more of our gifts made visible as an offering from our spirit-selves. I call out to all the nature kingdoms to watch now and offer protection as we lift up our hearts, I feel especially grateful for this opportunity to walk toward consciousness.

Being part of Nature, I pause to express gratitude for our Great Mother the Earth and give thanks for all the plants and the animals, for the waters and the air. I give thanks for bugs, birds, and fishes, everything, in fact, under the swirl of the Moon and our great day star, the Sun. Do you also feel grateful for so much good, wild company? Touching my heart space I toss this bundle of gratitude into the air so this little prayer will be felt and heard.

Dear Mothers, Aunties, Grandmothers and Mentors:

I invite you to think ahead. When your girl encounters Middle Childhood—the 'big' half of childhood before puberty—she will silently cry out for recognition. I call this a Passage moment and your response of recognition will be a ritual. This particular ritual, playful and earthy, sets the stage for a whole life of Women's Passage ceremonies. To hear the call of change heralding this new stage of development, tune your spirit in around age 8 when your girl's female hormones are produced and enter her blood stream for the first time. This invisible event will touch your Soul in a way only a woman can perceive. Acknowledging that something is different will invite more growth and change for you as well as for her. A small, ceremonial space to embrace her precious memories will offer a release into the second half of Childhood known as the Middle. As she changes and feels ready to release her Early Childhood, please see the spirit of change. It is always good. Ceremony invites change. A girl's Middle Childhood is completely exhilarating. Growth and change demand that everyone pay attention.

Between sleeping and waking, when change visits your daughter's pillow, she begins a silent call for recognition, for initiation. You wonder why she's cranky and she wants you to know she is different overnight. Change is the one great constant in the world. If we pay close attention to this call for acknowledgment and interpret it as a need for initiation, a celebratory life can be the way your family celebrates growth. Because Early Childhood is memorable our whole life long, a celebration honors these memories, and the arrival of Middle Childhood causes the spirit of this child to look forward to her next ceremonies.

Women's learned experience suggests the observance of a ceremony to acknowledge the change between little and big childhood, the important coming-of-age ceremony for puberty will be happily anticipated. I ask that you consider this remarkable, because I do. Without this Middle Childhood celebration, the First Blood ceremony and puberty teachings are often denied, skipped, or excused.

Add Fire to Make Ceremony

How can you help your girl remember she has a special connection to the natural world? Here's one way to excite and awaken her to deepen that connection. Teach her about women's ritual and ceremony elements: Earth, Air, Fire, and Water combine alchemically, and in combination create every single sentient being. Take that thought to its natural conclusion: These elements also create literally every material thing on the planet.

A sacred ceremony container for a girl stepping into Middle Childhood includes relations, near and far, related and not. Her stories and your emotions belong in the container. Places she has been, passions she has revealed, photos that hint at the bigger picture, these are all items only you know about that will create a sacred bundle she will hold dear all the days of her life.

Gather in a circle with those who will help you. Take time to look into one another's eyes, check-in about each other's pulses and passions. Then ask, will they help you create this girls' ceremony? At this edge, where little girls become big girls, now may be the only opportunity to celebrate the Early Childhood years. Embrace the days of routine, of singing and dancing, and days of play. She will be a woman for every other ceremony of her life.

Who has watched this girl grow? What does her Father want to contribute? This will be a community gathering. Should you invite her school friends to be celebrated too? As you decide to build a ritual ceremony for one girl or a group, offer thanks to all those who know your daughter. They want to hear that her girl-spirit has grown and has been safe in their care. Include the whole community; these ceremonies are great bonding opportunities.

Lingering on this growing girl for a moment, we hear Mother say, "She really is growing fast, she is no longer a small child." It's important for you to see this girl with new eyes, she's a big girl now and has new needs. Many of her needs are specifically mother-centered, as in woman-centered. She needs to know you see the difference.

Continue to watch for all the signs pointing to her gifts. In a dream-world without life and death challenges, this may be true: A child swims happily in the froth and fantasy of early childhood, moving through stages of toddler and pre-school and early education until a fresh stage arrives. Early personality quirks begin to show through your girl's fantasies and innocent meanderings. She almost stands on her head trying to reveal her gifts to anyone watching.

Girls at the Edge of Transformation

In a macro-view, ontogeny is the biological timing of our human development and this quick look will help you remember what you are celebrating. There are brain indicators, growth indicators, and neurological coordinators. The force of change is present and churning, so let's step into her natural story. Her baby teeth grew in and she walked when she was good and ready, on her own time. Then she was potty-trained just about the time she talked in full sentences, again when she felt ready. She learned to say the alphabet and read, then her teeth fell out, then they grew back in, and she learned to write. Finally, when she asked to be helpful and accepted more responsibility, she reached this Middle Childhood stage. As a developmental marker without a numerical age, this Middle Child Threshold offers a time to pause and celebrate all of Early Childhood because those precious events can be bundled as in the past.

Her Middle Childhood is coming, if it hasn't already arrived. Soon it is undeniably marked by a discomfort of being called little, or being left with the little ones. This can happen as early as 8, when those hormones enter a girl's bloodstream. Often, by age 9, the signs cannot be ignored.

Be not alarmed, this child is still very much a child. However, all the indicators reveal the Middle has arrived. This short, peak stage lasts until the signs of puberty overwhelm her with a distinctly personal biology. Right now she is ready for her Middle Childhood ceremony, because you read the signs and she asks for more responsibility. She becomes your helper of first choice. Because she has recently demonstrated this willingness, you gladly allow her to stretch her capabilities and applaud her accomplishments.

She grows more complex with each passing day. As a Mother or Grandmother of a Middle Child going through your own changes, you can hardly keep up with her changes. Awareness of change is made possible with regular check-ins to attend to the feminine in you both. For this Middle Childhood stage of development, change is less biological and more behavioral. Her spirit is expanding right before your eyes. New Mother/Daughter distinctions appear; almost daily, she differentiates in small ways. She has been your reflection, soon her Soul's job will be to become very different from you. We are often too busy or not well enough trained to notice every subtle change. Suddenly, it seems like she misses nothing and absorbs everything about adulthood. Her growing awareness is one of the charms of this stage and she celebrates noticing things you've missed. Girls either want to be grown-up or want nothing to do with the adult world. Which leaning does your girl have?

Beliefs may be a subject of intense curiosity for her. Do not be surprised if she questions and challenges your beliefs. If you prove to be inflexible, she may take it like a dare. All this depends on her personality. Your young daughter, to better understand her own edges, may begin to find and test your edges. This may be true for beliefs, morals, integrity, and your very IQ. Feel flattered if she interrogates you, but she may also test your intimacy. She wants to know you and as she throws out thousands of questions, notice that she wants to be engaged in full conversations. Mothers, decide where your boundaries lie.

Together with this expanding being, you will learn how to make those personally edgy choices.

Changing Girl

This may be an opportunity for deeper teachings about choices, and how making mistakes becomes the grandest learning experiences. Remember, this is a highly foundational time, her curiosity will be rewarded, but she is also tender and vulnerable. Teach her that fear is a healthy emotion and we all feel it every day, but courage is the antidote which comes from within. Often, fast growth literally produces growing pains that are real and cause discomfort. Times when she shows sensitivity in her spirit are good times to demonstrate the practice of stillness.

Several things are born of the new level of maturity she is showing. The first may be the discovery of your girl's shadow side. This is the collision of Nature and culture; your shadow self also appeared at this age. An easy way to view this initial shadow appearance comes through her story. You may use your own lenses of doubt or criticism to see hers and share from this common link. Does she have the brat, a princess, or perhaps the drama queen archetype? Find out as soon as you can what is beneath any shadow expressions. What quirks make you wrinkle your nose? She may drop the act once it's exposed, but she may have a deeper wounding that needs to be healed. She may also hide her shadow in the good-girl archetype. Notice if she tries too hard to please you at her own expense.

Shadows shape each one of us. Following the lead of shadow-selves take us to an honest and airy place we must look to know our true selves. Both shadows and bright lights belong in the bundle you create to help your girl remember her Early Childhood days. Mother and daughter, together, can take representational memories of dark and light, such as bullying or extra drama, and use the magic of ceremony to place any psychic pain in the past tense. Linger here with your trusted friends; ask for help if this resonates for you or your daughter.

In ceremony, a girl will meet her Higher Self as an aspect of her Soul who walks with her and challenges her to be better, smarter, fair and true to her newly forming ideals. Because Higher Self walks with high principles, each girl, indeed each woman, hearing and heeding this trumpet of conscience benefits from this learned skill. Every child has a conscious and a subconscious mind and this time of early maturity provides a great opportunity to begin exploring what that means. Through ceremony, a girl will have an opportunity to see herself new again, as her days of Early Childhood are remembered and celebrated.

In addition to shadow work, this developmental stage may awaken negative imagery common to both genders. Early signs seem like a weakening, declining self-esteem, increasing doubt, ungrateful expressions, and self-criticism. If your girl has none of these issues, at least they are named and you can stay alert for future places where her strength may be compromised. The sooner these issues receive your attention, the sooner you can repair the breach in her spirit. Sometimes the repair may be as easy as action: Take her to a soup kitchen to volunteer, or go pick berries, or walk along the beach gathering stones and shells. Think of what will represent a playful action that will take her mind off her negative feelings long enough for her to gain a fresh perspective. Provide the opening, the invitation to talk it through. These and other action steps will shift her energy, her perspective, and raise her up out of a false-funk. Talk to her about how to shift energy instead of focusing on the negatives that are born of faltering confidence. She will be glad to possess the skill of shifting her energy.

In many different ways, your daughter may face vulnerabilities of her rapidly growing and changing spirit. Call forth her courage with yours—vulnerability is a strength. Continue to explore the subjects and hobbies where she expresses passion, even if her passion-of-the-month seems exploratory. She's young, and unless she's a prodigy, her gifts are still coming into form. All her casting about at this stage will actually support her self-confidence as she eliminates things of little or no interest.

The future developmental stages ahead, pre-puberty and puberty, can be tricky to maneuver. Let her know you are always going to be her loving safety net. She knows that, but wants to hear it from you, her dear and closest support.

Truly when your daughter (or son) reaches the stage of Middle Childhood, the highest value to your child comes through your acknowledgement that a change has occurred. As the age of responsibility and accountability, Middle Childhood provides a symbolic opportunity to use the teaching tools of ceremony to mark this change as the prelude to puberty. Dare we look forward to that stage, the great and intense change from childhood to womanhood? The notation of this Middle Childhood marker, makes celebrating the arrival of puberty more likely. I merely repeat myself for emphasis, as age 12 rolls into age 13, a girl unfamiliar with women's ceremonies will more likely cave into peer pressure. One of the risks I wish to avert here is peers raising peers.

The act of celebrating markers of development, especially as a rite of initiation, is new in this culture but draws from old, old times before writing, before memory. I believe, searching through the oldest parts of our brains, we can remember. We come together in response to longings as old as those times out of memory. Each one of us knows how and what to do.

Let's make a ceremony! What is this particular ceremony? Her signs of growth and change reveal a spiritual maturity, indicating a new awareness and a soul quickening. This daughter is emerging out of her pretend world, taking exploratory steps into the fully abstract adult world. For each girl, her Middle Childhood ceremony celebrates the appearance of brain expansion more than bodily development. World religions have also recognized this age as something of competence. It's much more than a single word.

Before Ceremony Prayers

Making ceremony arises from heritage more than memory and encourages you to stretch to your future Elder-self. The ceremonial part of your heritage may be lying in the dust like mine was. If so, call forth the sacred in your imagination. Think of what might create a special day for you and for your daughter. You model and teach through your imagination, that doesn't change. As always, you lead the way and set the tone. A women's gathering to mark a girl changing from Early to Middle Childhood provides an opportunity to impart wisdom, to begin traditions like giving handmade gifts. You might offer a charm or a bead that will connect to future initiations. Remember, initiation honors growth and brings the spirit of recognition and a celebration of change. Commemorating the Spiral of Life developmental markers with a ceremony, whether it's simple or complex, will create your personal acknowledgment that her spirit longs for.

To open your spiritual response, say yes! This is the call of Rites of Passage. After the idea enters, initiations unfold in three steps the Indigenous peoples shared in the last century. The *first* is separation, *second* an ordeal or a test that proves the stage, and *third* is integration where the change feels most obvious in one's inner world. This last step, also called reincorporation, may last a full round of 13 Moons.

In every other stage, when the Initiates are older, a true separation would be a physical parting. Because this is a child-ceremony, psychic safety comes first, so separation may be in keeping with her fantasy world. Put a blindfold over her eyes and she separates without fear. An ordeal or challenge may be the central unifying force to effect change, only a little bit of energy is needed for this Passage. Her child's life review may be the perfect change-agent for honoring. Find the surprise for yourself in this review of her first three thousand days, and make special note of any of the places where she was wounded. Revisiting those ordeals already healed provides an esteem bump, see how you came through that ordeal, daughter? This ceremony time provides grounding threads her Soul will pull on her whole life long. This collective effort pulls her Mind-Body-Spirit together.

Gather with family and friends to let the child-spirit know that her maturity is noticeable. You will be gifting all her moments known as Early Childhood. Now cast as a group of memories, this bundle holds the many days since her first Passage, when she was born into this world. This pivot place of celebration serves everyone to recognize change. It's also the time when families heartily and cheerily tell the finest and happiest stories about the child so she remembers she was carefully watched. I feel passionate about how time is used for initiatory acknowledgments. Be sure to take enough time. In close communities, this first conscious ceremony could elongate to a potluck, but please, something more than her last birthday party. If this one ceremony tests your ceremonial mettle, start small. An initiation needs a separation and an ordeal. Super simple would be her blindfolded while relations recount her complete history, with everyone speaking about the obvious change they see in your girl.

Commemorating the entry into Middle Childhood as an initiation causes this girl to see herself differently, and after this ceremony she will be different. The final step in this three-step ritual alerts all who know your daughter: This step of reincorporation involves her close and extended family, everyone needs to declare how they see change and probably more than once. Like seeing into her whole self, acknowledgements coax her body-mind to follow the lead of her spirit. Do be patient, please. Some releasing of her little child self and accepting of her middle child self will break through its lingering resistance within a couple of months. Resistance is the doorway to the Divine, we simply must push it open. Integration, depending on how much work the spirit has to do, may indeed last several months.

Mothers, Grandmothers, Aunties, you are the guides; your child's first ceremony would best be instigated by a collective of you, and deepened by her community of family and friends as she integrates change. Here, I want to emphasize the extended family, the community that cradled this child from birth and continues to hold fast. Please let everyone know that our learning curve is a collective process. The next ceremony, the welcoming to early adulthood, lends itself to forming and strengthening, repairing and re-knitting community.

Watching girls (and boys) move through their Passage markers invites Elders to create ceremony. This is the way to circle back to remember our heritage as ritual expands our experience as it did for our distant Ancestors. Maturity rituals are offered in a zone apart from religions, beliefs, and those rituals. Ceremonies to mark biological maturity include mental, emotional, psychic, and spiritual development that have evolved over tens of thousands of years through tribal appreciation, recognition, and trainings. Incorporating ritual promises to slow us down, something everyone could use. Extended families notice one another's maturity moving through seasons together. When we watch with a consciousness, Passages will bring wholeness to our communities. There is great power in doing a ceremony to culminate all the watching and all the attending everyone has done. This recognition is one of the true gifts, another is the Soul's response.

For you, the women in a young girl's life, consider the essence of self, how often do you see the world through this Middle Childhood lens?

PREPARING FOR CEREMONY

Preparing you is step one. In the sense of having something you can give away, adult to child, do your own Middle Childhood ceremony. Start from your Birth Passage up to this Middle Child Passage, those 8 or 9 years, many characters crossed your path. Remember them. Consider what you believe. Right now consider this question, "Where do babies come from?" Where did you come from to be born from your Mother's womb? Walk yourself through your own Early Childhood. Imagine where you felt the awakening of your Middle Childhood place. Your memory of how you navigated this personal Passage is an important prelude. Keep in mind the wholeness you seek. Who will you choose to hear your stories? These ceremonies bond spirit to body and mind, so acknowledge this first level of maturity of your child-self; heal yourself deeply, and your circle of women friends and relations, through sharing stories. When you summon your own stories, something opens in you. Take all the time you need. These ceremonies are spiritually so essential no one should feel rushed.

Women and men make ceremony by stepping away from routine and by using ritual symbols. Please know, for your sons, these are easily translatable. First Peoples often used five elements: Earth, Fire, Air, Water and all of changing Nature; other cultures have included Metal and Wood. What do you choose? Women engage sensory delights: Candles, music, aroma, billowy colors, pillows, other women. Always, in our women's ceremony, we include food, culinary squeals. For commemorating all the great moments of your daughter's early history, I think a photo collage is a super gift idea. I wish I had one. Keep it simple—four photos, eight maybe. In our modern times, photos hold that memory record, but must be transportable too. I also like the idea of a precious little hankie to play the role of bundling tiny objects, symbols, and stories to tuck the whole of childhood safely away. The away-place is a visual image like a heart pocket or a physical bundle.

Everyone should agree if more than one girl receives this ceremony.

Consider what we have in the natural world that mimics and offers metaphors for change. A snake shedding its skin does so in its own timing although it may take an undetermined time to fit back into that new skin, which is different, fresh. Your newly Initiated girl comes through ceremony with an unfamiliar skin; she may not feel like it fits perfectly. When she feels comfortable with her change and her new status, she will glow with a luster you haven't seen before. Hold her close, she's about to surprise you with her most extraordinary essence. As you watch, even though this may take days or weeks, her spiritual portal will close and change will vanish. Your job as her ceremony leader is complete until her puberty comes knocking.

Five girls in the midst of their Middle Childhood ceremony found more than a dozen snakes, including skins. I call that metaphor writ large. Here is their story.

A STORY: FIVE GIRLS WELCOME MIDDLE CHILDHOOD

Before we could even dream this tender celebration of so many Early Childhood moments passing into memory, one Mother had to hear the call of one daughter, *I am different*. The great blessing of consciousness is the multitude of paper-thin levels of awareness available to each one of us. Moments that come with this silent call for recognition, a call from the cosmic spirit of change, produce life-changing choices with life-affirming results. Feeling no need for details, this woman from a far-away land, held tightly to her dream of an initiation ceremony for her daughter.

Hearing the call that penetrated the first level of consciousness had the possibility to create a Mother-Daughter, Grandmother-Granddaughter bond with spiritual adhesive for maturity and change. Right behind the first call, four more Mothers said their daughters were also ready. These women created the potentiated mystery of initiation by answering this first call for ceremony.

Within days of opening the window of opportunity to visit me, the one who stands as Elder, a perfect circle of girls attached a dream of their own. Throughout their busy spring and summer, five girls committed and held strong to their dreams for an initiation ceremony gifted to them by their Mothers and Grandmothers.

Preserve the Wild in Girls

READY OR NOT

Ready is an interesting concept and I spent some time on the phone talking about each girl's readiness. I found I did not disagree with any single assessment. How she walked in the world was my inquiry. Still, through interviewing Mothers, I learned only a little about each girl.

The magic of change enveloped everyone. Mothers, Grandmothers, and ceremony leaders worked through the process of design. Not even one of us had received this Middle Childhood ceremony when we went through our own portal of change from little to Middle Childhood. In rather dim memories, we could see change when we pulled out dusty, curly photos of our little Soul-selves. Beyond connecting to stories of our ancestral lineages, mystery had wrapped our former selves in cloaks of almost gauzy obscurity. We have no language for how our Soul remembers a few details but not others, bad feelings over good, or if there was a glimpse of now in that long ago time.

All together, the women leaders, the Mothers, and the Grandmothers considered the importance of our collective opportunity and the importance of setting the stage. In order to gather, everyone needed to travel far which offered time to reflect on their child's Birth story. The Birth Passage is the most dramatic for Mothers, and remembered often as life changing. This is the remembering place for the girl-to-woman series of Rites of Passage until adulthood arrives.

Each Mother agreed to share her girl's Birth story during drive time. When I work with symbols, as I have done with this stone Spiral, I begin with Birth as shown at the bottom. Follow the spiral around to each of the Nine Passages and you will find your place and see how far you have come. Whenever a young girl hears how she came to be here, that story informs and deepens her belonging to her family and to the Earth. Her very own Birth story transcends words and opens her spirit to a mystery dance between her small self with her Soul-self from the unseen world.

The Life Spiral begins at Birth

Most cities have open spaces; perhaps for ceremony, a small place in the corner of a neighborhood park needs to be claimed. Use what you have, this is the basis for ritual. When I lived next to a creek and a lovely river-rock bar, I used stones on the sandy beach above the creek for nine years of ceremonies. I used the Spiral for my own initiation when I wrote *Soul Stories*.[1] I believe in the intuitive messages received between Father Sky and Mother Earth, use what you have and it will be memorable. Photos and crowns, gifts from the Elders, these will integrate into a memory that will last her lifetime. Your daughter will feel like a fairy princess; that is the point.

Remember how the swirl took shape: Five girls and ten women. Suddenly everyone's personal tapestries began weaving with their future selves by using clouds of love, hope, and promises. With my spirit eyes, I could see this. Places where destiny and fate meet and play together, in the future, remain sealed in the nameless chapters of each girl's accumulating life story. This ceremony begins a life of awareness for change, where the intersection of development and circumstances open to her next call, and her next. For my grateful heart and the girls on their altar, women opened their hearts, their minds, and their spirits to the promise offered in this first ceremony. Stories matter, ritual makes them real and memorable, taking time for this pause to integrate changes, this could change the world. Mothers and Grandmothers will be alert and awake to the next call and the next.

FIRST STEPS

It was brilliant to bring our leader minds together the day before anyone else arrived. The three of us, Lorene Wapotich, Cassie Faggion and I, entered ceremony space ahead of the others and created a liminal bubble that everyone else stepped into. Our exercise of writing down a plan was good for our Western minds. We probably could have-should have ceremonially burned it. Spirit led us exactly where we needed to go; all we had to do was show up with a little trust. As we danced around the tipi, artifacts of past ceremonies came out of the box. I placed colorful, symbolic masks atop prairie sage bundles tied to each tipi pole. Our leader spirits harmonized one with the other. We felt prepared to create this earthy offering infused with a feminine spirit, backed by deep research.

Behind the scenes, in my prayer time the week before, I thought of each girl. I didn't know how her Soul had been welcomed to Earth, but I trusted love and good parenting. The Ancestor-realm offered a bit of fairy-dust to calm my imagination. I know well the spirit of the child self who peeks round Mother's legs and then quickly passes right into this Middle Childhood stage, boisterous and joyful.

Shy for Only Five Minutes

Our ceremony guests arrived along with the energy of Coyote (in Indigenous stories, Coyote is known as the trickster) and we felt laughter from the very beginning. Once the laughter started, Coyote who enjoys a good time, wanted to hang around for the whole weekend. Of course this is a metaphor, but a true one. As always, being well guided, laughter makes a better Plan B; women can always flex and improvise.

As we gathered for this Middle Childhood ceremony, I clearly saw those spirits emerge from their long car rides. One dear Soul ran toward me and placed a bunch of roses in my arms. Oh Allie!

Because my home invites play, I knew the girls, and the women too, would feel welcomed by my place on the planet. Everyone's faces told me they were ready for their first ceremony; I wanted to provide a ritual that would secure a marker in their conscious memory. With these threads to shape our tapestry, our weaving began.

Our design for this initiation included separation, a ceremonial altar, stories, a challenge, and two layers of integration. Wrapped all around and through our design was ritual like candle lighting and process, taking time for the story of emotions. Rather quickly, Initiates and women became playmates; we believe in plans that include play. As leaders who have lived and breathed Rites of Passage and initiation for ourselves, we told the women this was a teaching ceremony. We would lead the Mothers and Grandmothers through a little memorial Passage of their own and then they would wrap the bundle for their girls. The design was genuinely beautiful with the teaching piece that included a Middle Child experience and ceremony for each woman. It was filled with mystical surprises. We knew that once the women remembered how it felt to be 8 and 9, they would have hearts opened in the morning to gift the ceremony to their daughters in the afternoon.

THE GIRLS

Like the differences in women, the girls showed up for this ceremony displaying early signs of individuation. We were graced by two girls who were 8, two who were 9, and one girl who had been 10 for a couple of weeks. Differences in age seemed rather prominent to my eyes, but to the girls, experiential differences mattered not one little bit. Each one felt a readiness to step into her Middle Childhood. These girls showed excitement and nervousness to be in a girls' Circle surrounded by a women's Circle. Everyone's senses showed signs of alertness to learn about the mystery of a ceremony not yet in our culture.

Their ages and their girls' spirits made them fearless explorers. Mostly, they wanted to explore my intriguing woods' paths with the added thrill of a great creek. In August when cold water runs nine miles downhill over sun-warmed stones, it becomes delightful to play in. We gave them an orientation map as soon as they arrived, with no other instructions. None were needed. As a bit of a trick, we also invited them to go on a scavenger hunt to find the old tree house, a tent in the woods, and a tree with dark berries. Several of them made up their own game, crossed off items not found and wrote in items they did find.

Summer, Great Old Soul Just Turned 10

I watched them check in with their Moms again and again. They were big alright, as they went exploring on their own, yet one foot remained tethered to the careful conditioning from their little child days. I looked for the girls' collective readiness; they all displayed a desire to be recognized as a big girl. They squeezed around the women preparing food and wanted to be helpful. Yet, they were happy to chase back and forth to the tipi for this or that. They were edge-walkers, on the edge of being little and big, stepping with grace into both places. This is a tender time of life, but each girl felt completely ready to bundle her Early Childhood safely away.

Filled With Passion, Aresa

As I looked into one girl at a time with my Elder eyes, I saw the oldest was especially ready for prepubescent years of exploration and being in her body. Her name suits her perfectly, Summer is an earthy little Soul. When she looked out of her spirit eyes and into mine, we both knew she was going to have a good time with this next developmental step. She has an elfin smile, there's a trickster awakening in her. I thought, she will laugh her way through life if nothing wounds her spirit. Maybe we can teach her to heal any wounds that do come in, so she can stay light and in love with life.

The next oldest was Aresa with truly amazing red hair showing me her fire in wiggling and toe tapping. I saw how badly she wanted to run wild and free. She is a bit young to have such an expression, so she holds herself back. Actually, her lack of experience holds her back, but that won't last long. She's definitely got fire to work with as a metaphor. She will find so many facets when she looks within, she may have trouble choosing. I felt a kinship with her and immediately released her to the care of the matriarchal lineage that surrounds her.

Introducing Alethea, Horse Lover

I felt my heart go out to the girl with a love of horses to match my own. I smiled deeply within and swooned over the big red roses she gave me, her kindness touching me from the moment she sent her spirit out to greet mine. With the name of an ancient Goddess, Alethea will overcome whatever others deem an obstacle. I was not able to see her with spirit eyes for long; she has good boundaries and shields which prevented penetration from afar. There was a heart attraction that I still feel; I noticed her horse charm on a chain and knew we had a lasting bond through our horse friends. I want to say to her, "Let's be friends," even though more than 50 years separate us.

Aubrey, Heart of the Party

Another fire symbol showed through the fourth girl, I think she will burn her way through complications. Over and over, she revealed a volcanic force and then quickly hid behind it. Nick-naming her Beauty because that is what I saw when I peered inside, Aubrey seemed like a girl with endless personality who would add her comic relief and be the center of any party. Life is hard and Aubrey knows it. While she feels the whole spectrum of emotions, she will laugh all the way through, because her superior intellect will show her the underlying absurdity.

Always there's a youngest, this girl was happy for that spotlight. Immediately, I wanted to wrap Lena up in my arms and not let go. If there was one who would tough it through, but not feel good for even great accomplishments, it was this little fairy-queen, Helena, also named after an ancient Goddess. I believe she will outgrow her temporary setback of esteem issues. She is far too strong to be stopped and the force of her will lead straight into her watery passions. I have faith in Lena and her future and want to share my private action theory with her dear relations. Almost any altruistic action or creative act will serve to build self-esteem, action is a main component.

Introducing Lena (Helena), Youngest

I discovered a faith in every one of these girls; each one of them was my favorite. Their future selves need training for this world we have created, we of the older generations. As part of that training, these girls showed me how much girls need straight talk and kindness. I saw urgency in their emergence, they would soak up our well-oiled Elder skills and stories if we can only find ways to offer ourselves. Here is their sweet story about bundling their Early Childhood years and celebrating the arrival of their Middle Childhood.

We assembled in the beautiful tipi, the teaching lodge, crafted by Tipi-Lady, Debra Williams,[2] one of the Grandmothers bringing a girl to this ceremony. I asked the girls if they wanted to light the candles and the telling signs of helpfulness showed up right away. Still, they all dared to do something formerly forbidden to them and that makes me sigh with pleasure. There are just some things little kids do not get to do; one of them is play with matches. Big girls, asked to help with something formerly prohibited, received an immediate and unspoken sense of the change they were about to celebrate. They realized that I saw them as big girls from the first moments of our ceremony time and I am happy that such symbolic gestures appear. With the altar lit, we could begin.

Years ago, my husband gifted me with a long-fringe ceremony shawl, a Pendleton. Wrapping myself in it, I said, "I love to swirl this gift around me at least once a year." I asked everyone to stand with me to greet the Seven Directions and the guardian Ancestors in a salutation to invite in our sacred inheritance. My young leader, Cassie, drew from the Mohawk tradition offering their Thanksgiving Address[3] and sent it around for every person to express gratitude then send it on. Like other women's gatherings, this one was filled with old friends and strangers alike, so we introduced ourselves once again. This time around, we each offered a story-morsel from our own childhood years.

Author, Sharing a Moment

I gave thanks to Arianna Husband,[4] the Elder who gifted me with corn-meal and explained it was enlivened by cornmeal ground by the hands of an Apache maiden for her Moon ceremony. Wrapped in my shawl, loving the dramatic effect, I took the cornmeal and explained how the altar was set up as a Life Spiral. I said, "This is the reason for gathering," pointing down to the Spiral altar. "There are many ceremonies ahead and I want you all to see the whole picture."

"First, a Birth arrives in the East. Where that spirit comes from, we all want to know." Looking up through the tipi hole to the evening sky to em-phasize the mystery, I said, "Many think we come from the stars." All around the tipi there was a nod in agreement. "That means we travel far to have this great opportunity to learn lessons through a life on Earth." I left a pinch of cornmeal at the tip of the little marker for the East gate.

"Then comes this Middle Childhood time; the Threshold, once placed in ceremony like this one, marks maturity and invites a release of more than three thousand days of baby-hood," I motioned to the space on the Life Spiral between Birth and Middle Childhood. "After this ceremony, those baby sto-ries will be safely tucked away in your heart pockets."

Altar with Candles, Grandmother Stone, Womb-bowls, Circle of Friends Center and Cornmeal

Moving to the marker for the South, I said, "This whole space," gestur-ing from the Southeast marker to the South, "this playful place in the summer season represents all the days before puberty. The Coming-of-Age ceremony offers each girl a path of monthly visioning, a practice of sitting quietly through the time of her Blood to reflect and plan. There is much to learn from that quiet time with our deep selves." I dropped a generous pinch of cornmeal at the tip of that marker.

Motioning from the South to Southwest slice, "This next space, often called the end of high school, offers a great training ground before your wings sprout for Flight. I call the ceremony First Flight, because sometimes we return home with adventures and stories of life beyond our home nest. Yet, the Flight is just that, a testing of those two great wings at our back, our clavicles. Still, from puberty, youth lasts through the whole next decade and is often referred to as young adulthood. I say we are in training for Womanhood's Bloom." Dropping a pinch of cornmeal at the Southwest place on the Life Spiral, I pointed to womanhood.

"This place on the Spiral, my friends, opens to motherhood, career, or just good self-mothering, because now we're truly away from home. We must do everything for ourselves. Here we check in with the gifts we have to offer to the world and ask ourselves whether we are giving our gifts." With a swirl of my shawl, a bit of an adjustment to let my words sink in, I drop a generous pinch of cornmeal in the West place on the Spiral.

"Next on the Spiral is the place for returning to yourself. I call this time, Deepening Womanhood, and like straight across the Spiral to Middle Childhood, this is the place of Middle Adulthood. Often this is an empty nest, which refocuses on gifts of self. It lasts as long as we say, as long as we feel not-an-Elder, because the next ceremony on this long journey is the Elder Encore. We have so much to give at all places around the wheel, but this is the place where we look behind us and see who is coming around the Spiral and needs our helping hands."

I dropped cornmeal at the next two markers in a flourish and stepped to the place next to Birth. "We'd all like to reach this place, the Spiritual Elder place, and many blessings will be ours if and when we reach this delightful place. We may be ready for a rest, we may have lots of friends and relations by the time we get here, but most of all, each one of us will have a whole life for our enjoyment and review.

"With a knowing in my being, I reserve Death for its rightful place, in the center of this Spiral. Why the center? Because Death walks with each one of us all along this journey," I paused to let that reality sink all the way in. "If old Death comes early we call it a tragedy for all the other markers and ceremonies that will be missed, but through stories, we know Death does come early sometimes. We must respect the Divine and realize that we don't know much, we certainly do not know it all."

I sprinkled cornmeal around the center candle and stood still for just another minute. "Thank you for letting me show you the reason for doing this Middle Childhood ritual. This ceremonial mark on the Spiral, just past Birth, is the one to feed our conscious minds, as the first Rite of Passage, Middle Childhood celebrated sets the stage for all the others."

Looking to Lorene[5] for help at that moment, she stepped in on cue. I sat down feeling glad that I used the cornmeal in such a good and honoring way. She took us right into the introductions: Why we came, who we came with, and how we spend our lives back home.

Our life-story introductions effectively brought the girls into unity with the women who represented Mothers and Grandmothers, some present and some absent. With our memories synchronized, we became age eight or nine together and seemingly floated through evening routines. Each Soul went to sleep dreaming of all those days of early childhood.

CEREMONY DAY

Some of us had waited months for this day to arrive. It was much like a birth in that aspect and greatly anticipated. All of us knew that this was a rare occasion: So few ceremonies have been held for girls that none of the women present had any idea what to expect.

I crept down to the tipi before dawn's first light. My dog danced in the dewy grass until she was all wet and then pranced around every sleeping bag to give wet nose kisses to sleeping females. What a grand sight to see the spiral mosaic of women and girls, mussed hair, happy faces, squealing at the dog. That tipi space was transformed the very next time I looked, and I could hardly believe the alteration from dawn to after breakfast. What had served as a bedroom, now looked and felt like a space for women's spirits to do ceremony for a day to invite and celebrate change.

Our breakfast was a royal treat, one family offered scrambled eggs, homemade granola, and kept the toast coming until we were over-full. My house smelled like coffee and toast and my husband felt so at home with abundant female energy. Our breakfast was scrumptious. Being treated made it easy to open my kitchen and home to so many energized and expectant new and old friends.

As leaders, Lorene, Cassie, and I knew this whole idea of a Middle Childhood Passage would work best if the Mothers received a little ceremony of their own, after which they would build on inspirations received to perform the initiation ceremony for their girls. I knew a great story would emerge.

After a night of sleep, a morning of coffee and talk, we settled into the tipi space on chairs and pillows. For this Elder, there can be no more beautiful heart-warming sight than a large Circle filled with women and girls in ceremony. I was about to create this great story to inspire so many others—Mothers, Grandmothers, and other girls.

Our opening was soft and instructive. We sang rounds from a welcoming song offered by Arianna, our Elder sister far away and spoke to the anticipation visible on everyone's bright face. The leaders had a whole day planned but we revealed only the bare bones of our secret.

Girls Beading Gifts

Cassie took the girls away for the morning affecting separation—girls from women—one of the main ingredients for initiation. The youngers were going to spend some of their pent-up kid energy and make gifts. We have a few photos of the girls during this separation time so I felt like I spied on them. Each girl gave her full concentration to creation, they made gifts with a hidden meaning. I love this image, deep in the woods, the girls sitting with Cassie on a cloth from my Grandmother. As they strung beads, they were completely caught up with their creative selves. That focused attention with their muse will move all through their lives, as fire from their womb-space, their own creative spirit. If they stay open they will respond to many urges to create. I look at the photo images and can almost hear their chatter.

While the girls were gift-making in the woods, Lorene and I helped the women find the special spirit place of remembering details and specific feelings of being the same age as their girl. The bubble of early childhood sweetness and light, so alive in our imaginations, has already dissolved into a heart pocket before we arrive at this still tender Middle Childhood stage of life. Even though we may have been perfectly parented, the fairy-image we hold for all girls gets shredded by something. Every little girl already knows that life is unfair and can truly be painful. Their wounds and traumas need healing through art, through talk, through the fire of creativity.

Like women can do when sharing and deeply listening, we used up time way too fast telling the story of our child-selves. It's entertaining and still too rare to sit in a circle of women and share stories about a single time in our life. That was where we shined the spotlight and it felt really good. Since this journey began weeks before and memories were stirred up, women reached back to their own big-girl time of life and brought photos and artifacts to place on the altar. As the stories built from one woman to the next, our altar filled with images and symbolic depth. When we think of what we wish we had done for our big-girl selves, the energy flowed from us and healed a gap in our maturity.

What I heard from the women removed the fairytale of all sweetness. Like my friends sitting in our Women's Circle that morning, my childhood memories, true or colored, were not always perfect. Remembering even little imperfections brought fresh tears of truth and pain, the tears themselves salve for our wounds. For the simplicity of saying gratitudes: All of these women felt safe, secure, loved, and by the end of their remembrances, balance returned. No one showed or told of compounded or lingering trauma. For all of those blessings, I am grateful. More than sorrow, although we felt true sadness, we also experienced deep relief to be feeling the Passage of our Early Childhood in a sacred manner in the presence of so many loving witnesses.

Much wisdom emerged from our little selves in that morning Circle, and I hold the truth of deep sharing of those confidential stories. We shed more than a few tears, which is one measure for the good place we reached. Running out of tissues was another good measure. Also, we could have gone on the rest of the day, which means we felt safe with each other. The whole time we were in a sacred liminal space held by ceremonial intentions. We gave the one who spoke focused attention and she received empathy, compassion, and a knowing from every witness. That felt like pure golden love and was most healing. In our little way, we Initiated each other into this stage of life. Most importantly, we entered the frame of mind to be with our five girls.

Then, something magical happened. When we, the leaders, shared with the women that the girls would be back in only 45 minutes, every woman stepped up to the familiar pressure plate. In that very short time, we designed a plan for the Mothers and Grandmothers to perform a mystical ceremony for their girls, something both transforming and memorable. A professional face-painter sat in our midst and she made a kit for the other four women to use simultaneously. Masks have been a mystical transformer for millennia, so our girls' faces would be masked, honored, and revealed. We all agreed on the motion that would unfold after lunch.

Into the tipi rushed five flushed girls holding their secrets. In a quiet motion that said, "See this, don't ask," each girl went to her place on the altar and dropped her beaded anklet creations. The leaders had seen a metaphor for Mother's anklet holding all of her daughter's childhood memories. Each daughter would now step into her future wearing the second anklet. Back to the arms of comfort, the girls cuddled up to their Mothers and breathed excitement. They told more than they wanted and hushed each other.

I could see into the girls with my spirit eyes, how divine they looked at that moment. I had just been gifted a confidential download from their Mothers and Grandmothers. Now I could see girls about to step into their future selves. At this initiation moment, those girls realized they had been away and now they were different and that's exactly what they wanted and needed. The girls sensed their Moms had been through a change. They desired what we had in the tipi, a divinely feminine women's space filled with a spiritual stimulus that would be theirs.

Girls Returned: Women Hold a Secret

Here's what I saw: Coming back together allowed for time to breathe together, in silence. That was the gift from the Elders; we always feel it and know it when it comes around in ceremony. The transformative edge we seek comes in one second when the girls prance around the center to be seen-not seen. I know it's very rare to recognize it, so I am smiling into the reflection and feel thrilled that I saw it.

May we anchor the honor of her visitation—Changing Woman—both Mothers and daughters were altered in that very moment. I saw the shimmering of the invisible Threshold at the tipi door and how the girls had crossed over caused me to catch my breath. I felt highly honored to witness so many coming to their edge, crossing over in a second, and receiving their special gift of transformation.

In the flurry of women and girls with a common purpose, we all took a lunch break and every other kind of break. In less than two hours, loose ends bound women to creation energy. Food and party preparations held the excitement in suspension. We moved into the realm of festive celebrations.

Women and girls shared an incredible tuna salad medley, PB&J for non-tuna eaters, and all the trimmings. This was the edge. While we danced around the kitchen, one Mother said she felt like she had been through an initiation. I patted her bum like she was a young girl, and said, "You have." Thank goodness and thank the Goddess, our plan had penetrated superior skills of mothering and reached into her Soul.

I took an Elder Auntie out to my garden and we hastily gave thanks as we cut the stems to make five incredible prairie sage crowns decorated with flowers and ribbons. We had a really nice visit while we wove these crowns, holding rather delightedly the images of the five girls who would wear them.

On my dressing room mirror I had placed a sticky note to remind me of *empty presence*. The note was a gift from Arianna, my spiritual teacher who was with us in spirit. The holy and divine practice of slowing for that *empty presence* to arrive came while I changed clothes. That state of mind was a great gift and what I needed to bring the sacred back to the Passage ceremony of this day. This is the moment the girls were waiting for, the one they would remember long after their creek time melted into the puddle of play.

When I arrived at the tipi, I was probably a tad late, but I had *empty presence* with me and I was slowed. When I peeked inside, women were lined up in two rows, ready to make a portal of raised arms for the girls to move through on the way to their place on the altar. I put a match stick to my sage bowl, took my feathered fan, and smudged one round inside the tipi to dispel any negativity. Outside, the girls were held back so they didn't realize the deep inner ambience being created for them. I put my striker to the sage once more and worked the flame into a good smoke. I asked for oldest first and Summer stepped up.

"Have you ever been smudged?"

"No," she said.

"This smoke gathers your energy in a positive way and sends any negative thoughts or energies away. Does that make sense?" I waited for her nod.

Aubrey Tells the Others about Smudging

Teaching Girls about Smudging

"It's an ancient practice, so I begin with your crown chakra, your soft spot when you were born, connecting this smudge smoke to your spirit. Then I just cover you with fresh sage smoke, the plant energy does the rest."

All dressed up, little Summer had a blue flower in her hair and a hummingbird ally on a chain. She may be the oldest, but being petite, she had pixie energy. In the last moment before I released her, we shared a look that penetrated deeply through the window of each other's Soul. We saw that we would be long-time friends. It was her honor to be the oldest and go first; she earned this right through banged up knees and a broken arm. She earned it by nurturing her spirit in the woods and fields. As her friend, I could remind her of who she was when the chaos of adolescence took her away. "When I call you about this ceremony time, do you promise to tell me the truth?" I asked. Under the influence of smudge, she had to say yes. I passed her to the smiling Elder who presented her crown of transformation.

Stepping into next oldest, even though she wasn't quite the next, Alethea had watched the little smudging ceremony for her friend. When I asked if she had ever smudged before, she quickly answered, "No."

"Yes," one of the other girls shouted as our sacred bubble was distracted.

I put the striker to the sage to make smoke and started over. "I begin at your baby-soft-spot to connect to spirit, this is your crown chakra, and I use the feathers to smudge away any sticky negative thoughts or energies."

Alethea almost bowled me over with her dazzling smile. She beamed in the light of focused attention. I asked her to turn so I could refocus, there was much to share, much to say, but this wasn't the time. I sent my thoughts away and reached again for empty presence. I touched my lips and placed a little kiss on her forehead as a promise to keep our connection strong. I knew we had a lasting bond through our horse friends.

Behind my back, each girl received her flower-sage crown and a big hug from Kit, my dear Elder-helper. My attention returned to the smudge bowl. This was a sacred moment for the girls, both in anticipating their turn and re-grounding their energies after lunch. They entered ceremony with the dazzle of wonder showing on their faces.

Aresa stepped up to the place in front of me and we looked into one another's eyes. It's impossible to describe what her old Soul tried to convey to me. I had set the precedence, so I asked, "Do you remember being smudged at Grandma Camp?"

"Yes."

"I will begin with your crown chakra to connect with your spirit." When I heard a hurry-up message from her that she did not speak, I intentionally slowed down, and reached for the striker to begin again. Lots of smudge smoke would help us both, I thought. I asked her to turn around to change the focus so I could smudge myself a little. When she turned back around, Aresa's old eyes still penetrated my Soul. I touched my lips and planted a kiss on her forehead and felt so thankful for her Grandma and Great Auntie. She is like many girls, already flooded by her facets.

Little Aubrey couldn't wait for her turn. She stepped in front of me, wanting to talk and I shushed her, "Quiet now. I know you like being smudged. Let's connect with your spirit . . ." I trailed off as I smudged her with a happy intention to bring her heart and mind to the present. This girl is really good at being a girl and has received the great gift of her adult brain emerging early. She finds herself at that funny crossroad of being big and little simultaneously. When I planted a kiss on her forehead, I felt sure I had planted a seed for her future days as a big girl.

Helena had waited patiently for her turn to come, and gave me her biggest smile. Standing in front of me was one little girl ready to be big and very excited about that opportunity. Here was a girl who liked her body and already knew how useful it could be. She would be a natural, all-around athlete just for the fun of it. In fact, she would like her body and forget her spirit, so I intentionally upped the volume for her. "Smudging dispels negative energy, little friend, and connects your chakras in alignment with spirit. Can you remember that?" Oh, how her eyes sparkled. She nodded and as she moved beyond the cloud of smudge smoke, I turned to watch her receive her sage crown.

Gifted by that spirit-to-spirit connection with those dear girls, I followed Helena to the tipi opening and watched her pause at the portal opening to revel in the women's welcome. She barely got past one or two raised arms when the whole portal of women's arms descended around her in hugs and smooches. That was why we did this ceremony, that very edgy moment when one sweet girl felt loved more than any other day of her life. She would remember the feeling and see the photos; the memory will live on for her.

Girls on Their Altar

Girls sitting around the altar, expanded it, they became it. Crossed legs, with beautiful dresses illuminating their smiling and expectant faces, wearing flower crowns, and looking up at me; the whole radiant sight made me immediately weepy. The tipi circle had expanded to include several more Elders and Grand Aunties and Aresa's two Great-Grandmothers. All around an altar filled with candlelight, those five luminous faces beamed me directly into the realm of spirit. I realized they saw me as the Old One with the smudge bowl who had opened their spirits to this moment. I felt able and glad, and called forth to my purpose.

Blessed by two very capable leaders, they helped me with this moment when I needed to defer to them. I was overtaken by spirit so the blank I felt, I was supposed to feel. While I was left speechless and somewhat impaired, others stepped up. One of my Elder sisters was there in a supporting role as Grandmother to the youngest. When she stood in her glory, threads from all around the world emerged as a single golden strand from her heart weave. Her opening invocation, blended lands and beings that had touched her along her quest. Afterward, I fell to my seat in gratitude. All of my chakras had been awakened with her light and with the energies of girls on their edge. I love the re-grounding I received. I could only imagine that many of those dear old relations also needed re-grounding over the pageantry of the moment. The brilliance of ceremony rendered me invisible to myself, but I floated to the spiritual edge to observe how others were feeling and experiencing.

Fortunately, I also had the *empty presence* gift Arianna had given me scribbled on a sticky note. I lifted that note out of my pocket at this moment to pull me back from the edge. *Empty presence*, it said just enough. It could have said, breathe three times. I wanted this moment to elongate. Finding my voice again, I needed to be heard, because of several hearing aids in the tipi. So, connecting with many new faces, I said, "Welcome. Thank you for helping create that spiritual portal. These girls have entered the place of change and they know it."

With all eyes on me, I felt connecting energies coming from each woman, each girl. This was such a special time to say, "We have a few new faces and I want to be sure you feel welcome and supported. There is an ancestral way to introduce that we like. It will fill this beautiful lodge with our lineage and all those Ancestors who love a good party. Naming our Ancestors will set the stage and help the girls move smoothly across the Threshold we have created for them as they begin to integrate into their new selves."

Settling into my chair I said, "I am Gail, daughter of Fern and Leo, granddaughter of Flora and Harry, June, Hedley, and Fred." I motioned to the woman next to me, and around the circle our introductions preceded. All those who could see, noticed the tipi fill up with happy spirits.

Lorene, in her most elegant and welcoming way, spoke of the design that would unfold. That gave the women permission to position themselves and their girl in a comfortable space for sharing the stage simultaneously.

Aresa and Heather

This time of storytelling, when Mothers and daughters shared about each other's little childhood, and mask painting was beautifully accompanied by drumming and chanting to a rhythm like Mother Earth's heartbeat. What looked and sounded like chaos took over the tipi space but we all heard the drum. Ceremony leaders and our guests, sat around the edges and watched a magical unfolding. Dear friend and spiritual Elder, Eagle Woman[6] has worked through several initiations ceremonies with me and I was grateful to hear and watch her weave her own ceremony with ours. We had powerful spirits present to guide these girls.

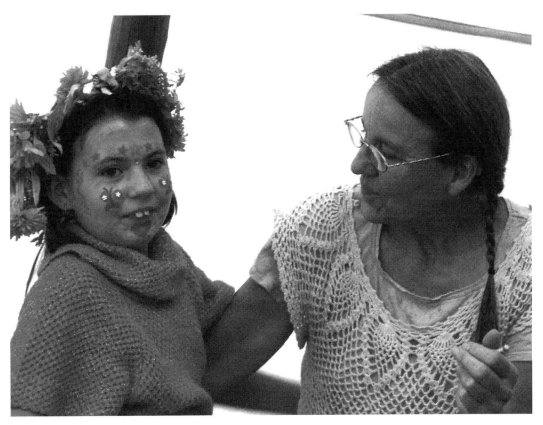

Aubrey Receives Grandmother Debra's Love

Then it was gifting time. Each Mother offered words and memories to cloak her child's spirit while she painted a symbolic design of many colors on the face of the changing girl sitting in front of her. Witnesses received tiny bits of the intimate sharing between Mother and daughter about younger years, and observed stories, photos, poems, and gifts exchanged. No longer her baby or her toddler, each woman was seeing her little girl grown up. For women and girls alike, this was the time of accepting change; the spirit of initiation penetrated every Soul in the tipi. Masks have been part of initiations for thousands of years. Behind each girl's mask, an emergence, a new being was lifted up to meet her new self.

We set up a stage in the tipi, beneath amazing painted flags for our awakening Souls that included Divine Girl Child, Blessed Maiden, and Sacred Mother, as if they had been made for this event. Sitting together on the stage, each woman formally presented her girl, telling a bit about childhood and what she sees now. The symbols she had created on the masked face of her girl helped each Mother to tell the childhood story and also expressed an excitement about meeting the new girl who would emerge from beneath her mask.

Each presentation was heart to heart, Mother to daughter, and a ceremonial sharing for all of us to witness. By watching, we felt the jolt each girl felt when she peered into the mirror. Just a little paint brought great expressions of approval and disapproval. One girl will never wear purple lipstick, she was truly aghast. Another girl wanted a whole new face painted right away; she knew just what she wanted, too. Along with being fun, as well as beautiful and poignant, those painted faces brought to the surface the conveyance of message from spirit. Every girl walked with her change already.

Alethea and Kelley

Helena and Kara

Summer and Michelle

We closed with a little more gifting. I told the story of watching the transformation of one local girl from the time she had her Coming-of-Age ceremony. I named Kaeli as the great maker of Unicorns who made one special for each girl. They were beautifully different and could be tucked inside a new little hankie to safely hold all of the stories of childhood. As I gave each gift, I declared, "This will be the best time," alerting each girl's spirit to the road ahead.

Impossible to Count the Blessings

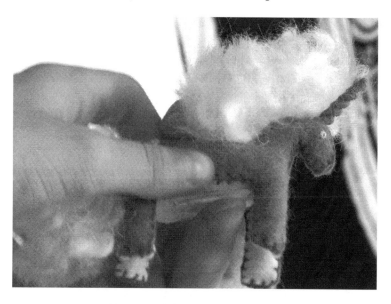

Unicorn and Crystal Gifts for Each Girl

Songs of Gratitude

That gave the signal to sing a closing song and begin the integration of change. We had rest and play time, we had celebration food to display and eat and we held one more surprise for integration around the evening fire. In less than one full turning of the Earth, these women and girls saw inside themselves as developing beings. We recognized our spiritual needs and met them with this lift in our awareness. We saw that we could do this for one another.

INTEGRATION: THE STRING WALK

Trees Hold Life's Stories

Saving the best for last, Lorene set up a challenge in the woods that began as a couple of balls of twine. She found one of my favorite places, an almost invisible trail I call CrossCut in honor of my sawyer Grandfather and Great Uncle. We reluctantly said goodbye to the visitors and Great Grandmothers who had attended the ceremony. Convening once again, we promised dessert right after and allowed the thought to trail off.

String is like life — Full of Tangles

One Grandmother objected to the challenge. We promised great support, close watching, and rewards greater than dessert at the end of this challenge. Once again the women were left with me to sort out their feelings as Lorene and Cassie took the girls to the one place they knew well, the Crossroads where they had made their symbolic anklets. None of the girls had discovered the CrossCut trail which began at the Crossroads. Here they were blindfolded and told they needed to use the string to find their way back through the woods. Not one single girl felt overjoyed, they were all rather terrified.

Strategically the girls were placed five or six minutes apart along the string. They were told the string would give them all the help they needed and would lead them where they wanted to go. Each girl had a different experience. As an individual, behind the blindfold and in the dark, every girl received the blessing of doing one very intensely hard task to begin her new stage of life.

The string walk was a great gift from spirit. Edgy and challenging, absolutely, but nothing in their life will ever be more demanding with quite that intensity. The girls were held by ten women, they were held by Ancestors, and they were completely free of dangerous hazards in my woods. Several girls met their own inner demons and quickly overcame those unspoken fears.

Explosive adjectives were used to describe their experience. I was stunned to silence by the amount of drama we created in such a short time. Tipi-lady served up strawberry shortcake, the best of the season, with lots of whipping cream. Finally, everyone agreed, this challenge was as good as it gets. I love that we could produce a transformative memory so easily. The integration ordeal came as the first and best challenge of their new stage, the best stage. "This is the best time," I said repeatedly and know it to be true.

In the morning, the girls could hardly wait to see their string-walk in the daylight and accused us of not following a trail. "Oh, yes, we did," it was my turn to protest, "and you each met some of my favorite trees along the way."

Everyone had slept hard with little dreaming and looked different in the light of a new day. We shared oatmeal topped with blueberry cobbler, feeling sad that our beautiful ceremony day lay behind us. I wanted to see the girls' change in the light of day after dreamtime and Changing Woman began to work together. I created a closing Circle filled with accolades for my dear friends and able leaders.

We discussed with the girls how to talk about the weekend. This carries an old-word, reincorporation, and means integration. I told everyone there, "Wait until the passion rises and tell that one part. In a couple of weeks, sit the family around a table and tell the whole story. Make it an honoring." These were all words of good cheer.

Offering one last tool, I spoke to the girls about paying attention to their inner voices and learning the difference between needs and wants this way. Boisterous girls are told to hush or be quiet. Their authentic selves are threatened by their need for approval. Lost in this battle, the spirit of self no longer speaks up and soon these early adolescent girls have a new risk as emerging women who dare not say what's true for them or consequences will bear down. Cassie took the girls away one last time.

For the Mothers and Grandmothers, Lorene offered a bit of the research about girl's voices and the need for girls to learn to ask for their needs and wants. This provides the perfect opportunity for Mothers to teach about the difference between needs and wants, one more time. We prepped the Mothers for the girls' return; they would be asking for something that signifies their new level of maturity. We asked all the women present to lean into this request. The girls had a rare chance of asking for more attention. I was honestly amazed that each girl asked for nearly the same thing, more time with her Mother.

I made presentations to my dear leaders, Lorene for being the one who came the farthest, for staying my friend and colleague forever, and for believing in this Passage as the one that begins them all. For Cassie, when I wrapped her in a synthetic, but really wonderfully earthy blanket, I thought of the babe in her belly and smiled deeply that our shared place was going to receive this baby. I am the welcoming Elder and I feel so deeply privileged. It doesn't have to be a girl, because we both love boys, but either way, Birth is the Passage that begins the journey through all of the others, for boys and for girls.

Now that the program was over, I had the hardest time saying the end, goodbye, when will I see you again? Two Elders and Lorene were getting on planes, the rest were driving far. If I let them go before lunch, everyone would be home by midnight. I released all of them with big prayers. We made promises to one another to stay in touch.

Beginnings and Endings

POST SCRIPT

Four days later, one of the Grandmas felt a pestering that had worked all the way through her Soul. "I feel nine years old and I want to walk the string, can I? Cassie agreed to help." Off they went to the enchanted woods, to the delightful place of self with self.

I, too, had wanted to walk the string. I, too, needed to feel the presence and absence of five beautifully challenged girls. I took my camera shortly after my Grandmother-Sister and walked with eyes wide open. I offer this for the girls, may you remember the inner strengths you discovered.

STRING WALK

I saw at the beginning the gigantic spider root,
Come along, help if you will, weave a story here—
This twine being just jute, swims between the worlds
Offering euphemisms, life is dark and scary, that is true
Looking at the back of a bandana, seeing nothing.

Girls cried over this, life is more down than up,
I think an untruth, it's an equal amount of both.

How about this one: if you fall just get up again.

On this String Walk, many times gravity just pulled
The force of the ground felt compelling, even good.
Metaphors serve real life in ways worth considering
Like, what goes round comes back ten-fold, remember
How many of my favorite trees you met along the way?
Can you imagine doing this in six months with snow
How about snow two feet deep? You're mighty lucky
For that string guided you from the spider root
Through a wood's ocean of lapping, slapping branches
Many tricky steps and trippy roots, even spider webs,
Here's the truth, not all of life is that intense or that easy.

One thing for sure, as the Earth spins and the seasons turn
Those trees will still be here whenever you come back
For another try in rain and mud, see how luck guided you?
Filled with fortune, life over-full with metaphors, invites
Even compels challenges; now that you're fully trained, just
Add humor. There never was a right or wrong way to do
Any part, big or little. Bring your tears, emotions feel great
We will always believe feeling is far superior to not feeling.

Bring your joy, like seeing the string in daylight laughter
No, there was not a set path. You getting back up, letting
Branches slap you, there was no harm meant, none done.

Whatever your memory, good or otherwise, you learned
About challenges, now go out there, get good at being you
Then tell us all how it feels to be your best self.

September 01, 2013, two weeks after
This is offered with my great heart of love,
Gail Burkett, PhD[7]

GIFTS FROM THE ELDERS: MIDDLE CHILD PASSAGE

Middle Childhood rituals will be **playful and earthy** as they set the stage for a life of Women's Passage ceremonies. Because Early Childhood is memorable our whole life long, the Middle Child Rites celebrates those memories.

The arrival of Middle Childhood causes the spirit of this child to look forward to her First Blood and First Flight ceremonies. This change releases Early Childhood.

Gather with family and friends to let the child-spirit know that her maturity is noticeable. This **pivot place** of celebration is the time when families tell the finest and happiest stories about the child so she remembers she was carefully watched.

Prepare for ceremony by stepping away from routine and using ritual symbols. What do you choose? Create a special day for you and for your daughter.

Consider the **essence of self,** how often do you see the world through this Middle Childhood lens? As the adult, try to walk in your own eight-year old shoes for a day.

How can you help your girl remember she has a special connection to the natural world? Consider how the natural world mimics and offers metaphors for change.

Teach her about **ceremony elements: Earth, Air, Fire, and Water;** these elements also create literally every material thing on the planet. Using these elements will help your girl stay connected to her Spirit and Soul.

At this edge, where little girls become big girls, now may be her only opportunity to celebrate the Early Childhood years.

Continue to watch for all the signs pointing to her gifts. Early personality quirks begin to show through her fantasies and innocent meanderings. She almost stands on her head trying to reveal her gifts to anyone watching. Help your girl open her curiosity, where she finds her fire.

She is ready for her Middle Childhood ceremony because she signals she is ready for more responsibility; she becomes your helper of first choice. Several things are born of this new level of maturity. The first may be the discovery of her shadow side.

Who has watched this girl grow?

What does her Father want to contribute?

✳ Does she have the brat, a princess, or perhaps the drama queen archetype? Speak about sexual predators, can anyone tell a personal story?

Do you see early signs of declining self-esteem, increasing doubt and self-criticism? These inclinations of pubescence can be derailed through a service project, giving to others really boosts self-esteem. The repair may be as easy as action: Think of what will represent a playful action that will take her mind off her negative feelings. To shift her energy, she may need free time to be with her curiosities.

Caveat: Throughout the budding years of Early Childhood, including infant, toddler, and 4-7, I recognize the cobblestones, how photogenic the stories are, and how crucial the foundations of these ages. Almost embarrassed, I confess to my own inexperience with the whole topic. I must relinquish Early Childhood to developmental specialists such as *Parenting from the Inside Out* (2013) by Daniel J. Siegel and Mary Hartzell (gender neutral) or especially for boys, this poignant research *When Boys Become Boys* by Judy Y. Chu with foreword by Carol Gilligan. For toddlers, Cassie Faggion, the mother nearest and dearest to me, suggests author Janet Lansbury's book *No Bad Kids: Toddler Discipline without Shame* (2014). My lovely friend Deb Hart Gift raised two boys and recommends *Big Spirits, Little Bodies: Parenting your Way to Wholeness* by Linda Crispell Aronson *(1995)*.

NOTES FOR MIDDLE CHILD PASSAGE

1   While ceremonies swirled all around, I took the journey of double-tracking through my own personal stories guided by the drafted manuscript for *Soul Stories: Nine Passages of Initiation* (2015).

2   I have lived in cities much of my life. My calling is to do ritual to celebrate growth, and for five years I experienced the enormous privilege of using a magnificent teaching lodge tipi made by one of the ceremonial Grandmothers, Debra Williams (www.sagebrushtipiworks.com). When the tipi went to the Burial Grounds, we used the blue dome, the night sky, and the cool indoors fluffed with fabrics and pillows. For your girl's ritual, please use what you have and know that it's perfect, that is where home and comfort lie. Women need not cross cultures to do ritual ceremonies, I no longer use a tipi. I use Nature because the sweetness of the people standing between the Sky and the Earth is our common bond. Draw from your Ancestors and the lineage of your daughter. This is important!

3   Cassie Faggion, a deeply experienced leader in nature programs, learned the Thanksgiving Address from traditional teachers and offers respect by opening ceremonies with connections to First Peoples.

4   An Elder and Soul Sister, Arianna Husband has gifted many things, including the potentiated cornmeal ground by an Apache maiden for her puberty ceremony.

5   Lorene Wapotich came from Boulder, CO and Feet on the Earth programs to fill out the leadership team, www.feetontheearth.org. In 2009, Lorene introduced, through a master's thesis, a new model for supporting girls' development through all female mentoring for Rites of Passage.

6   Eagle Woman, aka Debra Duwe, a local Elder has worked through several initiation ceremonies with me. Trained by the Deer Tribe in the metis tradition, I pull her in again and again as a gifted ceremonialist.

7   Researching for my master's thesis, I interviewed Mothers and daughters about truth telling and sharing everything. *Gifts from the Elders* originated there, in that research, when I realized the closeness that Mothers hope for is best secured with an intimate and regular women and girls' circle from age 8 to 18. After I finished graduate school, I published my first Rites of Passage book, Gifts from the Elders: *Girls' Path to Womanhood* (2004). It is still available through Amazon.com.

COMING OF AGE: FIRST BLOOD

THE INTENTION:
GIFTING WOMEN'S WAYS AT PUBERTY

When I speak of we, I include the many women who have entered this conversation with me, each of us bringing life, breath, and a newness to Women's Ways. Most of these women are Initiated Elders in an advisory and council way with me. We use humor for our long conversations because we differ so dramatically. Cultural repair is our reason to come together. We wish to raise the Divine Feminine to an accessible concept for our daughters and granddaughters. Our search has been long and continues. With this opening, we wish only to give Great Mother and the newly emerging Divine Feminine, a greater presence in our lives.

I give thanks for the Blood of my life, for the memories of being a bleeding woman. I give thanks for my Last Blood, witnessed only by my dog and the Ancestors. In deep gratitude for the natural world, I salute the birds most visible and rejoice at undulate tracks so numerous. With my heart-mind full of animal sightings and fish stories, my prayers encircle the seen and unseen who make our world worth living. Please share with me in giving thanks to Nature's great, wild diversity.

Dear Mothers, Grandmothers, Aunties, and Mentors:

Every woman looking down at the face of her newborn baby girl reviews her own life. As your girl transforms from Early Childhood to Middle Childhood, and then becomes a woman, you and your relations will remark about all the changes, and how fast time passes. Many Mothers wish for something more for their little girls, an improved version, especially at the tender juncture where childhood meets puberty and she is pushed into womanhood. Baby girls become big girls, prepubescent girls become newly bleeding young women.

Moving through the myriad of biological changes from height, weight, pubic hair, armpit hair, acne, enlarging breasts, and finally First Blood, each new young woman collects instructions on how to receive her womanhood. Long threads of advice come from Mother, then Mother's sister-friends, Grandmas, and teachers in school. She begins to say, "I know, enough already!" But, we're really just starting to weave. The old ways of telling a girl she will bleed and showing her a napkin, leaving her to tend, those ways and those days are falling away.

What can replace the complete secrecy of bleeding? Women of the tampon era have carried on like nothing could stop us. I was surprised by this news and these new ways as you might be, but I am determined to share for your daughters and your granddaughters. Our old ways made us cringe, something new yet very-very old has peeked over the horizon. This is about to change the world, Mothers, a very simple action.

BACKGROUND

The evolution of Herstory around menstruation is turning back to sacred ways for women. Hundreds of years have passed since women took the Red Tent or Moon Lodge for their very own time of visioning and gathering, wrapped within a tightly knit tribe of women. Every woman's lineage offers a unique and different answer for when their connection to these ceremonies became a lost art. Women's stories have not been well recorded. The Herstory that I would love to share here has been so fragmented it is impossible to piece together. Our collective sorrow has been experienced for so long, now we choose to simply change Woman's Way forward. We may give thanks for the Moon, la Luna, our ally in the night sky; she teaches women to count days between Moontimes and has been a constant companion for women's blood-time through eons beyond memory.

Women may think our history is clear-cut, but it's still murky. Long ago, first menstrual cycles occurred in young women aged 15 and 16. This middle teen marker held strong for millennia. From the origin of our species, sacred menstrual cycles flowed through women as the evolutionary gift for birthing the next generation. As humans awakened to speech, women's mysteries were viewed as too powerful. Taboo was one of the first words meaning sacred. When enough time passed, taboo became associated with dark mysteries and was seen as bad. We barely understand the great power of our Blood mysteries or the fear of women's sacred time, past or present. Through many generations, women's marriages arranged by tribal leaders or parents were keyed off a woman's first menstrual cycle and her adult-like behavior. Older women took this time, early teen years to 14 or 15, to train each maiden for her womanhood. Today, even the idea of womanhood training is rather astonishing. The reasons are legion: Women working second and third jobs lack the time, teen culture, Internet information. Why do you think our culture lacks specific trainings for womanhood?

Research now reveals an alarm surrounding this sacred cycle. The average age for a maiden's First Blood cycle has dipped to 12, even age 10 is increasingly more common. Menstrual blood is hormonally driven and extra hormones have entered into her blood stream from the food web. We do not accept this change without emotion. I wouldn't say I am happy about the lowering of the average age: I hope for 13. Still, change is undeniable, and now this has forced a re-think of ceremony and training for new young women.

WOMEN'S VISION QUEST

Rising from Indigenous roots is the Women's Vision Quest Way. This is a dreamy fragment coming through me from a beautiful Alaskan Elder woman[1] by way of a casual comment. She said, "Don't you know? In Alaska, we use our time of bleeding as Women's Vision Quest time. The vision quest possibility is only a part of a woman's whole Moontime experience. The Moontime focus is inner reflection as well as connection with creation ... with cleansing, purification, reflection, and regeneration and renewal."

Now this almost whispered secret has circled the planet a few times. Because of the great value to psychological and spiritual growth, Women's Way brings a halt to agendas. Businesses run by women are the leading edge of this change. Our Way now takes time off for visioning.

We know from our own personal experience that menstruation changes everything for a young girl. Her feelings run deep about the approaching monthly cycles. Often those resistant feelings are counter to reality. If she expresses androgynously as a tomboy, like many of us did at age 10 to 12, it's likely she will think her womb blood and the discomfort of cramps will just get in the way of other fun. Perhaps you're tempted to remind her of this absolute truth as an attitude adjustment: Every woman bleeds so she is in good company; every day that she bleeds, many millions of other women are also bleeding; and, sitting in stillness, those women ceremonially review their lives in the quiet of their own sacred space.

Your daughter may already know this Way forward, news travels fast these days. Her most welcome entry into this world of women is in the midst of its own seismic change. Tell her that during this quiet Moontime, women take stock of our dreams and polish our personal visions of the future. One simple action will change the world: Women's Vision Quest, practiced monthly, and practiced by millions, simultaneously, all around the world, this is Women's Way.

THE WAY FORWARD

Long ago we moved from our tribal contexts to agrarian, and now most women of the world live in city dwellings. What were once Women's Ways in hunter-gatherer contexts have dissolved, released so completely we can hardly find the thread. Somehow we must connect back, connect our wombs directly into the Womb at the Center of the Universe.[2] Our intuition tells us this is true, what women on the edges have begun to whisper, "There is another way." Let's use our imaginations and our intuitions to bring forth this Women's Vision Quest, bring it into the mainstream. Let's gift it to ourselves first, then to our daughters, and to our men, then our neighbors and employers. Take this viral!

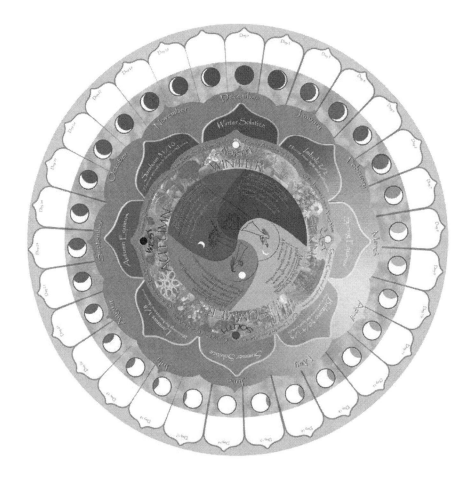

Moon Dial

Women are now demonstrating how this Women's Vision Quest happens during their blood cycles. Complete rest and rejuvenation may be just the hook to turn her Moontime into a sacred time, into a practice that she plans the rest of her life around. Tell her how lucky she is to be on the first wave of completely new ways of approaching this time of her life. Can a girl hear these words? Mothers can and here is where minds are changed. A few moons of experimenting will cause both a girl and her Mother to adopt this teaching together. This may be the missing link.[3]

Planning with a Moon calendar, an area where women excel, can smooth out all obstacles. Thanks to conscious menfolk, this new Way for women becomes a rest time for Mothers of small children as Moon cycles resume after nursing is over. During this rest time, Mothers begin to dream of bleeding with their daughters. When a girl's biology indicates signs of puberty, Mother begins to share her space, being welcoming and instructive. Women's Way will work around stubborn and strict employers and all other complications in modern lives. The Moon calendar makes this possible. Many women have left the complications behind already.

The world will hum in the presence of the Divine Feminine if we just make this prayer to ourselves. For over-stretched and over-stressed women, this may be a life-saving prayer. For the new generation, the First Bloods, this may also be life-saving. Consider deeply, the wholeness that awaits each woman inside of this word: Rejuvenation. Would you like to change the world? Sit in stillness on your Moon. You may soon synch to the New Moon or the Full Moon, and all of the world's women will bleed together, in stillness, practicing sacred rejuvenation—phenomenal.

Start wherever you are this month. Everyone will be in a slightly different place. Maybe you need ceremony for yourself first, maybe you and your daughter already bleed together, but maybe you still have that time in front of you. Look to the Moon; make a date with yourself on the calendar and a prayer-pledge to keep a date with the next New Moon. This may be the most important first step all of us will take to bring us together in Moon energy, in Sister energy. Soon every bleeding woman and formerly bleeding woman in the world will be sitting in silence in the dark just before the New Moon. We may call her Grandmother Moon as women of old times did. Women and girls could pay closer attention and renew their gratitude for her descending Crescent reminder. In the early morning hours, Moon's waning expression of Sun's reflection, announces the Dark of the Moon that comes just before the New Moon. Blending observation and intention brings a blessed release of Blood into synch with this holiest of Moontimes.

Once you know your own flow pattern, Mothers, then your modeling will become a powerful force for your daughters. Teaching comes before learning. For help with planning, we have the Moon to thank. She is completely dependable and for most women, that beautiful orb in the sky, la Luna, will help plan this sacred ceremony into your lives. Monthly and dependably, our bodies synch with the Moon. Her lunation cycle is exactly 29.5305882 days. She helps us become excellent planners. Closely watching and inviting the Moon's light to fall directly on the iris of your eye will help create the synchronous rhythm. Said simply, encourage stillness to become a regular part of your life and sit in vision time for some or all of your menstrual bleeding. This new Way of observing monthly cycles comes as a gift from the Moon; it's our women's Moontime.

If your own Moontime is very regular and synchs with the Full Moon, then celebrate your personal power and learn to rest while basking in Moon glow at the height of her expression. Women who are especially charged with inner fire may always bleed with the Full Moon or it may be a particular decade when powers are heightened. You will only know your patterns when you begin charting. This is the potent model you wish to share.

Before we consider your daughter's ceremony, we may need to change your perspective about how to proceed. For you to get in step with this Women's Way, please allow me to propose a personal ceremony to celebrate you. A season of Moon ceremonies will catch yourself up to these Ways and teach you what you wish to pass along to your daughter so that you may begin modeling this practice. Make personal experience your ally.

From *Soul Stories,* Rituals for Catching-up

Quickly and together, we have reached the crux of our work: Transforming this time of women's bleeding from the First Blood to the Last Blood, from the silent curse with a rag, into a sacred Moon-guided monthly vision quest with the Divine Feminine inherent in woman's nature. Consider the intention of this change in how a woman experiences her time of bleeding.

Blood time is women's most holy time, alone and blessedly quiet.

Women, feel what is right for you and enter a ceremonial process to find your true place on the Life Spiral. I am the encouraging one; I hope to inspire you. Women, Mothers, do your catch-up ceremonies in slow time. Begin before memory, at Birth; if possible, learn the story of your own birth. In my Council, we called this double-tracking, reaching back through time to re-story and do our Divinely Feminine ceremonies where they were missed, because no one imagined them, or they were forgotten while crossing oceans and continents to capture the last frontier, or in the rush of raising children, or simply surviving in wild and irreverent times.

In my way of knowing women who did all these things, my Ancestors, I have found the thread they left behind. I reached back through my lineage to discover the women in my tribe. Other women in my Council did the same. As an opening to identity awareness, Mother and daughter may also do the same. The basic question is this: Who are the Ancestors of your Mother and Father?

As a gift of knowing, the Council's ceremonial work around me and with me, gave rise to the book, *Soul Stories: Nine Passages of Initiation* to be used for double-tracking while catching up ceremonies. We put our seal of approval on the method to bring an honoring to all women from 30 to 100 who missed Rites of Passage through their early years. You see, this First Blood-time is the third of nine Thresholds of development; the road ahead is brighter than you can imagine.

Consider the memories of your own Early and Middle Childhood times. Our Ancestors used Earth, Fire, Water, Air, Nature, and handed these down to us. What needs to be called forth in your heritage to be renewed in ritual? Consider how to blend your inherited ritual elements with those of others. Make yours a conscious collaboration. Gather one or two friends to create a new Circle or convene your Women's Circle, light candles, sing songs, shake rattles, and share stories to commemorate all the days of your own childhood up to your First Blood. You may begin with a review of your life, call forth and heal every day, every major event of your childhood, ease away any lingering pains. Sit in a circle, pass a talking piece and tell those stories to your circle of women friends. Your daughter needs you to do this work; your healing will heal all of womanhood. Then you can help her create a practice for herself.

You only need to focus to catch yourself up, step into this ceremony, if only a little bit ahead of your daughter. The gift that follows will come from you and circle back to you. You will set up a boomerang energetic, what you give you will receive ten-fold. This will keep her with you always, even as she individuates to make herself different from you.

CEREMONY

Now that you and your friends have reviewed and bundled your development in a ritual, we return to gifting the same initiation to your daughter, as a gift to her Soul. I will focus on the not-yet-bleeding maiden, but I include every woman. The inner Divine Feminine comes to a woman the very first time she sheds menstrual blood. By habit and by perspective, we still call her a girl, but not for long. Quieting ourselves, opening our spirits for wisdom, the presence of a sacred Mother-Goddess comes to call at Blood-time. Feminine instructions come into each woman for direct visioning. This is how to foster the Divine Feminine and invite her to return to be with us in the world.

I propose a coming-of-age ceremony for girls to celebrate this auspicious event whenever it does come, and I call this her First Blood ceremony. Young women's first menstrual cycle (any one of the first 13 Moons) must be a celebration so every girl will have this Vision Quest Way to look forward to. Release any grief you may feel if her sacred Blood comes while she is still a girl, give her a story to carry. Neither the ceremony nor the celebration needs to be dramatic. Mothers and Grandmothers, set the tone for your daughters, perhaps soft and quiet, musical and memorable. You will lead your daughter or granddaughter through a training that focuses on her special time.

This is Women's Vision Quest time. That is what the Alaskan Elder woman said. We are all blessed once each month with an opportunity to calm down our busy-ness. Visioning invites us to be still. Quietly, we raise our conscious minds and reclaim a sacred time for the ease of looking back and looking forward. As a monthly review during Moontime, journals and art get caught up, the inner critic and judge come back to a resting place, and holy intentions—good healthy daydreams—begin to take shape, Moon by Moon.

With reverent focus, become part of the answer to this question: "How can women create a consecrated, Divine ceremony for each one of your daughter's eggs?" Softly, I say, honoring Moontime is Women's Way forward.

A coming-of-age ceremony is a gift that acknowledges the Mother-to-daughter bond. Every blessed change you have seen in yourself now reflects through your daughter. A little thought and a little focused training will open the edge of her womanhood in a way that causes her to consider who she is becoming. Who was she born to be? As a sacred practice, she will use her time of Blood, every time, for the purpose of looking a little back and a little forward and building her life, one Vision Quest at a time.

Beware: 21st century women and girls move at high speed. It's a cumulative energy—we do because we can. Our brains have evolved into beautifully tuned orchestras, even multitasking is passé. During blood-time, Moontime, tend to your Soul and its need to quiet all the way down. This is when women gain the most direct attunement with our inner selves. Even your most brilliant self needs this recharge. Grant permission on your schedule to seek spiritually delivered intuitive messages. This is a modeling, a practice, at its most powerful. In the grand scheme of things, every new young woman's most profound blessing is this idea of 400 nearly consecutive Vision Quests. When she synchs with one of the Moon's expressions, New or Full, she never needs to miss a time of visioning. This is Woman's Way—in quiet candle light, with little care about time, you will be rewarded direct access to your Soul's instructions.

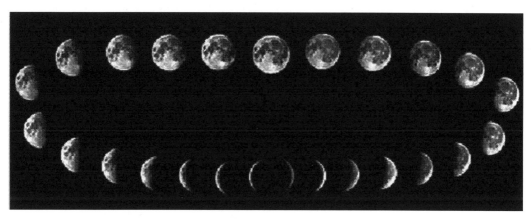

Moon Watching Connects Back to the Grandmothers' Spirits

REJUVINATION

Your Woman's Way of living-being-doing all those things on your wish list comes to you on your cycle during your Moontime. The unbelievably great gift of quiet and calm days comes when your sacred red blood flows, but only if you grant yourself permission. Allow your bleeding days to be a time of absolute quiet to connect all your highly energetic activity, past to future. Recharge. Listen. Evaluate. Dream. Two days, three days, parts of four; can you give yourself permission? Can you share this gift of rejuvenation with your daughter?

Mothers, you open our Elder hearts with your devotion to your little girls. See into our Elder Circle as we wrap our arms around you. Our sacred prayer is that you may rejoice and release. During First Blood, your girl becomes a woman, whole and beautiful standing next to you, still clasping your hand. Except she now bleeds, she may even bleed when you do. Now we turn our hearts and minds to your daughter's First Blood, when you become mother-teacher-ceremonialist. Ask your friends to help, there are Mothers and daughters nearby who want to do this with you. Cast your gaze around your community, there are Elder women ready to assist.

Your instruction and example of setting aside time for stillness, for a sacred interlude, will be her greatest benefit of learning from you. Many things about your life will be sourced, researched, remembered and awakened in the quietude of this bleeding time. You will want to teach and share all the obvious and all the obtuse things about womanhood. What do these things mean to you? Consider—blood, sex, men, women, struggle, passion, pregnancy, childbirth, motherhood, intimacy without sex, pleasure with her body, competition, love, jealousy, oppression, lust, betrayal, oracles, sacred Nature—women know about these things and girls want to know. Find your own support for the sex and pleasure topics, gather a round-table of other girls and Mothers to ease the awkwardness.[4] Your teachings are as diverse as your experience and you will design her ceremony your way with your beliefs, hopes, and dreams. Still, every girl wants to know about one key fact of her life: How the Moon guides her flow. So, begin with Moon teachings, they are fun. When you are both well versed, consider teaching her father and brothers about the Moon.

Being at least 60%, perhaps closer to 70% water, women connect deeply with the Earth's waters, especially the tides. We love all waters in every form, streams, rivers, lakes and ponds, even water from the faucet is precious and rare. Like great waters around the planet, our bodies respond to the Moon. The Moon pulls women through our cycles. It's the Moon's pull that causes our cycles to be regular. Let's say, mostly regular, since every woman is different. That's where this new term originated, Moontime.

Water of Life

The Moon even helps us stay hydrated by holding and releasing bodily fluids. With the Internet, Moon images abound, but whenever possible, connect directly with the Moon in the sky. She's visible in all her phases as a floating pale orb, seemingly washed and white against blue. See if you can follow her faded self when the Sun is bright. Her beauty is nearly as stunning in the subtlety of her washed-out reflection. Moon's power comes directly into us through our eyes. To begin to synch to her rhythm and learn cosmic time from Grandmother Moon, women only need to lay eyes on the Moon whenever possible. Become a Moon tracker, she is always there, somewhere. Except on the dark days, her powers grow most sacred when there is literally no-Moon. You will only know if you are on or off track with the Moon's cycle by actively tracking. Rest with your Moontime and discover your truth in 13 Moons. We need to create our own lore about this, dear women. We will change the perspective of the culture as soon as we change our own. Moontime teachings begin in the admiration of the beauty of Earth's Moon.

Teach about the stages of the Moon and her language. Some language has been offered by the astro-sciences, but I like the women's version. Women I know find great joy in noticing how we synch with the Moon. Your daughter's women relations—Mother, Aunties, Grandmothers—need to practice and introduce the sacred side of this menstrual Moontime. Women are raising the Divine Feminine through our small personal acts, shared one on one and in small circles. Depending on your rising level of intimacy, this sharing will become all the more sacred.

First, prepare a space. Is it a room or a corner of a room? What needs to be there so its stillness will feel inviting? Probably candles or softened lighting will create the ambience of awe. Colorful pillows, for sure will accompany meditative tools, a sitting cushion or a chair. Add your Moon journal and other books, mandalas for drawing on, and your favorite music. This is a space to move into for sleeping, for deep visioning, and for our new favorite word, rejuvenation. What are your elements and cultural symbols for ceremony?

Now that you know what you know, the rest is up to you. I am happy to share the following story of a 3Moon training for a First Blood maiden, but only to inspire and encourage. Rituals drawn from your lineage and from your Ancestors, work through your imagination. I have a space to share on www.ninePassages.com. Share with me and I will share with you. This is Anathea's story.

Nature Inspires Learning with this Symbolic Yoni

A STORY: MILLENNIAL GIRL'S FIRST BLOOD CEREMONY

When a young Mother asked me for her Womanhood Ceremony, she did not hide her reason. She wanted Moon teachings and womanhood teachings that she could share with her three little girls. She had attended our ritual celebration of the Great Catch-up Ceremony and presented me with my Elder's Shawl. She too, wanted to catch up on her missed ceremonies, because her daughters were growing up fast. Her timing was impeccable.

One year after a beautiful Medicine Woman from my inner circle, Debra Duwe and I fulfilled that Womanhood Ceremony for Mother Accalia, her oldest daughter Anathea showed definite signs of puberty. Beginning on the New Moon of April and ending on the New Moon of July, Mother and I timed her ritual ceremony and celebration to finish one day prior to Thea's thirteenth birthday.

Request for Ceremony, to Grow-up, to Separate

Before this Millennial child came to my creek-garden place with her Mother and two sisters, I felt anticipation build in me. Then, our eyes met for the first time. Our hearts twisted, one around the other, like vines. Looking down, shy as shy can be, she requested a ceremony because she was close to her time. I introduced her to this unique combination of words, First Blood, so she could look forward with an energy of eagerness. That old veil of secrecy about this first womanly fact finds no place to hide near me.

Before we enter into ceremonies, which designate great change, we must locate our respect and our center so we can begin. She had come on a New Moon day to make her request of me. Thea and I will always remember the freshness of the air and the long-sleeping daffodils nodding their heads; this spring season marks the place where we first went deep in our relationship as Elder and Initiate.

We felt the personal impact of uncovering ancient practices—Elder offering Women's Ways and maiden requesting basic training. She and I would work together to create a framework story for others. We would best begin with prayer ties. Anathea came to create a story for herself and for girls many generations into the future. This sacred way of beginning—with personal prayers, good thoughts for family, community, and prayers for the planet—symbolized an important link between the opening of Anathea's 3Moon training, begun on the New Moon and closing on the New Moon three months later.

Her Mother, Accalia and two other daughters made ties and spread smudge smoke over prayers with Thea and me. A teaching was shared about what might go into each little red bundle of fabric and tobacco. A prayer is a sign of gratitude and a way of slowing your racing mind. When you find the place inside yourself that feels thankful—go ahead, give thanks for safety, yes, health, yes, maybe some little personal prayer—that's the moment the pinch of tobacco is dropped on the tiny red square, just big enough to be tied with a string.

I explained making prayer ties is a ritual handed down from the Native peoples all across our country, maybe from around the world. Into our red bundles, we offered an exchange with the entities responsible for hearing prayers of gratitude, prayers of hopes and dreams, prayers asking for family wellness, all secured in a pinch of tobacco on a square of cloth bound by a string. A mixture of dried plants and cornmeal would be a fine substitute. Once those prayers are strung together like beads on a necklace, they create a bundled offering to hang on a bush or tree branch which allows the Sun and the Moon and all the cosmic energies to act on those prayers. Inspired, I decided we could tie ours to the naked legs of the tipi.

Anathea, a bright and sunny twelve-year-old blondie and oldest of the three girls, played the big-sister guardian role and shared her chair and the spotlight. All three sisters were going through change and needed recognition. Although I only signed on for one Passage ritual, I welcomed an entire household of females going through drama and change for themselves. My Elder eyes recognized all the signs.

I shared the word *intention*. I said this carefully so Mother might repeat this teaching later, "Speaking an *intention* creates a place for your hopes to dance. You might ask for good Moontime teachings and feel satisfied."

I like the number seven for the four wind directions, plus the above, below, and center energies, so we each made seven red prayer ties, beseeching to the spirit world, to the God of our understanding. Those little bundles of prayer energies would hold our space for this 3Moon ceremony.

Although the season rains had not yet stopped and the skin of the tipi had not been placed around the poles, we went to the tipi space and each one of us, Youngers and Olders, selected a pole for our bundle of prayers. Tying our prayers above our head height, we admired those ties that would later be burned at our closing ceremony. The Navajo *Walking in Beauty*[5] chant guided our tracks in the mud as we circled around those tipi poles; five of them were adorned with prayers made sacred.

Moon Dial for Journaling[6]

With beauty before me may I walk.
With beauty behind me may I walk.
With beauty below me may I walk.
With beauty above me may I walk.
With beauty all around me may I walk.

That first day I passed on this beautiful Moon graphic to Anathea, saying, "This graphic shows you the many stages of the Moon and will also show the many stages of you, if you pay attention. It is a gift from all the Elders, from all the women who have entered womanhood before you. We will examine the Moon in great detail in the coming weeks." To complete this gifting time and close our ceremony, I offered a Moon Journal to go with the graphic. That closing released us to the creek to play in the water.

Then, dancing to the cadence of the *Walking in Beauty* chant, we trailed through the woods to the beach above the creek to see the spring runoff. All three girls loved playing in the sand, middle sister displayed Genius creativity with design and construction and little sister lost one sandal in the fast waters. They felt the natural draw of the noisy, exhilarating creek, fast and cold from melting snow.

Seeing with my old woman eyes and also with eyes which remembered being 12, the biological signs of readiness shined through this woman-becoming. Oldest daughter revealed herself as a completely differentiated Soul, thinking for herself at the tender age of 12. She felt the holy influence of both parents and their spirits, and she took in all she could, all she was supposed to absorb. She reveled in their security, but she also declared herself to be the decider in her life: She will decide what to think, she will decide what to believe. I could see her Soul self, her Higher Self emerging though that safety net of dependence still wrapped around her.

As the Earth released winter and began skipping through spring, I took my solace in each new dawn, each bud, every natural sign directed me to catch a message from spirit. Our 3Moon ceremony unfolded easily because I received help from the natural world. Eggs, buds, and occasionally seeing the Moon, kept it all in motion as I held the important questions: What did Anathea need to know to make her more comfortable right here, at this first gate opening to her womanhood? What will pull her through the early teen years and prepare her for the Passage after this one, the emancipation gate I call First Flight? What will this story mean for other young girls, for their Mothers, and for their Grandmothers?

I knew practice was one key. In teaching Anathea the practice of stillness, she will create her own ritual of attending to her spirit during her flow of blood aided by her own ancestral lineage. Her Blood-time would be matched to her practice of sacred visioning, this holy idea felt like an energetic earthquake to me. I reached back to Judith Duerk's[7] question, the haunting one: "How might your life have been different if there had been a place for you, a place for you to go to be with your mother, with your sisters and the aunts, with your grandmothers, and the great- and great-great grandmothers, a place of women to go, to be, to return to, as woman? How might your life be different?"

I am closing in on an answer for myself and offering this to maidens coming into their conscious minds, their choice-making minds. Creating conscious sacredness around women's flow and practicing intentional stillness will build an incubator of depth and meaning for women's enormous creativity. The dual powers of Soul and Others, all those in relationship, radiates into a single woman who sits alone. What's the one thing I wish I had known? I wish I had known that millions of women attended their Moon days at the same time I did. I could have used that connection. Women hold this understanding now, it's a practice worth passing along. Make this imagining a practice for yourself and find yourself in dazzling good company. Sharing keeps us connected and in the river flowing along together.

Delicious conversations happened in my head between the Wednesday afternoon visits from Anathea and her family. Almost every day became a

Medicine Walk for me, as I focused on the spirit of Anathea and this edgy place in her life. That became a theme for our shared time, this edge. She was on the edge of her childhood, so we celebrated every day that brought her giggly, frivolous joy. I reminded Anathea about her child-self: Her beautiful smiling joy-filled bundle of a wee girl would live in her heart-mind and be there for her musings and her imaginings whenever she put her focus there. Now, we looked together to her edge of becoming a woman.

Swelling Cottonwood buds reminded me of this formerly flat-chested girl, her breast buds beginning to emerge, a girl becoming more like the trees. When her time is right, biological changes lead up to First Blood—brain expansion, pubic hairs, armpit hairs, sudden growth spurt, and breast-buds—these biological events happen on a unique timing for each girl. A force, the creative center of the Universe, perhaps the Womb of the Universe, caused her spiritual uniqueness. This truth floated around Anathea to deeply protect her inner Soul. Every girl-to-woman journey is beautifully different. Unique unto herself, each woman is remarkably different from every other woman, and a miracle.

Nature's Metaphors are Easily Found

Sky blue eggs nested together waiting to hatch. I made the natural connection between those delicate little treasures and the eggs born inside each girl child. I would tell this to Anathea. Between 300 and 400 eggs reside patiently inside her woman's labia waiting for a turn through the Moon cycle. Those eggs were inside her Mother, inside her Grandmother, waiting their turn. Evolution made this so and we have evolved to know this.

Month by month, a single egg will release into her uterus, her womb space. Protective blood gathers around each egg awaiting fertilization. Potency is often a state of being; the blessed combination of intention, luck, and timing of her Moon cycle helps decide the journey for each egg. Young women, at their earliest cognizance, need to completely understand the complications and responsibilities of their sex drive. They need a mature understanding of sex long before they feel lustful. Women have evolved to reproduce so we have hormonal urges that can barely be controlled. Culture can only offer a little control; the girl herself must provide the rest.

WOMEN'S VISION QUEST

Yes, women, there is a spiritual connection that will deepen with the practice of tending to your womb's request for quiet. Women's Ways are changing from the industrial frenzy and a need to act-as-if nothing is happening. Rather new, changing one woman at a time, Women's Way is the deliberate celebration of Blood-Time, around the world now referred to as Moontime. Personal peace and power depend on contemplative rest while seeking one's deep inner intention that wants to come to the surface. This is the quest for a vision, month by month. When the youngest new women receive this teaching as a practice and see it modeled by their Mothers, quiet time will lead to increased power for visioning our lives. Psychologically, we hold enormous amounts of grief. Sitting in the spiritual company of millions of women creates a perfect cradle for all our collective grief. Release it, deliberately, and as soon as possible. So many women have looked squarely into this sacred intersection of blood flowing with the Moon's power. See this obvious connection for yourself, especially at First Blood, and create a reliable practice with initiation. Receive this gift of Blood with your heart-open. Welcome to womanhood. These teachings will change the culture for women.

I held a question more immediate because of the innocence before me: How do I share this 'big picture' concept? Most women will experience a timed release of one egg after another for over 40 years. My more wizened intuitive self told me to tell her straight, even though she is a tender and wide-eyed 12 year old. Anathea is a woman-becoming. I may not have been able to hold such a wide view myself at 12, but I would have appreciated being told. The information found its way into my understanding, but it took a very long time. Mothers, consider sharing these facts with your daughter at some point in her teen years. Maybe here is the best time; you decide as you prepare her for her Moontime practices.

Although Anathea's First Blood had not yet arrived, her time for this great change was imminent. She walked the trails through the woods with her developing body each of the Wednesdays in May and June, leaving a bit more of her childhood in the path behind her. The woman-becoming grew more visible.

Over the next weeks teachings were shared, Elder to Initiate, and Anathea and I grew closer. The whole family practiced being quiet with me and we spent time in the tipi listening to Clarissa Pinkola Estés'[8] powerful storytelling voice weave its spell in the ear-bones of our hearts. Laying in a circle on the floor of the teaching lodge, we put one of Clarissa's recordings from *Theater of Imagination* in the center, each of us ready with our watercolor paper and brushes. When we pushed the play button, we agreed to be silent with our artful selves.

Girls Know Altars are Holy

Each of us felt something rise from deep within. We practiced quiet while we created mandalas with water colors. A precious combination of storied art in the quiet of Soul-seeking provided us something special, an experience and a model to move our lives forward. In the heart of our time together, I gifted Anathea ways to know her Higher Self. Meditative mandalas were hung on the tipi poles to remember quiet time. As a practice, mandalas can be filled with painting and writing. Doing this play practice, we followed the precise recommendation for Woman's Vision Quest time.

On altar day, I taught Anathea and her sisters about sacred ceremonial elements: Earth, Air, Fire, Water, Nature, Wood, Metal; any combination of these will hold sacred energy and form an altar. Metal may be a bell, that may be air also, or a flute could be air. Earth could literally be soil from a gopher mound or ashes from a sacred fire. Water could be a beautiful bowl with a floating flower next to a candle for fire. The water could be present in a vase holding a summer bouquet.

Nature weaves through everything. The same altar or a new one each Moon will create a personal place to practice silence and prayer for monthly visioning time. I taught her to take time, hold a prayer in her heart, use the sacred element of quiet to design an altar, these bring the essence of spiritual to the mundane. Enriched with sacred items from her unique cultural heritage, something from Mother, Father, Grandmothers, Grandfathers, these items will add depth and meaning to her experience.

Creating a sacred space and calling it an altar, sends a signal to her brain to quiet down. Slowly the language of symbols begins to emerge. This symbolic language connects us to the Ancestors, to the constellations in the heavens, to all the oracles ever practiced, and to the heart of our creative imaginations in our womb space. I suggest young women begin their ritual experience by building an altar.

Anathea and her sisters practiced building an altar in front of the hanging mandalas, using the elements we deemed sacred. The girls and I noted that these sacred elements were gifts given directly from our Ancestors, still used by all women doing ceremony. I asked Anathea to look around and tell me what she could see that was made from something other than these simple, sacred elements. That challenge rendered all of us mute.

Anathea teetered on the edge of her womanhood. For some time, perhaps as long as a year, she has pointed her mind and her body toward this edge. Coming to womanhood is like falling off a cliff, when I said that, her eyes grew as wide as saucers and we both laughed. I told her as the biology of her body releases childhood, the amping-up of her hormonal juice causes her Blood to flow with the Moon. These hormones blend with new brain chemicals to begin to form a woman's psychology that is different from childhood.

This is what it feels like dropping off a cliff. She would fall deeper into her womanhood with each passing Moon, and she would know herself better if she put her attention there. *Focused attention* is one of life's great secrets, in fact it is a foundation stone. I told her I became an Elder before I heard those two words put together in a meaningful way. *Focused attention*, just think about that, women's creative energies represented in one simple concept.

Looking straight into her Mother's heart, I said, "Anathea wants to know what you know. Share everything. Your child-rearing for her comes to a gentle end right here and your woman-to-woman sharing begins with her Moontime. She will have a different blend of passions, but you have woman-hood and blood in common, that combination offers a lifetime of sharing."

Every child, teen, and adult desires focused attention. That is the pure golden proof of love. I told Anathea that to love one's self, a person need not be narcissistic and focus wholly on one's self. That came out as a bit of a caution, because I know adolescents can be self-absorbed. I am clear that women need to focus more attention inward on quiet, self-love during their Moons. This sounded good to Anathea, she can spend her focused attention to prepare herself through reading, meditating, and using oracles for self-discovery.

Women, notice how your own rhythm swings from quiet, restorative Moontime to the highest productive output of Superwoman. We are all of these energies and can chart the highs and the lows well enough to design our lives in this spiraling energy. Everyone benefits when women focus attention inward. Think of this: As the Moon follows the Sun through 13 lunar cycles in one solar year, we move through 4 distinct seasons with many ups and downs. Benefiting from this elegant cosmic pattern, women can become fully-aware energy designers. This awareness begins with First Blood, guiding women to be with the cosmic and symbolic language of Earth. Belonging is at the heart of this awareness.

I wondered about those days each month when she would bleed: How do I demonstrate, even talk about this beautiful time she has yet to experience? She hadn't started her cycles yet, but she said she was ready because her best friend had started. This is the way of early teens; they share everything with one or two friends. Women know the effect of blood-time on one another, synching, sometimes even starting days early because of the proximity of other bleeding women. Plenty of stories exist telling of the ultimate power of Moontime. Women 2 or 3 years into menopause have been pulled back into bleeding by other women. Surely, synching to each other's rhythms would be true for close girlfriends. As the guiding Elder, I decided perhaps my teachings might trickle down through Anathea to her friends. I worked hard to be clear.

With all the early signs, including new pimples, I could visually see change coming to Anathea. Her neurological pathways had a certain construction. For several years, Anathea had been watching other women; her Mother and step-Mother, the women in her church, and the teachers in school. I call her shyness, her hesitancy, the twelve-year-old hush. The child inside gradually quiets her voice so this intense watching and synthesizing happens naturally. Perhaps women even told her to hush. By watching, Anathea had stepped to the edge and just barely begun the age-old practice of forming and inventing herself. Her hand movements and the way she looked without raising her head, those were just like her Mother's way. As she gathered so many other influences, she individuated from her Mother, she made herself different.

I saw other things in her. Anathea quickly became invested in my teachings about womanhood and wanted to learn everything in three hours a week. Turning back my memory to be thirteen, I revisited the feeling of this really interesting human event, puberty. I remembered being where she is, going through the stage of tweens, pre-puberty, before my woman's body filled all the way to its young woman form. I found myself revisiting my own time: Who was I just before my First Blood? I looked out through thirteen-year-old eyes with odd familiarity and felt a seamless connection. She had heard her Mother's description of the coming event, her bleeding time. She knew there was more to it than red blood soaked up on a pad. Anathea wanted to know all there was to know. She pulled it out of me over time. All this danced through my heart-mind while we played, like tweens together, in the water by the creek.

All through the 1990's, a research team of psychologists led by Carol

Gilligan[9] from Harvard revealed that the twelve-year-old hush is also heavily influenced when girls discover that males are culturally favored. Of course, all of this—the influence of puberty, differentiating from Mother, and feeling an essential power struggle with boys and men—make life harder for every twelve-year-old girl.

Each week as my sensitivity grew more acute, I realized I lacked her history. Along with this first realization came another: Moon trainings and womanhood trainings need to be Mother and Auntie directed and community supported. The reminder once again, that I was filling in for a society with a deficit of women's ceremonies, gave me great joy. That fact alone makes this sharing necessary and possible. With Anathea's help, I reawakened to my role as the enthusiastic one who empowers. I do not need to be the instigator. Mothers, Grandmothers, Aunties, I pray this is awakening your own enthusiasm. This womanhood training is what we wished we had had before our First Blood. Every woman alive has wished for something more. Together, Anathea and I will help shed the secrecy, even the shame held by so many women. With her girlfriends, Anathea will replace that Moontime secrecy with quiet, joy-filled visioning.

Announcing true-story time, I placed Anathea in front of me and shared one of my own personal experiences from 1998, before she was even conceived. While I wondered exactly what to do for my second career, I went on a week-long backpacking trip called, *Dancing Between the Worlds*[10] in September 1998. Eight miles from the trailhead, dear friends and I danced our hearts out on an exquisitely polished granite dance floor. This was remarkable because I am not a dancer. At the end of our wild dance-fest, we sat under a tarp in the desert and waited for the rain to stop. Falling softly all around, rain perfumed the desert landscape with the sweet, blended odors of soil and sage. One woman guided our group of ten women on a spiritual journey.

This Shamanic journey took me away in an instant and back in time more than 100 years. From far away I could see myself seated at the edge of an

Indigenous Village. I had traversed time and space while holding hands with my own Great Grandmother Sirah Bledsoe who showed me the traditional Coming-of-Age passage ritual for a young Village woman of the Cherokee Nation in the Carolinas. I watched as this Grandmother Spirit and her Village women completed a ceremony for one girl's first time bleeding.

All the women gathered around and welcomed the young woman, pulling her into the light of day from the dark space of a tiny Moon lodge. Her Mother and Aunties gently stripped off this daughter's sheath, washed, dressed, decorated her, and combed and tied her beautiful hair. Then, oldest to youngest, they spiraled out to the fire circle. Round and round they danced, this was their celebration of a new woman. After a long time of dancing to drums beaten by the Village's men and boys in one far corner, the women collapsed to the ground, oldest first. Left dancing was this beautiful and breathless new-woman for all to see. Just before this vision-journey ended, I saw food being carried to the fire circle on a large hide.

That was when my traveling spirit came back into my body, but my perspective about my future direction had completely changed. I cried tears of joy and recognition and surprised all the women watching and listening. Each telling, I gain a bit more clarity and a fire of determination for all Nine Passages but especially this First Blood Passage. Re-entering this vision, I touch on my life work, teaching the importance of marking ceremony. I believe Circles of women and girls making ceremony can shift the paradigm and completely change the world in Divinely Feminine ways.

"This time we spend together for your teachings," I told Anathea, "is inspired by that vision. Our plans are similar enough to that ceremony to make a connection. All those women took a turn to tell the maiden what she needed to know about womanhood. They told her as I am telling you, the time when your woman's Blood flows out of your body is a sacred time. We will call in many women to help you celebrate."

Moon is the Bridge to our Ancestral Lineage

The Moon is the bridge between the ceremonies of Indigenous cultures and our culture. I want Anathea, indeed all of us, to become translators of ways of old into our modern lives. Even if we are post-modern with capacity to examine things in their smallest parts, we still have biology, emotions, and brains almost exactly like our old Ancestors. When we translate Moontime to young girls-becoming-women, we can hardly place them in a dark little hut and teach how women observed their blood-time as young women did 100 or 1000 or 10,000 years ago. Maybe we cannot duplicate a ritual from a vision, however, we can translate this sacred ceremony to fit our lives today. We can quiet our spirits, allowing our feminine side to accept *being* and release *doing*. Women can learn to slow our tempos, and gift to ourselves and each other our most valuable offering *focused attention*. Through playful challenges, we can discover a practice of self-care. As our own witness, month to month, we can track growth and expand on our deepest dreams. Wherever we locate quiet, there is where we dare to dream.

To observe this time as a Vision Quest, as a quiet sacred time, this practice can be put in place at any time along our 40 year continuum of cycles of bleeding. Even beyond the blood-time, in Moonpause, women still long for a practice. The Moon cooperates; no matter how long we live, descending, waning, and retreating to the deep quiet of her dark side, in renewal she begins again as the New Moon. Like a drum beat, we follow this rhythm of the Moon: New-Half-Full-Half.

Clay Womb-bowl, a Playful Creation

Women entrain and swoon over the Moon as we believe our Ancestors did. How would it be if all women, at blood flow, quieted down to a vision for their life? If we synch and in harmony, our flows could come with the New Moon and begin to fill again toward the Full Moon. Our cycles are unique and common, depending whether we are emptying or filling, releasing or gathering. The role of the Moon, our guide and power source, adds potency to these many millions of monthly events.

This great night orb, our Moon, is a wonderful partner for women. She waves at each of us individually as she goes through her own cycle, following the Sun across the wide sky. For Moon teachings that will be guided by her beautiful little Moon graphic and her Moon journal, I asked Anathea to watch, draw, and enter into a relationship with the Moon. I felt like the encouraging Elder, "If you cannot see her, you can still know her. A dedicated Moon watch will synch your body to cycle with the Moon. Watching causes this entrainment through the iris of your eyes." We feel especially lucky in the Pacific Northwest when the skies clear for Moon gazing.

Moving through our teaching Wednesdays, one afternoon Mother brought clay and we sat together in the tipi space, now the canvas cover delighted our eyes and accented the blue-sky hole in an uplifted way. Looking at Anathea, I said "You're the second lucky maiden to get this teaching."

It seemed good timing, the Moon was New again. I told the First Story when I made a womb-bowl with another maiden. This went back around the world it seemed to me, to a different time. That story is told in *Gifts from the Elders: Girls' Path to Womanhood* (2004). Two dear friends helped me put together a Rites of Passage ceremony for one single girl. Sneaking a peak at Anathea, I said, "This maiden also had two sisters."

Intending to repeat the umbilical separation ritual during Anathea's ceremony, I reached into this old, true story to give her a fuller anticipation of release that comes with moving into womanhood. "In the cradle of that beautiful Sawtooth Valley, before we held our little goodbye ceremony, I tied this beautiful piece of rope around Mother and daughter in an infinity symbol for a releasing ceremony." I whispered to Anathea, "We called this rope the umbilical cord," and I showed her my piece of that very soft rope, kept sacred all these years. I always put it on my summer altar.

"Mother Geri and her daughter Lauren said a few words to each other, about love and separation, then I handed the scissors to the daughter. We told her it was time to cut the cord. When she did, her Mother and sisters departed for one whole week."

Anathea was listening. Abbreviating the story, I said, "One of the treats during the week was a trippy little jaunt to the lake where we set up our camp chairs at the edge of the water, so our feet could splash and play in the waves while we pinched clay and talked about wombs. A woman's womb is a completely magical place. Not only is that where babies grow, it's a place of filling and emptying, a place where energy erupts with women's creative juices."

Clay is enormously fun for hands. We can almost forget we have a thinking mind. Putting our minds just on our wombs, this intentional pinching and stretching, wetting and smoothing, causes our womb space to come into view. The rise and fall of two main hormones, estrogen and progesterone, work through a woman's blood, and with the waxing and waning Moon, raise her personal power known as creative energy. She moves out in the world as she fills and then quiets herself as she flows. Somehow, every woman finds a rhythm to claim as her own. All her life long, she has access to this creatively energetic rhythm.

"Anathea, your womb-bowl can be anything you choose. Allow your creativity to flow, it's all yours. Every creative act of your life comes from here, the juice, the energy of your womb. Your source, your juice, will turn on very soon. It's a good idea to think about these things in advance of the time your womb drains of its blood."

The following week, we shifted the energy in keeping with a rhythm, alternating inside work with outside play. I pulled a piece of string from my pocket and asked, "Are you ready to see this whole Life Spiral?" I directed

Anathea to step into the center of the cleared space on the beach. "The planet spins right here about 900 miles an hours, but due to gravity, mostly it feels like the world turns around your center." Just to make her eyes sparkle, I said, "We also travel 67,000 miles an hour around the Sun because the solar system is big, really big."

Using a compass, I showed Anathea how to find the directions. There is a certain amount of logic in orientation, but the closer we get to Summer Solstice, being so far north, the perfect logic of a circle skews by 18°. I admitted my limitations, with a sly smile, I said, "Well we all have limits in what we know for sure."

I used the string to measure equal distances from the center and Anathea built a beautiful cross to our directional markers, connecting North to South and East to West. She held the string at the center while I drew a big enough circle in the sand to demonstrate the seasons of our lives. Anathea soaked up my words. While she pondered the circular design of life, her Mother helped me gather stones. We handed her one river stone after another to define the spaces of life's remarkable spiral which marks maturity. Around the outside circumference, we talked a little geometry and Anathea closed the circle playing with the placement of big and little stones.

Wheel of Life, of Seasons, of Medicine, Another Ancient Bridge

"East for Spring, South for Summer, West for Autumn, and North for Winter. While the Earth rotates and spins, it also takes a full year to tilt both ways on its axis. That movement creates our seasons. The tilt and the seasons, and women's 13 Moons make this circle more like a Spiral, so that's what I call it. You may even call this a Medicine Circle. You're in for some fun if you pay attention in geography class," I said, "and you can learn a lot from asking Google questions."

When she felt complete in her task, I grew weepy. She had built a gift of lasting remembrance, a scaffold I could use for my daily prayers to the Ancestors. Had I been a girl, I would have leapt three feet in the air and clicked my heels together. I dance that same jig in my imagination on moments like this one.

After Anathea built the Spiral of Life on the beach, I told her I called her the Girl of Summer in my journal. Now she would have that anchor as her internal vision for herself. She was in that South place, but moving through the Spiral with each change of season, around and around the Earth turns, up and up the Spiral goes. As the Girl of Summer, she would always locate this time of change and this story as the way her womanhood began.

I presented flowers and ribbons and we decorated her Wheel just a bit. To connect back to old ways, we offered a little sacred cornmeal to each direction feeling thankful to the Elder who gifted us and to the Apache maiden who ground that potentiated corn. Feeling satisfied with our efforts, I stood her in the South and showed how she had moved from the East of her Birth and passed the Southeast of her Middle Childhood.

We faced North, together. Standing behind, I wrapped my arms around her and I asked her to focus on the North place where I now find my comfort. "Girl of Summer," I said softly, "always look across to your Elders for their help and for reflections. We have been all the places you will go, felt similar feelings, and we have had unique challenges. Some of our challenges were just like yours and some different. Every one of us wants to help you."

Her Mother stood in the East, the place of Birth, sunrise, and new beginnings to tell Anathea, in gorgeous detail, the story of the moment she was born. As first child, hers was a long and easy birth with tons of welcoming and support. Mother felt the joy in remembering, in telling, and in being heard. The poignancy of that moment, so filled with smiles and tears, so alive with honesty will live in our hearts to the end of time.

During the Full Moon of June, six weeks before her thirteenth birthday, Anathea experienced her First Blood. She started her Moon cycles that would define her womanhood. At the very moment the Moon came into fullness, so did Anathea. She can always claim that first Moon as her very own because as she awakened to being a Girl of Summer, she crossed over her Threshold of First Blood taking her first steps into womanhood. She felt prepared by her Mother and her Elder to be in full ceremonial acceptance.

The trickster, always present and looking for an opening to offer a twist, made certain that Anathea was with her Father for this first time so he would have to be involved. Fathers need their consciousness raised and Anathea's trickster sent him to the store for Moon pads. Men, who enter beginners' mind with their daughters, can be of service to the Divine Feminine on the other side of this First Blood Threshold. They can also entrain and anticipate the sacred time each month when their daughters need to be quiet for their visioning. In the rebalancing that is occurring all around the world right now, men can step up and fill in being helpful while women take a down-time rest for their Vision Quest. When that's the way it is, that's the way it is. Whisper this to the men; they will get it because their best interest is in keeping women happy.

Girls need the strong shoulder of their Fathers and men need to be reminded of their feminine side. Without question, a new intensity, a hormonal intensity, comes along with every pubescent experience. Suddenly, the Father-Daughter relationship transforms when a daughter changes into a woman. Deeper conversations may emerge during the sacred visioning time when she bleeds. This will cause everyone to open to the sacred event, which may serve as the great re-balancer. When young women feel the support, the understanding and pampering from their dads, other female to male conversations can follow. Consider the potential for bonding, Father to daughter, which will lead to young women adept and able to communicate about tender subjects in future relationships.

When I looked into Anathea's eyes again, it was a woman-to-woman look. Now my teachings would focus on what I wish I had learned when I was a young woman. I re-read Judith Duerk's book that opened with one deeply penetrating question. I personally consider this question the foundation for the Red Tent movement, which is rising with the Divine Feminine. As a reminder, *Circle of Stones: Woman's Journey to Herself* begins this way: "How might your life have been different if there had been a place for you, a place for you to go to be with your mother … a place of women to go, to be, to return to, as woman? How might your life be different?" Honestly, I do not know a way to form Villages of like-minded young women in support of each other's Moontimes. Society has not cooperated in that way for young women. Structures have not been erected in support of Mooning women in the way society has built corner churches. I hold hope that someone will do the work of gathering women in ceremonial Moon centers. This question is both daunting and haunting. Until the culture shifts, women, wrap your arms around your daughters and granddaughters when they are First Bloods like Anathea, and demonstrate a few of these quiet practices.

Feeling light and gay, we all went to the creek. After high water passes, a rocky bar shows up making river stones into play things. Heading for a powerful visualization, we searched out a womb-stone for ourselves. I talked about the First Blood somewhat abstractly knowing Anathea would translate to the personal for herself. A womb-stone, the object of our search, leads our way into symbolic language. A summer warmed stone placed on our womb space can focus our attention to the creative energy found there. I said, "Pick out a stone that wants to go home with you."

After her first few Moontimes, as her anticipation settles into reality, Anathea will feel more informed about the cycle of her flow. When does ovulation happen? When does the blood begin to slough away? Understanding the biology is one part. The other part is spirit time, understanding how and when the focus narrows to intuitive and creative energies. A new woman's Moontime lends itself to quiet visioning, to the slower pace of self-care.

"Spirit cries out from the Cosmos," I said. "Listen to your womb and take the intuitive information that comes into your body-mind as a gift. This conscious connection will teach you how you might direct your life. Receive your month-by-month vision to guide your life and build your Soul connection."

For my teaching, hoping she might be listening and absorbing, I told her to focus on passion as a feeling like fire and follow wherever that inner flame ignites her curiosity. This practice will lead her to the core of herself. Is she ready to find out who she is, to see deeper into her Soul? She can use this womb energy like a creative fire.

Good for Manifesting, Womb Stone

Everything I told Anathea flowed through me intuitively as we searched through stones and stacked a few into prayer cairns. I said she was in good company. Simultaneously, millions of women bled with her last week and spent meditative time re-focusing on their life-purpose while they lounged in a quiet space caring for themselves. She will be the teacher for her younger sisters, and with her Mother, their strongest role models. Together they will join the legions of women who seek answers to their spirit directed questions: Is my life on track? Am I working toward my higher purpose? Do my spirit sisters need to hear from me? Did they have a vision on their Moontime? Have I found the personal keys to happiness and fulfillment? What do I need? Questions are paramount for growth.

At a crucial time in my life, a close woman friend asked me, "What question are you holding?" I have never forgotten how that stopped me in my tracks. Energetically, I felt like she had asked me, am I on track with my hopes and dreams? Whether women are alone or in the company of their Moon Lodge or Red Tent sisters, that matters less than their visioning. What question are you holding right now?

Just imagine having a clear record of 400 Vision Quests in quiet succession. This is what I feel is most profound. I asked Anathea to be alert to any distractions that might derail her practice. Her life will find its constant Northstar direction if she devotes herself to a monthly practice of visioning.

Back in the tipi, we laid head to head, Mother and daughter and Elder, and closed our eyes. Talking enough already, I quieted myself and took us into a journey process: "Count yourself down to a soft breath, 10, 9, 8… and clearly visualize a tunnel with steps leading beneath the two big Cedar trees, 7, 6, 5 . . . down, down, down you go. Find your way slowly as your eyes adjust to the dark, 4, 3, 2, 1… ask who wants to support this womb-stone journey? Ask your helpers to step forward." I drift off into silence for about 7 or 8 minutes.

Then I said, "Bring yourself around by wiggling your toes."

I counted again this time from 1 to 10, "Climb back up the Cedar's roots with your inner eye."

I say, softly, "Open your eyes and soften your gaze. Enjoy the reflection of your vision and this quiet time." I allow another 7 or 8 minutes to pass before I stirred my body from lying to sitting.

I appreciated the quiet. Using the 50-50 principal, planning enough to fill only half our time together, the whole time goes by very relaxed. We talked about the practice of using the womb stone for visioning. I did not tell Anathea she must sequester for three days, although I did tell her I wish I had given myself at least three days each month for quality realignments. "When you track the Moon, you will find most of your blood comes in three days and you might synch to the dark before the New Moon." I also said, "Make an opening on the calendar for your vision time, make a note of your question of the month, and the rewards will show up in magnificent ways. There is no better investment than you, Anathea. Catch up on your journal, turn you lights down low, and use aroma therapy. Invite a look back over the past month and a look forward to the next month. This is a way to gather personal power to your Higher Self."

Before ceremony, we had a bit more work to do. Together with Mother, Anathea and I planned her celebration and invited women to come as her guests. At ceremony time, she would stand before her witnesses and cross a Threshold that would give her permission to declare her womanhood openly and proudly. A tipi full of woman would nod and applaud their agreement.

The week before ceremony, I wanted to talk about oracles. Women who learn to use oracles, open doorways and bring creative ways of seeing and new ways of knowing the deeper aspects of self. In my life I have used oracles to open new vistas and questions about characteristics of my inner life. I know they are valuable for that simple little reason. There are many oracles and each differs from the others. I like using several in combination and I invite the spirit of play to be with me when I pull out the Tarot cards, and when I keep track of planetary relationships. For Anathea, I introduced my astrological chart and my latest numerology reading. These are ancient tools and have been used by men and women for millennia. "Only you will know if one or several of these will help you see your personality and life events in a deeper way," I said. "Look around, you will find your teachers."

Oracles Reveal Inner Secrets

The night before her ceremony Anathea came to stay overnight with me. A separation from Mother is crucial to an effective initiation, and she needed to cross a Threshold. Those two important steps needed to be done away from her Mother and sisters. I picked her up and she showed great confidence in me. One last day before her transformative celebration, Anathea helped me clean and decorate the tipi. I began to talk about her interior life, her spirit life. This central theme of spirituality was the core message for Anathea's Coming-of-Age ritual.

Crown Chakra	Spirituality
Third Eye Chakra	Awareness
Throat Chakra	Communication
Heart Chakra	Love, Healing
Solar Plexus	Wisdom, Power
Sacral Chakra	Sexuality, Creativity
Root Chakra	Basic Trust

©2016

One of the ways to understand one's self in spirit is through the energy system known as chakras. They line up our spines as lower energies to higher energies. Chakras are vibrations unique to our inner life; self-churning and rebalancing centers, each one offers a perfect focus for a meditation during Moontimes. Anathea said her Mother told her about chakras already. So I thought great, she had a scaffold for visioning. One of my early teachers was Stephen Gallegos.[11] Through his book, I learned about the chakra totem pole. I find that it prevents loneliness and provides a personal council for problem solving. In telling Anathea that her Blood and her Moontime were portals to her Soul's awakening, I wanted her to remember tools to guide her to her inner life. I taught this chakra totem pole to Anathea so she would have a tool for imagery.

First, she and I went to the creek. We played a little and I told her what we would be doing during this time together. Drawing a line in the sand, I asked Anathea to step over it if she was ready to accept womanhood for her very own. When she oriented to the land and felt grounded, I put a blindfold over her eyes and began.

When she took that step, I held her hand and led her through the woods moving from one tree to the next. Each tree, adorning the woods with above ground parts, offered roots for grounding and visioning to help her call forth her power animals. Soon she was building a totem pole. We talked of the specific energies that are associated with the first chakra, the root chakra belonging, family and home, for example. I asked her to lean against the tree, feel its strength and follow its roots down. "What animal wants to come and be your helper for the energies of family and home?"

When she was sure an animal was willing to help her, I asked her to re-member it and I guided her through the woods to another tree. For the second chakra, the attributes of creativity and sexuality are the driving energies. As we worked our way through the seven chakras, Anathea leaned against a different tree for each and followed my visualization to build her totem pole with seven animal guides who will be a council for her anytime she calls on them. I said, "There is an energy alive in this little exercise and its main value is in the practice. You will have this meditation to use throughout your teen years."

I asked if she could remember her animals, but I didn't ask her to reveal them. I simply said, "Use these totem animals to help you whenever a problem arises. My totem pole seems to climb out of my center and sits around in a cir-cle with me; each animal gives me a different point of view about the situation on my mind. There is a solution for everything. This group of personal allies will help with visioning too. Remember this from my wise friend, what ques-tion are you holding?" We wished each other good night and slept dreaming with our power animals.

Mother Leads Daughter to Ceremony

The next day, Anathea said she was ready for her guests to come and celebrate with her. Her ceremony would be simple, standing with her Mother as woman to woman. All around the circular space of the tipi, women sat in witness to welcome Anathea to womanhood.

Choreography is rarely flawless, I did not get the sage crown on her head before her exuberance overcame her. So excited and surprised by some of her guests, Anathea spontaneously circled the tipi, hugging each woman. She had made little gifts for everyone. She slowly and shyly circled round a second time to receive their blessings and presented each witness with a handmade gift. She had learned the heart value of generosity and I was thrilled.

In the quiet interior space of her Higher Self, Changing Woman would continue to work transformation through this new woman. Being less than a central force in this family's day-to-day lives, I let go. Anathea would be celebrating her thirteenth birthday at the water park with girlfriends. The 3Moons we had spent in this womanhood training gave me time enough to go deep and discover my true Elder self. Changing Woman had worked through me and not so long ago. The following day, in the stillness of the New Moon alone with my thoughts, I cleaned the tipi and burned tiny little prayer ties. Adjusting my heart and my mind, inner vision showed me the way to bring these teachings to other girls.

Changing Woman completes the acknowledgments by working through family and community. This recognition of change known as *reincorporation* closes the liminal portal. Girls slowly integrate through a couple of cycles of bleeding. Acceptance seeps in through dream-time and girls begin to take on a hue, a glow, an attitude of chameleon.

Cutting the Umbilical Cord

Already on the way to her First Flight, the emancipation Threshold, each new young woman copies all other women as models to shape a unique personality. My sincere hope for every new young woman is quiet visioning during Moontime that will shape and deepen her inner life.

POST SCRIPT
MOTHERS, GRANDMOTHERS, AUNTIES AND FRIENDS:

You can plan a week or even a full weekend around these ideas and blend in your own teachings. Allow personal experience to revisit this cusp place, be thirteen. The supporting cast needs to conduct an acknowledgment ceremony for the time right after First Blood—up to a year after. Please remember, Changing Woman visits each night before and after First Blood, Second and Third Blood, all through the first year. Then change feels complete, even for the really young bleeding girls, their new normal eventually arrives. This is known as *reincorporation*. It is very hard for a spirit to accomplish *reincorporation* without this acknowledgement and the ceremony that opens to the initiation.

Moon Dial to Guide Maturity and Dreams

Once Across the Threshold, Changing Woman begins Integration

GIFTS FROM THE ELDERS: FIRST BLOOD PASSAGE

Blood changes everything. Moving through the myriad of biological changes to First Blood, each new young woman collects instructions on how to receive her womanhood.

"Don't you know? In Alaska we use our time of bleeding as Women's Vision Quest time." --Alaskan Elder Woman

"In other cultures and other times, girls who were entering womanhood would be welcomed by their tribe. They would be told the secrets of womanhood, they would be tested for their strength and courage. They would be blessed and celebrated. For generations this has been missing from our culture." *Reaching for the Moon* – Lucy Pearce

Moontime used to be called periods which used to be called menstruation which used to be called taboo which used to mean sacred. Perhaps our Women's Way could ease into a ceremony of mindfulness for girls already bleeding. Invite them to love where they are now.

Let's use our imaginations and our intuitions to bring forth a new teaching about **Vision Quest for women**, bring it into the mainstream. Let's bring it to ourselves first and then to our daughters.

Two ways, both good, celebrate the First Blood of a girl becoming a woman. **The first way,** Mother is confidant and helps her girl through, in privacy, with candle-lit baths and welcoming womanhood sharing. **The second way** is a gathering of beloved women relations and family friends for a ceremony of sharing and airing: First Blood happens to every woman.

So much healing happens when there is **a place for the girl's story** to be nested with women's stories. One among the group may offer the teaching of the Women's Vision Quest in the middle of this chapter.

Sit in stillness on your Moon. Rest and rejuvenation will return the sacred to your Moontimes and into a practice your daughter plans the rest of her life around.

* Tell your new young woman that during this quiet Moontime, women take stock of their dreams and polish their personal visions of the future.

* Tell her how lucky she is to be on the first wave of completely new ways of approaching this time of her life.

Mothers, an early blood cycle is just that; there are layers of causes and consequences. *The New Puberty*[12] is an excellent reference. For an 11 or 12 year old, the consequences may be self-loathing or for athletic and tom-boy types, bodily rejection. These need processing and are handled like a psychic wound. For girls age 9 or 10, 3rd or 4th grade, the responsibility of early puberty and self-care need special balancing to keep childhood innocent and fun.

NOTES FOR FIRST BLOOD PASSAGE

1   The name of the Alaskan Elder Woman who was at the Rites of Passage workshop is anonymous; I am deep indebted to this connection to her lineage.

2   A new meme in women's cultural lexicon, the *Womb at the Center of the Universe* may be a reference to God, to Goddess, to the Divine Feminine in all her forms. I have used this often in the past four years since Arianna Husband shared it with me. I often shorten it to the *Womb of the Universe*. We are told by Indigenous Aleutian Elder, Ilarion Merculieff: "Women are sacred because they (we) carry the original instructions from this place, the *Womb at the Center of the Universe*."

3   Lucy H. Pearce has written *Moon Time: Harness the Ever-changing Energy of Your Menstrual Cycle* (2012) to inform women all over the world about their own Moontimes. To introduce a young daughter's journey Lucy wrote *Reaching for the Moon: A Girl's Guide to Her Cycles* (2013). Both books are straightforward and meant to shed light on women's collective Moontime connection. She sells mandalas for tracking la Luna at http://www.womancraftpublishing.com/, This Moon Dial is made by Zoe Shekinah (her website is http://www.earthlightcollective.com/silver.htm).

4   One of my early influences for self-esteem and confidence (*Schoolgirls*, 1995) came through journalist and researcher, Peggy Orenstein. Her newest research involves conversations with girls about sex. Two books are important to the conversations between women and girls about sex: *Cinderella Ate My Daughter* (2012) and *Girls and Sex: Navigating the Complicated New Landscape* (2016).

5   *Navajo Walking in Beauty* chant is borrowed cross-culturally from Navajo Ancestors and comes in several versions and lengths.

6   An Elder from California, Bethany Staffieri, has a tradition of gifting a little graphic with all 28-Moon stages in a circular image. I say thank you to her and to the Elder who passed them onto me, Arianna Husband.

7   Judith Duerk imprinted thousands of women with her haunting questions from *Circle of Stones: Woman's Journey to Herself* (1999).

8   Clarissa Pinkola Estés, one of women's foremost teachers, is a Jungian and Cantadora, a keeper of the old stories. She uses her voice to draw out our Souls' truths. Her library of offerings is vast, find books and recordings at your library or at www.soundstrue.com.

9   Carol Gilligan was influential in my early training. Interested in the nuances of voice and resistance, Carol Gilligan published research about the moral structure of a woman that begins with a girl finding her voice: *In a Different Voice: Psychological Theory and Women's Development; Making Connections: The Relational Worlds of Adolescent Girls at Emma Willard School*; and *Meeting at the Crossroads: Women's Psychology and Girls' Development*. No longer at Harvard, she continues to help break through more barriers of patriarchy; she most recently published *Joining the Resistance* (2011).

10 Women offering breakthrough programs for other women are becoming more common as our glorious gifts emerge. Evolutionaries™ I met early in my search for kindred spirits, Lorene Wapo-

tich and Lenore Anderson gifted this desert backpacking trip to my friend Diana Eldridge, and me, along with six other women. We returned to the site of my 1996 Vision Quest, Fish and Owl Creek in the Canyonlands Wilderness. Nothing is finer than women dancing together in the wild, polishing aspects of our Soul-selves on the polished floor of Great Mother.

11 Eligio Stephen Gallegos wrote a beautiful little meditation guide linking animal allies with the chakra energies, *Animals of the Four Windows: Integrating Thinking, Sensing, Feeling, and Imagery* (1991).

12 When one of my dearest friend's daughter began her Moontime early, I found my only solace in research. *The New Puberty: How to Navigate Early Development in Today's Girls* (2015) by Louise Greenspan and Julianna Deardorff rescued me. Like the invisible tsunami of climate change in our world, the changing landscape for girls, in terms of early puberty and early sex, women must be balanced and level for the fallout.

FIRST FLIGHT

THE INTENTION:
OFFERING THE GIFT OF WOMANHOOD TRAINING

*I speak directly from the heart of one who was once a girl. Mothers, I share these words for your girl to hear with her heart. I hope I can speak bluntly. Please **share** this conscious training with your daughter along with your own instructions for leaving the nest. You may want to fly back to your own teen years with a ceremony for yourself, maybe with other Mothers, using Soul Stories: Nine Passages of Initiation, designed to help you remember this time filled with your own stories. The muse says, address the young woman between her two Passages; First Blood and First Flight.*

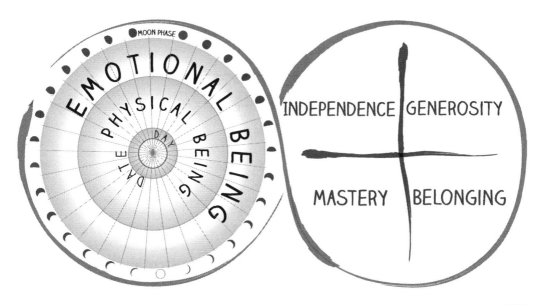

©2016

Dear young woman: These suggestions, words between you and me, will help you build skills and stretch your brain to prepare for your own emancipation story. Write about what you think as you read. Everything you write will help you grow-up. Here are the teachings I offer lovingly, as an Elder with arms around you — Gail

Entelechy is a word that holds promise and potential: This is a Soul symbol.

This entelechy symbol represents the intersection where your inner potential becomes a reality. Follow along and your dreams will come true. One circle offers the cosmic rhythm of the Moon, which belongs to the Divine Feminine. The other circle holds the ancient teachings of Indigenous values. For sheer delight, I connect these circles together with colorful and strong silken threads. The threads, or secret insights, provide flexibility for your life design. Silk is strong enough to hold the unbidden forces coming into your body; you need to know about them.

The Grandmother in me sees like an Eagle far into the past and into the future. I want to wrap every fourteen year old girl in circles of silk. Imagine this symbol, surrounded by multicolored threads, two circles meet and continuously flow one into the other. Secret insights are nestled among the silken threads. Choices and passions will lead you down a winding path of growth. Love each one of your decisions with all your heart. Silk is strong, earthy, and so are you my dear young woman: You need a design for your life to serve your long and amazing future ahead, all of your womanhood.

THE EAGLE'S VIEW

I sit in stillness with you. I acknowledge how hard and confusing this time feels. Insights to help you through your transformation ahead come from various perspectives. The most important is your own, carefully watch for changes; you are fluid at this time in your life. The next perspective closest to you is your Mother's. Watch how the concentric rings, just like a drop on a still pond, begin to build. Your closest girlfriends will be as fluid as you but also offer helpful perspectives on all kinds of things. Maybe the most valuable ring you could reach would be a circle of your friends together will all your Mothers.

Every woman alive went through this same biological metamorphosis from chrysalis to butterfly. It's mystical and magical. Colorful and strong silken threads bind circles within circles to remind you of your power. I offer thoughts about these two circles and their intersections to give you a place to begin your training. With a circle of Mothers, all of you together, will be able to expand and improve on these design ideas for your womanhood. Welcome to your womanhood training. Soon you will take flight.

FALLING WATER

Do you remember being a girl of ten and eleven who ran and played? She was a miracle and freely expressed her genuine wild Soul. We also remember our teen years right after that; for some of us, a paralyzing energy turned that girl on her head. I wrap Elder arms around you, my dear young woman, and peer into your world. In this time between your First Blood and your First Flight, I offer my best wisdom for your developing womanhood. I turn this conversation to intimacy, like into-me-see.

Dazzling Light on Water — Like You

Let's begin with play and the importance of play all through life. Then, I will offer up the Moon teachings and la Luna's ways of revealing your inner life. Finally, I dish up the great news about your increasing brainpower, which will give you abilities to think for yourself and weigh risk. I will tell you about the nature of womanhood, timeless and forever true, to prepare you for leaving home. You can teach me too, I would like that. I know only a little about the details of your teen life and how you change your world every day. This is our starting place.

Many women stand beside me and we know all there is to know about womanhood. We offer a crystalline bridge, alluring, inevitable, and clear. To help you across this bridge, these insights will illuminate a design for your life that may serve you for decades. Think about that, an interesting workable foundation and a design for living, this is what we wish we had when we were your age.

Sure as falling water, you have grown in competence and confidence and have gathered secret, earthy clues that belong to you. Your big-girl-self has language skills, emotional awareness, keen observation, and a huge desire to explore the world. You have favorites: Quiet places in Nature, body-moves that feel wonderful—dancing, riding, skiing, skating, volleyball, soccer—and you have figured out how to survive the ridicule, rejections, and judgments of mean-girls at school. When you hear music you dance, you might even reach for instruments to jam.

In Nature, you can be led by the occupation of a bee into its tiny world to help gather flower pollen. When you eat food, you might delight in some new taste you would not touch as a child. Some girls discover the miracle inside of a seed and learn how to grow delicious food. Is this you?

How does your Soul whisper in your day-dreams and night-dreams? Have you completely outgrown your Middle Childhood time when you explored worldly wonders with wild abandon? What marvelous wonders belong to you now? What do you long for?

Soul is always a girl's companion and guides you to what you love most and all that belongs to you alone. Are you paying attention? Soul awakens gradually and begins to convey your purpose and reveal your destiny, bit by bit through your experiences. Your life path seems to emerge out of darkness, awakening from forgetfulness, wanting to show you the way. When you have an insight or an intuition, when you swoon over something you've always loved, this is your Soul tapping on your shoulder. Soul-purpose always relates to what you most love to do. Something occupies you so completely that time disappears. This is why I begin with play, it's very Soul-full.

Your future—mysterious and unknowable—depends on a few foundation stones that you create. While still in your home nest, use the warmth and safety of home to play while you learn.

PURE PLAY, POOR PLAY

Life is playful, funny, and comic as often as it is serious and driven. Growing up is learning how to balance it all, so let's turn again to play. As you learn about the inner flow of intelligences—emotional, moral, spiritual, intellectual, and physical—play is the delightful ingredient to help you align with all that you love. Your creative juices need play to balance the serious nature of school. Explore everything that gives you joy; for you to thrive, remember what feels light and frivolous. You will always be rich if you have laughter.

I am a play specialist: I play with words, I play with my camera, I play with my dog, Rosie, and I get down and roll around in play with my grand-daughter, Kestrel. Pure play has no hooks and no competition. You do not need to be first or best. Play can be solitary or with one or two others who absolutely love making up rules to suit the moment. Play improves relationships through kindness and love. Very often play involves art or invention. Find the crack between the worlds: Attend to what you love in play because the passion you feel comes from Source. Use play to discover your Soul and your purpose. This is the priority contract during high school.

Experience is beyond value but seems to be a secret. Your gift of experience when you feel light and playful and when you are deeply happy exploring the world, may be offered to a younger girl who would be happy to play with you. Reach one hand out to a younger who will value your experience while she helps you remember pure play; and reach your other hand out to an older woman whose experience you value. You now have the secret, use play. Building your life around playful relationships is primal and essential.

Official
Permission To Play

This *LICENSE* Permits

The Bearer

to play at will, at length, at any speed, in any case, for any reason,
in any place, for better or worse, alone or with playmates,

Forever

© *Joseph W. Meeker 1993*

What do you most love to do? The primary clue that you are growing up nicely is when you nurture the relationships around you. Play will help you find your tribe. As a foundation stone, play shapes and defines you and offers the juice of life experiences through the burning fire of creativity. By playing with your heart you will also be shaping your future life.

My play Mentor, Joe Meeker, used to say, "Poor play," with a great exhale.[1] He explained how the serious side of culture has forgotten play or discounts play as childish. Then he taught me this secret—play is life's balancer and keeps you close to your Soul. Play is very active; so don't confuse it with laying around, watching television. I immediately adopted these playful ideas and became a play specialist, and invite my women friends who love to play: Unplug! Come out! Let's play! My life moved from surviving into thriving as fast as I could snap my fingers. I learned that play is an attitude as well as an activity. Everyone loves to make up rules. With practice, you can move through life in touch with your playful Soul.

GIFTS OF EVOLUTION

Evolution from girl to woman can be tricky waters to navigate. When your First Blood came along, maybe you and your friends hushed each other and you all allowed blood to dampen the extreme joy of being great girls together. Just after the swirl of hormones caused breast buds and then breasts, pubic fuzz and then hairy legs and underarms, another internal chemical blast comes from your body producing compounds to supercharge your brain. Around 14, a natural chemical cocktail swirls inside of you and floods you with confusion. You really want to know how to handle the muddle. I will show you how Moon tracking will teach you about your inner life. Great gifts will rise out of those muddy feelings.

Underneath your skin, your neuro-networks are busy evolving multiple intelligences. I hope you learned about those in elementary school,[2] the many ways of learning. The actions inside your body are unique to you; your particular heritage and gene pool holds triggers for different rates of maturity in you than in your friends. This is only part of the nature of individuation. How your identity is shaped depends on environmental forces, at home as well as time you spend in Nature; it depends on social interactions and on your psychological disposition. Every single day, change comes into you from one of these directions.

You might remember the life of a Turtle born of the Earth. Her Mother buries her before birth and emergence happens slowly. Gangs of little Turtles begin their journey in the comfort of the ocean—floating, exploring, playing. Being of two worlds, like teen women, each Turtle finds her way back from Mother Ocean to Mother Earth. When she does, her swirling confusion is gone. She has explored the depths, learned about herself, perfected play, and feels prepared to use the elements of Great Mother Earth to make the world a little more interesting, a little more playful, a little more beautiful. The similarities of a girl and a Turtle continue.

One gift all women share is the precious Moon. La Luna invites you to quiet all the way down when you bleed. Another gift, believe it or not, is emotional intelligence. Early to middle teen years are the training ground for your EQ (emotional quotient means emotional intelligence). Many books have been written about emotions, learn all you can. For as much as a million years and certainly the last hundred thousand years of evolution, your brain *begins* to mature at 14. A final and profound gift from the Ancestors, you receive a super-computer at this age that begins to network through your whole body. This neural network at your service for the rest of your life takes another ten years to completely develop. You feel the inner swirl where hormones—estrogen, progestogen, testosterone, and adrenalin—combine with brain chemicals—endorphins, epinephrine, and serotonin—to make your early teen years the most challenging time in life. What you are going through is so dramatic that every woman remembers because we have received these three gifts.

I give you permission to be a Turtle. Sit quietly on the Earth and focus inward.

WOMEN'S ALLY, LA LUNA

Train Your Brain to Follow the Moon

Probably many Moons have passed since your womb released your First

Blood. Now you feel practiced and maybe even regular. Discovering your personal rhythm takes some settling. When you look up, you will see a great number of Grandmothers who circle round you and all girls during Moontimes: We wish to tell you about your personal power and how you can find it, hold it, and expand it.

Rhythm is the reason for taking a personal retreat each month. I view life as a musical instrument dancing to 4:4 time. There are 4 seasons, 4 Moon phases, 4 winds, 4 directions, and 4 ways of being—introvert, extrovert, introverted extroverts, and extroverted introverts.[3] Deep inside your genome map and the biomechanics of your body, 4 trillion human cells depend on change: Rhythm is one of the great secrets in life.

Our most visible and rhythmic indicator of continuous change is la Luna, the Moon, present and predictable, moving from the tiniest crescent through her First Quarter which shows a Half Moon overhead, to Full Moon and back around showing the other Half, growing gradually dimmer. Luna is always moving away from or towards the place called the Dark of the Moon. Before she is receptive of the Sun's light, she is dark and quiet. She offers mystery, lingering in darkness for three days before her tiny crescent shows again. At this dark place of incubation, before the New Moon actually shows herself, Luna's cycle begins again, renewed. New. Many women plant seeds or intentions for incubation during this place of darkness and then apply action to help those seed-thoughts grow. Luna mirrors your cycle. With attention, you can know yourself.

Before tracking your Blood cycle on your Moon chart, before you feel this rhythm, you will experience what I call settling. (By settling I mean the process of learning before your understanding grows strong and trustworthy.) Count day one of your Moon as the first day your Blood appears. On days 10 through 16, give or take one or two days, you can get pregnant all around your ovulation because your vagina produces mucus, which protects sperm. For up to six days, sperm can survive inside your body. You need to understand as all women do, but, no babies yet, not if you are 14, not until you decide when. This bluntness is meant to empower you.

Sacred Moon teachings have been saved and cherished from other cultures and other times when people lived a Village life. To update them, we surround you with streaming music, twinkling lights, hot tea, and colorful wraps. After a string of about 26 Moontimes or 2 years, your Blood serves as the catalyst for change and transforms you into a woman. In this time-tested rhythm, hormones meet brain chemicals, making your adjustment feel radical. Women emphasize Moon teachings so you will remember to honor yourself and enjoy your Moons the Women's Way in a monthly Vision Quest. This is our common practice.

We live in a fast moving culture but *women's practice* intentionally slows things down. Even on very full and busy days, attend to your Moon rhythm to slow down. Women's Ways go counter-culture like the Moon turns counter-clockwise; both highlight the desirability of slowing down. Moon teachings are much deeper and much older than anything else in culture. Using her ancient, ancient design, we weave this old Moon philosophy in a modern way. Your Moontime invites you to explore, la Luna guides you to unlock your personal knowledge.

Moon So Like You, Mysterious

Get to know la Luna. Sometimes I call her Grandmother Moon because my Ancestors did, she belongs to all women. The Moon serves as a guide and confidant for all women. With a rhythmic motion, Luna pulls on the Earth's waters drawing out the tides twice a day. Moving through her full cycle, Luna does the same with your Blood once a month. Each time you bleed, your Moon invites you to quiet down for your monthly Vision Quest.

Visioning and questing with the Moon is uniquely a woman practice. Take a personal retreat for yourself for as long as 4 days. Sleep, find new music, make art and ponder the immediate events of your life. Use your imagination to track each tiny egg all through her cycle. The presence of eggs is like having an inner Goddess; she may feel crampy, but only to get your attention. She is teaching you about self-care and revealing your inner world. Tracking all through your Moon-cycle will inform you and empower you. Soon you get to know and trust your yoni, your womb. She is the source of all your creativity and your ability to procreate. Allow your womb's connection to the Moon, the gorgeous bright orb in the sky, to illuminate your dreams and passions.

A Womb-stone Helps You Remember Your Foundation Stones

Turtle enters again. Feeling inviting, luscious, and mysterious, Turtle invites you to pay attention to your egg as it flows out of your body with its protective blood. This flow is precious and can nourish the Earth. Because your blood is life giving, you may sit, turtle-like, on the Earth and nourish Great Mother. The more you talk to your Mother and other-Mothers, your Aunties and Grandmothers, the more you will discover how other girls are changing their experiences of Moontimes.

Emphasizing *permission* delivers a big change to the old cultural norm. Women give you permission to experience deep visioning to call forth inner quiet so you might express your passions. Quiet is your personal power source. Every woman in my generation missed this in our teens, but we find quiet for ourselves now. In our high-speed culture, one of the emerging crises is great noise about time. Do not fall victim to this. You are the one in control. Carve out time; we give you permission to learn to think about your life's passions, Soul-work, and design your daily practices. This is the power piece that every woman longs for, permission to stop and enjoy a Vision Quest time.

Discover for yourself why I play with 4 as inspiration and guide. Follow these 4 practice steps:

* Make notes on your Moontime worksheet every day.

* Take a long Medicine Walk with the Moon on her New and Full days.

* Use play and your art journal as your Soul connection.

* Find deep quiet for visioning when you bleed.

These are 4 foundation stones. Play with them as your personal self-care guides. Go ahead.

MOONTIME
WORKSHEET

©2015 NinePassages.com

Copy your own Moontime Mandala from the back of the book or from www.ninepassages.com

Changing Moon provides you with a scaffold for self-examination. Your personal practice might begin with daily reflections: Every day, do a 10 minute check-in with la Luna, use this Moontime Worksheet or another Moon-tracking chart. Scan it, make copies, and share them with your friends, your cousins, and your sisters. Daily tracking of your inner world, your sanctuary of private thoughts and feelings, will introduce you to your deeper psyche. Over time your womb will become like an intimate confidant. Charting your moods and emotions throughout the month will guide you to know yourself and this thing called ego. In your quiet space, you will make friends with all of your inner parts. Read about anything that fires up your curiosity. This is a lifetime occupation, getting to know yourself and learning to hear your Soul messages.

THE EMOTIONAL INTELLIGENCE FACTOR

On the Moontime Worksheet, you will notice emotions cover the broadest swath for tracking. This is because women are blessed with the widest range of emotions and those can be tracked, as a way to self-knowledge. La Luna is women's helper. Plan ahead so you can devote hours to Nature connection, and especially during power-days, on the New and Full Moons. Whatever the wild swing of your moods and emotions, they can be improved with a walk. Walking as a wanderer where you're safe (please) feels playful, fills you with wonder, and will draw out your curiosity. We call this a Medicine Walk, time wandering away from the digital world and into the natural world. Walking in la Luna's rhythm will place you in cosmic time. She takes about a week from her New Moon phase to reach the First Quarter. Appearing to float through the Cosmos as a Half Moon, in orb geometrics, only a quarter of her surface is visible. In your planning, you may walk daily or match her rhythm of exaltation, and take a Medicine Walk in synch with la Luna's rhythm. Check your Moon calendar.

When you can carve out a time longer than your daily 10 minutes, open your art journal. A journal and art-materials become the go-to choice for playful visioning whenever you feel like it. Be surprised by what emerges from you, the running story of the day or week or month may turn into a story to share. Multiple levels of knowledge become accessible to you when you share with another, when you hear words fall from your heart. Your Mother, your Mentor, a girl coming up, or a Grandmother, these are perfect listeners. Human brains are hardwired for storytelling and after playing in your journal, talking is your most important action step. Clarissa Pinkola Estés, an extraordinary storyteller, says, "I don't know what I think until I see what I say." Ask someone to listen to your inner discoveries.

With the resurgence of storytelling, I ask: Are the Ancestors reminding us of the strong evolutionary connection we had to the central fire we came from? You can deepen the power of your experiences by simply sharing your story. After enjoying your deep quiet personal rituals during each New and each Full Moon, adopt a practice of telling the stories la Luna teaches you about the profound connection between emotions and blood. Every young woman needs a confidant besides her womb, who is yours?

Look back over the past month, was it all you wished it to be? Look ahead to the next month, what is your holiest and highest intention? Paying attention to the Moon is paying attention to yourself: Allow her four stages to shape the chrysalis of your inner life. Something inside wants to come out. What is it?

WHY RETREAT

Radical acts of self-care will teach you more of your body's sacred nature and how much there is to love about deep kindness. This is pure invention, Dearheart. Not one of us will tell you what, this is for you to decide: Whatever feels good to your heart, your spirit, and your body, do that. Self-judgments slowly begin to fall away when you practice compassion by giving yourself time. Judgments that began early in puberty will begin to dissolve when you discover more about your inner beauty. A profound friendship and loyalty will replace self-loathing with inner power. Liking yourself as your own best friend is one sign of maturity.

Self-care for your body envelops more than your body of course, this is woman's essential secret. By caring for yourself, remember to include your emotions, your spiritual self, you cognitive self, even your playful self. This is survival advice; there are plenty of moments ahead that could potentially feel very lonely. Being lonely, as in discontent with your own company, can be a real bummer. Break through with talking therapy, workout therapy, and share emotional experiences—even negative ones—to feel better. Learn and practice self-care; it's one of the most essential habits to learn before you leave the nest. Living fully and wholly, you will find the sacred in everything. Everything that feels nurturing— yoga, massage, manicures, brisk walking, gardening, and Nature explorations— can be experienced solo or shared with your Mother or Mentor.

Two Words Naturally Go Together: Ritual and Play

A woman's practice uses the energy of intention to create worlds within worlds. Your greatest inner power peaks when your Blood releases, the veil between the dimensions grows gossamer thin. Inspiration comes through easily in the quiet of your Moontime practice so you may commune directly with your Soul. Listening in the deep quiet of Nature or the corner of your bedroom, you will feel, hear, and appreciate how intuition guides your dreams. This is peak time for creativity. Review your Moon chart with your highs and lows. Your outer power peaks during ovulation. You want to be out in the world doing many things. Even the busy-ness of your life deserves a little quiet to listen inside. Intuitive messages can be missed if the noise in your head ignores any part of this sacred, treasured women's power practice.

Shedding one egg and then the next offers you a design that revolves around the Moon and your month. Women are brilliantly designed, egg-by-egg to work and play and check-in using both. Inside this design, a bridge from month to month has been illuminated. Your greatest discoveries wait for you in rest and retreat. The first days of your Moontime you have the opportunity to explore the details of your life design; using clues from your heart-dreams, you can plan how to build something. What adventures call to you? Have you filled your heart with Nature? Do you want to build a strong body? The deep quiet of your Moontime offers this ever unfolding treasure: You exploring your mind and your Soul.

La Luna holds the seeds of your creativity. She teaches you about you, about harmonizing with cosmic time and natural flow. What you feel depends on other factors, like your home and school environments and how well you have developed emotional intelligence for yourself. When my mood swings, my family becomes vigilant. Deeply personal discoveries sometimes beg to be shared. I have discovered how my Moon in Aries works with the other cosmic forces, the Sun and planets, to affect the energies of my emotions. This is complex, but I keep learning by observation and study. Gifts from the Cosmos are not part of the emotional intelligence found in books.

Our great Mother Earth is one of the heavenly planets. See for yourself, look up *My Orrey* on YouTube[4] and you will learn how Earth, one of the many planets spinning around our day star, the Sun, rotates as a heavenly body. To advance your personal development, what else is there but discovery, growth, and joy in this great spiritual adventure?

Of course! Love emerges through discovery, I love being in heaven on Earth. I love being in a state of love. I love knowing about the planets and la Luna, all of them have taught me so much about myself. I circle you back to emotional intelligence. Using your emotions, especially love, to learn about yourself will provide you with facts and lead you to higher use of your brain. As promised, your platinum brain power begins to arrive at age 14, and will be discussed in a few pages.

GOOD MEDICINE: THE CIRCLE OF COURAGE

Two fat circles seem to dance, side by side. The rhythmic cycle of your Moontime chart meets a second circle, called the Circle of Courage. I call their meeting place *entelechy*, the force of good. I line up your Moon chart with this circle of good medicine because both have round natures and beautiful synchronicities. Each supports the other. Together they help you evolve your potential into reality.

A Medicine Wheel is a circle divided into four parts and all parts are equal in emphasis and necessary for wholeness. Spirals and layers of ancient meanings of good medicine can be found in the wheel, including the 4 winds, the 4 seasons of life, even power animals. Medicine Wheel symbolism and teachings are old, old like Moon teachings. Ancient wisdom has been carried by Indigenous peoples all around the world. Watching taught these people and can teach you too, my beautiful Turtle.

Four More Foundation Stones

Inside this Circle of Courage[5] that I show here are 4 big ideas waiting for your embrace. These words will enable you to focus your attention on growing up, and after the rage of hormones and brain chemistries settle down, these ideas will lead you to balance and wholeness. The 4 big concepts inside your Circle of Courage are **Belonging, Mastery, Independence**, and **Generosity**.

Belonging rises out of our spirits. Look within, you know when you do and when you do not belong, you sense it, you feel it. This sense is an emotional intelligence, a knowing that begins at Birth. To explain Belonging requires warmth, comfort, and positive feelings of home. Belonging to the Earth as our Mothership and other-Mother offers values like awe, sacred, unity and playfulness to deepen this knowing, I belong.

The action of belonging is a simple embrace, relationships work two ways, making kinship with others. Belonging is the psychic key to being, when you feel love and attachment to family and friends, you understand how kinship and loyalty are connected.

Psychologists love this word attachment; many social theories spin on how well you bond in your relationships. Lining up with the East on the Medicine Wheel and with Birth on the Spiral of Nine Passages, belonging is a personal value to practice with those you love that will enrich every single day of your life. Focus on deepening connections with those who love you.

Moving through good medicine, **Mastery** is a whole concept to occupy your teen years. More than anything in the world—what do you want more of or want to know more about? Answering this will bring you closer to mastery, especially if you persist to get the answer. What is uniquely yours to give the world? In the body and spirit explorations that created your 'great girl' between Middle Childhood and puberty, your curiosities revealed a few early passions. Beyond puberty, your dreams begin to rise like yeasty bread and grow. Passion, a thread from your Soul which can nag through your intuition, must be pursued because this directly aligns you with your Soul working through your dreams. One of my Coyote Mentors calls this Genius,[6] and I do too, it's the place where your dreams meet your Soul. Michael Meade says. "Every person is a genius at being yourself."

Even believing this, you may need to ask for support to follow your dreams. Without reservation, I define mastery as your alignment with the cosmic rhythm of time. Ten thousand hours of devotion to one or two passions will build the foundation for all of life. This is a lengthy devotion to yourself. Even if you have to sleep with this mantra: *What do I want? What do I want?* Your answers will float to the surface because your inner Genius is the passion that lives in what you love. At this South direction and First Blood on the Spiral, you discover clues to your future by reaching for mastery.

Between the Dark and the Light—Independence

This metaphor is growing in strength: By the time the Moon comes to Fullness, the third concept, Independence, naturally appears as a reward. This circle is now becoming value-laden. Independence includes two interacting values that cascade like falling water. Where self-discipline and self-responsibility intersect, this cross-point creates independence. To find support and encouragement for your independence, hang out with adults who model and discuss values—risk assessment, decision making, and responsibility—to build your confidence and honor. Out of deep discussions, you will begin to feel competent to take up the challenge to make decisions and use inner discipline to create your own challenges. This will give you just a glimpse into your future where you will next reach for the Womanhood Bloom Passage on the Life Spiral. When you act consistently and realize mistakes are wonderful teachers, you will begin to feel a growing sense of independence. Action builds self-esteem and experience and feels exhilarating.

Generosity completes the Circle of Courage and like the Moon in her final Quarter, her waning stage, giving back has a personal flavor. Generosity includes caring, attention, and empathy, which arise when you share time with others. When you practice a rhythm of generosity, you start to feel more and more worthy. When your feelings of worth gain traction, you eliminate lack and the need for a therapist at the same time. By learning that giving is equal to receiving, and for emphasis, receiving is equal to giving, your heart unlocks the secret of good relationships. Your reward is a higher personal regard.

Although accumulative changes turn you into a woman, this enormous and remarkable metamorphosis from chrysalis to butterfly does happen gradually. You never have to know it all. Human evolution begins to flower in you as your great gift of change between 12 and 18. This is the first half of adolescence. No other six years contain such drama or cohesive energy as your early emotional and intellectual systems integrate with social and sensory systems.

YOUR ENTELECHY: THE FORCE FOR GOOD

By giving yourself deep quiet and time to pursue your thoughts and discover your dreams, you can actually watch your thoughts take form. This is known as entelechy, a vital force directing the growth of your life. Entelechy moves heart-thoughts from potential, as in a dream, to actual, as in a thing. Entelechy is part of your Soul, teaching you things through thoughts. Blend these vital heart-dreams to create a good design for your life in any way that feels right for you.

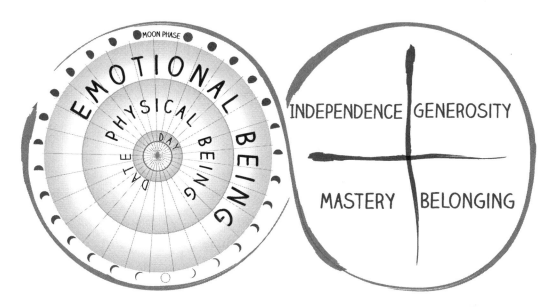

Look Again: Entelechy is Your Moontime + Your Skillset ©2016

The Genius in your Soul causes a thought to grow into an action and take shape as a thing; that is entelechy in action. Through entelechy, what you dream comes true. Like baking, you simply blend: Form an intention, create a plan, and add action. This is your silk thread! Very often you will need to ask for help.

The intersection where the Moon helps you track your inner potential to make something happen seems like magic, but look around you. Women constantly make things happen, make things appear out of practically nothing. Begin to notice others' process, ask them about how they manifested their dreams. Entelechy is this force inside of them and inside of you.

Follow the silk thread for a minute. Go with the flow of your cycle and wrap your heart around the 4 Indigenous values that are important for teen focus: **Belonging, Mastery, Independence,** and **Generosity.** A force of personal courage begins to rise inside of you. This is entelechy, your very personal and very vital force. Now you know more about life design than I did when I turned 30!

I have a little story: Just before I turned 16, I suffered the death of my best friend. My sophomore year was filled with grief. The following summer, my parents sent me to my California grandparents for six weeks and I returned supercharged. I picked boysenberries with my Grandmother and attended the short summer session at Modesto Junior College with my older sister. At the beginning of my junior year, I announced that I would graduate from high school early, as a junior, and I did. How did this happen so easily? It was only a thought from the berry patch, but I held onto it, tracked the potential of it, made a dream out of it every day through all the Moontimes of my junior year. Those two things—time with Grandmother and with higher learning—built a fire in my belly and the day-dreaming was Divine, as from God. You can do anything you dream, when you learn to track with your inner potential, your entelechy.

PLATINUM BRAIN POWER

Fourteen is a peak age of undeniable complexity in ontogenesis. That's the fancy word for the biological timing when your hard drive finally arrives: Your adult brain. This new and better than gold, platinum brain power, begins to download at age 14 and never stops.

Play with Ritual: Learn about Your Soul

Let's unpack this complexity: Your female hormones now meet your new brain chemistry. While you might long for your former light, playful child-self, you discover a new longing at the same time. You long to be grown up and be treated as a woman, you long to make your own choices and your own mistakes. Your brain has just expanded to adult size and power, but you haven't yet learned how to use it. As a self-defense mechanism, you must act like you have it together. Simultaneously, you feel and see a new awareness with your inner sight. When you lay on your bed or on the Earth, you wonder about the presence you have begun to sense. She is like a regal watcher; your essential and mysterious Soul awakens on a higher platform, like up in the tree-tops.

This gift of Soul has been quiet since Birth. For a few, the inner companion awakens in Middle Childhood, but Soul becomes an urgent force when the adult brain arrives. Now, especially when you sit in the quiet of your Moontime, or you float awake out of your dreamtime, or you enjoy the silence in Nature, you can feel the presence of Soul. You deserve to explore your Soul's inner nature. For Soul explorations, deeply immerse yourself in what you love. Beginning to feel masterful, use your Vision Quest time. How you use this gift of quiet will shape your life. Before you leave home and take your First Flight at age 17 or 18 or 20, your cosmic clock delivers another 50 Moons when Blood comes to quiet you and help you connect to your Soul and what you love.

Learn how to track emotions and compulsions that feel scattered and undirected. When you really learn self-love, judgments and criticisms dissolve back into pure exploration. Every woman has many facets, so do you as the youngest among us. Some of us run helter-skelter, wanting to polish a dozen passions at once. The entire world needs to be explored and you, with the high privilege of having a home nest, you deserve to fall into endless, timeless joy with your explorations. When parents provide a home they intend for you to shape your identity, discover what you love, and use every opportunity to become strong and resilient enough to fly from the nest and thrive.

Play with Meditation, Make it Yours

MAKING INTENTION SACRED

A practice of deepening meditation begins at 14 when the gift of human evolution offers you the brain power to consider the abstract. Learn to be very Turtle-like, basking in the Sun. Dare yourself to unplug. Find quiet inside your mind. As you begin to practice meditation, quiet mind seems rather abstract. Entering the realm of your mind to meditate, you find your mind quick and noisy with thoughts, so looking for quiet can be frightening. Try laughing at this monkey of a mind and begin again. Many of the wise, experienced meditators say, "Follow your breath, in and out."

With persistence you will soon succeed. Meditation is rest for your busy mind. Follow your breath in and out. I like to light a candle to set the mood. You could ask for help, find a woman who knows about meditation, perhaps a yogini will become your ally. On-line, Sally Kempton or Pema Chodrin[7] are both master teachers who offer help for you to begin a meditation practice. When meditation is over, even ten minutes each day, growing to twenty minutes twice a day, you will quickly notice how fired up you feel. Your brain likes rest. Circle back to your Turtle self.

Just out of your deep state of meditation, pay close attention to your intuition—each message delivers gifts from your Soul. In your Vision Quest time when you bleed, focus on the messages of your heart-dreams. During your Moon is the most excellent time to become relaxed and practiced with meditation. Sometimes, in barely discernable whispers, you will receive reminders of what you love most, which gifts are yours alone. Singly or several woven together, your gifts deserve to be cultivated, in fact it's what the world is waiting for.

Gifts rise from quiet, like a dream floating out of the mist, when you commune with the deepest part of your Soul. From there your sacred intentions find their power in entelechy because they arise from the quiet potential in your heart. Dreams begin to manifest, step by step, egg-by egg.

IDENTITY AND RISK

While the Earth turns 2000 day-to-night rotations, your consciousness expands with the help of your wild self and your tame self. Identity formation finds the balance between your wild and tame extremes while you physically mature. In the cultural view of early and middle adolescence, a chasm opens as wide as the Grand Canyon and many people just label it chaos. Girls cast off labels, as should you. What is really going on?

If identity is the puberty project, chameleon energy is the game that delights you and your peers. This chameleon game causes you to experiment, so you're one way with family, another way with teachers, and yet a whole new way with your peers. These different ways you invent make you feel talented, secretive, and wild. Sometimes, you literally change every day, which can be exhausting, but you can also see through this to the other side. Deep down, you know the world is a stage and you are the lead actress. Soon one true self will emerge and you will like her.

In adolescence you align with a wide array of risks and need someone to tell you the truth about risk. Your Mom has been trying, but it's hard to listen when she loves you so and spins a positive twist at the same time she points to danger ahead. Who is the person who will tell you the truth and who will you listen to deeply? I am not kidding, risks are those things with consequences, hard to see and often dangerous. The cultural risks that involve your body and easy to name, like substance abuse and sexual experimentation, carry hidden costs that you cannot yet understand so parents and teachers hold out punishments for them. I am going to teach you how to weigh and understand risk so you can decide for yourself. You and I intend to prevent the psychological damage that can cause scars for life.

You have already learned to keep yourself safe from harm. Some of that, knives, scissors, fast moving cars and bicycles, even extreme sports, skateboarding and skiing, have taught you about risk. Early and Middle Childhood filled you up with experiences—if you were like me—you have needed more than one trip to the emergency room already.

Ask a Tree to Be Your Witness

Learn advance risk assessment now, like you are parenting yourself. Ask these questions about potential harm: What trouble lurks? Who takes the lead? How would anyone be harmed? What penalties will result and what are my personal consequences? Is death a penalty? Is jail a penalty? Are my moral standards involved? Weighing risk, would I choose the same friends? Besides my body, what other parts of me might be harmed? Can my spirit be harmed?

Develop a two-column chart, list "do this" (pro) on one side and "don't" (con) on the other side. Now, being totally honest with yourself, answer each one of those questions. Sorry if this pros and cons list seems adult-like behavior. Even from your point of view, risk assessment is all about keeping yourself safe, which is very adult-like. This will also teach you to use your adult brain and learn to think. The last question is about who: Have I thought about who cares? How do my actions ripple out to others?

Learn to weigh risk successfully and you will have more control of the inner and outer parts of your life. With risk assessment, your potential for harmony in relationships will increase and you will begin to think like a woman. Honestly, this is the conversation that parents long for so be proactive. Every successful transition from early adolescent to the middle where you have more control includes asking yourself: What is my risk and how does it show up for me? Risk weighing, the analysis of choices and decisions, light up like signs of maturity.

THE WITNESS

Over time, women acquire tricks that might be useful during and after high school, so why not learn them now? The first two tricks are mindfulness and resiliency, slightly different techniques for mastering the ability to absorb the little and big shocks of every day. You are all too familiar with inner turmoil, and you know about contrary energies that you receive from peers, teachers, and even your parents sometimes. Resiliency is your innate ability to bounce back and to recover a calm, tranquil state. As an internal energy which you can trust and strengthen with your mind, resiliency is a bounce-back energy that works very well with mindfulness. Many people, who focus on the intersection of mind and body where you think and feel, teach that mindfulness is a way of training your mind to pay attention to the present moment only. Both re-siliency and mindfulness are abilities to handle stress caused when your mind judges things as negative even before they happen. A little saying: Be mindful and kind to yourself rather than judgmental and critical. This is self-care.

To remain upright through life's storms, knowledge comes to your aid. Follow routine and automatic behaviors may lull you into a sleepwalking state. You can learn to *pay attention*, even if you write this on your hand for a few days. If you forget, you fall back into mindlessness. Paying attention only to the present moment, being mindful, you are more sensitive and open to surprise. Most of all, practicing mindfulness avoids mindlessness. This is a big duh! Huh? It came from Dr. Ellen Langer,[8] she is the Mother of Mindfulness. I tell you this because I want to quote one tip she offers: "Today, identify three things you don't like about yourself. What is the positive version of each of these traits? Can you reframe what you don't like to create a more positive interpretation of your qualities and traits? For example, are you 'slow' or merely contemplative? Are you 'impulsive and rash' or simply spontaneous? Are you 'obstinate' or determined and tenacious?"

Oh, how I love that reframing. This is emotional intelligence at work. Paying attention to each moment, mindfulness, twisted around an attitude of resiliency, gives you control over the ups and downs that come from interacting with all other people. When something or someone—even you—knocks you off-center, these two energies, mindfulness and resiliency, work together to return you back to your center with much less stress or anxiety. Reframing is a great strategy for mean-girls, too. Play their game with kindness and playfulness. Many an old Mother has said this: "Confuse your enemies with kindness."

With practice, you discover that you can trust yourself more when you engage with all that is happening in the moment in front of your eyes. Even blame dissolves when you let go of past hurts. Trust is the reward of paying attention to your inner knower and her witness. This expands your emotional intelligence. You have built-in capacities for paying attention to the moment and for witnessing your own actions and reactions. This is part of consciousness and identity. Practicing mindfulness will bring you peace.

What are you trusting? Yourself? Your connection to all that is? Consider what happens when you awaken your mind in every part of your body. Can you be a tuning fork for the Universe? Perhaps there is much more to trusting yourself as you are an integral part of the whole. Yes, God and Goddess would agree with me. Trust turns into faith with practice, be your own witness. Prove this to yourself.

Ellen Langer, as I have introduced, has worked the past 40 years leading the research in mindfulness. She has spent her adult life combining and recombining questions to bring this gem to our attention: Mindfulness. One summary statement goes like this—all of our problems, personal, interpersonal, professional, and societal stem either directly or indirectly from mindlessness. Noticing more is an antidote to boredom. I love knowing this is true because I really dislike those times when I feel bored or boring!

Your inner witness reminds you that you already know a great deal. Sometimes you don't even know how you know things. Being mindful, not zoning out, gathers up all your past experience so you can learn more from each moment. Challenge yourself to acquire these tools and they will be yours. Best of all, tools like meditation and Moon retreats are free. Encourage your antennae to stretch and grow. Your wise inner self and witness are always present and will offer up this advanced wisdom anytime you reach for it.

Gain control and take charge of yourself before your 15th birthday. For this to happen, practice mindfulness and demonstrate accountability. You want this and I want this for you. By staying close to the light side, your passions will begin to line up.

NATURE, ALWAYS THERE FOR YOU

While you remain in the nest, the time from 14 through 17+ contains 1500 days for play and learning. Nature connection began when you were a wee baby imprinted with furry bumble bees and flittering butterflies. Your heart connection to Nature becomes more important through your teen years. My friends remind me that time in Nature brings solace, smooths the edges in our emotional bodies. Nature is a gift you give yourself.

Summer and winter I am a tracker, paying attention to who shares my world. I call these the tracks of the sacred Others, because I seldom see the critters, but I like knowing they are there. Seeing fresh tracks means I have company. Connection to everything in the natural world deepens our feelings of belonging. Learning about ecology will anchor your place in the Cosmos. Change is rolling through all of Earth's environments and seems to be speeding up and must be embraced.

I like the image of an ecosystem pictured as an intricate spider's web delicately swinging in the breeze. Every tree, every animal, every bird, every little plant, every water particle, everything is connected by that web. Everything is related. Like you in the center, all of it is delicate. You are related to each one of these parts and your life depends on knowing all you can learn about how relationships and interdependence works. All these ecosystem pieces belong to the Earth, often called Gaia from Greek mythology for the Great Mother Goddess. Luckily you have at least six senses to enjoy Gaia's gifts. Your senses will help you locate your gift for Gaia.

With a little sensory practice, you can learn the perspective of our First People here on Turtle Island, their name for North America. We are all related. We are all one, an intricate part of the whole of life on Earth. When you know in your Soul that you are related to everything you lay eyes on, your perspective changes.

Consider how your senses work together: When you blend sight with hearing both become infinitely more powerful. Blending senses is one way of strengthening all of them and to feel the connection they need to be strong. This requires a "dirt time."[9] Simply stated, dirt-time is your regular devotion to going outside, to firing up your curiosity, kissing the Earth with your bare feet, and moving as you are one with Earth's magic. What you receive is belonging, balance, and outrageous joy. Let's begin a campaign to give back to Earth for all she gives to us; I like the idea of Gifts for Gaia. What can you feel inspired to do for this Great Mother who will hold you all the days of your life?

FINALE: WRAP THE BUNDLE

Transformation is Complete

Maybe you can feel my great gratitude for the evolutionary force that makes leaving home possible. With all the preparations of the last couple of years, you know now that you are ready to leave home; your knowing is driven by an urge for new ordeals. When this first half of adolescence is complete, with it goes most of the drama of change. Your butterfly wings are dry and tested. The second half of adolescence is harder, this is true, but you have secret tools that no other generation of women has bundled together.

You have a rhythm to watch your changes through your Moontimes and through the Circle of Courage. I want you to feel comfortable with entelechy, your inner power, but that comfort comes through practice. Endurance and resilience have been part of these early years of adolescence: You learned about yourself and your passions, you learned about risk assessment and gained appreciation for your super-charged adult brain power. Like the day a baby bird leaves her nest, you will always remember the day you fly on your own.

Now you are ready to receive blessings from your Mentors, the Aunties and the Elders. More than ever, you need a supporting cast to hold the nest while you fly away. Invite everyone who helped you.

I advise you to simply ask for a very special Rites of Passage ceremony. Invite all of the women who have been your supporting cast and turn the ritual over to them to create. Each woman will offer a piece important to your ceremony. Set a firm date so that you and your Mother can take a breather. By simply exploring your inner desires with these women friends, a Rites of Passage will be designed just for you. They have been your community, the generations ahead of you in age and stage who have pioneered their own lives. Ask them to include an away place, a challenge, and a means to bundle your story up to now.

A DRUM-ROLL PLEASE

Leaving home begins with the drumbeat of consciousness. Primary self-parenting means you hear the inner voice of moral authority before making a major choice. I love the model of Maslow's hierarchy of needs.[10] First you need food, water, and shelter. These needs are so real that creativity will often engage every fiber of you to solve them. Your drumbeat quickens around age 16 and allows time for expression and discussion. The drumbeat of your Soul may send you exploring the practical possibilities of early autonomy, a beautiful word for self-sufficiency or independence.

We could honestly fill another chapter for your womanhood training if we included body image, relationships, sexuality, wild-within adventures in Nature, musical intelligence, personal rituals, more about self-care, brain health, more about emotional intelligence, social graces, chakra music, sensory awareness, meditation, compassionate self-parenting, religious intelligence and peacemaking. These were all on my Elder-friends' lists of most prized knowledge before leaving home. This list is yours to use, to begin conversations. You will find the intersections of experience and research which will ignite another layer of curiosity. You will learn things by asking that will help you with real life experiences. Your action step involves taking the time to ask what others think and feel. Dear Fledgling, each woman has learned about these headliners and we will talk anytime you ask.

On the Life Spiral, each Passage includes dozens of birthday ceremonies and holiday celebrations that add great joy to a whole life. First Flight is Passage No. 4 and includes the bundle of everything that came before. Assembling the parts and pieces for this ritual begins with a review from Birth and moves experimentally and experientially through Middle Childhood Rites and First Blood celebrations. If you experienced those earlier ceremonies, my heart is glad.

Just in case you draw a blank on ritual: A Rites of Passage ceremony is perhaps the oldest ritual on Earth, and is now returning to the culture. Your initiation ceremony is a dramatic catalyst of change that shows your people you have reached the end of one stage of development.

Bundling experience all of your challenges and ordeals from age 12 to this Passage now provides an honoring for your life. To perform a ritual requires a quiet state of mind, a space made sacred with your thoughts and actions. It's good to light candles to invite ambience. Treat your senses to incense, to colorful fabric for an altar, smudge for cleansing, photos in memory of yourself, poetry you love, bells, music, drums, and rattles. Each ritual item honors you and elevates you into an altered state of being. Initiation "reveals yourself to yourself," in the words of Michael Meade.[11] Do your bundling then let go. Your supporting cast will create a ceremony that honors all your early days. Time stands still for moments while you respect the memories of all of your joys, all of your trials, and all of your dreams so far.

For every woman, ritual draws from her personal ancestral well of experience. Those are the foundational pieces for this ceremony. I always add Mugwort to invite the dreams of life and Prairie Sage to invite the Ancestors. Trust your supporting women, they know what to do.

I cannot emphasize enough the importance of wrapping your bundle. You will carry this honor through all of your life. The ceremony will be regal and powerful and you will flow into the next decade like falling water.

THE STORY OF DIVERSE FLEDGLINGS

More than a thousand million graduation parties are held every year; we live in that storied landscape. I offer this story because it lives in me; my Soul truly understands how it colors my perspective. This First Flight ceremony is the rarest in my personal experience, but I have helped create two Fledgling ceremonies ten years apart. I am only the common thread in each young woman's story of their Passage from the first half of their adolescence into the second half.

Dee came into my life first, just as she turned 10 years old. I observed that hope lived in her spirit in a way that seemed eternal, often that was all she had. As a teen-age girl with big check marks in most at-risk categories, she still held onto hope. I was her 'big sister' for two-and-a-half years, and then I was her advocate. Finally, after she had traveled a long, long road of trials, I became her foster Mother for her senior year in high school.

In the middle age of our lives, my new husband and I jumped through the hoops to move Dee from Colorado to Idaho sending shock waves through us and our relationship. Dee had the hardest time adapting, because she had been in 15 different group homes in 5 years and survived a fostering system that controlled her with drugs. She was almost feral and certainly angrier than a caged animal. As part of her commitment to come drug free to our home, she had refused her medications for two months. My constant questions were: How could we use one little year to fill in so many developmental gaps? How could I give her all that she needed?

When it came time to fledge her, the ticking of a clock was the indicator rather than experience or maturity. She was half a year past 18 and needing to go. I had taught her to drive, she had successfully interned at the local animal shelter, and she needed more, probably more than anyone could give her. Dee and I walked the neighborhood and talked about life. She needed to experience for herself. She was about to walk out on the gangplank into the school of hard knocks and I was going to push her.

Introducing Kanga, Formerly Dee / Deirdre on her Gangplank—She Called it Emancipation

A very nice dinner party lavished gifts on her that she had no way to value. She needed a car since we lived in rural Idaho. Dee needed a computer because her first step on her own was to check into the dorm of a small college. In no way could we fill in her great need for love and belonging or for the social graces in relationships. Only she could find her intelligences emotional, spiritual, and motivational.

Basically, we breathed uneasily when my husband and I released Dee to her dorm room. For one year, only one year, we had treaded lightly with each other and learned about resiliency in our spirit-selves. We did let go, that was what everyone needed.

Rebellion and confusion made the next couple of years a real challenge for Dee. Stories of her escapades floated to us along the mysterious grapevine of social connectedness. She struggled mightily to keep herself upright. Whenever she felt hopeful and positive, she would call and give me news. Those hard years made her stronger and resiliency is part of her core strengths now. I feel very grateful she stayed connected to me, she is a big part of my personal story.

An Earth Momma, Always Offering Her Heart, Always Helping Everybody

In the middle of her crucial teen life, I wrote a graduate essay on how resilient she was throughout her experiences in all those group homes. That resiliency which she had earned blended inexplicably with her inner spirit, the fire of hope, so now ten years later, Dee is upright and doing very well. She provides a snug little home for champion dogs and laying hens. She reads voraciously and is a culinary wizard. Always a night owl, she has liked working the night shift.

Another Threshold has appeared for Kanga and with her whole heart she is stepping up to training as a foster parent. In a new place, a new life and new job, she uses joy for her fuel. I find the light in her voice encouraging and her hope infectious. I love this relationship and include her in my prayers.

Maybe in our humble strivings, we can make a difference in another's life. This was all I ever dared to ask for, that I could make a difference. I know that love has been the bridge between a young girl and me, almost 40 year's difference gets stuffed with laughter, tears, understanding, and so many prayers that begin with Wow.

PRACTICING RITUALS

Ten years later, another teen named Maya came to me and asked for help. I was more than happy to provide her with a college prep writing class where we worked closely together for six months. In a home school/on-line accreditation system, she added this class to her credits. Maya found tremendous inner strength in applying discipline and working hard to please her inner critic. She wrote for herself and I merely supplied a rudder.

A beautiful woman's ceremony 'wrapped the bundle' for her Rites of Passage to send her far away from home. Elders, Aunties, and Maya's Mother designed an overnight retreat for Maya to serve her in memory all through the transformative first year out of the nest. First, our celebration circled around food, which is always superb at women's gatherings.

A Gathering of Women and our Symbols to Gift Maya a Box of Love Notes

Maya loved the feast and was very surprised by the temple we created for separation and an altered state of being. Mother told her Birth story and journey as heart-companion to Maya's Soul from Birth to now. I really liked giving the stage and the spotlight to Maya, the bud of a new woman, but I scared her by telling her to come prepared. Everyone enjoyed hearing about highlights and ordeals and how Maya wrapped her life inside a story. Aunties and Elders listened carefully and wrote on sticky notes. One by one, as all of her Mentors mirrored highlights back to Maya, we carefully wrapped her story into a small, wooden, gift box and offered accolades to Mother.

This initiation ritual still feels amazing to each of us women. The Divine Feminine in our different offerings blossomed into a beautiful flower. We didn't talk about what to do or rehearse; we allowed ritual practices to flow out of us and harmonize. The glorious high point of Maya's Rites of Passage ritual resulted in a Soul-filled bundle of storylines and affirmations. Inside her gift box, each one of our sticky notes traveled away with Maya, our newly fledged young woman, to keep her company throughout the year while her transformation completed itself.

There are many ways to bring a ceremony like this to a close, but usually a test of wits, a swim across the pond, a blindfold walk to the sound of a drum, even a string walk would be a small demonstration of the ordeals ahead that she will encounter alone. Saying adios to an old self provides an initiate with a little "d" for death; a ceremony could include some of that flavoring.

We could not locate a blindfold, so Maya's jacket literally wrapped around her head like a turban. In that dark place she felt drowsy and warmed. Her two nearest and dearest Aunties took her to the bottom of the road and let go. They guarded the edges and told Maya to follow the drum. When she finally came to the fire we sang songs and then everyone went skinny dipping, ate too much pie, and fell into deep slumbers. Symbolism of finale happened in the morning with henna paint that marked her change amidst great giggles.

Maya flew from her comfortable home nest and once in college wrote an essay about her experience.

Here are her expressive words:

Driving home, I told my Mom how grateful I was for all of the time and planning she had devoted into my Rites of Passage ceremony. Although there were no physical differences besides the henna when I was reintroduced into society, I was spiritually and mentally impacted. I value my bond with my Mom and I know the ceremony helped prepare me for my solo journey away from home. I am the only person I know out of my friends who was given the gift of a Rites of Passage ceremony and I want to carry on this tradition to my children. I am my Mother's daughter inside and out and I know I will carry her teachings with me wherever I am.

I love my Momma.

Like Maya, each of the women in the Circle felt the ceremony flow from our hearts and form a memory essence that remains with us, sweet and enduring. To close out the first transformational year away from home, the formality and long preparation of a Vision Quest could function nicely to close the portal. The symbolic Death of the former self and final grieving for those 'nest years' could give a stamp of a formal closing for the whole Passage. This is for reincorporation: Gather the women again to share about your true ordeal away from home. We will reflect back to you, fledged woman, that your change is significant and permanent.

Student of Life

A GAME: FIND MY PASSION

A woman named Sogini demonstrated this game, playing with a group of girls.

Simple rules, on a large piece of paper, draw a star burst with your name at the center. Then, use this list to remind you what you love. Write and doodle, think and create, then admire your passions, as fiery as the Sun. Include everything you feel curious about. Re-do if you like, several times, admiring all that you love. This is your shine.

Animals (real, imaginary, stuffed – what do you love? What have you loved?)

Plants (house, nursery, wild, include your favorite trees)

Theater (costume, pretend, musicals)

Writing (stories, poetry, comics)

Reading (fiction, non-fiction, comics)

Drawing (doodling, zentangles, pen and ink, pencils)

Painting (crayons, water-colors, acrylics, pastels)

Music (playing, singing, listening)

Dancing (modern, mystical, ballroom, ballet, jazz)

Sports (playing, watching – name all that you love)

Photography (portraits of people and flowers, scenery and memories)

Nature (wandering, naming, discovery, wondrous or scary, soothing or hazardous)

Logical science (math, chemistry, physics, biology)

Health science (medicine, nursing, herbal, alternative, integrative)

Food (cooking, growing, cross-cultural)

Sex (pleasure, lust, games, orgasms, safety for your Soul, LGBT)

SNEAK PREVIEW

Your adolescence extends all through the decade of your 20s. Your adult-like behavior accumulates between the ages of 18 and 29, but your full adult maturity coincides with an astrological symbol, the return of Saturn.

Saturn is an apt symbol because of this question, "Who were you born to be?"

The decade of your 20s requires you to strengthen each one of your systems while your brain finally reaches maturity. You will use all of your senses to feel belonging and love and to integrate your fine mind by discovering where emotions live in your physical body.

I call this next Passage, Womanhood Bloom and want to share new secrets ...

about your shadow-work
how to understand your beliefs
acquire problem solving
develop personal analytic skills
manage your habits
experiment with various risks
engage in movement and body works
explore various divinations to open you up
stabilize your emotions through good self-parenting

When you are ready, I feel confident to share more of the secret building blocks of womanhood. I thank you for this privilege to inspire your inner guide.

Emancipation Begins a Journey of Soul and Self

GIFTS FROM THE ELDERS: FIRST FLIGHT

Dear young woman, curiosities, choices, and passions will lead you down a winding path of growth. Love each one of your decisions with all your heart.

This Passage speaks in a different voice to the young woman herself. Mothers, read this chapter with your daughters. My natural voice, the voice of Mentor, offers tools to help you find your way through the maze.

When your parents provide a home, they intend for you to shape your identity, discover what you love, and use every opportunity to become strong and resilient enough to fly from the nest and thrive.

Your most profound gifts rise from the quiet:

* Do you meditate? Do you dance? Do you sing?

Learn to weigh risk successfully. Ask these questions:

* What trouble lurks?

* How would anyone be harmed?

* Are my moral standards involved?

* Have I thought about who cares?

With **Risk Assessment,** a young woman's potential for harmony in relationships will increase and she will begin to think more like a woman.

* What is my risk and how does it show up for me?

Resilience is bounce-back energy: **Mindfulness** is paying attention to the moment. These are the abilities to handle stress caused when the mind judges things as negative even before they happen.

* Be mindful and kind to yourself rather than judgmental and critical.

Today, name three things you don't like about yourself:

∗ What is the positive version of each of these traits?

∗ Can you reframe what you don't like to create a more positive interpretation?

∗ Have you practiced self-parenting and self-care?

∗ Have you learned to trust yourself and your passion?

∗ Do you admire another woman's process? Can you ask how she man-
ifests her dreams?

Nature will always be there for you. Nature is the connection to everything and deepens your feelings of belonging. You are Nature. You are related.

∗ Can you begin a campaign to give back to Earth for all she gives to us?

∗ What can you feel inspired to do for the Great Mother who will hold
you all the days of your life?

NOTES FOR FIRST FLIGHT PASSAGE

1   You may have noticed the dedication page. Joseph W. Meeker changed my life when he asked me to write my play history. He was Mentor-in-chief on my doctoral committee. Joe presented me with this certificate when I completed that eye-opening assignment. Begin as soon as possible to create a play history for yourself. Nurture your personal experiences with play. Make a presentation of a certificate when you feel willing to surrender to play.

2   Howard Gardener, an Education professor from Harvard, was the first to write about multiple intelligences, and because I was a student, I paid attention to *Multiple Intelligences: The Theory in Practice* (1993). I am happy to say when Gardener added Nature intelligence to his list, I could accept his theories, although like everyone, I learn by blending two or three together.

3   Susan Cain wrote *Quiet: The Power of Introverts in a World That Can't Stop Talking* (2013) to explore all the ways of being from introverted to extroverted and the in-between states of being. She felt the extroverts were getting all the attention. This will probably always be true.

4   We have influences that can only be felt, explanations can be tricky. My study of Astrology has been validating and satisfying. The depth keeps me interested. *My Orrey* takes some of the guess-work out of how the planets interact. I have learned a much deeper sense of the Cosmos by doing rituals with my husband on the Equinoxes, Solstices and cross-quarter days each year. Ken Condal built an Orrey in 7 months, see at www.zeamon.com or search YouTube.

5   *Circle of Courage*® was first introduced to me in 1995 by Larry Bentro. Information can be found all over the Internet but the original website, Reclaiming Youth International has become www.starr.org to help kids at risk, especially. The Circle of Courage founders are real heroes.

6   At the Mosaic Multicultural Foundation, Michael Meade hosts the Genius Project, see mosaicvoices.org He offers many YouTube talks about mythology, mentoring, and Genius.

7   Many meditation teachers are available. On-line and searchable, Sally Kempton or Pema Chodrin are both master teachers who offer help for you to begin a meditation practice. Brain scientists recommend this practice but only you can give this gift to yourself.

8   Ellen Langer PhD is the first woman to be tenured as a professor of Psychology at Harvard. An early researcher into *Mindfulness* (1989), her pioneering book of that time is enjoying a 25-year anniversary. We can continue to benefit from her major groundbreaking discoveries as she shows the mind connection to aging. Counter Clockwise: *Mindful Health and the Power of Possibility* (2009) explores her research on reversing aging with the power of mindfulness. See www.ellen-langer.com

9   I love this play on words, dirt and time connected. As soon as I heard Jon Young use dirt-time, I claimed it for myself, except I heard it first from him in 2004.

10 Abraham Maslow, a psychologist who wakened cultural consciousness with the conversation about needs, published a famous pyramid that placed a priority on needs. When I have been with slim resources, the basic needs do stand out the most, food and shelter.

11 A workshop with Michael Meade in 2013 deepened my understanding of initiation in the culture

today. These words, "Initiation reveals yourself to yourself," became a takeaway after a full week-end of storytelling. After that I read his two books filled with the mythical stories that Michael Meade carries: *The Water of Life: Initiation and the Tempering of the Soul* (2006); and *Fate and Destiny: The Two Agreements of the Soul* (2010). I recommend the stories in these books as a sharing, Mother and Grandmother, to spark conversations about Soul and destiny with the young woman ready to fledge.

WOMANHOOD BLOOM

THE INTENTION:
EMPOWERING WOMEN FOR THEIR JOURNEY

My prayer: Stories contain lessons whether from the light side or the darker ways of being human. I pray we can honor all women's stories.

Cobblestones fill the space between each imaginative symbol which represents change, usually biological change. This Life Spiral offers a metaphor for the stories of your life, each stone preserves something of value for you. Memories often relate to another memory that came before or after. Side by side, these cobblestones show a life filled with stories. Sometimes your stories were consciously intended, often they were not.

The Life Spiral

Locate Your Soul in Time and Place

With my squinty eyes, I see life's events among the cobblestones on this Life Spiral. Each cobblestone, bubble-like with firm boundaries, holds the secret neuropathway to a memory, sometimes throbbing, wanting to be remembered. The momentous occasions of your life, held safe and secure inside a stone, connect to another story nearby. We are made of stories.

It's absolutely impossible to plan a life down to the finite detail. There is an old proverb that says: "If you want to make God laugh, just tell Her your plans." Being flexible like a willow is part of survival. You can plan to be happy and you can practice to be in balance, women will teach you by example. Intention contains a spiritual power; setting and holding intentions helps God and Great Mother help you. (Women use prayer for the winds of change and we use intention to align with our Souls.)

THE EAGLES' VIEW

The road ahead is all yours now, exhilarating and exhausting, festive and hauntingly lonely, filled with peaks and valleys, sometimes all of these at once, but this is your very own path. You cannot do it wrong. Relax in the stillness of your pillow-talk, you do not have to figure out your whole life all at once. Spend time with play rather than worry. Learn what play means and how it feels in your 19 and 20 year old body. Remember your playful self at 10 and 11 to rejuvenate your spirit and deepen your connections to play. Pure play provides the best cultural anecdote for serious women and the best dare I can toss your way. Connect your Soul to your body in the arms of Great Mother and you will fulfill the challenge to find balance through play. When you do, share with those you love. Call them out to play with you. This is a Gaia Gift, the Earth needs balanced women.

I am both fierce and tender as an Elder guide. Take from me all that you can work with and leave the rest. This is a joy-ride, this decade and those that follow. I offer you a strong shoulder and the best gleanings from many lives observed with love. Remember to play!

We all want to see where we are going, what is the path ahead? A wide-angle viewpoint relieves anxiety from not knowing in the midst of change. Welcome change. If you are gifted with sight, cultivate this gift. Especially if you are a city-gal, practice Eagle-sight with your imagination to see your path ahead.

Ancestors going all the way back through time have mimicked the strengths they found in their wild neighbors. Consider what First Peoples learned from watching and living with Bears and Wolves. Women can learn about mating and family by watching Geese. Do not forget that you will need a strong connection to the wild to find all of you.[1]

To help you fully blossom in this Passage, I share secrets with you about personal skills to analyze and solidify your beliefs. This is very big, so you likely will be a work in progress beyond this decade. You will feel more mature every year, managing and even evolving your habits, problem solving, experiment-ing with various risks, self-parenting, and understanding yourself enough so that you are able to stabilize your emotions. Your adult brain finally matures around age 25, find the awe and mystery of this news; neuro-pathways run through all parts of your body, which means you are somatically intelligent.[2]

Everything seems to have a root in this decade between 20 and 30—love, ambition, high adventure, and twists of fate. Your passions mingle with the spirit that breathes through all things and leads you to your destiny. I chose a 5-year marriage as my platform to learn a few lessons and the heartbreak was a profound teacher. Through work, with other weekend warriors, I found good company to explore wilderness where I met up with my own inner wild self. I love that I learned about my wild self. She is with me these many decades later as an inner capacity to feel comfort everywhere. The Earth became my true home in the decade of my 20s, even though far deeper feelings of connec-tion came to me in later Passages. In the Eagle's view, this is your destiny, too.

My ability to feel solace and belonging from Nature helped me cultivate the perennial flowering of me to do the work offered up by my shadow parts—processing, loving, forgiving, and accepting that masked by pain, pure gold is the alchemical miracle of profoundly dark places.[3]

Your very long road of trials will reveal personality parts previously hid-den. Dream journaling will help connect you to your vast subconscious self. Discovery and nurturing are dual focal points for your expansion during this decade, wild will happen and you will cope. Somehow, you will. Proceed slow-ly if you can and know that is the Woman's Way. If you feel judgments for yourself or others, fears or anxieties that prevent you from enjoying your life, this calls for shadow work. Go alone to a quiet place and sit. I was taught to observe a foot square of Earth and find help there.[4] I promise you will find gold in your shadow-self and much relief in welcoming back all of parts that once wanted to be denied.

Your Tree of Life Begins with Your Roots

Eventually, Elders offered me such kindnesses that I learned to love my whole self. Through Nature connection, I will show you how your wild Nature self will reveal and heal your shadow self. I encourage you to cultivate your girl-gang, your Women's Circle, and especially Elders.

Farther down the path of your life, just before you turn 30, all of your unbelievable experiences from this 20's decade need to be bundled, wrapped in gossamer threads to fuel your transformational fire. At the end of the decade, the time known as the Saturn Return serves as a fine delineation between the far end of your adolescence and your Womanhood Bloom. Saturn takes a nice long path around the Sun, about 29.5 years for one complete cycle. Interestingly, this also marks the Threshold of adult maturity. This planetary influence is a powerful catalyst for change; actions and decisions at this Threshold have a long lasting effect on your life. Your inner muse rules change, it is your responsibility to be informed. I hope and pray you have Mentors and

Elders who will show you this Threshold, enclosing you in a liminal space and offer you a ceremony. When you turn 29, this is your assignment. Pull in your Village, be the wind of positive power for all you have worked for, and celebrate yourself with plenty of spiritually minded women, your kindred spirits.

A second full circle of Saturn around the Sun, another 29.5 years will bring you to your Elder Threshold. Development slows and time speeds up, it's one of those koans in life. Five Passage Thresholds filled your first Saturn Return and two will fill your second. This is because biological change slows all through menopause and finally reverses.

Reinvention is possible throughout your life. You can always renew or reinvent yourself with a clear plan for very different kinds of purposes. Make these changes with conscious intention: Have a baby, expand your family, start and stop relationships and businesses, get married or divorced, move across state boundaries, and experience trainings of all kinds. In my 20s, I reinvented myself by changing jobs three times. The miracle of human evolution is free will. Every single day brings change of some kind; graceful change expresses the nature of living and connects humanity together along a common thread.

I use this Eagle's view to deepen your understanding: Initiation happens step-by-step, day-by-day. Invite change in, make friends with the nuances of change. It is the one thing you can depend upon, change is constant. Watch the Moon, the seasons, and yourself for proof of change. Re-read the early Passages to be sweetly reminded of how completely you've transformed, at least four times already. Use the power of your own example to fuel your New Moon intentions.

You are actively building a life! Now that you have this Eagle's view of the days, years, and decades along your timeline, let's overlay a design that will lead you to the next Threshold ahead, your Womanhood Bloom.

As you think about building a life, I return your thoughts to *entelechy*, activated potential. This Elder-wisdom was planted in my heart and took root.

Potential has been a continuous thread in the weave of my life, yours too. This is your *entelechy*.

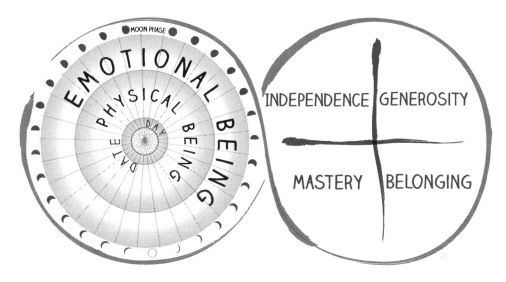

© 2016

Your practice of watching the Moon, dancing with la Luna feels like breathing. You simply do it. On the cosmic surface, the Moon is present enough to imagine or find in both the day sky and the night sky. Many layers deeper, all of the planets have an influence on earthlings. How deep you go is up to your curiosity. Your Circle of Courage becomes layered with values freshly minted through experiences. This action of entelechy, on the move, actively seeking your true potential, will help you track your Genius, your Soul-self, and all that it means to be human.

RITUALS ⁓

Every experience that moves through you can be held in a cobblestone, our visual metaphor for the bubble surrounding memory. As your brain continues to mature, experiences begin to intertwine, to cobble together. This increases the value of your Vision Quest rituals practiced on each of your Moontimes. Take time to reflect and wrap a ritual around your meaningful experiences to hold them in a sacred way. Take every advantage of the heavenly opportunities to be a visioning and rejuvenating woman each time you shed your womb's blood. Your inner life will become rhythmic with your cycle. Make a record of yourself; put a date on your dream-log, your art, and your journal. The progression of your maturity will be visible and encouraging. Playfully mark these quiet moments of your life with ritual. The sacred elements of Earth, Air, Fire, and Water combine in infinite ways to mark a moment of your day with quiet.

Remember when you made a wish and blew out the candles on your cake? Candles represent intention. Light them often.

Mentoring and Friendships Make all the Difference

A curious mind and rhythmic practice is how you develop your spiritual intelligence. Only you can develop this inner sense of yourself. As often as I say to myself, slow down, I would like to say the same to you. When I use the word ritual, I mean deeply personal, and rich. No one but me needs to understand my symbols and the meanings I place on them. No one but you needs to understand your inner life. Use quiet, symbols, and rituals to investigate your depths.

I pause here long enough for both of us to be smart: If a therapist or counselor is needed because the knot of our lives feels too tight to unpick alone, definitely use the services of Divine listeners or energy workers. I have asked for help many times through the course of my long life. If the option of a class for study is needed to open you, to free you, to unlock your creativity, sign up! The possibilities to receive more joy out of life are truly endless. Notice when you feel strongly about something exciting, this is passion rising. As my most wise friend Kathleen says, "Listen for your Soul knocking. Give yourself permission to choose."[5]

Ritual brings the gift of slowness into your heart and will enrich every aspect of you. As simple as watching the Moon, and swaying in a dance rhythm you can deepen your feelings of spirituality with a remarkable, beautiful cadence that is quiet.

My practice has many layers. While lighting candles and smudge, and rearranging my altar, I allow thoughts, friends, and loves to float through my heart space. My mind slowly disengages. Before dawn I sit in my meditation chair. I feel prayerful, mellow, and in touch with my Soul. Using my Moon altar, I gain insights about my life that cannot be coaxed out any other way. I find my four sacred elements penetrate into journaling and walking. They complement each other. I need them all to see inside.

RETURN TO THE CIRCLE OF COURAGE

Remember the four foundation stones of early adolescence: **Belonging, Mastery, Independence**, and **Generosity**. You first learned about those four values during your teen years; the Circle of Courage[6] laid down the first layer of self-awareness to help you understand risk. Now let's add *woman-power* to make the Circle of Courage more meaningful for this Passage. This is good mentoring, helping you examine values.

When you noodle around with **Belonging**, you may sense that it's elusive. A few values will give it more depth. Sometimes you feel a sense of belonging, sometimes you don't. When you accept the power that is yours, belonging becomes part of your mental health. It requires effort on your part to build a community around you. That is the hidden ingredient in belonging. To feel kinship, you must give mindful attention to those you care about. Attend to everyone you have a relationship with, everyone.

Look closer, what do I mean, attend? Look at a baby, what makes a baby thrive? My friend Arianna taught me that *focused attention* was the special juice that all babies need to thrive. I say, that's what we all need. Attention is how bonds are made stronger. To define kinship, first you feel an energy; you sense a positive charge from someone new. Besides attention, you might think about and write about what you notice in appreciation, even how you might collaborate. Appreciation and collaboration both define attention in new ways, which leads back to belonging. Helpfulness and playfulness are powerful energies that make every bond stronger.

When you seek solitude, the awe and intimacy of a quiet wood may teach you about your own spirituality. By meandering around with me, I invite you to wander. Invent for yourself the simplest concepts to expand your sense of belonging. For me, trees hold me and I return the deeply rooted feeling of being held offering a hug, often.

Wherever you live, an entire bioregion waits to be explored, alone and with friends. Belonging attaches to place, as in knowing the place you live, as it does to the people who live with you in this place. What other words, feelings, and values help describe belonging for you?

Mastery implies devotion to one or more of your inner fires and the passion for creating something that comes from you. Introspection and dreaming will help gather ingredients necessary to pursue mastery of the things you love. Audaciously and boldly you locate your inner flame. When you push fear aside, the fire inside of you will light the way into your unexplored inner wilderness of talent and gifts. Fan this inner flame to reveal the source of your Genius.

Certainly, it's more fun to have someone cheerleading your brilliance, but only you hold the vision and only you need to believe in your abundant abilities. Only you can follow your Soul's entelechy.

In seeking mastery, your Genius is fully engaged. When you play with your Genius, you will find your purpose. This needs only your focused heart. Soul and Genius are synonymous for the stardust that you brought with you at Birth. Increase your awareness to notice how modern culture has dumbed us down. Rise up in personal rebellion to defend your inner Genius. What help do you need to express this Soul-essence of you?

I offer the values associated with mastery: Devotion, excellence, audacity, originality, focus, dreaming, and most of all passion. These are the powers you draw into yourself for the 10,000 hours you need for true mastery. When you are brave enough and bold enough, you will discover that your self-respect depends on you choosing this path of mastery. Find that one thing or weave several things and hold on for the ride that will bring only smiles to the experience of your inner world.

Independence is a much bigger value than it first appears. What exactly does independence imply? Can you find self-reliance and financial security in there? How about adventure? I find the true depth of independence in optimism and humor, in preparedness and integrity. All of these values wrap around Courage itself. Feeling brave enough to take a risk for growth will help you find and feel independence.

You will feel the power of your independence in bare naked honesty. Revealing the truth of independence will straighten your spine, you already possess many of these values. Peering into your independence, you claim the powers of acceptance, integrity, and resilience. By claiming these inner powers, you will find the delight—and the chutzpa or nerve—in recommitting to your own fearlessness. All of the values of independence give you lion-heartedness, the core of courage to live your life.

Once you feel this core value of independence for yourself, you will discover the interlocking value of interdependence. Every one of these building blocks of life work this way—they are interrelated and you're strengthened by all the others in your relationship sphere.

The final quadrant on your Circle of Courage that generates so many good feelings worth pursuing is **Generosity**. The essence of altruism is heart energy. If I direct the energy of generosity inward, I find care and warmth, along with silence and rest. I need those soothing energies to feel generous to myself. When I turn that energy outward, my imagination runs wild. Wondering how I might be useful or in some small way, in service to another, I think of respect above all with loyalty, surprise, and usefulness nestled among patience, extravagance, and empathy.

I encircle your symbolic wheel with *woman-power* to energize your Circle of Courage, a circle filled with good medicine. Check-in, breathe deeply, and see how your energy is flowing, around and in and out, moving gracefully as your breath. Hopefully, you will feel inspired to make a drawing to explore your own values. Embellish. Use art and poetry, song and dance, to make these values your own.

NATURE CONNECTION

In one sweetly compact way, your Mind-Body-Spirit and wild emotions coalesce. You are a miracle of evolution and your long ancestry lives in your genes informing you with instinct and intuition. The one place where each human, each woman feels most at home, is out in Nature. This statement is true even if you were (1) raised in a city (2) deprived of deep Nature connection throughout your growing years (3) freak out over the thought of a spider and/or (4) seek more of anything in your life.

I know that *Nature Connection* begs the question, why Nature? Being a Soul wanting and needing an Earthly experience to advance our lessons, you and I chose this planet where Nature flourishes in thousands of millions of forms. Nature is our primary home and our inspired teacher. Earth, where Nature is friend and Great Mother to all, provides our one and only home in this lifetime. This is a truth known to women and men alike who have touched into the core of our Divinely Feminine selves.

Maybe your Tree of Life looks like this: Who Are You? Who Are Your People?

For just a moment, consider where ideas come from: Inside your gorgeous, somatic computer-brain or from outside to inside? I don't mind how much credit you take, or how long you sit at the drawing board or keyboard to originate an idea, your greatest inspirations come outside to inside. Great Mother and Great Mystery source all ideas and then provide the energy and the raw materials. To receive your dose of inspiration, go outside and tune in.

Healers have long known about the essence of Great Mother and Great Mystery to soothe, to perform miracles through herbs and waters, and to transform inner brain imbalances back into a calm heart. Each human is sourced from stardust which is our tuning fork. Deep Nature connection returns your focus to your heart where stardust has settled. This holy stuff of the Universe is your personal fuel. You can easily recreate this connection within yourself, but first, silence your chatty mind and open your heart. Step outside and find the awe in air. Awe—feel the inspiration in this word. Pure delightful awe is the reward of your curious mind. Your connection with place is all about feeling awe, which is heart work.

Sit with your back against a big old tree, one who has been around for a century or two. Do this in the physical as often as you can and in your imagination when you must substitute. Invite her to become your tree of life. Send energy down through your tailbone to wrap around her roots and allow your heart to soar up into her branches. This is medicine. You need this Earth and Sky medicine. Open your heart space and use your senses. Quiet your brain and repeat daily if possible. I use this ancient shamanic practice, a meditative practice, to ground myself back to reality and to reclaim a mindful state.

Restoration of your essential self can happen anytime you discover this miracle of dirt-time. All of your Moon walks give you dirt-time, any time you wander with a curious mind, communing with the Earth on a park bench, this is dirt-time. I recommend quiet, inner quiet, even when the city deems otherwise. Having spent decades in career-mode and citified, dunking my feet in a stream and closing my eyes always gives rise to tears and brings me back to myself. Recovering from the years I call my mindless decades, I wondered what was missing and now I know—Nature restores; we all need Nature to move from a state of surviving into thriving. Dirt-time, just as it implies, gets you out with Mother Earth. I go every single day and say prayers for you; that you may feel inspired to awaken and heal yourself, that you may find sufficient stillness to welcome your Genius.

HEALING THEN AWAKENING

First Blood and First Flight were Thresholds of change, delivering evidence of your womanliness. In the years between these early Thresholds, you rarely used these two words, woman and womanhood. Laughing, crying, dancing, you still feel the adolescent roller-coaster inside of you. Yet, every day, magically, you create more *woman* in your body and in your heart-mind. Some of your joys and dramas may feel like they happened yesterday. I welcome you to this interesting time, parlaying all that you have learned, using your dreams and your heart to heal and shape your woman-self.

Let's say this is your Heart: Wet, Wild, and Beating for Love

Coming to consciousness is your great challenge; this is how you will shape yourself with the cleanest brush-strokes of your Soul. Remember from the Circle of Courage, values are hidden powers. Your woman-power puts your unique and influential stamp on your whole environment, the culture that surrounds you. By understanding this power and influence you see how you can be a culture-maker for others. Each woman has exceptional powers to create and together we are truly a force. When you speak these words, woman and womanhood referring to yourself, you awaken the desire to connect to your powers and to your purpose. You will find no ordinariness in following your own Soul.

Society has produced expectations that belong to no one woman. Be vigilant for superwoman who can overtake you at any time. Take the time to heal your inner perfectionist. Healing opens the way for consciousness to expand. Ask Elder women who have experienced the transformative fire of initiation, what awakened them? Usually, they will begin with healing, then reclaiming personal power through sacred rituals.

Healing requires an intention, a focus from you. Therapists call this process which means seeing inside your memories for how choices led to consequences and then finding ways to completely unhook your attachment to the hurt. Energy healers and therapists will help you move your psyche through any rough patches. My teen years were challenged and therapy would have helped me, but I was stubborn and blinded by my false-self. My paycheck, a sign of being driven by ego, seemed to report success. I didn't understand the values in Circle of Courage or learn how to be quiet with my visions. I was led around by ego and shake my head remembering how long that sleep-walking persisted. Because my passion remained dormant, so did my entelechy, my potential.

Attention and intention will heal your heart. Look deeper where you find barbs and hooks and any attachments to the past that hold you there. Personal attention will help you reclaim the Soul parts which you gave up to please someone else or gain approval. You need all of your parts to feel whole. Some parts were sliced off to be likable in school or gain a teacher's endorsement. A fair amount of Soul moved aloft in false support of your self-image. Anything that hurts now, feelings, attitudes, memories, those still need to be healed. Growth and healing depend on you doing this work for your psyche.

Discover the trendy practice of mindfulness. It is parallel work with healing. Mindfulness is brain training: Your present moment practice grows with repetition. You literally train your brain to pay attention to your heart.

Every person wants and needs love. The neediest part of your psyche may have compromised important parts of yourself to feel the love you wanted. Those compromises left your Soul out of the equation. Look deeper and deeper. My friend Diana taught me about peeling the onion to recover my Soul parts. When I first began to look back so I could heal, my way of dredging came through my physical body while I chopped wood for my stove. When I shared, Diana allowed my pain to pass right through her.[7] Who will hold you while you do this inner searching?

Use all available tools, talking therapy is wonderful, so are the woman-tools of journaling, art, and dance whirled together your way. Your family will always be your family and will remain your home safety net, but you are shedding the snakeskin of dependence. After processing your teen experiences, your First Flight Passage transformation will feel complete and you will be free to be you.

Find ways and means to release what no longer belongs to you. Do not continue to carry pain of the past around. Releasing it may take some effort, and be well worth it. Intention always helps. Candle-lit prayer ritual, writing down my tears, and then burning the pages and offering the ashes to the river, this is what works for me.

Please allow wise old women, your Elders, to teach you the art of letting go. See the path behind as the only way you could get to where you are now, nothing more. Be mindful of the pain of regret and ego conflicts. You need to tend to your pains and heartbreaks like a Medicine Woman placing salve over your own wounds. This may be the most important work of your life. Healing requires skill that you learn and then use to deepen the rest of your life. You become your own Medicine Woman. This psychic healing process reveals to you the wonders of your inner life. Do whatever it takes!

This is the time, earlier the better, to examine self-parenting. Rather than mimic your parents, go deep into your memories and begin to parent yourself mindfully. The art of self-parenting is part of your identity formation. As an art, the day-to-day permissions and coddling you give yourself need to be conscious and evolving. Learn about love, tough love, and wounded love. Do not avoid the school of hard knocks if a challenge crosses your path.

Lessons that come the hard way may be fabulous blessings and provide the clearest teaching. Remember that play and laughter can heal those knocks, and mistakes often provide a good laugh along with a great lesson.

At times, escape is all that you can choose for yourself. Wave a flag of exhaustion, invite yourself to surrender playfully. Read a great book or two, watch a movie or two. Escape means entering an altered space. Play is one of the finest creative acts of our animal natures. What activity moves you closer to bliss? A wise man, Joseph Campbell, instructed us to "Follow our bliss." He was talking about finding bliss where your Soul feels playful.

CORE BELIEFS

Your core beliefs are what makes you, you. I tread on sacred ground here, but in a most gentle way. Many beliefs may feel quite rigid, but if you are able to relax and search out what you believe, learning to track your thoughts, you may find your very core is fluid like the Earth's. Thousands of sources will catch your attention and help you understand your core beliefs. Be patient.

When you practice with a peaceful, introspective ritual of looking inside for ten minutes each day, you will find that many of your beliefs have been inherited. Bring your parents and grandparents into your mind and fill in the blank: From her or him, I inherited _____ : Write page after page. Your manners, your gait, and many of your behaviors have been directly inherited or influenced. Every relationship has shaped you and added to your core beliefs in some unique way.

A broad stroke of *human ecology* created every one of your core beliefs. In 1907, this term was first used by a woman, a home-economics teacher. Ellen Swallow Richards defined *human ecology* as the surrounds of human beings and personal effects within those surroundings. Since Birth you have been encircled by people and symbols. Without you realizing it, they have all been teachers. As girls, we loved watching women for clues about who we might become. Your parents carefully taught you things and mostly with pure heart-intention. Your Grandparents, Aunties, and Mentors have all taught you things, sometimes by modeling, or as an offering like, "Here is something interesting for you to learn." This is how we found the fun inside of sewing, cooking, or gardening. Every environment you shared—churches, wilderness, home, and shopping malls—provided icons and symbols to sift through now like grains of sand.

Tree of Life and Death

When you evaluate your core beliefs with people and objects as outside influences, you learn about your personal psychology. You may see this as another layer to be healed. Search through your beliefs with playful curiosity. This is your human ecology. The seeds of your past become your present; the seeds of your present become your future. My editor and wise friend Janis says, "Only in silence is pure knowledge."

Begin with observable topics, those that are religious and spiritual in nature. Look also at your political and social beliefs. You may discover that you inherited feelings of pain and general emotional patterns. Keep only what belongs to you. Beneath every belief is a principle, begin to discover yours. Be patient, this may take some time because beliefs can be sticky and deeply engrained. I know you will spend years learning from your inner-self what you believe about Birth and Death and God, what you believe about love and partnerships. Relax into this as a process, hold the questions until answers arise from inside of you. You have time, blessed time.

In this broad and deeply personal arena of core beliefs, you will find foundation stones you didn't know you had, the very bedrock of your life-dance. This is the most private work. Allow your inner smile to flow through your breath as discoveries settle into you. Explore with an Elder Mentor and you will learn about trust. How you fill in the blanks about your core beliefs may lead you to begin again to search for teachers.

I recommend that you focus on your Soul as an influence. Your inner mystery found only in deep quiet will reveal so much to you. Quiet, the secret to listening is where you connect to your Soul. As you search through your core beliefs, I urge you to doodle-art with your passions, all the things you love that light your way. I call this guiding light, Soul; it's also called your Genius and your Higher Self. I bow deeply to your Soul, the essence of you that per-meates your skull and your heart muscle and your fingertips. I believe in your Genius but do you? Let's coax her out together, shall we?

With all my heart, I believe in the creative Genius who lives within you. Train your mind to focus on what you want most. At one time or another, we all realize the answers are found inside. Because your Genius is hidden among all your core beliefs, search carefully for your basic passion, the Soul-full ener-gy connected to your Genius. Search youtube.com for Michael Meade, he has launched a Genius Project through his Mosaic Foundation.[8] As a proponent of Genius, and one of the more accessible Elders, he directs your attention and discovery of Soul through story and mythology.

I am rather direct on this subject: Soul and Genius are your stardust and came with the first breath of spirit into your wee body at the moment of your Birth. Your Genius is an essence readily available to your senses when you focus your attention there. Your Soul is waiting to be acknowledged. They are the same, Soul and Genius. See how all of this fits into your core beliefs. Your Mother wants to believe in your Genius. Anyone who hesitates has not yet connected with their own deep passions. This teaching is very old; see how your core opens and feels receptive to this emerging Soul-self.

My Soul sounds a gong that wakens me in the morning and causes a smile to float up from my heart. She is the essence that causes me to smack my lips and head out for a walk because I need to stop thinking and feel the mind in my body. The Soul of me is my dearest companion. I took a long time to find her, only to discover she was there all along.

You only need to believe in what you most love to do and have always loved. The world needs you to find this inner fire because your gifts are near. That is why you are here on Earth right now. Look into all of the facets of your passion and you will find your Soul. You know I begin with play. What gives you such joy you can only call it play? To locate your Genius, this is where you begin. What do you love? How does it all fit around your core beliefs?

Every ounce of your passion, every drop of your capacity, all your talents and interests wrap around the little star-seed inside, your Genius. You have plenty of time, many Moons, to dance with these parts until you feel you know your Genius. Searching to find this core of you is your personal 10,000-hour project. This inner fire deserves your focus. Opportunities will appear before you because holy, spiritual energies are attracted to this kind of focus. I invite you to gaze at the cobblestones and imagine them beginning to take form out of the mist. You are building a life of meaningful stories, one and then another.

You May Need to Revisit Beliefs before You See Your Way Through the Wilderness

SENSES TURNED ON

You will sharpen your brain in search of your core beliefs while you learn to assess risk. Each time you combine these simultaneous tasks, your neurological network elongates and creates new connections. Through practice, your abilities will expand and then weave back together. Practice your inner capacity to weigh decisions, to self-parent, and to understand your belief systems. Practice mindfulness, which is inner self awareness. To increase your confidence, practice being totally in your body and not so much spinning your thoughts. When you choose quiet for yourself and take charge of expanding your neurological connections throughout your body with focused thoughts, you build this into a skill. Practice is required.

Women learn a powerful bundle through sex. How is your sexual intelligence? You deserve pleasure. Ask yourself, "How has sex informed me and shaped me?" More to the point, I ask, "How would you describe your sexual life?"

Just like motherhood for women, thousands of sources inform us about sexuality. Advertisers spend billions of dollars to capture your attention, reminding you that you are first and perhaps foremost, a sexual being. Examine your story and if necessary, adjust your intentions. The bloom of your woman-self is just beginning to open. You will be sexual for decades. Can you be mindful about sex and pleasure?

Consider motivations and distractions, and all the other ways of learning—emotional, social, cultural, and sensual. At 20 or 25, it's very difficult to know how you know all that you do know. In your triune brain, many beliefs and skills hold a genetic clue, maybe even a turned-on gene. Other ways of knowing are deeply primitive. How do you know all that you know?

With your finely tuned old-brain-parts, you can smell trouble and feel in your gut when something is good, or off, or dangerous. With all of your sensory powers, you see, feel, taste, and touch the world in miraculous ways that perhaps you have not considered. If you are midway through this Passage, your brain has finally matured and you can trust your decisions. This inner work is another way to know you. When you know yourself, you will trust and like yourself more. The word mindful leaps out like a gazelle, this concept brings everything together. You will feel spiritual in one moment and emotional the next, then gazelle like, your body feels like leaping in the air. By watching yourself with an inner eye, you will soon see how each of your senses and all the different ways to learn something, combine and recombine. The way to wrap together these parts and pieces of being is through mindfulness.

Allow Nature to Inspire Your Evolution

When you become deeply involved with your personal evolution, if you will use true patience and clear persistence, your intuition will mature and your meditations will grow more enjoyable. To help shed attachments that no longer serve you and begin to understand obsessions, begin with mindful evaluations. Teachers, coaches, mentors, or therapists can be valuable guides to help with this inner exploration. How the right guide at just the right time comes to you or crosses your path may also be an interesting story—coincidence, fate, or merely mystery.

Once you become a practiced and loving evaluator without judgment or criticism, with kindness and compassion to guide this journey of your life, self-trust begins to expand. You can relax and make good choices based on your beliefs about yourself. When you hold fluidity and flexibility as sacred companion attitudes, time will bring you opportunities to practice your core beliefs.

Before you go too many steps down a new path, hesitate and check-in with youself to ask, does this fit with what I really believe? Why? Soon you will automatically see both sides of a question, pro and con. Your brain is powerful and growing every day; you can almost feel your neural systems expand and spread throughout your body.

Seeing your environmental surroundings as influences on your personal ecology, you now choose with your conscious mind and heart. In practical assessment and quiet meditation, examine your core beliefs before you come under the influence of new teachers. While you are still pliant, moldable, and susceptible, you will benefit from this baseline look inside. Everything begins with a thought, including your experience this day. In the wise words of one of my Dearhearts who remembers this decade with clarity, Kim Gridley, emphatically said, "You do not need to figure it all out at once."[9]

TEACHERS: INNER AND OUTER

To deeply honor your unique Soul, your inner power needs to be stoked, supported, and mentored. Maybe you do need to stretch your wings all by yourself or maybe you will find an all new girl-gang. Truly, you need a grandmotherly type who, over this entire decade, will listen as you discover what you think by what speaks through you in story, in beliefs, in philosophy, in morals, in desires, and in values. Find a girlfriend, a teacher, a mentor, and adopt a vital and wise Elder. Take us for a walk and talk, that's all.

The essence of you that is beyond biology, beyond the blended gene-pool of your Mother and Father, is your inner teacher and guide, unique to you. Listen to your dreams before you leave your bed, write them down. What resonates from this deep sub-conscious part of you? Listen as your intuition fires up with your chakra practice. Pay close attention to your Moon. There is so much to learn about your inner life and the multitude of guiding energies who support you.

Learning to listen deeply is primal and essential. Stillness is your greatest teacher, always and in all ways. Your inner world is creative, juicy, and emotional. Your elemental nature grows from earth, air, and water and mixes with your stardust to fuel a seemingly endless supply of power and energy. I am edging closer to the next great teacher: Relationships.

Working their way with you through a circular timeline, many people have crossed your path. Here is where you begin to consider their importance. The first step for your psychological well-being is listening to your fired-up inner-self; talking to another, someone sacred to you, is the important second step. When you add another body made of stardust, you will learn even more about you. With this confidant, one special other person, talk about things, all kinds of things. Become a little humble and practice respect. The honest truth about becoming more human, more upright, more of what you desire, living and growing toward your worldly dreams is one long quest. Become curious. Right after your friend listens to all of your musings, turn the talking stick over to see what you can learn from her or from him. This turns up the volume, the heat, and multiplies the possibilities.

Mentoring from Nature

I have been a Mentor for the past 20 years, deeply watching and holding possibilities. Watching how my little Doves have made choices and how easily a few choices backfired. I wrote this poem to the Dearhearts who call me Mentor, one especially:

THINKING OF YOU

No one but you can sail your boat.
No one but you can make your mistakes.
No one but you can feel what hurts.
Celebrate feeling what others cannot, then
Ask a healer to help you find balance again.

No one but you can fall in love with love.
No one but you can practice personal care.
No one but you can ask your questions.
You are never alone even in solitude
That's when the angels gather around you.

No one but you can meditate for you.
No one but you can keep your body moving.
No one but you can express your gratitudes.
Experience how the world changes perspective
When an attitude of gratitude lights your way.

No one but you can set intentions for you.
No one but you can hear your Soul's cry.
No one but you can set your course straight.
When destiny comes calling, and you're sure

Do you plan to answer or ignore your gifts?

© Gail Burkett

I believe in the saying, when the student is ready the teacher appears. Native Americans widely share their ceremonies and spirituality as a recovery practice to heal from the past four centuries of oppression. Eastern mysteries are openly accessible through yoga classes, ashrams, and Buddhist retreats. You cannot read all the books on any subject found at your local library, but you can try. Investigate the esoteric side of everything that appears along your path.

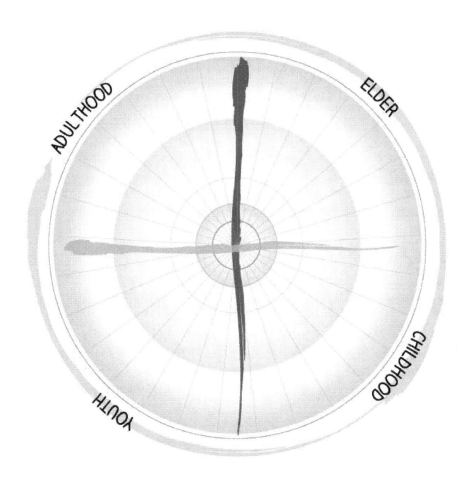

Relationship Wheel for You to Fill with Names   © Janis Monaco Clark

Take care with your discovery process; find the patience you need to be open and flowing through your days. If you feel tense and anxious, your Genius will crawl under the covers and wait for your growing pains to subside.

Feelings are key to discovery. Emotional intelligence is the new permaculture of human ecology. You must consider yourself responsible for your feelings as well as your thoughts. Focus on mastery of what you love the most and how it can lead to your right livelihood. Only you know the answers. Perhaps you will discover how this relationship wheel mirrors your heart.

SHADOW AND CONSCIOUSNESS

If you are lucky and stay alert to find caring teachers, you will receive help navigating this decade of your 20s, your late adolescence. Each coach or teacher, in fact each person who comes in close, will change you and will help you reveal your essence. Experience is most valuable when it reflects back to you what you love, feel, believe, trust, and hope for in the future. Carefully consider what experiences will lead to a deeper consciousness. This wakeful awareness, an indefinable essence that feels like your chest is expanding, helps to cultivate your gifts and talents. Such a deep heart connection is needed with anyone from whom you receive teachings, stay open to receive from another's Soul. Remember, you are solely and personally responsible for activating your Genius and developing your Soul's purpose.

As you reach for maturity and Womanhood Bloom, consider yourself the consciousness project with your mental, physical, emotional, and psychological aspects activated. For decades, scientists have been searching for the nature and science of consciousness. Probably, it's not their job because it's closer to pure energy than pure science. The mind has a controlling influence over the immune system and in reverse, placebos, sugar pills, cure disease because the psyche has been deeply engaged. Many of the leading edge intellectuals agree—your Genius, the Soul of you, radiates from your heart-mind. Trust only those who use the language of the heart to tell you about these philosophies of living.

The world of positive and negative charges known as dualities—shadow and light, male and female, good and evil, hope and despair—seem to be opposites, but often contain wholeness like two sides of a coin. Dualities, many times defined as opposites, will often blur into one another to become a whole piece. To recognize dualities is one thing. The trickier step is to consciously recognize that judgments cause energy to hold dualities rigid instead of fluid. I have learned from dualities and judgments all my life, they are great teachers. I have learned that my capacity in the shadow side of my Soul-self is as deep as the capacity of my light side.

So I ask this question to surprise you: What troubles have you touched in on already that, through carefully looking into the dark side of your personal story, have something to teach you about your shadow self? Usually, trouble finds us to teach about shadow. Sometimes the characteristics or tendencies which reveal the darker side of your nature will become great personal teachers. Clearly, tendencies toward addiction or narcissism for instance, reveal what you would rather not choose. This is a great thought to contemplate: Exactly what do you dislike and why? What do you fear and why? What troubles have found you already?

Cross over the Bridge to your Whole Self

We are all touched by whatever comes close to us, that is a law of energy and often we invite the energy to move from outside to inside. Whatever you intensely dislike in another person offers you a clue to your hidden-self; contemplate and write about this until your own truth comes out. When my girlfriends learned this secret within shadows, we consciously used "mirroring" to reveal more of our truths to one another.

Everyone has hidden selves, shadow selves. Pay attention to how another person reflects these aspects back to you. At the height of my career, I noticed every homeless person on the streets. My job took me to large cities in 44 states and I saw so much I couldn't process. I absorbed and practiced something like mindlessness. See how that energy got close to me, under my skin. I had to be homeless myself to know and value making my own home again.

That year, 1990, effectively removed all of my own judgments and deepened compassion for myself and others. Where else can such great lessons be learned? For me, being homeless without a place to rest my head or to wash myself or my dish was a twist of fate; I have experienced so many twists and they were all great teachers. I invite you to be watchful of how your Soul delivers lessons to your doorstep. In all ways, observe how fate works within your core belief system. You may find you believe in fate, in coincidence, and in Soul-contracts that hold them both. My twists of fate are those great teachers that are without parallel outside in the world. I would not reach for them for myself; my Soul chooses them for me.

FACETS, CHAKRAS, AND ORACLES

Women have so many facets we cannot possibly see them all at once. Let's explore what I mean by this word, facets. Think of a gemstone, cut and polished. You may even have a favorite cut that you prefer to represent facets of yourself you want to explore.

Remind yourself of the expedition: Self-discovery. Simply add "self" behind any of these word combinations and these many facets will begin to appear and surprise you:

Wounded and Well-self

Tame and Wild-Nature

Bleeding and Visioning

Motherly and Protective

Tender and Sexy

Dreaming and Planning

Warrior for Peace

Activist for Justice

Seeking and Finding

Sensuous and Sense-aware

Partner and Solo

Opened and Closed

Creative Genius

Flowing and Resistant

Womb and Cosmos Aware

Superwoman and Little Spirit

Some of these dual ways of being or ways of perceiving yourself form a combination of thoughts that evoke facets of you. I am quite certain you could grow this list using your own ideas and energies. Am I right? Professional career, marriage, and children may surprise you and call forth additional self-parts to nurture. Each aspect that genuinely belongs to you will demonstrate the most patient essence in the Universe. Facets wait for their time because they carry an essence that came with your Soul. You are much more than you appear, even to yourself.

Allow play to be your trickster. Play with art, acrobatics, dance, music-making, singing, and martial arts to engage the imagination of your body. Your body-mind is fuel for your intuition, and connects with Source to remind you who you were born to be. Yes, it's very true, you can be anything and anyone you choose to be, but I urge you to discover who you are first. That authenticity will surprise and reward you with luscious depths. Only the Elder women know this truth. Allow your true self to emerge in play, go on a treasure hunt for clues.

The culture needs to evolve so that you can continue to grow your Genius, so prepare yourself to be a cultural creative. The quality of the next 50 or 60 years of your life depends on how you take up this challenge. Although you do not need to go to college or remain in school unless that is in your heart, I invite you to dream your biggest dream.

The nurturing facet, caring for our physical selves with body-work is one of the easiest things women let slide when work and family begin to fill in available time. Your body practice might include yoga, walking meditation with prayer, running or martial arts, and weight lifting. You can get a great workout dancing and singing. So many different practitioners will help you find your own practice, but only intention will make it yours. I like to avoid getting in my car for body-work, so I lace up my boots or tennies and walk out the door.

A Sliver of Her Former Self

In the First Blood and again in the First Flight Passages, you learned how to use the Moon to guide your inner tracking. I invite you to keep up this habit, make it life-long: Write in your journal to see what flows out of your pen or crayons in freestyle, in a flow of consciousness. Let's take this up one or two levels now. The mystical Soul that came in at Birth longs to speak to you and through you. Quiet rhythms of your Moon practice have birthed spirituality, that which belongs to you and only you. The art that you do reveals first to your heart that which your Soul wants you to know. Play with art and include la Luna, these are the warp and weft you weave with on your life loom.

For subtle inner body-work, deepen your work with your chakras. This is energy work and opens your inner core beliefs as a guide for senses sight, hearing, and especially felt-sense. Chakra work is body-work that reveals your inner energy world. As pure energy, chakras can be sensed as open or closed, as flowing or blocked. If you reach 20 or 25 without knowing about your inner energy system, then you grew up sheltered as I did. I learned about the chakra system through girlfriends whispering in yoga class and laughing while soaking in hot springs. Consider this scene, girlfriends, hot springs, chakra; it must be kundalini energy that made us all laugh. Well, that was how I was introduced. When my curiosity is engaged, I dive into books.

Already you know I have a curious nature and for years I practiced with the chakra totem pole I introduced in the First Blood Passage. Then my old friend and teacher, Kathleen, taught me how to move that playful energy through the central channel. She called this 'running energy.' That opened my understanding and my felt sense of chakras. Then I searched out all the information I could find.

This body-work with your subtle energy system invites creative juices to flow into and through your power and heart and visioning centers, your seven internal chakras. Our bodies are dense and we accumulate stress; without a working awareness of the flow of energy, one or more of these energy centers can become blocked. Have you ever felt stuck?

This is a brilliant, built-in system for understanding yourself energetically. As an ancient gift, chakra roots go back thousands of years to the origin of yoga. When you devote yourself to a regular practice, a switch will slowly turn on to reveal your whole inner life. Your felt-self will literally pulse with new energy when your centers are flowing clear.

Since this awakening began inside of me, I have learned how beauty and power deliver transformative energy to initiations, helping to complete a Passage on time and not become stuck. In these last years of chakra work, I have kindled an internal creative revolution. I became curious about the Goddesses found throughout the women's cultures of the world. These spiritual figures and archetypal teachers found in art and texts might be endlessly fascinating for you.[10]

Practice is a word women use to cover a wide variety of topics. Deeply engrained habits like a yoga practice may or may not include lighting a candle, a piece of smudge, or a long meditation. Your woman's practice may use inner creativity to discover what you feel about what you say on paper, in art, or a blend of those two. It may be purely somatic like running, trance dancing, or Qigong. For your Womanhood Bloom, your inner practice provides a personal forum where your wild self and your many other facets can contribute to your whole self. Use your personal list of facets to do this good work on yourself.

In my daily practice, I meditate with breath and with a particular Goddess on my mind, chanting silently. When I sense the awakening of my spinal fluid, I know that is chakra energy. With my quiet mind, I observe the inner spiral, the kundalini coil at the base of my spine. My mind is often turned-on high in the morning, so I use the salve of patience and forgiveness to set aside my thinking mind.

The chakra energy centers can be meditated on singly or as a shooting little fireball of energy from the base of your spine up and out the top of your head. Chakras influence your self-regard which is my reason for bringing them to your attention. I am not the teacher and want you to know that others know more than I can possibly know. My practice with the chakras began very playfully in 1995 with my first awakening. Chakra teachings are still on the edge of our culture. Many good things come in very slowly. You can intuit the energy invited by your intention. The basic instructions and oldest Eastern teachings of the chakras are described in Judith Anodea's book, *Eastern Body Western Mind*.[11]

Crown Chakra — Spirituality — 7 Self-knowledge

Third Eye Chakra — Awareness — 6 Self-reflection

Throat Chakra — Communication — 5 Self-expression

Heart Chakra — Love, Healing — 4 Self-acceptance

Solar Plexus — Wisdom, Power — 3 Self-definition

Sacral Chakra — Sexuality, Creativity — 2 Self-gratification

Root Chakra — Basic Trust — 1 Self-preservation

©2016

When you dive in deeper, your inner world of subtle energies will reveal more information about subtle aspects of yourself. Seven in all, these aspects, from self-preservation up through self-knowledge are neatly packaged along your spine as chakra centers with renewable energies that will offer you a lifetime of inquiry, observation, and guidance. Use these seven aspects in your journal art. These subtle energies offer you a map for self-discovery. I practice to transform stuck energy into flowing energy. Notice how subtle these flowing energies relate to your Moontimes, to continuous change, worldly discoveries, to core beliefs, and your potential for greater maturity.

You alone are responsible for the ritual life you lead and how your spirituality awakens in you. Do you use ritual in the quiet of morning or light a candle in the evening to awaken your subconscious, maybe both times? When can you imagine meditation working for you, morning, afternoon, or night? Anytime you sit on a yoga mat is the perfect opportunity to begin consciously moving energy for balance, for juiciness, and for endless self-exploration. Beautiful and wise Janis puts it this way, "Relax. Be comfortable. Breathe deeply. Be still. This is meditation."

Prayer Ceremonies for 8 Holy Days Marking the Seasons

CONNECTIONS

As I write, the cross-quarter day for quickening is dawning. I invite you to know the seasons and their cultural gifts. I offer healing prayers for the Earth and on the eight days of seasonal celebration, I do ceremony with my Earth sisters. The seasons offer another map for going deeper with ritual. Winter Solstice begins winter and Summer Solstice begins summer. In all of South America, Africa, Australia, and all geographic locations south of the equator, the seasons are exactly opposite the Northern Hemisphere. On the Equinoxes, all peoples experience the Earth with no tilt. In the northern hemisphere, the Vernal Equinox marks spring and the Autumnal Equinox marks the beginning of fall. In between these four days you will notice four more days mark the center of each season: Imbolc on February 2, Beltane on May

1, Lammas on August 2, and Samhain on October 31. Each season is 90 days long. By observing cross-quarter days, women all around the world observe how these enormous Earth changes help us build our communities. Ritual ceremony is prevalent in Earth-based cultures. As lovers of ceremony, many women have overlaid this map into their spiritual lives.

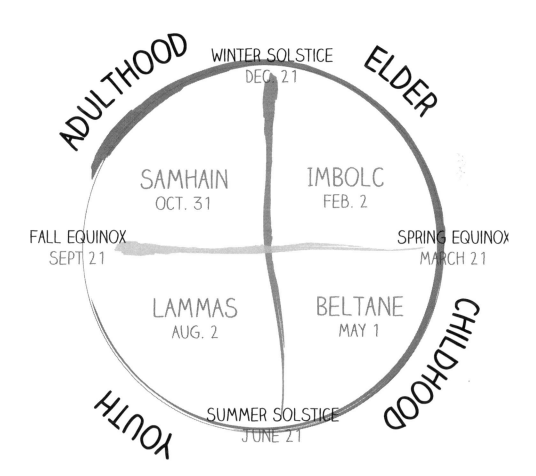

WHEEL AND SEASONS OF LIFE

I find oracles, often called divination tools, endlessly fascinating for seeing deeper inside my nature. Honestly, these are great fun to use in small groups: Oracles offer intimacy, as in into-me-see. They help women friends see deeper into one another's true natures. This requires a certain level of vulnerability. Brené Brown[12] encourages every opportunity to live our lives daringly. The deeper inquiries of oracles are playful but they also require vulnerability between girlfriends. Expect aha's to come, those you will want someone to witness.

I track la Luna with an overlay of Astrology because the information available is uncanny, persistent like the Moon and often accurate. I find that speaking this language of the Cosmos gives me a sense of knowing I am part of something very big and powerful. Astrological newsletters come into my email inbox, I like to learn about the planets and cosmic relationships. Wouldn't you like to be surprised to raise your own awareness in this way?

When the Moon crosses into and out of certain astrological signs, I notice my biorhythms engage with Earth and Water signs differently than with Air and Fire signs. Each Moon phase gives energy of initiating or completing. Almost every day offers an energetic and psychic twist from a planet influence. You might enjoy looking for the psychic, emotional surprise waiting to be discovered through this cosmic dance.

Do you see this layering? I use my attention for a quick check-in to see if one of my chakras has been engaged by planetary action. This is inner knowledge, accessible to you, only by you. It's personal and enriching.

When I am searching for inspiration or an answer, I will draw Tarot cards and do a spread. I like to draw Animal Cards; I have read those for years because I have lived on the edge of the wild and often see animals. Do you wonder about these oracles? Besides Tarot, many women play with Runes and read the I Ching. The broad purpose of these oracles is to reveal more about your inner facets; what would you like to know more about? Who are you, separate from your family, your career, and your partner?

EMBRACE SPIRIT AND SOUL

Look into the squinty eyes of any Coyote Elder and you will discover that we like to present challenges. In the East the teachers provide koans, in our culture, we offer irresistible challenges. Like Nature's law of elasticity, using these personal enrichment oracles will strengthen your intuition. You have opened your core beliefs, you have learned the value of chakras and oracles, now let's layer in how you learn new things that will tie these all together.

Women-centered Learning: Dialogue, Intuition, Relationships, Connections, Gift Exchanges

Depending on your personal wiring, some of your teachers seemed more inspirational than others. Give thanks for all who brought you this far, shaped you, added something to your quiver, and sharpened your assessment skills. Now you will become your own teacher. Hopefully, you understand which of the multiple intelligences work best for you. This has been taught for several decades, but is worth a look since growth is your focus. Learn how you grow your body-mind. Update what you learned in school.

The totally unique way you acquire new knowledge is powerfully serious and great fun to discover. However you blend these various energies of learning and knowing into a daily practice for health and growth, defining a personal system will create your own true map for change. Choosing how you use these learning systems will give you depth and maturity. As the years progress, you will discover that women become more unique, not more alike.

By creating a design for myself, I became more valuable to myself; my curiosity has remained engaged far beyond school. I am fairly certain your method of learning differs from mine and from your sisters'. To solidify learning new material, reading reinforces writing. These two ways of acquiring utterly new information can then be reinforced physically, often through walking and talking. I seem to need Nature to collaborate with, and find myself sharing with stones, water, wildlife and birds. Eventually, I share my writing with all my friends, but I work it through my personal design first.

How do you learn something you consider difficult? Skills and knowledge freely shared is one of the great secrets to strong friendships. What are your personal methods for learning on a deeper level? Your quiet reflection on these questions will reveal that knowledge is power and change comes through both.

As long as there have been cultures of women, we have shared learning maps like these and the chakras to make us endlessly fascinating to one another. Look at the relationships you might discover between these systems. With your Genius, you can create something entirely new.

RELATIONSHIPS OFFER FLOWING ENERGY

Be a culture-maker, be the one who shares all that you are learning. When I talk about sharing I mean, enrich your girl-gang. In my 20s, my work friends were my gang. In my 30s, my best friend was a bachelor who simply loved women and was looking for his special one. We were friends, and even though he crossed in 2001, I consider him my friend still and talk to him sometimes. I learned about girl-gangs around the time I adopted one. With my women friends, I feel safe and surrounded by love, forgiveness, laughter, which produces a juice in me that I call thriving. I have worked to create a Village where all of us have adopted one another like family. Through my 20s and 30s, I migrated all over this beautiful country, moving and seeking my place of belonging. When I found my place, I knew I belonged because my girl-gang lives here. I was quickly embraced! Home means hugs and laughs in great abundance.

Of all the ways you can know yourself, relationships offer you the very best mirrors. In the process of mirroring, you see your shadow in the face of the other. You do not need to like every bit of another woman to like her a lot. Remember this wisdom about shadow: Often the part of another that you really do not like is a shadow part of yourself. Mirroring is a reflection freely offered for you to look deeper. This mirror may help you out-grow some part you no longer need. Maybe you and your friend can talk about it and work through the edginess; this is known as peacemaking. Give an edgy feeling your gift of introspection.

Sex, lust, and heated affairs are such a part of the culture now, I see we were probably never without sexuality, but in my lifetime, it opened gradually like a flower. There were times when flirting was a high art and could be brought back. These are ways to get to know yourself, sometimes you will discover you really want to know the other, your partner in the affair. Be kind and gentle, be playful, become friends who share and you will find a different kind of mirror for learning something new about yourself. Qualities emerge in a life partner that will fine tune acceptance and tolerance in you, for example.

Rarely are women successful enough or powerful enough to change another; find the change inside of yourself or find another life partner. Trust the mirror of your beloved relationship for all that feels triggered inside of you. That includes growth, understanding, challenges, and change. Sometimes the spark becomes a flame, sometimes the great wind flutters back into a mere breeze. Look for the Nature metaphors and take your questions into your Moontime, your answers can be found in the quiet. I live with a Lion, a true Alpha, and when he stirs, I merely turn sideways and allow all that wind to blow past me. I have learned so much about myself in this love affair with my Lion-hearted man.

Some people are simply not part of my Soul-cluster and I am glad to know that. What if I was truly a stone rolling, gathering moss and closely tracking every person I met? Oh my goodness. I have known many people who cannot love me without overlaying their judgments. I wish them well, I send them along with love. I hope this example will teach you to love as well as you can love and find yourself growing through mirroring with your friends, that you may find and know your true friends.

Accept, encourage, and create change; this is how you live harmoniously with your true Divine nature and with Nature herself. Invite your gang, your Women's Circle to join you outside beneath a tree. Talk about change, talk about systems, open your core beliefs and learn something new.

With my Women's Circle intact, I feel a safe sense of belonging even if we do not see one another for weeks. I have been able to finally heal some of my sexual wounds and talk about promiscuity openly. I knew I was home once I was able to step through the wall of shame around my secrets and talk openly and freely. This is the value of true girlfriends. Authentic relationships provide a feeling of deep belonging where you feel responsible for kinship because good healthy relationships go both ways. In giving and receiving, you feel both enriched and generous.

Notice how change flowed beautifully and gracefully through childhood. You remember being a fairy princess and a dragon, getting dirty, exploring the land, climbing a mountain, and rolling down grassy slopes. You do, don't you? Remember getting pubic hair and breast buds, and feeling how those marked womanhood as they grew fuller? You have changed over the years and didn't think a thing about it when you were a child of Nature, a child of the world. Now you are a woman for sure, you have a woman's body a woman's spirit, and a woman's brain with supernatural powers. I hope you invite change and love change; it's your attitude about change that you control, not change itself.

Finally, before I step you across the Threshold, I want to help you find perspective about work. Women find work through what emerges and connects with heart strings and/or meets our needs. You may have a dozen different jobs to finance your basic needs and your personal discoveries. Like all other ways of acquiring knowledge, the world of paid employment can be like stepping stones that offer you different gifts. Work forms an ecology around you long enough to be an external force that shapes you and changes you. In return for your talents and the juice of your life, you offer conscious power to shape the organization.

Remember to return to your personal 10,000-hour project. Mastery includes confidence and self-esteem; what two *ideas or energies* can you weave together to make something the world has never before seen? If you are on purpose with the enthusiasms of your heart, what you learned during your teens plays directly into this second half of your adolescence, your 20s.

From your Eagle's view, put wholeness up on a pedestal, use the assessment skills of your finely tuned brain to look at your mind, body, spirit, and Soul. Examine your motives. Notice how your New Moon intentions shape your month. Play with your internal multidimensional, multilayered, theme-park to discover who you really are inside. Be open, be curious, and be creative!

Before we bid your decade of growth adieu, I offer a couple of Coyote assignments. Begin to write your play history. You will want to track this through the next decade of your life, begin now. Write your sexual history, for your eyes only and prepare to adjust your attitude as maturity settles around your heart.

Finally. I have used the metaphor of trees, liberally and visually in this Passage. Here is another one you might use to begin an art project called your Tree of Life. Free-form this thought, you need only a few sparks from me. Do you hang your values, your events, your shadow-lights on the tree?

WOMANHOOD BLOOM THRESHOLD

Women's initiations are slightly more common than other Passage rituals because of the conscious awakening of women. As a long-time advocate for women, I can say this ceremony is crucial for women's evolution. In order for this Threshold to serve well, women need to gain the Eagle's perspective about life. Claim the heroine's crossroad where struggle meets joy. Process the past and its grief with Death rituals, releasing each Threshold including Birth. You know well the babe you were, the girl and big girl. You also know the pubescent maiden and the darling who gave her virginity to an experience. Since then, your growth has been exponential, year by year. A rattle and a drum will serve you to hold a ceremony of release, a Death ritual for the illusory nature of your former personas.

Rituals observed outside the box of time, relaxed with senses engaged, reveal this deeper truth: We all deserve to observe and to feel our maturity. Personal evolution differs from the science of evolution. The sheer effort to become an upright and fully functional human being is beyond understanding. So many forces, so much testing, hundreds of relationships, thousands of experiences have shaped you and each one was necessary. We can join hands and smile from the inside of this Eagle's perspective, only you know the whole truth. By releasing the element of time, we women gain access to our Soul-selves and Genius-selves. This will call forth the gifts that Gaia needs now, gifts of exalted and Initiated women. You have never been more needed in the web of life.

This Passage Threshold marks the end of adolescence and wraps a ribbon around the bundle of joys and sorrows of the human variety. As a marker for maturity, the Threshold appears because you as Initiate have done your work. Spiritually understanding the crossroad ahead, an Initiate acknowledges that change is a force of Nature. At least one year past the Threshold will be needed to integrate this spiritual experience. Enjoy the peaceful pull and the comfort of knowing just enough for now. Failing to cross this Threshold would cause arrested development. Even with a Death ritual to bring up the fire of transformation and release the past, no pain compares to stagnant growth.

Be the inviter: Invite your Mentor, invite the Elders and the Youngers who create the constellation of your community. Ask for the help you need. Women who initiate receive support through the processing of their life experiences.

The community needs this ceremony, because for everyone participating or watching, this Passage celebration reveals the future potential for their own personal growth.

Our collective purpose is growth and its natural extension, maturity. By the time a woman has grown into and learned to challenge her fully mature brain, she has discovered the power within accumulating skills and experiences. She has made friends with her body by practicing self-care. A well mentored young woman will have completed at least one and possibly two 10,000-hour projects to master her gifts and reveal her Genius. Perhaps Mothering has become her project. With the help of many other women, she will have become a heroine to herself. She will feel confident, brilliant, strong, and clear about her direct connection to her Soul. Her Genius has fully awakened when she reaches out to younger women to give back what she received from her Mentors.

In this giving back for all we glean from life, initiations breathe new life into all women. Through a spirit of generativity and reciprocity, young women and Elders remain connected to vitality and evolution. Guiding adolescents into fully blooming women is psychically joyful and satisfying.[13]

Each woman I have guided through this Womanhood Bloom Passage has been my teacher. My own process has been sometimes clumsy; I admit, very willing Initiates have taught me a powerful amount. By using the dust of our Ancestors and their imagined or real lives, women are teaching women how to be courageous and interdependent. In this reincarnation, I am the Elder guide, the trickster determined to bring Rites of Passage back to the culture in my lifetime.

AN HONORING: RACHEL'S STORY

Womanhood Bloom Threshold

A gift came to me and I knew her as a blessing when I saw her. In my mind's eye, I can still see her coming up my driveway; she is Rachel Ruach at 32. After a series of women's ceremonies and a profound Vision Quest, and after deep trainings with the Nature Connection community in California, she decided to walk to Idaho. When her original idea didn't meet her expectations, Rachel cleared her head and chose again. She came to me in an honoring way, a number of respected Elder men had directed her me. Laden with emerging gifts of her own and a finely tuned spirit connection, she carried the bare bones, the beginning of a cultural map for women's growth and maturity, a map for initiation and spiritual evolution specific to the Divine Feminine rising in the world, now.

Intertwined around this special introduction, I had helped lift up a circle of women who called ourselves the Inland Northwest Women's Council. Rachel was one of our early presenters. I had seen the outline of her cultural map and recognized both its luminance and its promise. She was giving birth to something new. She held great hopes for her gift: A Cultural Map for Women's Rites of Passage.

Rachel asked me for a Womanhood initiation for herself. She was the first to honor me in this way. I felt my cells awaken to the challenge that her question posed. I needed to extrapolate all that I had learned from many First Blood ceremonies for girls. This was a sign of growth for me and I said, "Yes, absolutely, who can help us?" Personally, this is true to my way of being with the spirit of Earth's women, I always say yes to their requests for spiritual assistance, I say yes to ceremonies. I never hesitate.

"First, I need help planting a field of wildflowers." I saw the need for relationship building. I never charge for ceremony even though a positive response on my part requires that I set aside at least two months for preparation, for dreaming the creation, for going deeper into needs and wants, and to listen to the spirit of the endeavor. Then I need two more Moons to find a new normal for myself and discover the deeper teachings within. Initiation is such a powerful force, time is needed to embrace the essence of the woman, to gather the community for support, and to align myself to energies stirred that need to be contained. Planting seeds would support both of our journeys.

We arranged to meet next in a driving rainstorm. We suited up to be outside, rainproof is particular to being in Nature so women may truly touch the wild within ourselves. Something new was going to emerge from a wheelbarrow completely full of good compost holding about a billion carefully collected wildflower seeds. My husband had planted a new arboretum, the trees were babies, the soil had been stirred and weeded once. Rachael came when I said, "Ready." Soaking wet, I shared a little plan, "Spread evenly," and winked as I handed her a shovel. For that wet and sacred moment when we both leaned on our shovels and looked into one another's eyes, Rachael and I both knew we were planting the most important seeds of our lives. We could not imagine how those seeds would grow, but we could cooperate with Nature, open our hearts to receive the Earth's gratitude for our care, and build our dreams with hope while we danced between the raindrops.

Across the Threshold, Friends Waited

A woman's initiation summons the energy and gifts of transformation to enliven the holy Soul which wraps each cell in one's body. Every bone cell, every heart cell, every neuro-transmitting cell will come through a transformative fire of change during an initiate's first year. This is inner work which requires the deepest quiet, deserving silence. Once connected, the initiate finds, lying dormant, the silence is where the Divine Feminine lives. God and

Goddess, side by side, merge with a woman's Higher Self. Other forces and energies are ancestral, some are from current culture. How can anyone describe anyone else's holistic experience through change gifted from ritual and ceremony? What are the universal forces coming to assist?

Rachel and I were friended by the same wild woman, Lauren Gonsolves. I introduce her into this story for intersections needing to be honored. Lauren cleaned those seeds that went into our wheelbarrow, a billion, representing delightful wild woods adventures. Those seeds, gathered by me, cleaned by Lauren, planted by Rachel symbolized the mindful moments ahead when we would all be harvesting. We are more deeply connected, every single thing is really alive and connected. That is how Rachel and I began, with wildflower seeds, because they sprout underground in the winter.

A magnificent red-headed fiddler, Karen, stepped into the role as my assistant and began to meet with me and Rachel. Appropriate for women's most serious endeavors together, we met at a diner and planned over plates of food and hot tea. I felt like the stickler for logistics and safety, but once I was satisfied we had met those basic needs, Rachel was ready to step out into the wild to be alone. I shared the steps involved to complete a Rites of Passage in a good way: Severance, separating from her life for a time; crossing the Threshold into liminal time where the portal to the world beyond is accessible by silence and prayer. I would help with the last step, reincorporation, and would speak about that later.

Rachel's was a journey into herself, seeking the Divine, bonding and listening for the places where inspiration, intuition, and ancestral gifts intersected. Inviting change, using the liminal space between her wild camp and her little yurt home, she chose eleven deep winter days to be alone on White Mountain. This is perhaps the edgiest scenario I could have imagined.

In December, before the snow arrived, we hiked to her camp site. "Follow me," she said up a sheer rock face, decorated by lovely, emerald green moss. We dodged boulders that loosened, When I lingered, unable to find my next step, the Fairies invited me to stay forever. The easy, vertical hike required focus to navigate, and delivered wonder at each step. It was a very beautiful location; I knew this place would offer deep visitations.

This Womanhood initiation of days and nights across the deepest northern winter, began long before I handed Rachel a shovel for seeds and looked into her eyes. It had been in both of us as a dream. She had searched for her sacred space and discovered a womb-like bed with a natural fire circle. When the three of us saw the space, it was not completely ready. Rachel said she would stack wood around two sides, perhaps a cord deep. Imaginatively, I could see where the tarp would go, where her body would curl into Earth's little curved bowl, and where she would sit in firelight contemplating her life.

Rachael's Soul was prepared to take a journey back in time and forward to now, the spiritual inheritance from her Ancestors was the longing in her Soul. Her seeking stretched far into the future of cultural change for women. In each moment, she would listen to discover how these two forces, past and present, shaped her future. She would have plenty to do, I didn't worry about that. She showed me a gallon jar of barley, for making her porridge each morning, to last her through the day. She hoped no predator would be attracted by the smell of grain. Karen and I, the Ancestors and Guardians, and Rachael herself, we would all hold a strong enough container for this whole-spirit work to be done in safety.

Still, we were all projecting on her behalf. Karen jiggled for the adventure, I did too. A younger version of myself felt the wild, the rush of adrenalin, and felt wonder for woman's deepest and unknowable mystery on Earth: Initiation and emergence through the darkest darkness. The February Full Moon had me on edge, either it would snow a foot or, with a crystal clear Moon-lit night, the wild animals would have a good visual fix on the camp. I knew the bears were hibernating, but wild cats, especially bobcats and mountain lions rarely sleep and often have a litter to feed through the hungry months. Those thoughts caused a worry, with my prayers I wove a spell around the campsite. We all love wildcats, I had no doubt they would be nearby, it's the nature of her place on White Mountain.

We met at the trailhead, checked our logistics one more time, agreed on the day for closing the portal that had just opened to the spirit world. It was time for her departure ceremony, silence, rattle, last connection, pledging our devotion to this sacred time with our whole hearts, and Rachel was off on her own. Karen and I watched until the bravest of women reached the top of her skid trail, waved and disappeared. Eleven days suddenly seemed long, too long, an eternity.

A message tree doubled as a way-station for water, and taking turns with Karen, every single day a gallon was delivered. Miraculously, every single day a gallon was retrieved and the empty jug returned. When it was my turn to deliver the gallon, I drove 5 miles north of home and 3 miles west to the base of White Mountain. I hiked up that skid road previously used to slide down logs when conditions were right. It was cold, there was snow, but I didn't need snowshoes because no new snow had fallen. I reached the tree with some effort. I looked up at the rock face, I could sometimes detect Rachel's fire, usually not. Invisibility was key to her process.

Crossing Back across the Threshold

Karen and I provided a container for transformation, we held strong and prayed we had done enough. That this story was created to be held by a community of women and told to our daughters is perhaps the highest purpose for any Rites of Passage experience. We draw from the mythology of transformation, using the same alchemical magic found in mythology and stories; then we go further, we make it personal, powerful, and intergenerational. When women go into themselves, in the deep interior quiet where silence mingles with possibility, Soul and Genius hear the invitation for an awakening. I could never really tell another's story; I paint the portrait of the space for the transformative fire of spirit to find the heart and Soul of a woman. With all my heart, I pray that Rachel tells this story occasionally, to inspire others. More fires live within her, more darkness, and more light. The seeds planted for this journey will ignite those new fires as her journey path discovers more maturity.

Since we had agreed on an end time, I invited everyone I knew who knew Rachel to come to her closing ceremony. Karen and April went to the message tree, gathered up Rachel in hugs and smiles. Then shushing each other, they blindfolded Rachel so she would return her focus to the drum of her own heart beat and find the blessed silence where she had become a tuning fork for the Womb of the Universe. Those 11 days, that is the story only Rachel can tell.

The three walked around the corner and arm-in-arm, slowly floated down the skid trail. A drum beat gave her Women's Circle waiting a connection to Great Mother and offered a grounding sound for Rachel to find her way back. Women had gathered at 7 a.m. on that February morning, sharing thermoses of hot tea. With a spirit blanket laid down to circle around, the raw Earth served as our altar, as always.

As a carrier of ritual, I knew this was the opportunity to plant another seed. I asked Rachel to be seated at the West edge and face the rising sun. Women gathered in close. I gifted her with a woman's power symbol to carry her memories in a large leather pouch, hand worked by a woman, decorated with tiny bells that would jingle a joyous sound. Then, as I placed a crown of flowers on her head, clapped my hands together, and in my squinty old way, I announced the spiritual and psychic integration of all that she gathered up on her mountain will require at least one year ahead to fully understand.

Crowned and Gifted, Integration Begins

"Use this crown as your broomstick, because I know you are going to fly away now. Integration must begin, right here in your community. The final stage, reincorporation, will last up to 13 Moons and begins by you telling this community of women something of your experience up there on White Mountain."

She gasped, "Really?"

"Yes, we came to hear from you so you may plant the seed in our hearts. Share with us."

This is where the rest of the story belongs to Rachel, but I can tell you her transformation was as peaceful as any fire can be. She accepted the ancestral gifts she had received from her mountain vigil and spent the next two weeks in her tiny yurt in seclusion, writing down all that had awakened in her. Rachel's Soul had become a receiver of ancient wisdom, a gift from her Ancestors. Sitting on the blanket that morning, she told of messages she had received, some came to her in the original Hebrew language. Her Women's Cultural Map is being refined and used in California as a guide for women's journeys into themselves, including all of the mystery in Rites of Passage ceremonies.

One final ceremony wrapped our experiences together with a dazzling ending. Rachel came to the little cabin where I lived with my husband and cooked us a very fine meal. She put so much love into those preparations that I will always hold that occasion as the most sacred way this story could end. Even though this was a major life event for Rachel and me, it's now enveloped and lives as a little story we once shared. Rites of Passage, in its most holy way, wraps all of one's life experiences into a bundle, so the emptying, the release, the empty vessel, may be filled with fresh, new offerings from one's Soul. This intentional swaddling, pausing in the liminal space to awaken and enliven herself, created a new stage for the dance of her life.

You see, this is not the end of the story, but the awakening of a woman's true self. Enormously deep experiences filled Rachel's bundle before she came to me. I only held them for her while she paused and emptied herself so new gifts could enter. With the buckskin pouch, she received back her previous bundle of experiences and launched her Womanhood Bloom in the transformative dream waiting to be delivered by her awakened Soul.

Glory of Initiation

Rachel Ruach's whole dream is now being held in Sonoma County, CA in a new container, *Infinite Wild* by name.[14] She gifted me, you see, by seeing the Elder in me even before my own initiation. From her I received a symbol of our story, a perfectly round and hand-size knapping stone of brilliant black flint. When I need to remember my journey, I touch this stone in gratitude for being seen. One of the highest honors of my life, of all our lives, is to be seen. I bow in deep gratitude to all the tiniest seeds waiting for their time to bloom.

GIFTS FROM THE ELDERS: WOMANHOOD BLOOM

Your practice of watching the Moon, dancing with la Luna feels like breathing. You simply do it.

Your **Circle of Courage** becomes layered with values freshly minted through experiences. This action of *entelechy*, on the move, actively seeking your true potential, will help you track your Genius, your Soul-self, and all that it means to be human.

Remember the four foundation stones of early adolescence: **Belonging, Mastery, Independence**, and **Generosity**. Those four values practiced during your introduction to the **Circle of Courage**, laid down the first layer of self-awareness to help you understand risk.

Invent for yourself the simplest concepts to expand your sense of **Belonging**. Belonging attaches to place, as in knowing the place you live, and to the people who live with you in this place.

✳ What other words, feelings, and values help describe belonging for you?

In seeking **Mastery**, your Genius is fully engaged. When you play with your Genius, you will find your purpose. This needs only your focused heart. Rise up in personal rebellion to defend your inner Genius.

✳ What help do you need to express this Soul-essence of you?

Independence is a much bigger value than it first appears. What exactly does independence imply? Can you find self-reliance and financial security in there? How about adventure?

✳ Ask a Mentor about interdependence.

If you direct the energy of **Generosity** inward, you will find care and warmth, along with silence and rest.

✳ When you turn that energy outward, how might you be useful or in some small way, in service to another?

Nature Connection: Why Nature? Nature is our primary home and our inspired teacher. Earth, where Nature is friend and Great Mother to all, provides our one and only home in this lifetime. What are your Gifts for Gaia, the ancient Goddess name for Earth?

Reclaim any Soul parts which you gave up to please someone else or gain approval. You need all of your parts to feel whole. Anything that hurts now, feelings, attitudes, memories, those still need to be healed.

Those compromises left your Soul out of the equation. Look deeper and deeper: Who will hold you while you do this inner searching?

You become your own Medicine Woman. This psychic healing process reveals to you the wonders of your inner life. Do whatever it takes!

✳ What activity moves you closer to your bliss?

You may discover that you inherited feelings of pain and general emotional patterns. Keep only what belongs to you. The seeds of your past become your present; the seeds of your present become your future.

You only need to believe in what you most love to do and have always loved. That is why you are here on Earth right now. Look into all of the facets of your passion and you will find your Soul. To locate your Genius, this is where you begin

✳ What gives you such joy you can only call it play?

✳ What do you love?

✳ How does it all fit around your core beliefs?

Be watchful for Divine guidance: How the right guide at just the right time comes to you or crosses your path may also be an interesting story—coincidence, fate, or merely mystery.

Teachers: Inner and Outer: Listen to your dreams before you leave your bed, make a record. What resonates from this deep subconscious part of you? Pay close attention to your Moon.

I ask this question to surprise you: What trouble can you get into that will teach you about your shadow self? Sometimes the characteristics or tendencies which reveal the darker side of your nature will become great personal teachers.

✳ Exactly what do you dislike and why?

✳ What do you fear and why?

For subtle body-work, begin to work with your chakras. This is energy work and opens your inner core beliefs to guide your senses, sight, hearing, and especially your felt-sense, your emotions. Chakra work is body-work that reveals your inner energy world. As pure energy, chakras can be sensed as open or closed, as flowing or blocked. Remember, chakras are a brilliant, built-in system for understanding yourself energetically.

✳ You alone are responsible for the ritual life you lead and how your spirituality awakens.

✳ Do you use ritual in the quiet of morning or light a candle in the evening to awaken your sub-conscious, maybe both times?

✳ When can you imagine meditation working for you, morning, afternoon, or night?

When I am searching for inspiration or an answer, I will draw Tarot cards and do a spread. Do you wonder about these oracles? Besides Tarot, many women play with Runes and read the I Ching. Their purpose is to reveal inner facets.

✳ What would you like to know more about?

✳ Who are you, separate from your family, your career, and your partner?

Skills and knowledge freely shared are among the great secrets to strong friendships.

* How do you learn something you consider difficult?

* What are your personal methods for learning on a deeper level?

NOTES FOR THE WOMANHOOD BLOOM PASSAGE

1 Paul Shepard (1925-1996) was an early influence on my thinking about human ecology and the life cycle. By reading his major works, I learned about evolution, my place in the Universe and humans' place coming from the wild to make culture. Shepard's books demonstrate how our cultural consciousness has developed and matured as have we as a species of thinking animals. *The Tender Carnivore and the Sacred Game* (1973); *Thinking Animals: Animals and the Development of Human Intelligence* (1978); *Nature and Madness* (1982); and *The Others: How Animals Made Us Human* (1996).

2 Neurologist Daniel J. Seigel wrote *Mindsight* (2010) and many other books to teach about the workings of our brain. He wrote this one to inform adolescents about the power of mind and intention to re-sculpt neuro-pathways; this information is transformative at any age in life.

3 An African folktale, *Maggots and Gold* is retold and preserved for our psyches to plumb the depths of our shadows, by Michael Meade in *Fate and Destiny* (2010). In the shadows, we find the true gold.

4 A Mentor at a turning point in my life, Rick Medrick, took this one teaching about the small space right in front of me to teach a profound meditation technique. Studying the Earth is a delightful and soulful way to take your mind off yourself. I am amused at the Divine Masculine influences I have claimed as Mentors. Rick Medrick also gave me the word *entelechy* as a seed thought and it grew.

5 Most of my Mentors have been my wise women friends beginning with the original, Kathleen Bjorkman Wilson. Our spirits visit often, like the two little statues sitting around in Nature. Mentors need not be older, Kathleen is 50 days younger, but has always displayed an ancient wisdom and I am the beneficiary. Listen to the women, profound truths may be harvested from talks and walks in Nature.

6 At a psychological symposium in 1995, I heard Larry Brendtro speak about his new book, *Reclaiming Youth at Risk* (1990). Co-authored with two colleagues, Martin Brokenleg and Steve Van Bockern, the foundation created around Circle of Courage has widely dispersed the principles of this Native American model for youth development.

7 Once in a while a woman crosses your path that you must hold on to, with all your heart, forever. This is how it was when I met Diana Eldridge in 1991. She continues to evolve how she shows up for me, as saint, savior, and wise woman, we've moved from great need to great love.

8 The Genius Project is a contribution of the Mosaic Foundation led by Michael Meade. From the website, mosaicvoices.org, "Each person carries a unique way of seeing the world, and it is this rich diversity of perspectives and styles, talents and aptitudes that is the greatest resource we have as a global community when it comes to facing our greatest challenges."

9 Kimberlie Jean Gridley was in the first group of Initiates who helped with the groundwork for *Nine Passages. Soul Stories* was drafted while her initiation story unfolded.

10 Marija Gimbutas (1921-1994), a Lithuanian-American archeologist, introduced me to the Goddess through women studies programs. Through the 1990's, many scholarly women referenced her groundbreaking book, *The Language of the Goddess* (1989). Marija's excavations from Neolithic times introduced Goddess first from an academic perspective and left my imagination to unlock the spiritual mystery. Donna Reed directed and Starhawk wrote *Signs Out of Time: The Life of Archeologist Marija Gimbutas* (2004) an accessible video on YouTube about her life and work.

11 In 1996, Anodea Judith published her classic book about chakras: *Eastern Body Western Mind: Psychology and the Chakra System as a Path to the Self*. She offers lots of experiential workshops through www.sacredcenters.com/.

12 Brené Brown, a graduate professor in Social Work from the University of Houston, has changed the face of shame, vulnerability, worthiness, courage, and showing yourself to your community. Backed by amazing research, she continues to publish her discoveries in consumable form. *The Gifts of Imperfection* (2010); *Daring Greatly* (2015) both meant for self-discovery and *Rising Strong* (2015) bring the conversation into the wider spheres where life revolves around others—home, work, church, and community service.

13 In *The Life Cycle Completed: Extended Version* (1998) Erik H. Erikson and Joan M. Erikson posthumously published the ninth stage, an elaboration of their famous theory about the life stages. By the time I came across these stages of psychosocial development they were practically a cultural belief, although more will continue to be revealed. As generativity is understood, Elders and Youngers collaborate through mentoring to make the lives of both better.

14 I am pleased to pass along the website showcasing Rachel's work with women, http://www.infinitewild.org/

DEEPENING WOMANHOOD

THE INTENTION:
BECOMING A CULTURE-MAKER FOR THE VILLAGE

I see and honor the amazing energies that flow in and through your body, sometimes you are Fire, Air, Earth, and Water; occasionally two of these energies merge. All the more beautiful and stunning, every day your woman-self is changing, challenging, creating, and different from the days that came before. Looking back to the last Thresholds you crossed, now far back in your rear-view mirror, fire burned through you to bring you here and now. You finally understand that womanhood holds secrets slowly revealed—moist, ecstatic, earthy—as you realize more and more brilliance in yourself. Because you laid a foundation in your teens and twenties and burned through the pain, your transformation was complete. You are ready to receive the full power of your adulthood throughout your thirties and forties. This is your life. Live your dreams and share your passions. Do what you love and do it often. I am your Elder inspirer, always in your corner.

EAGLE'S VIEW

You have stepped over a Threshold perhaps you thought you'd never reach, but now you are over that milestone, beyond 30 and blossoming. This is the age and stage of your life when pure creative powers emerge. To help you spin your dreams, call on your resiliency and curiosity to reveal new things. The brilliance of your 20s comes into this decade so you may literally stand on your own shoulders. Feeling vital and alive, you love growing, always wanting to be something more, because you know there is more in you. You will spend time with the Saturn question: "Who were you born to be?"

Smiling to yourself each morning when you wake, you will have a bigger taste of life when you use your Moon days to observe the unfolding of your dreams. Seek the sacred in the ordinary to discover that ordinary is sacred. You are the change agent and have the power to create and change absolutely anything.

Personal and spiritual development becomes your prime directive because your physical body, your temple, has completed its development. This is true, until pregnancy changes everything. I call this Deepening Womanhood because now is the time for Passages within Passages. So much will happen as the seasons turn, you will soon understand deepening and then deepening some more. Passages layered and always going deeper, this may ring a riddle tune. That is fitting of this very long, prime stage, your womanhood.

Consider the common thread to all of womanhood: We are daughters first, sisters often, and we continue to grow into the roles of wives, partners, Mothers, and culture-makers.[1] Because these outward manifestations seem to define us, we long to stretch ourselves out of these bounds for our Soul-selves. In everything you set in motion, seek to balance being and doing.

When you locate the inner acceptance of being 30, other people will also observe your development and see you as a fully mature adult. As a woman who knows her own heart, you integrate lessons, blessings, and opportunities. As a seeker and creator of joy for yourself you discover laughter and make that a quest. You are a culture-maker for your family and community. You rest when there is warm sand to lie on. If you haven't already, you will discover there is more to do than you can manage. I hope to help you find heart-ways to merge work and play so you can release the cultural curse of busy-ness. This is a false myth for women.

I see you walking along the beach alone, climbing mountains, flying kites, turning cartwheels with children. Radical in your self-belief and your fierce love, I smile when you find your niche and fill it for the entrepreneurial fun of it. You and your friends celebrate woman's variations and potentialities as you make plenty of time for each other. High-energy activities stir your body to its truth. You talk to understand how you feel, what you stand for, why it matters, and how you can make a difference. You love the Earth and give yourself over to Gifts for Gaia.

Honor Your Teachers

You use rituals to honor your Moontime in a flowing rhythm of self-care. Each one is your own quiet initiation into the depths of you, your desires awaken, and your curiosities lead to passions to reveal a little more of yourself each Moon.[2] As inevitable as Moontime is for you, the Vision Quest you observe faithfully each month guides your heart's intentions, unfolding with la Luna in the deep quiet of rejuvenation for yourself.

In the Eagle's view of this era in your personal development, you become a heroine to yourself and to others. Half close your eyes, become squinty-eyed like me and look into that far distance; see how you might shape relationships and build rapport with others. Being a far-seeing visionary, you build your life with eyes forward and take great care to be on purpose.

This Eagle's view includes all or most of the next two decades. I believe as the Navajo Diné women, that the middle of womanhood, the first Deepening Womanhood Threshold, arrives around 52. While you are still squinting, see that the exquisite 50s will be the very middle of your life, a glorious decade indeed. Figuratively of course, the end remains elusive, too far away to imagine. When you add 100 to the year of your Birth, you will be closer to understanding how life will go for you. Your own Soul is the messenger and will deliver that faraway Threshold with grace and good news.

Ahead the distance is farther than the Eagle can see. Walking beside you, heart-to-heart, together we will look into this time and space capsule from 30 to 52. We will not count again until the next Threshold appears. As worlds spin around other worlds, the multiverse comes into you; amazement becomes cliché. Before you hit cruise-control, understand that your Soul is laden with Coyote's twists. Sometimes flying in like an asteroid, twists of fates and hidden blessings will enrich and surprise, so find your willow-like core. Trials that test this inner resilience are your Soul wanting your attention.

BUILDING A LIFE

As a woman, you are gifted with the rarity of rhythm. Ovulation and shedding blood are the two life energies of every woman.[3] To increase your consciousness, build your life around your Moontime, swinging between these energies. In the deep quiet of your Moontime, when you lie cuddled beneath your hot water bottle, intuition and inspiration meet to reflect on the little slice of life since your last Moon. This way, your stories become bracketed by your cycles. Only you can carve out this Vision Quest and quiet rejuvenation time for yourself. This Moon and the next one take you deeper into your interior life where you are a wise, brilliant woman. You train yourself to open to your Soul's calling and to receive guidance. This rhythm is how you build your life.

A chasm of age separates us, Elder to Woman in Bloom. I am thrilled that I can talk woman-to-woman and celebrate your youth as you celebrate my age. In fact, my intention is to celebrate you, be with you, encourage you, and cheer you on through your every action. As ever the Initiate, I hope you continue to waken. Everything you do feels wonderful to me. Every time you step outside the boundaries of your regular habits, I feel a special excitement. When you feel even a little bit daring, it seems contagious, and I feel braver and more inspired.

Still a Long Life Ahead

I crossed this same Blooming Threshold and clearly remember my moment basking in the glow of thirty. I would have benefited from this holistic view and would have enjoyed having an Elder in my corner to smooth my ruffled feathers. I see with clear sight how the Great Mystery, with the help of many Goddesses, carried me thorough hardship. This is a changed perspective from being in the muddle. We will work together to shine light into the enigmatic building of your life. I have gathered the wisdom of many Elders who all

266

encourage you. We invite your Genius to come out to play. Know the heart of women is to give, give, give and with great love, I remind you to put on your own oxygen mask first. Your own inner Genius also known as your Soul, needs tending first, so you don't give from continuously empty places.

I provide a rather earthy, sensuous, and practical way of seeing into the mystery to call forth your authenticity. In many ways women are alike—we have heart and passion, we have history and personal demons, and we have gathered skills and relationships. In just as many ways, women are different, more unique almost every day. Beneath the agenda of each day, the Divine light of woman's spirituality shines occasional beams of dazzling light.

Being real, showing your true self as you become known to you, is the same individuating energy you perfected when you separated from your Mother. Your original effort of individuation may have been filled with hesitation; this advanced effort seeks to discover how much more of your authentic brilliance may be filled with endless delight. Your gifts and talents have been kneaded and massaged, work and play histories combine to reveal an interesting story. These are the elements I will help you work with as you craft your beautiful womanhood.

SEEING SHADOW

Remain vigilant for how life presents itself to you. Mischief may be one of the adventures of these two decades, but adventure is something quite different from shadow, a vast uncharted territory inside of you. Even though I have known great darkness, hidden from view like the inside of an envelope, my shadow-self has become one of the knowns in my quiver. Shadow is a great informer and a springboard for change. When I looked inside the envelope, my story emerged with blessed clarity and even wisdom. My destiny became light over dark. There's so much to learn about yourself: Inside of every dislike, every negative view and every judgment you harbor your own shadow. Those are gifts to be exposed, to be brought to the surface and acknowledged. You do not have to spend a ton of time with your shadow self, but know that shadow cannot be denied. When I revealed personal magic by facing my shadow-self, introspection became fuel for my authenticity.

I learned comparison, one of the darker aspects of shadow: I watched others enjoying highly active lives, enjoying their bodies and their relationships. A certain mindlessness of self gave way to a darker force for my womanhood; I focused on career development and missed enjoying many parts of life. I went further into darkness by focusing on what I did not have instead of simply locating the inner power that I did have. This is a true Scorpio mannerism. When I went back to graduate school at 44, I went seeking all those things I missed during the time I had lived in isolation yoked to the corporate mirage. Fortunately, I had learned well how shadow fits into my personality. In the very middle of my life, I knew everything needed a closer examination: Heart, assets, beliefs, spirituality, gifts, talents, loves, desires, relationships, self-care. I chose silent seclusion rather than isolation and learned the difference between those choices.

Occasionally your life is too big to hold. If you need to, choose special silent retreats. I recommend contemplation and deliberation for spiritual relief and Soul-full adjustments. Writers have given me permission to be introspective.[4] One early inspiration was Anne Morrow Lindberg who inspired me to slow down; I gave myself to the mountain, rather than the sea, and allowed something new to arise out of that stillness. Another influence was *Creative Visualization* which describes building a life for yourself, our theme-song, by locating and following the desires of your heart.

Women have many ways of knowing. To unwind the knot and harvest the goodies inside, I began to explore all these ways of knowing. The entire world is your stage; the multifaceted and scrumptious parts in this slice of your life live in you because you are the lead actress in your own play. You cannot possibly see all your facets or understand how to feed your Genius. As a personal gift from the Elders, please trust this is true. Facets are aspects and assets, talents and rare gifts. Put yourself in the middle of a star with rays and remind yourself of your strengths, your special qualities, your facets. Perhaps you will discover your own artful expression. Remember, you do deserve these personal strokes.

Before the Moon descends into darkness, a tiny Crescent begins your Visioning Time

MOON FOR VISIONING

Give yourself permission to design your life with visions and dreams, with imagination and creativity, and with incredibly hard work. This will bring deep rest for your Soul each night. With this one wondrous ingredient, *permission*, you will experience your life through a unique lens and immeasurable freedoms. Almost daily, you will see the many ways your gifts can be woven together. At any time, you can stop, dig in your heels, turn your direction a few degrees or all the way around, and begin again. You have every woman's permission.

By the time you reach 30, you have used half of your eggs to build and vision your life to now. In the brilliant design of woman's nature, you still have nearly 200 remaining Moon visions to design your life your way. This visioning is your opportunity to understand your Soul. Visioning opens your Divinely Feminine portal of receptivity. If your antennae are clear of psychological junk, the God and Goddess of your understanding will deliver the whole of the

Universe, but you must be quiet and present to receive all the inspirations that belong to you, Moon-by-Moon. As the power of your passion is revealed, take the action steps to build your life in an inspired way.

From the worldly intersection of Great Mother and your wild nature, Earth offers the inspiration you seek as your intuition expands. So many people have dedicated their lives to protect sacred pieces of land so you may now go there for the inspiration you need to discover more of both—your inner nature and your wild nature. Women do not keep this secret, wild Earth is our collective source for great inspirations. Singly and in small groups of adventurers, we simply and tenderly find our way to the deep quiet in places that hold special meaning and good energy. We nurture ourselves with Earth's offerings for personal reflection, lying on her tender body, absorbing Earth's regenerative energies.

The pure, revitalizing energy from Earth Mother is ours to receive every moment we genuinely connect with her Nature. Many women go to Nature to create private Moon ceremonies; what we do always feels deeply spiritual, often secretive, and always nutritional. We repeat this as often as each Moon calls or whenever we are able to dip into this spiritual well for Soul-full nourishment. By falling deeply in love with a place, you become one of its protectors.

Consider the intersecting energies of Nature and your Moontime. By far, my deepest spiritual experience came when I received the inspiration to bleed on the Earth and acted on it. I would like you to grasp this simple gift—inspiration invites action. In my contemplative solitary years, the heart of Mother Earth came into me. When my Moon began skipping months, I was deep in the silence of my Moontime and feeling the wonder of it. Within this time of exquisite quiet, I found Mother Earth to be the very heart of inspiration. With such a gift I felt a responsibility to take an action step. I stepped out the door and went up into the woods to a mossy spot to experience the intersection of Moontime and silence, of inspiration and action.

FOR THE GIRLS OF GIRLS OF GIRLS

I stripped naked and asked my dog to watch over:
I received this message, from Higher Power,
From God and Goddess, from the Womb of the Universe
And Great Creator: Share this story with women.

Share it with girls, advocate for all women,
Moontimes filled with silence.

As my dog lay near enough to stroke
Thoughts transported me into the future
Where the Seven Generations would unfold,
Girls of girls of girls;
Tears fell down my cheeks.

Sierra sat up, gave me her paw,
And leaned in to taste my tears;
Giving my well of regret to the Earth,
I wondered why this inspiration
Had never come to me before?

As it would be, this was my last Moontime.

Opportunity forever closed the door
For an egg to be planted in my womb
Blanketed with blood and nourishment.

I had become a Crone.

I made one delightful Moon-story, a touch-stone.
My beautiful companion Sierra,
Named for the daughter I never had,
Helped me create this story, so women will be inspired

To find the silence inside their Moontime.

I offer you a place in my Circle
So you may speak for yourself
And you may build on my one little story
With Moontimes filled with silence.

©Gail Burkett & Janis Monaco Clark

Revering Nature

That was not the last inspiration I have received from spending time on the Earth feeling the Moon. In my Moonpause, I have doubled down. I now give la Luna the long attention that a close relation deserves, especially when she exalts. I call this rhythm, New-Half-Full-Half. I adore cosmic time, knowing and feeling what our Ancestors felt; in holy relationship with Earth and earthlings, the Moon presents her energetic gift of inspiration. This exquisite rhythm from New to Full and back has taken me deeper into honoring the gifts women have received for millennia from the cosmic language of time. I have learned the truth about the distinctly different energies of these four phases of the Moon and the subtle energies in the Moon's different seasons. I am now learning to blend Astrology with the ancient messages that come from the Moon just for women.

I go outside every single day, sometimes twice a day. Prayers for the Earth and my Sisters call me out. I walk in an empty meditative way with my dog friend Rosie, successor to Sierra. I feel how the season expresses; I feel the energy of the Moon kissing the other planets in our solar system. Wandering in the woods creates a blank slate inside of my heart-mind, I send my antenna out like a butterfly's. Being an enthusiast, I always come back with photo images, but on Moon days, I am most astonished to receive profound inspiration for Passages. This is a long recovery process, dusting off all the Passages for women and offering them up to the Moon and to you.

When the Sun reflects nothing at all on the surface of the Moon, earthlings call this a New Moon. She is dark and feels so mysterious, holding promise and potential for at least three days. This is a good metaphor for life: Not everything is light, but darkness serves incubation. Intentions seeded during New Moon phases, received as inspiration from her darkness, feed your Soul. The waxing phase from New to Half to Full provides building energy to sprout ideas and projects, exuberance for creation. Each day the Moon changes 13° which offers numerical magic and inspires growth and change in you. It's all magic energy. Watching the sky for the expression of the Full Moon, the Earth's people, especially women, are captivated by the sight of her. We swoon, we find love, we feel love, and we fall in love.

She is out there in her Full Moon glory even on cloudy nights to teach us about love. I am convinced of this fact: La Luna verifies what my friend Diana taught me before I could believe this truth, "Love is all there is."

La Luna's capacity for relationship is so big, she guides our hearts to pump blood, she helps us release water; Luna regulates the flow of all women's cycles. She illuminates the fire inside while pulling out our love song. Moon reminds us we are given this high privilege to dance on the Earth; how wonderful life is for awakening women.

Whatever the vision or inspiration you receive during your Moontime, give it the honor of a single action step. Even if you never find the opportunity to bleed directly with the Earth as a way of giving back to our Great Mother, use the inspiration she offers inside your silence to give something of you back. A nurturing practice for many women around the world is bleeding on cloth, rinsing blood from the cloth into a bowl and offering this Blood of your life to plants. I am grateful to Rachel Hertogs for being one of the leaders of this change so needed in our relationship to our Moontimes.[5] You do not need to be an Elder to verify this spiritual promise: Open to receive the gift of sacred inspiration which adds fire to your passion; then give something from your heart. In giving you will receive tenfold.

DIVINE RELATIONSHIPS

The distinguishing characteristic of this Passage is caring for others. Looking outside your Soul-self, you will see who else has joined your journey. Accompanying your beautiful woman's journey, sacred Others—a partner, a child, beloved friends—become your teachers. Because of the sensual and giving energy within your womb, this long journey through your 30s and 40s very often involves Mothering, whether you have none or if you have one or more children. Your most enduring teachers helped you come into this life, parents and grandparents. Among your teachers of choice, the ones you also hold sacred are your partners and your sisters. Slightly different than your experience as someone's Divine child, you and your friends and lovers teach one another. Hopefully, personal evolution enters your mind regularly: How do you become more human?

You gather your teachers in unity with your Soul. Offer care for these sacred Others in exchange for their love and lessons which reflect and inspire your trials: What did you come to learn, to do, to be?

Besides your great giving energy that nurtures your tribe, seek until you find intimacy and companionship. A few Others will hold your secrets and support your Genius: These Others will track your growth, and teach you more about wild Nature. The Divine energy of teaching and learning, of giving and receiving, supports your inclination to grow through your whole life.

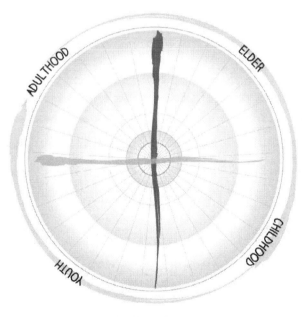

RELATIONSHIP
WHEEL

© 2016

Truly Divine, the sacred Others in your life bring you play and work, they bring the gift energies of sharing, guiding, inspiring, and the melodic laughter of joy. I have used the word "Divine" lavishly and intentionally.

Nearly every other Soul who crosses into your sphere will bring you a gift, a spiritual gift that you cannot source for yourself. I invite you to bow to these Divine gift-givers for their generosity. Notice how their stardust matches and how it differs from yours.

Learn to see your concentric circles: You, at the center, draw sustenance from the juice of these swirling energies—nurturance, learning, sharing, connecting—to discover more about the threads of your passion and exactly which of those threads lead to your purpose. The characters on stage with you will distract you or support you; at different moments, you may feel the power struggle of time and attention. Your animus, your natural masculine self who feels drawn to action, to doing in the world, is healthy if you see the energy as just one part of the whole of you. You do not imitate men and you receive your nurturance within your Divinely Feminine silence.

Whenever I deeply feel such struggles of power, I raise my own awareness by seeing into the dueling priorities. None of us do this well or even gracefully all the time. When yin and yang struggle, I am never in balance. Something must give way for my attention to return my focus to the energy of my passion.

POWER TO BE FREE

Try singing, "Freedom." This is your song, "Freedom." Declare yourself free of shackles: *Should* must go. The need for personal approval must evolve and every expectation turned inside out. Freedom is women's uphill struggle. Consider the vast implications of your personal freedom song.

FREEDOM SONG

Baby, you tell me this and that
How I ought to be;
Let me tell you what I think,
Don't lay your should on me.

© Janis Monaco Clark

Increase your awareness around another single word, power. In relationships, this incredibly large word, power, can elevate all of your connections once you understand, and with reverence, attend to its pure energy.

We joke about alpha males and alpha females. Put your attention there for just a moment, can you feel the attraction of this power? Respect for power—whether you have it, feel it, or observe it—makes relationships sacred. Helen Luke[6] speaks of humility which rises from the word and feeling of humus. We are of the Earth, receptive and nourishing. She wrote about women's aim for equality in *The Way of Woman*, with a corrective aim that at once elevates and preserves women's difference.

"If we are to stop the wreckage caused by the disorientation of women, by their losses of identity under the stresses of the new way, then the numinous meaning of the great challenge they face must break through from the unconscious; for no amount of rational analysis can bring healing."

Consciously sharing power, and as equals who acknowledge our differences, makes the jokes funnier, allows for the possibility of freedom, and causes relationships to rise to higher levels of love, compassion and personal growth. Return to the humus of your receptive nature.

When power offers beneficial empathy that feels equal, you thrive. Power also has a troublesome side. I would be correct in saying power has a historical reputation as a trouble-maker. I may even be correct in saying the dark side of power, which is control, has a personally historic context for 95% perhaps 100% of the women in the world. Women have all felt a controlling power over or through us. This deserves reflection. Power-over is oppressive, it shuts us down, it steals from us, and we run off the stage that is rightfully ours. Raise your awareness about oppression; it is a global epidemic and no woman is immune.

In relationships, do you strive for respect or control? You have learned about these two energies through all of your felt senses. Because of its attitude and its intention, when you feel power-over someone, the essence of that energy is control. To keep your children safe, you use control because you must. The other side of this power, the felt sense, is respect. Between your heart and your mind is an intersection. You have the emotional intelligence to know which of the many roles power plays in the theater of your life. The characters on your stage change over time. Parents have the main influence in childhood, peers and teachers throughout your adolescence. Woven in and around all of these influences, Nature and love both have starring roles. Consider what influences money and sex have in your relationships. Each one of these elements has a power and a spice component. If growth and enrichment are the driving forces through life, you will discover that power and spice make the going either smooth or not.

Consider that only you pull the puppet strings as you dance on this life stage. Many times in my life I would have laughed or even scoffed at this statement. Those were the times when I allowed someone else to have control over me; my choice was buried beneath my fear. I did not have the awareness to understand power as belonging to me, so I gave it away. If the squinty-eyed Elder in me teaches you nothing else to guide you through Deepening Womanhood, I wish it to be awareness about your personal power. I have deep experience in the theater of oppression so I know that women can wiggle out from beneath its force by understanding power.

Like leaves on a tree, review your many gifts.

One of the Geniuses I have studied in my desire to understand power is Riane Eisler.[7] I stand on her shoulders to offer up this distillation about relationships and power. Her work dives deep into the nuances and historical perspectives about the two sides of power, which she calls domination and partnership. I invite you to explore your personal history with power. These words alone may be self-explanatory. I gave my power away to men, then to corporations, then to fear. Look into your experiential memories for the energy that Riane Eisler calls domination. You may see something similar in your historical relationship with power. This is one of the clear differences between the genders. Go into your own stories, harvest what you have learned. When you become the sacred observer of your life's experiences, you will see how power influences your life. It's far deeper in influence than your partner, your parents and other relationships. Power plays its game through competition and can be especially difficult between friends. Look to employers, all levels of government, and power-plays between countries for a deeper understanding. In the many ways that power colors your story, you can wield it as a force for transformation. Women are never without personal power.

With you, I practice reverence and respect. This is the most Divine of all the personalities of power. I ask you to notice how power offers lessons into and out of your core. This third chakra is the inner core of you and your personal power center. For women especially, this place of power in your core draws your sense of balance closer to earthly power. I am endlessly fascinated how the inner energies interact; use personal respect to be your own witness. The interaction between your heart energies and your inner power center is always active, but not always conscious. How do you dance with these very unique inner energies, power and love?

Those who you pull into your inner circle receive your love and those farther out receive your Genius. Your stage may include the public sphere and the world sphere. You have a role to play in all these spheres and will recognize that role when your own people help you find your purpose. When you share a sacred cup of tea and a candle, you may feel compelled to turn the spotlight on your sister sitting beside you in support of her Genius. Allow her to shine the spotlight on your Genius; this is the respectful nature of power shared and the deepest beauty in relationships.

Consider that we all start out in the place of beginners, although our Soul is ancient. For most earthlings, we forget so we believe we know next to nothing. We learn by exploring, talking, and observing. Exactly what does your Soul know and how does remembering become a source of learning? From your inner realm, feel the spin of entelechy, your pure potential. Become the one who teaches all the sacred *Others* what you have learned about power, potential, and purpose. Respect for your relationships offers these 10,000 lessons on a shiny silver platter. Become an observer of power, inner and outer power. Meditate on your intuitive powers and all that your Soul does know.

ENERGY AND GIFT EXCHANGE

In this precious package you call self, something is always cooking in your energy field. You receive and hold a special capacity for balance in the juice flowing through your central energy channel. Take your understanding up a level, the yogini practices have focused on healing and spirituality through the parasympathetic nervous system. Every woman has capacities for healing others, there is no greater gift. Now that you have the benefit of maturity, your next action step will often involve others—cooperating, leading, and giving to others. Consider who needs your hand to lift them up.

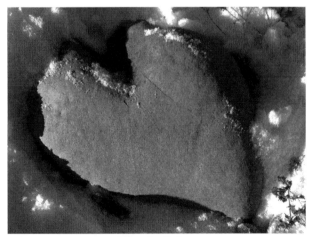

Heart for Giving

The natural energy of women, womb-energy, draws you deeper into generosity. When you give from your heart, in return you receive the golden sustenance, the energy you need to live. Your exchange might be for gift or for money, in every way, all of your giving feeds you. This one truth is worth discovering and practicing: Giving shines like light through a gemstone—all that you give heart-fully and without hooks or attachments comes back to you. Perhaps you will not recognize it or even trust this golden drop of truth until you try it out. Then, it becomes such a spiritual experience that you will find, like an Earth Mother, thousands of ways to express your gifts. Giving without expectation, giving without need of reciprocity, giving because it's your Soul-food, this is one of the simplest ways to discover sacred connections which build community.

Did you feel the twist? Here comes the Cosmic Coyote with her multiplication. First, you need to give intentionally to yourself; extreme self-care has its relationship to consciousness and survival. Then you expand to give to another, a sacred Other or others with whom you feel a special kinship. Turn by turn, you begin to feel the divine inner glow of relationships expressed among your family and your sisters because you learn the higher value of giving. In giving you receive, it's a spiritual law.

In this luminous, holistic capacity of Deepening Womanhood you find yourself sitting on the web of your own design. By your creation, you feel at home in your Village and you begin to pull the strings to draw people in. Because you feel the magic of giving, others feel it too. You discover this juice together, it's heart juice and deeply crimson. I call this the formula for Divine relationships: Giving with heart and opening your heart to receive. It's a gift exchange. This is the love that makes the world go around.

By your delightful modeling and generous sharing, a sense of trust begins to grow in your community. It happens when you play in the water and sit around the fire; it happens when you feel the air pass by your lips in song and story. You feel your family growing. The communal feeling that people share as vital members of a throbbing community spurs everyone to cultivate their gifts.

In this juice, celebrating Earth's creatures and communing with Nature become easier. You have moved through survival into a pulse of thriving and you like it. Your efforts and your action steps begin to return the dividends to you and your family. You begin to trust that everyone in the community who feels the recipient of your gifts will discover ways to surprise you in return. Elders have been teaching this gift-economy our whole lives, no one escapes our teachings.

This is illusory with a dream-like quality, this exchange of energies. Yet, I ask with all sincerity, who lives with you in your inner circle and the next layer out? Who gives you the juice of their life in exchange for yours? Connection with your family, with your community, and with deep Nature cause a satisfaction like no thrill can provide. Are you exploring and sharing your gifts?

Connection holds an opposite energy, disconnection, once explored in depth by Jean Baker Miller for women.[8] Since I studied with her, I have been the cultural observer—a student of disconnection in relationships. It's happened in my own relationships and seeing it seems to double the hurt. In a whisper of ego, a disconnection happens. Often an abrupt end to the flow of energy feels like a little tear in the fabric of a relationship. Words have invaded the culture, like busy and schedule. Such words tear at the heart of well bonded relationships. Soon, without repair, a fade begins, and your once cherished relationship enters a risky place. Will it survive or end? As members of the gift economy, women need to take responsibility for our sacred gifts of connection.

BE A CULTURE-MAKER FOR YOUR COMMUNITY

Earth Mother conspires like a Cosmic Coyote to offer seasons to celebrate. Some of the glue for thriving relationships and the communities of concentric circles, the idea of gift exchanges wraps around the Divine Masculine, those sacred *Others* we each hold dear every day. Come together for the eight special days when all earthlings feel a celebration rising. Many of these celebratory days came before the holiday calendars of our parents and grandparents. Once you see the beauty of this design, a quickening happens. Something truly irresistible ties women to men to children. Celebrating the Earth and her journey around the Sun is a warmly held reason for gathering, to have a potluck party and maybe even a bonfire.

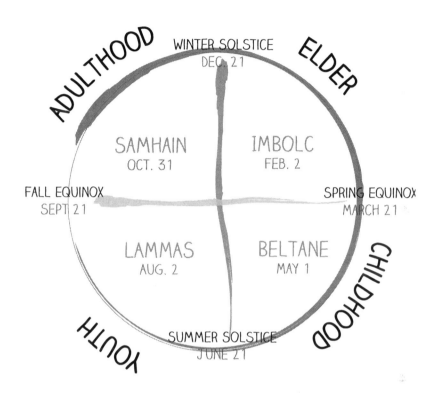

Change is a holy thing, and every year Earth Mother shows us the grace and joy in noticing. When you see change in yourself, you will begin to see how entelechy, the beauty of human potential, spins inside of everyone. Use your wise eyes to learn to see into those you love. The essence of community fills with divine passion and with an earthy spirituality that honors each other's Genius. Gatherings become the rituals for honoring community members in need of a ceremony marking their change. When the deep well of inspiration and clear sight reveal growth and maturity as the holy bond for communities, a shift will be certain.

The multifaceted strengths lying as hidden gems in your neighbors are waiting for you to discover them. These kindred spirits share love of place and many other things. In permaculture, these folks are known as friendlies, but they are so much more. When you feel the vibrancy of this web from your place on Earth, you will begin to feel the emergence of your special purpose also. The comfort of cultivated relationships will hold you when change comes into you. Gaia awaits the gifts we each have to give back. Allow your community to support your Genius.

In the world where half the women are Mothers and half are Aunties or Elders, the magic of building a community is having the support you need to express your purpose. You have experienced self-care so you understand the on-going nature of giving to yourself over your lifetime. Paying close attention to you is an ever evolving talent for regenerating your mind, body, and Soul-self. You have felt the heart of a girl-gang, your sisterhood, and have felt the many ways you throb together. You may have finally discovered the beauty of community festivals as the holy markers where women can see change as a deeper intimacy, as seeing into one another.

By flowing through one Passage and then another, you have become an active participant in your life. Sitting in silence to vision with the Moon, exploring and practicing the elements of Courage, you prepare yourself to take all the next steps. This is the time when your penetrating vision looks within and outside, shifts towards making the culture you want to live in. Leadership shows up for you and your friends. Please remember to ask for help before you find yourself alone with your vision.

In post-modern cultures like ours, we find it rather easy to deconstruct things, just like we were taught in high school biology. We are looking for the intersection of science and art; this may help you find your way to your greater purpose. When I say, find the art and science intersection, I am giving you permission to allow your imagination to run free, to explore these crossroads that have been strictly separated for more than 400 years. If you follow either the art or science thread, you will gather skill and polish those into a craft. Since the world's people thrive on creativity, examine where art crosses your science or vice versa.

Deconstructing and Reconstructing Self

Some people miss seeing their gifts altogether so they seem to always feel a quest in their hearts. What you love the most gives you the biggest clue. This is where to look for your purpose. Inside of what you love is a passion like no other, maybe two passions, maybe an art and a science providing enough fire for you to go deeper but never feel lost. You will actually find yourself; this is true passion and it needs something from you. This passion needs your faith, like a seed needs water and sunlight. Trust yourself—inside the very thing you would love to spend the rest of your life doing lives the very thing that you were born to bring to life for the rest of humanity.

Inside of this trust you might find a prayer worth repeating. Never be embarrassed to say, please God. This needs only be the God of your understanding, your Higher Power. We all have one, I actually have many. Sometimes my God is the huge Cottonwood tree that stops me in my tracks when I am thinking about my passion. This tree sometimes just sits me down and I must dream about what I love. Maybe she is channeling God, I don't care how it works. The Great Mystery conspires to help you and me through inspiration that feels just like magic juice. That feeling reminds me why I care. This is known in French as raison d'être, the thing most important or the reason for existing, now used in ordinary conversations as a cultural meme. Have faith in yourself and you will find your purpose.

Part of passion is prayer and part of prayer is trust. I want to return to that Cottonwood tree. Have you ever watched a tree grow from seed? I use this to demonstrate the patience you need to grow yourself and your purpose. Once a seed receives just the right amount of encouragement, like water and sunlight falling on Earth, two things happen: A root goes down and a shoot comes up. I can hardly express the miracle of a seed bursting, it seems like su-per-natural intelligence. You have such a seed inside of you. Under the right conditions, you will send down tiny little root hairs like feelers, testing the soil for nutrients. If you don't find the conditions right, you will crawl back inside your seed-shell and wait. You are waiting for the right conditions. Maybe you need to dream a bit more and use your imagination to discover the right in-gredients. Maybe you only need to talk and receive loving, willing reflections from neighbors and friends.

Like stardust hidden in your fingertips, all of the essential ingredients, pieces like patience and persistence, can be learned and practiced. Once you understand them, you will use them to design your life around passion and purpose. To deconstruct the parts and pieces of living, see how you have or may have a spiritual life, a practical life, a physical life, a married life, a sexy life, a creative life, a family life, a Village life, a dreamy and powerfully purposeful life. Which of these parts already belong to you?

Once again hold and behold your Soul question, who were you born to be and what were you born to do? Beneath your adolescent's mask you asked this sacred question: Now, crossing your Womanhood Bloom Threshold into Deepening Womanhood, Saturn brought this question back. Look deeply into these many different aspects of life rolled into one you. How do you fulfill your Soul's urgent request? How do you imagine your life story and shape it to serve you while you serve others? Can you find the spiritual opening to receive what you need—love, juice, nourishment—from the sacred Others in your life?

Emerge from the Darkness

MOODS AND THE AGE OF AWAKENING

Sometimes in equal doses, life is dark and light. Some days you're dancing in the cherries and another day you're in the pits. When life's path inserts a sudden curve, it may feel like darkness takes over. Let's look at moods, their sources, their power, and their magic. I will reveal my personal red-flags, gathered over the years of being a cultural lover and critical observer.

We all know moodiness; it became fully engaged in adolescence. Maybe you have literally felt the shifting of moods from light to dark, from positive to negative. These polarities rarely stay for long, mostly moods reside in an in-between territory. Look introspectively, look very carefully at your own sources. What causes your positive and negative moods? Do you have stories you will not share? Do they haunt you? How about the stories you treasure, some of them even make you giddy. Do you share those freely? On the outside: What bugs you? Can you fix it? Should you? Have you practiced the Serenity Prayer?

Serenity Prayer

God, grant me the wisdom
To accept the things I cannot change
The courage to change the things I can
And the wisdom to know the difference.

All around the world, women have found journaling to be useful because writing often surprises and leads to deeper self-knowledge. To wrap a cloak around moods, the culture has begun to sprout new fields of study—positive psychology, happiness coaching, emotional freedom techniques, emotional intelligence, mindfulness training, and an integration of all of these called interpersonal neurobiology. To these I would like to add personal observation. The over-culture has become too helpful, even offering too much advice. During times when our balance is off, sometime we do need guided spiritual and personal growth.

Remember always, your inner power grows stronger in silence. See for yourself if exploring, contemplation and meditation in Nature offers the kind of spiritual help that only needs silence and your attention.

To know your moods better, begin with a raw timeline and lay out your stories by year; put the positive ones above the line and the negative ones below the line. Your dance will show up when you walk with the New or Full Moon, moods up, moods down, up, down. This will be an exercise that leads to harvesting. Be patient enough with story to allow this richness to fill and satisfy you. No one is ever all one side of the line or the other.

My most enduring and eloquent teacher has been Clarissa Pinkola Estés.[9] I was sitting with Dr. E. when she said these words, ". . . we were made for these times. Yes. For years, we have been learning, practicing, been in training for and just waiting to meet on this exact plane of engagement."

In this fast changing culture, your spirit may be at risk of being crushed or fractured. Find just the right combination of personal practices that will weave you back together. Maybe movement and dance will dispel your despair and stimulate your intuition. You have dedicated hours to honing your skills and your gifts needed by this seemingly uncaring culture. This risk that I call fracturing is the reason I focus on your Moon practices to unearth your purpose.

We were all made for this 21st century, for this Age of Awakening. Thank you, dear teacher. Remember patience and persistence, we are all challenged to find what is ours alone.

I have been cynical about culture, the over-culture can truly be crushing. One example is how we think we can see right through advertising if we try. We must be powerfully vigilant to avoid the psychic influence of something we didn't know we needed or wanted. Advertising is one thing we can agree on, it's a red-flag. Be vigilant about personal advertising. The Internet thrives on the strong narcissistic thread of social media; learn to see it and use your vision to keep your selfhood and your sisterhood healthy.

Competition among women may be on the same dark side of culture. See the red-flag of this energy. What is it, why is it? Look inside your own ego and your own shadow; hopefully you can find and tame this demon in yourself. Do you compare? Do you need to keep up or 'best' your friends? Reach out to other women in the kindest and gentlest way you can. Talk through these questions. Competition is a felt sense and when its shadow appears, the energy feels like betrayal. Beware of comparative words; more than, better than. See these red-flags before they materialize into something unimaginably painful. I always say, "There is no peace in comparison." This reminds me to return to my heart's desire: Peace.

Sometimes our dark moods come when we simply speak criticism about our culture. I am so very guilty of this. I use care to not pass my cultural critiques down to the personal level. Shake your head in wonderment, dear Makers. As culture-makers, we still have the over-culture squeezing in around the edges of our very special communities. This is the Age of Awareness, what change do you wish to see? Practice kindness every day and know the picture is so big you can only see your little part. No personal criticisms please. It's much too hard to be a woman in this big over-culture. Positive feedback is always welcome, when it's kindly delivered.

Laziness is your welcome respite during your Moon and during any time you need to exhale. However, trust me when I say that deep laziness can lead into a darker hole and fester more negativity. If it's the dark you need, dive deep inside to discover what the darkness has to teach you. If you need to, let the darkness know you are searching for answers. Journeying is a method I wish to learn. Just a glimpse into Shamanic practices brings one little exercise for you: Imagine the darkness surrounding trees' roots. They are all connected below the ground by threads of fungus carrying and sharing nutrients. These connecting threads are mycelium interconnecting trees below the ground to one another. This is a freeing and healing image. I suggest that you make a symbiosis with mycelium. Honor your darkness, for there is richness to be harvested around the roots of yourself. Every woman knows this place. Only you can wake yourself up if your lazy mood is habit forming. We need you to rise up, we all need you and your gifts. If you need the darkness, then you do and no one is judging.

I invite you to see these other deeply feminine aspects that our culture so often judges. Because they are personal teachers, the final explorations of women's moods need to be harvested. I received much of this muck through relationships—moodiness, cynicism, competition, guilt, betrayal, criticism—and I have practiced laziness. Deep experience with suffering, alone in the darkness, now helps me see everything. Only when you are ready, the Earth is waiting for your gifts. I invite you to rise up to your fullest expression, like your balloon perpetually filling with helium.

By our example, yours and mine, those beloved women who make up our girl-gang will begin to use these pieces also becoming fully luscious culture-makers. We do need to vision the world of our making, together. You are fertile inside, when you increase your curiosity, you increase your awareness. What is yours alone to bring to the world? Mary Oliver developed her personal convergence with Nature and poetry, out there, with wild Nature.[10]

WILD GEESE

Whoever you are, no matter how lonely,
the world offers itself to your imagination,
calls to you like the wild geese, harsh and exciting
over and over announcing your place
in the family of things.

RESILIENCE

Watching a one-year old baby learn to navigate the world around her, I watch her stand up, fall down, sit down, and get back up again as perpetual motion serves her. This practice has gone on for days and weeks and months, her practice of resilience. I have seen this very same motion in pre-teens and teens. They seem to have curiosity in their hearts and sometimes their world explorations cause suffering. From the very heart of suffering, resilience is the practice of your Soul. Use the energy of hope and nourishment that this word offers, you have it in you from when you were a baby learning to navigate.

Face of Resilience

You've likely heard that all things begin with a thought. All things actually begin before the thought. All the inventive things the world needs begin in the sauciness of energy, in the earthy fire of the first three chakras.

Things may actually begin in stardust and the creativity of childhood when you were making forts and finding bugs under rocks; when you knew no limits and you were grandiose along with your friends. Your seeds of greatness were planted under the blankets behind the couch in make-believe and in mud puddles and staring at blades of grass where the tiniest of the insect world lives. Even if you feel your ideas now are too grandiose, like your inner 11 year-old's, they may in fact be your leading edge. Perhaps those seed ideas only need the green juice of affirmations and the willow-like strength and endurance honed from your inner resilience to fuel emerging passions.

To understand the very beginning of the audacity needed for greatness—wrap a ribbon around your incredible first mud pie and all the imaginative fantasies of your dreams. Inside you lives a fertile and receptive integrated energy system for passion. Just as you can dream with the same fluid boundaries of your child-self, you can also be assaulted by the floating memes in the over-culture to squash your dreams. At both ends of your capacities, where you know your Genius and where you doubt your Genius, you are especially vulnerable.

See how this works: Privately, you receive inspiration from who knows where; God and Goddess connect to your receptive self. You nurture this inspiration until something in you has made a thought out of it and it might become a thing. When you doubt or criticize your inspiration, using words like hard or outrageous, that over-culture meme which stops thoughts from becoming things, shreds your idea to bits. Does this make you feel vulnerable, as in weakened? Take heart. This is a place of opportunity. It may be a choice place—do you follow inspiration or the meme of doubt? Are you bold and courageous or worried about what someone might think? Do you see this as an opportunity to gain a deeper understanding of yourself? Remember these two things to help you decide: Mistakes or failures are sometimes the only way to learn how to move forward and the Earth needs your Genius. When doubt overcomes you, read or re-read Brené Brown's three books.[11]

From the quiet inside of your prayer and time in meditation, you may find your great idea. Rising to a sweet place of service to yourself, your family, and your community, maybe you need to nurture inspiration without self-imposed boundaries like supplies, money, assembly, time, or help. Have you accepted all these or other super-adult realities as personal limitations? What if they weren't there, what if you could source all of them? Do you have the kind of juicy passion that contains persistence in generous doses? Is your passion the kind with patience? Does it keep you awake or wake you up, have you prayed over it? Do you have faith in yourself and your idea? Well then, you see what I mean, people may call you crazy because you are so close to the leading edge. Your greatness, your Genius comes from your Soul; it's in you from the beginning of time. If you have molded your inspiration into a thought already, it may be holy, like this book you hold in your hands.

COMPETITION

Equisetum Arvens – Horsetail – Competing since the time of dinosaurs while standing in relationship

Exposing the evolutionary truth of competition, let's choose to understand it rather than practice it, I want to deconstruct where women learned competition: In women, this is the shadow expression of the inner Animus, the Divine Masculine.

Competition in sports teaches about physical possibilities and team-work. Competition between women is much more insidious, hidden, and often propagates deep feelings of shame. Many phrases are still part of the over-culture and have pushed every woman—win at all costs; there's a war out there; you are better than that; be first in your class; break through that glass ceiling—can you think of other phrases? Talk to yourself about this pattern of competition between women and talk to your friends. Talk, talk, talk. One of the antidotes to competition is now a cultural meme, be the change you wish to see in the world. Let's evolve competition so we can see it for what it is, the winner of one and the destroyer of the other.

Frankly, some of life's best lessons come through a darker lens. There is more power in your Genius than you realize, and that may feel like something to fear or run away from. Look back, sort through your experiences to find and use the power of your passion. Your path began with the work of your 20s, finding your firm foundation and knowing what you believe. Polish up your daily practices, work with prayers to your unseen God and Goddess. Discover all the ways and means to heal what prickles you. When you can be authentic with other women, your Soul expression, the Genius that wants so badly to emerge will find no more resistance.

ON MOTHERS

To honor Fern, thank you.

I write because of my Mother, and when I think of her I always say a prayer for her Soul. I was raised by a Mother who was different to me than to my three sisters. There was some karmic connection between my Mother and me that gave her permission to be over-powering and still feel safe enough to reveal her dark nature to me.

I write because of my Mother, to repair the breach between some Mothers and daughters. When I didn't get what I needed, or what I thought I needed from my Mother, I looked everywhere else before I circled back to understand what and why. I feel grateful for truth and validation; I feel compassion for the darkness my Mother carried. I feel relief that I have her genes and have located that over-large capacity in my Soul to carry more than is mine to carry. That is what she experienced too.

I write because of my Mother, she lived with such a void inside of her. Never was there an ounce of recognition for her Genius beyond being Mother to six of us and wife to an extraordinarily powerful man. I know she had a frustrated Genius because I was with her for two of her last three years on Earth. At the age of her Spiritual Elderhood, and especially her last 13 Moons, she finally quieted her demons and grace cloaked her. She left when she wanted to leave, on her own thought-wave.

I write because of my Mother, women have had it hard for centuries. For equality to mean anything, women's hardship must be dissolved. We can work together to empower ourselves, to hold our sisters' and friends' Genius up to the light. By searching, we will find ways to cast off what is not ours, like competition, petty criticisms, and judgments. These dark threads were born of cultures that have been toxic to women. They will dissolve when we applaud one another for pure courage and brilliant insights. This is the New Way for women; we can rise above our hardships by standing strong together and recognizing Genius in each other.

I write because of my Mother, and to change the culture that surrounds women. The most holy exchange between women is recognition. I wish to show myself to you as excitedly as if you were my BFF so that you will show yourself to me. After our sharing, you will receive Anne Lamott's three essential prayers: Help, Thanks, Wow! I promise.[12]

RESISTANCE

I am having a love affair with resistance and so can you. Whenever I have a grand idea, resistance is the director who shouts, "Cut!" I adore my ideas. We are culture-makers, you and I, taking care to create a home environment and a luscious community for ourselves and our dears. Satisfying your Soul is part of making culture. Weaving your inner world of passion and purpose, rise before dawn to find what is yours to do. If you go to bed just a bit earlier, the dreamy dawn time could be yours alone. All the rest of the day, create opportunities compatible with your outer journey.

Learn to recognize resistance as pure energy. Sometimes your spirit may sense that it's attached to a negative feeling; often the feeling is oppressive, and just as often that oppression is born from memories rather than what is true right now. That thread to the familiarity of your past is why it delivers a spark of recognition. Feel the jolt of resistance because its source is entirely inside of you. This energy may give you pause, sometimes for days. We call this procrastination. See it for what it is: Resistance puts on the breaks, creates the voice of doubt, behaves as a real stopper overlaid on your creative, inner Genius.[13]

If something wants to emerge, you have to love it and love your resistance to it. The trickster in resistance hovers over your head like an umbrella. On the other side of resistance, an entirely new level of your being waits to meet you. Usually, it's a higher level and with it, a felt sense that you have touched authentic Divinity by persevering on your own behalf. See and feel the oppressive thought, the feeling of resistance, and the love that pushes through as the Creator. God and Goddess are waiting for you to push through resistance and appreciate the grand sigh of relief. Feel a deep willingness to push through your energy centers, alchemy of will begins to merge with love when you reach for the next level. Your idea pushes through to a higher level; it works every time.

All your hard work puts you in touch with your core growing like a tree, gathering rings in the rains and casting shadows in the sun. You are both parts, small and scared, bold and dedicated, light and shadow. Feel the love dearly, it's in you, inviting you to feel every ounce of resistance, harassing you. Do not be stopped by yourself any longer. Have a secret love affair with resistance. Love always wins in the end. I pray that these words may be wisdom for you.

GRIEF AND REGRET

I deeply love the women who model this stage of development, filling its varied cobblestones with the deep imprints that have built their lives. A Threshold looms, Deepening Womanhood, one that deserves a ceremony fit for Elders-in-training, for those cobblestones beyond belong to the next phase of life. With all my heart, I believe Divine Feminine is wrapping her arms around all of us women of the 21st century.

Your two decades of Womanhood elongate from 30 to 50, so you may experience the fullness of being human as you ride the roller coaster of ups and downs. This ride often brings very real feelings of regret and grief. Among the more reflective of feelings is regret, which will move right on through when you recognize the choices you made were right at the time. Invite this idea of movement to help you. Although these feelings carry different energy charges, sometimes grief and regret accompany one another. If something happens that begins with regret and later ends up causing grief, use your friends and talk, continue reaching out. Write down your feelings, get help from an energy Medicine Woman, and find your way to relief, but not alone.

Grief over loss is an emotion of honoring, take the time to feel deeply. Go below the surface of your life and into your memories. Allow your thoughts and your body to feel the essence of slow time. All that ever was feels shattered and shaken. The deep grief of loss teaches all of us about impermanence and immortality. I have become philosophical about Death, it is the one event that no one avoids and every Death is a lesson for the rest of us. Death walks with us through every day. Grieve well, my daughter. This is my blessing.

Everything you have learned about yourself adds to your core strength; no one can take that self-knowledge away. If you feel regretful or grievous, slow all the way down until you can cope. If you have an unplanned dark-night-of-the-Soul, of course go deep enough into that darkness to feel the whole of it. Honor the darkness with your presence and your patience. If you are safe, stay with the darkness until you need the light more. If you are not safe, seek help and protection in your community.

BALANCE IS KEY

I am audacious enough to offer this Elder counsel: All you need is inside of you and no, that's not original from me. The Eagle's view offers a thrilling design for you to consider. In this slice of the Spiral of Life, the whole of your adulthood lays out before you. Beautiful events year after year will define you just as childhood and adolescence have done. As you design your life, you will grow ever stronger from experience but need to remain willow-like because twists of fate wrap around your destiny.

Locked inside the mystery of coincidence, synchronicity, and Soul contracts, you cannot know these twists ahead of time. All the rest, you have complete control over, where you sleep, work, and play, and whom you love.

Remain open to the spice that will come sweeping in or sneaking in, and give a nod to the Great Mystery when something surprises you. In a very long succession, all of the twists of fate in my life taught me to be adaptable, open, and watchful. In reflection I see that I was hardly ever quite ready when Coyote came calling.

Your life is not a total give away, but here is a question for you to consider: How can you improve life for another, several others or many others? You are privileged if you have pulled the pieces of your life—mind, body, and Soul—all together. After you have traveled this far with me, I ask you to keep up the good work, remember to acknowledge your gratitude, and gift yourself some special training once a year. I believe in reaching for the brass ring, what teacher do you need to experience next? How can you build on your experience to be of service to yourself and others simultaneously?

All women can perform miracles with the creative juice of our wombs, whether it's the actual miracle of making and rearing a baby or blending new juice with skills already in our quiver. Those with a particular energetic charge, do both! Soften all edges and blur your vision, sit in deep meditation on your Moon, and allow your imagination to seek out the art and science intersections where passion may be lying dormant. You have entered the power decades. If you are as lucky and as gifted as in your dreams, you will truly become yourself. That is no small task.

You may be inspired to do one little thing for peace and justice to help others focus on personal healing. In your way of visioning, watch your own influence ripple out like a pebble dropped in a still pond. If you can see how the word, *dysfunction*, first used in 1916, has grown and infiltrated families, organizations, and whole countries, then you can offer up prayers for healing and take one step of action.

In your lifetime, people will re-imagine and form mini-Villages. Many immigrant peoples who remember Village life now live among us in our mobile, melting pot. We do not have to reinvent the wheel to come together as

Villagers. From my home Village, I lived next door to teachers, post masters, and doctors. I grew up with the model. Within a bicycle ride, we had bankers, grocers, and every kind of farmer. I would like to re-activate those dormant genes that truly knew cooperative sufficiency. We can dream it into being. Even if we live in a high-rise apartment building, we have a common address with dozens of others. How can we become cooperative? Isn't that the elemental definition of a Village, feeling we belong because we cooperate, first by greeting one another, then finding more common threads?

THERE IS NO END, ONLY A CONTINUUM

You have an opportunity to see and live for your Soul-self. When you make listening to your Soul a conscious decision, your modeling will be seen, even felt, by all the other women, younger and older. It's all sensate, live with your Soul activated and feel fully alive. The Youngers will feel their own genes awaken and the Elders will sigh with joy and relief. As you collaborate with other women to build community, offer Rites of Passage to the little sisters, your personal reservoir will fill to the rim.

When you feel the irresistible energy that signals change, delivered through a catalyst, turn into that wind, it will blow for you. If you can imagine the next Threshold, it will appear out of the mist. Make preparations for a retreat, a personal ordeal, and a time away with yourself. Ask your loved ones to prepare a ceremony to welcome you back. They will do this for you and receive your journey story as well. May I personally welcome you across the Deepening Womanhood Threshold and into the mysterious and luscious training ground for your Elder Encore.

Consider a Death Ritual to transform this Life Stage and prepare for your Elder years

LAURA'S TRIPLE INITIATION STORY

Gail: In a rather anxious but daring moment, I took a draft of *Soul Stories*, to Laura Wahl's house to invite her to consider being the designer for the book. We had lived in the same town for years but we had not met before. She was sitting at the tiniest picnic table, I remember her Blue Heeler eyeing me suspiciously while I shifted from one foot to the other. I told her *Soul Stories* is a guidebook for a woman's journey to reclaim her Soul through her stories. I was really surprised by her response, I swear all the planets were in alignment. She said, "I want to do this!" which put me into shock at her clarity and immediacy. Simultaneity became our theme-song, mine and Laura's. I said, "Five other women, plus two in California, are crossing the Threshold next week, on Summer Solstice."

"Can I bring my girls?"

I had been zinged; perhaps the surprise was readable on my face. She stood up from the tiny table, gave me a generous hug and offered me a cup of tea.

"I love girls the most, how old are yours?" When my palpitating heart slowed down, I realized the Cosmos had blessed me with a new girlfriend and someone I truly needed. I had not known the power or emotional response of my book until Laura's honest reaction; I had secretly hoped for that. I had not known how writing had caused me isolation and Laura's genuine warmth covered all my holey needs with the sweetness of honey.

While we investigated our common threads, we found overlapping circles of friends and overlapping afflictions: We love through hugs and encouragement and example—Laura and I have each found the spirit inside of addiction. Together we have almost 60 years of sobriety, she has 34 years herself. She has literally been practicing life wisdom, intentionally increasing her consciousness, for all of her adult life. She faces the world with bluntness and fierceness while she lavishes love. Laura calls herself a party girl and when I'm around her, my definition for light takes on a clearer shine.

Her power cord gets plugged into recovery where she sees and feels the suffering of others, where she knows too well the powerful potential of addiction for destroying lives. From the inside, where her bone marrow is made, Laura has felt the deepest thrill of loving another suffering human being and watching their lights come back on.

Mother's Prayer to Carry Across Her Threshold

Laura: As a single mother with two girls, one entering high school and the other in elementary school, life sometimes felt 'out of my control.' Once upon a time I had fantasized about being a Mother and imparting to my girls all the "wise" lessons life had taught me. Reality was different. The years sped by. Work sucked up too many hours of each day, months, years.

I made mistakes. I was too demanding in the garden, insisting their rows be straight, that the seeds be placed just so, neither one will garden with me. I took them on hikes that were too strenuous and they whined; I put them on horses and they got scared.

And then I began to notice if I stepped back and allowed someone else to do the teaching and demanding my girls brought their accomplishments back to momma with pride. I needed to open my arms and let other women help me raise my girls.

So four years after separating, divorcing, and being on our own I noticed Mason (my oldest daughter) was attracting friends from similar backgrounds; broken families, with histories of addiction and denial among other things. How could I stir up the strength, empathy, compassion that I knew was in my girls? How could I reroute this energy before it got angry like my adolescence was...?

Into my world walks "little Gail," as we refer to her. Her first sell was about the healing transformation and discovery that initiation offered. Go through this process, connect girls to their Moontime, teach them ritual, become an Elder myself. Thank-you, little Gail, for entering our lives at the exact moment we needed you.

Gail: Laura gifted me the overwhelming power of affirmation. When I met her girls the following week, I saw how all of their threads connected and I saw something else. The girls are connected to Nature. There is something obvious about kids who are comfortable in the woods and around wild water like the torrential creek that runs through my play space. But, there is more: Mason and Sage are also fluent in the language of birds, in the purpose of spiders, and in wild weedy plant medicine. I am also, so I asked a couple of questions and began to deeply appreciate that Laura's kids have been raised knowing the conscious dialect of Mother Nature. Sage was 6 and Mason was13 then, but they were growing fast and I could see their changes coming.

Mason took all the photos for our Soul Sisters' Threshold crossing. This was participatory research for *Soul Stories*. Before we launched our guidebook for women's initiation, we needed to give it a test drive. On the beach, with my stone Spiral, I explained how the Sun and the seasons would mark our movement through each of the Passages we have already lived through. There are stories needing to be recalled, even healed, and bundled together before crossing each Threshold.

Introductions to the Spiral

Taking a moment to look around the circle, peering into the Souls who stood with me, a sense of pure love for women and girls was reflected back to me. Besides the girls, Laura had brought her partner Nancy to be an anchor for the journey ahead. I realized the Divine Feminine was present, digging her toes into the sand; I felt her energy. I have faith she is always present when women stand in ceremony offering our whole selves to regenerate Women's Ways of being and knowing. When we stand in ceremony, we trust Divine guidance. I also knew that three other women were elsewhere doing ceremony to be with us in spirit, to take this journey to recover the stories of their Soul.

We smudged each other with sage smoke. I smudged Sage, and made a joke about how her name covered all of the women with a blessing. Girls are welcome in my Women's Circles, I would like to say always, but that's not quite true. When women offer Circles for girls and raise girls with the ritual of sitting in a Circle, in quiet, waiting for their turn to hold the talking stick, the dynamics of consciousness will shift all around the planet.

Laura: Mason was going on 14, not very interested in my "old" boring friends sitting around a tipi doing "hippie" things. I asked her to participate as an artist and photographer for the day and she agreed. Once we got to Gail's for our opening ceremony, I saw it was time for me to step back and allow relationship to develop.

Shift to Sacred Time with Smudge

Mason and Sage both connected with Gail's dog, Rosie, and they watched Gail through veiled glances. Gail tempted and teased them with marvels from the garden, rocks from the creek, plants in the woods and she finally won Sage's wonder with a deck of Tarot cards and a book that explained things in words Sage, at 7 years old, had no way to comprehend, yet she was hooked.

The girls left Gail's, as became the habit, with treasures in their pockets and in their arms. And thus we all began our journeys, each on a separate path, all to a similar place.

Gail: In the following months, when I checked in with Laura, she would report that she had lagged and always, her sweetest smile followed. Her life is huge. She was getting what she needed and she was in immersion whether she kept up her journal or not. We moved around the life Spiral meeting regularly with another Soul Sister, Janis, because now we had become the book team and wanted to polish *Soul Stories* for publication. We met and talked and bonded through the journey and through the book project. We practice the way of women, all things simultaneously.

When Laura told me that Mason was going to do a Rites of Passage journey, I was thrilled. Suddenly there were two females in the same house involved with initiation rites. How sweet is that?

Mason came out to my place with a gift and asked me to be a Mentor

for her journey. I felt another jolt, an honoring filled with surprises, and without knowing more, I said, "Yes, of course." Women other than Mothers have special gifts for these budding young women we still call girls, they still call themselves girls, but the truth is emerging day by day. If we give them only time to talk, if we give them the blessing of listening, that is a huge gift.

She gave me the date for her ceremony and asked me to come. I said, "Wow, so fast." Then, I thought, What about womanhood training? That can come after. Mason at 14 was an eighth grader, bursting with energy to match her beauty. She knows a few of her gifts and is on an intentional discovery path to know more about her body and her Soul-self.

Feeling the Change

At the initiation ceremony for six teen girls, I was present as Mason's Mentor. Watching, I was impressed with the pomp and pageantry as these young women crossed back over their Threshold after being away together. To anchor their energy, the young women-becoming built an evergreen arbor as their ceremonial portal; they crossed through this Threshold for the community to witness. I saw each girl ducking a bit coming through the portal, it was like her prayer to Great Mother, a nod of an initiate's head. Yet, standing together, each girl felt the power of her accomplishment, she had finished. Let the celebration party begin!

I watched Laura and Mason together, absolutely the rarest spiritual experience in our culture, Mother and daughter going through Rites of Passages simultaneously. Because I have felt the special power of integration, I have been listening to and watching as Changing Woman does her secret work. The final step— formally known as reincorporation—requires a year, 13 Moons, before reflection illuminates the bridge of change. Reflection is an unusual trick, but looking back now to before, change becomes evident.

Initiates Addressing their Community

As a Mentor present for Mason at her ceremony, I was called on to give these six girls a final blessing. I cupped my hands into a clamshell and spoke of the pearl each girl would find inside herself, when she focused on her inner world. Of the six, I only knew Mason and briefly, but I could feel the magnitude of this message, each girl received a pearl image of herself. I opened my hands to each girl, showing her a metaphoric pearl. I felt it was what an initiating Elder needed to do for this young circle of darlings. My experience gives me privilege as a seer. I am certain such a ceremony invites change to become felt, even noticeable.

Laura: Once again I stepped back to be the Mother and allow someone else to work the miracle. On her own without any prodding Mason asked Gail to mentor her through her Rites of Passage (ROP) with the group she spends her summers and weekends with, Twin Eagles Wilderness program. At first she resisted involvement in her own ROP but was eventually swept into the current. Her words at her own emergence ceremony (after her initiation weekend) were wise and strong, She had found her strength, faced her fears and realized "together" they could endure and emerge. She was becoming the strong compassionate Soul I had sensed in the shadows.

She carried on into high school that fall with a new grace and understanding of who she was. Her friends have begun to change as she finds ways to reach out to other young women unafraid to reach outside her comfort zone.

Gail: Maybe it was the ceremony in the yurt, but soon Laura shared an epiphany with me. Sage's eighth birthday would come in August, she asked, "Is June too soon?" Once again, I could not resist my Guardian Angels bringing another invitation to me, to walk my talk.

I know this for sure: A Middle Child ceremony celebrates the change within childhood and adds an emphatic, so far. For a girl, when responsibility enters her desires, sometime between age 7 and 9, a ceremony prepares her psyche—her watchful Soul—for all of the coming ceremonies to celebrate her maturity. Built around play, a celebration is especially powerful when friends are present to witness and be celebrated too. A Women's Circle thrills the feminine psyches in their very young Souls, and they want more ceremony forever! Research indicates this Middle Child celebration is the ceremony that makes all the others possible.

When Laura asked me to help with Sage's ceremony, I was already inside the wonderment that had been created by Laura's initiation, followed by Mason's Rites of Passage ceremony and standing on my own consecutive Thresholds celebrating all the changes in my own life. I said, "Absolutely!" We were in ceremony together when she asked and we were working together to put *Soul Stories* together. Our own closing ceremony date had not even been set. "When, exactly?"

Six weeks before the girls' ceremony, our time came to step across the last of our Thresholds. Laura and Janis and I gathered to complete our year-long ritual with a celebration six Thresholds for Laura and seven for Janis and I. We joined our hearts together to close the portal and say prayers of encouragement for our other Soul Sisters. I had found my final Threshold in

February and eddied up until we gathered in early May. Waiting is one part of nourishment, like the Earth waits for rain.

Laura: My six Passages covered 9 months. From the beginning there was trepidation about the commitment. I had a full-time job, raising two girls, a partnership that often suffered from lack of quality time.

But I heard the promises of healing and felt the truth in what Gail offered and I wanted it.

So during the Passage phases I put pen to paper and wrote, not every day like she hoped but often enough that I worked through each phase, spending time with self, listening, telling stories. The biggest realization was that there was a new story here. I had heard my Mother's version of my birth, filled with her own disillusionment and feelings of being overwhelmed, but when I sat down and wrote my story, I wrote about the characters that surrounded me. It was a different story than the one I thought I knew. This was my story, filled with love and wonderment and I preferred it.

Each month I shared and listened to other women's stories. Each month we took an hour out of a Sunday morning, it wasn't hard. If I was home with the girls I went into my room with a candle. If I was out somewhere I found a quiet place to sit. After each talk I was warmed with a blanket of connection. Sometimes the women reached out to me with words of advice, encouragement and sometimes I had a kind word for someone else.

My sixth Passage caught me up to where I am in my life, at the beginning of Elder-ship. I can't say I feel confident in being a wise Elder, but I can see getting there one day.

One day one of the sisters in response to my share of recent heartbreak and loss said something to the essence of this:

"I envy that you were able to drop so many balls and fall so completely apart. It allowed you to change everything that wasn't right." She saw strength in my journey, not just loss, and slowly I began to roll that song into my own and learn to celebrate the growth not the loss.

An Elder's Meditation: Spiral Ceremony of Gratitude

SAGE'S MIDDLE CHILD INITIATION

Gail: The heat came early in June. I made this Spiral to express my gratitude for the New Moon in June, for the 360 days in ceremony with my Soul Sisters, and for the girls coming in a couple of weeks.

With barely a pause in all this swirling energy, we settled plans for the Middle Childhood event. Meeting once with the three Mothers, we dreamed drama into the plans to make a big story for three little girls. Sage invited two of her friends to share this day with her so they could enjoy their own spotlight. Each ceremony takes its own form, but special to Middle Childhood is play and Mother-daughter time.

Let's Play!

The Sun baked the Earth at the end of June, 2015. Keeping to the ritual form, I welcomed three beautiful little Initiates and their Mothers. Arrangements had been made for other responsibilities and the pause button was pushed on their busy lives for two whole days. They offloaded their gear inside the tipi poles, minus the cover. Then, with just a little orientation to the land, I introduced my husband, Kenny, and my dog, Rosie.

We always open to play first. Everyone changed into swimsuits and headed for the water. Ordinarily, late June is pretty high water, but danger had passed, peak water and heat had come early, so the water was Sun-warmed. Girls know about play and help women remember.

The next day was reserved for ceremony. This all-play day sets the stage for togetherness, for the pure spirit of play to be part of the story, and for bonding the women and the girls. Since the girls were friend of Sage, the Mothers were long-time friends with Laura. This is the nature of close communities. They would be there to help one another throughout the next year.

On ceremony day, the mood changed. We made relations with all others who come to stand in celebration of the girls. We gathered around brunch the next morning to meet Grandparents and other best relations.

Before the high heat of the day, I led the group through the woods to the beach to stand in ceremony and cross the girls over their Threshold. We passed the smudge bowl. Out in the open, standing on the sandy bluff over the creek, there was no place for refuge from the searing heat and perspiration began to drip. Nature was cooperating in her way, the atmosphere felt immediate, everyone's energy was altered.

I felt the feminine spirit of change envelop the witnesses and each young girl. Saying words that would not be remembered, I was intentionally formal, delaying our rush back to a cool sanctuary. I thought of how the Mothers and daughters would remember this feeling and would remember the spirit revealed through long moments under the hot Sun. We were each like our standing friends, rooted to the Earth and absorbing love from our day star until we were almost cooked. I knew the heat would be remembered and I hoped the spirit of the moment would be easily recalled. I dearly love to watch the faces of each girl because when the spotlight is solely on them, something begins to shift. It's subtle, but their inner light takes on a new glow.

Initiates on their Middle Child Threshold

When I looked around to the faces of Laura and Mason, I was met with dazzling smiles and the force hit me. Three Souls journeying through life together, Mother and two daughters wrapped with the same gossamer threads to celebrate how living brings change and change invites maturity. To be fully wrapped into the weave where Soul announces a new level of maturity, each one of us only need to have our lives celebrated when change appears. This is the value of ritual.

A LITTLE CATCHING UP FOR THE ADULTS

Nancy and Mason took the girls away for some solo play while I gathered the adults in my 'cool tea room.' Setting the stage for memories to emerge, we rearranged the altar and lit the candles. Nine adults passed the talking stick for one question that seems small but lives large inside, "Can you tell your story of you at 8 and how you were greeted by change?" This question causes spontaneous engagement. Unexpectedly, strangers hear intimate stories of change. Listening to each other, we appreciated on a deep, Soul level, what this ceremony means to those three girls.

As culture-makers, women are on the leading edge of offering Rites of Passage to young and old alike. This edge is where people are just beginning to recognize the significance of Rites of Passage. This edge of a cultural paradigm shift believes in marking change. Early in this new century, many Nature connection and related organizations are offering Rites of Passage for youth only. I remind myself, this is an edge, like Nature's ecotone, the zone where two well defined and differentiated ecosystems meet and blend. The ecotone represents the best parts of both and creates a unique and sacred third ecosystem. On one side, the uncelebrated, on the other side religious offerings like communion and bat mitzvah. In the middle zone is the ecotone,[14] where ceremony thrives and is beginning to grow into the culture. Just look at Laura's story, imagine the holy way spirit moved through her to create this story for herself and her girls.

Laura: The younger Middle Child ceremony took me outside my comfort zone, as I wove generations and families together. My family who live in the midwest and miss so much of day-to-day of our lives were invited to join in the ceremonies. I wanted this connection for my girls. And like my family does, they rallied. We built our summer vacation around Sage's closing day of her two-day ceremony and Mason's "Give," six months after her ROP ceremony as a gratitude dinner. Not until I was making the final itineraries of who goes where at what time did I realize how much each of us would have to bend. Things we take for granted like walking to the creek, sitting in a Circle, smudging each other, passing a talking stick and then presenting a dinner for over 20 people became a rather huge mountain of logistics.

The temperature heated up to over 100°, my Mother was immobilized by a foot injury, my 84 year-old Father and my urban executive sister would be asked to sit in a Women's Circle in a half day ceremony. Nancy and Mason along with cousin Alexander from Chicago would be asked to take the three little girls for part of their day into the woods. I realized too late how far out of everyone's comfort zone this was. But like troopers they all showed up because I asked them to. These two days were not about me or them but being a momentous part of my girls' lives; it was a lot to ask; perhaps it was good that I hadn't been discouraged by how much or I wouldn't have asked.

In the end, we all enjoyed a fine meal of salmon and the three young girls and their Mothers all beamed at such attention lavished upon them. For a moment in each of their lives they were special and valued and loved. The connection between Mothers and daughters were woven and strengthened. Each girl, voicing gratitude, at eight years old! **Proud Momma.**

MASON'S "GIVE"

As a sort of conclusion, Mason's ROP included a "Give" as in a give-back gratitude meal to her family and friends. We waited until my family was here for a week to pull it together. Mason drew up the menu, helped prepare and served each guest. Her Grandparents, her Mentor Gail, as well as her

Mentor Jeanine from Twin Eagles, my partner Nancy, her brother Autry, sister Sage, and Mason's Aunt and cousin Alex.

After dinner, without giving details of her Rites of Passage, Mason told her story and what it meant to her. She had gifts for all involved.

It was a moment of pure gratitude and appreciation. I smile as I think of the courage it takes for a young girl to stand and address a crowd of peers (siblings and cousins) and Elders. I smile at the awkwardness that will not remain as she finds her voice. I felt in my heart it was just the beginning of the emergence of the young woman to be. **Proud Momma.**

The Inner Beauty of an Initiated Woman

Gail: To celebrate change and spiritual maturity, Laura knew that each daughter needed to be pulled out of their mundane, ordinary lives and placed in a sacred container for a time away. This was their Threshold time. Such time away in Rites of Passage ceremonies may be hours or days; if the ceremony is carefully done, all that is offered to the feminine can be interpreted symbolically so she may be imprinted by her own story. Each initiation will complete itself in the 13

Moons that follow. The ecotone becomes more holy over time.

Now Laura knows the value of initiations for women and Rites for girls. She has lived with change for the full round of 13 Moons, watched herself and her girls, watched the spirit that moves through a family unit, bonded in ceremony. The change is more than noticeable, woven into their conversations, it is welcomed and remembered. There is more change ahead for Laura, for Mason, and for Sage.

I like to notice and write about women who hear the call and take action. My friend Laura was a quick study. After a full year, all three females in the house had Initiated to themselves, transformed, and felt the joy of change as a welcome companion. Each journey was individual, unique, and very beautiful.

Viva la difference, Laura, you are an Initiated woman, and now a baby Elder! As an Initiated Elder myself, I say to anyone who asks, transformation isn't easy, but neither is resistance. She is called Changing Woman for a reason. A Rites of Passage ceremony smooths out fear of change and erases resistance.

Laura: Gail's gentle prodding, pushed me to eek out a little time for me, for my journey and my healing. Both of my girls have their own journeys; I am not soley responsible for them but I can guide, I can praise and I can provide a way for them. My load is lighter today as I learn to share it with other women, but maybe it's also because I have become stronger. I have found joy and laughter in these Circles. It was beautiful to wrap the lives of Sage's friends and their Mothers, my dearest friends into this journey. It's fun to grab the girls and head out for an adventure. They are friends, it's something they are sure of. Not everyone gets that at 8 years old.

GIFTS FROM THE ELDERS: DEEPENING WOMANHOOD

Consider the common thread to all of womanhood: We are daughters first, sisters often, and we continue to grow into the roles of wives, partners, Mothers, and culture-makers.

You talk to understand how you feel, what you stand for, why it matters, and how you can make a difference.

* Your original effort may have been filled with hesitation; this advanced effort to discover how much more of your authentic brilliance may be filled with endless delight.

* As the power of your passion is revealed, take the action steps to build your life in an inspired way.

Discover your inner Nature and your wild Nature. Women do not keep this secret, wild Earth is our collective source for great inspirations.

* You gather your teachers in unity with your Soul. Offer care for these sacred *Others* in exchange for their love and lessons which reflect and inspire your trials: What did you come to learn, to do, to be?

Try singing, "Freedom." This is your song, "Freedom." Declare yourself free of shackles: *Shoulds* must go. The need for personal approval must evolve; see how every expectation can be turned inside out. Freedom is women's uphill struggle. Consider the vast implications of your personal freedom song.

Respect for power—whether you have it, feel it, or observe it—makes relationships Divine. Shared power causes relationships to rise to higher levels of love, compassion and personal growth. Put your attention there for just a moment:

* Can you feel the attraction of power?

* In relationships, do you strive for respect or control?

✳ Consider what influences money and sex have in your relationships.

If the squinty-eyed Elder in me teaches you nothing else to guide you through Deepening Womanhood, I wish it to be awareness about your personal power: With you, I practice reverence and respect. This is the most Divine of all the personalities of power.

✳ Giving without expectation, giving without need of reciprocity, giving because it's your Soul-food, this is one of the simplest ways to build community. In giving you receive, it's a spiritual law.

You begin to trust that everyone in the community who feels the recipient of your gifts will discover ways to surprise you in return. Elders have been teaching this gift-economy our whole lives, no one escapes our teachings.

By flowing through one Passage and then another, you have become an active participant in your life. We are looking for the intersection of science and art; this may help you find your way to your greater purpose. What you love the most gives you the biggest clue. Have faith in yourself and you will find your purpose.

Like stardust hidden in your fingertips, all of the essential ingredients, pieces like patience and persistence, can be learned and practiced.

Look deeply into these many different aspects of life rolled into one you.

✳ How do you fulfill your Soul's urgent request?

✳ How do you imagine your life story and shape it to serve you while you serve others?

✳ Can you find the spiritual opening to receive what you need—love, juice, nourishment—from the sacred *Others* in your life?

✳ Look into your stories to discover what is there for you.

✳ What causes your positive and negative moods?

✳ Do you have stories you will not share? Do they haunt you?

✳ How about the stories you treasure, some of them even make you giddy. Do you share those freely?

Mistakes or failures are sometimes the only way to learn how to move forward and the Earth needs your Genius.

Do you have the kind of juicy passion that contains persistence in generous doses?

✳ Is your passion the kind with patience?

✳ Does it keep you awake or wake you up, have you prayed over it?

✳ Do you have faith in yourself and your idea?

✳ Freedom: Power | Control vs. Power | Respect

Increase your awareness around power. In relationships, this incredibly large word, power, can elevate all of your connections. First, you must understand power and with reverence, attend to its pure energy. We joke about alpha males and alpha females. Put your attention there for just a moment, can you feel the attraction of this power? Respect for power—whether you have it, feel it, or observe it—makes relationships sacred. If you feel bound, limited, or small, you may need to ask for help to relieve your oppression.

Shared power, consciously and as equals, makes the jokes funnier, allows for the possibility of freedom, and causes relationships to rise to higher levels of love, compassion and personal growth. If you are emerging from a cloud of oppression, find comfort in starting again. In *The Power of Partnership*, Riane Eisler provided comfort when I needed to understand power.

CLOSING BLESSING

After you have traveled this far, I ask you to keep up the good work, remember to acknowledge your gratitude, and gift yourself some special training once a year. What teacher do you need to experience next? How can you build on your experience to be of service to yourself and others simultaneously?

Choose your battles carefully, but choose one. This may be your Gift for Gaia. These top women's issues listed by MsFoundation.org may include an opportunity for you to express your gifts and heal dysfunction. What are your top issues?

- End child sexual abuse because it's the worst form of abuse imaginable

- End domestic violence because we are all related

- Work for immigration because most immigrants are women with children

- Work for reproductive rights for women because choice is so precious

- Work for equal pay for women which has inched up from 56% to 77% in my lifetime

- Work for affordable child care because Mothers' struggle builds the future

Your Village needs this conversation and demonstration of courage. Everyone you know and love needs to feel the freedom of their imaginations.

NOTES FROM DEEPENING WOMANHOOD

1   *Moon Mysteries: Reclaiming Women's Menstrual Wisdom, A 13 Month Journey with the Cycling Moon* (2010) is a reference for women of all ages and for Moontime rituals. I have high praise for the creators, Nao Sims, Nikiah Seeds, and Eyan Myers because I learn something new with each reading. On the book's website, they offer abundant generosity and celebration: http://www.moonmysteries.com/moon-cycle-chart

2   I owe so much to women who helped me mature, but I must begin with Judy Grahn. By the time I picked up her opus, *Blood, Bread, and Roses: How Menstruation Created the World* (1993), the historical basis for women's mysteries, I had already shed 350 eggs. Many women experienced this same oversight; we were raised without a woman-centered origin story. We can correct this with the generations alive right now, our daughters and the daughters of our friends.

3   I give thanks to Lucy H. Pearce for her fearless presentation of Moontime. She opens the conversation to the sacred mystery of our wombs. She writes about women and Moontime. Find her imprint and her remarkable books to share with Youngers here, Womancraft Publishing. http://www.womancraftpublishing.com/

4   Influences to feed your transformative fire: *Gift from the Sea* (1955) is a woman's journey to herself. Even for the briefest time a retreat is restorative as demonstrated by Anne Morrow Lindbergh. Silence reminds us of the value of silence. Shakti Gawain wrote several books that began to open me, *Creative Visualization* (1995) and *Living in the Light: A Guide to Personal and Planetary Transformation* (1998). I accepted these books as gifts from my great friend, Diana, who taught me that women influence one another with love, love of life and sharing.

5   Rachel Hertogs guides women and girls in ritual. Ceaselessly energetic and living off the grid in Wales, she runs a little online store for every woman's Moontime needs, including pads for bleeding and pads for incontinence, an Earth conscious way to fall in love with your yoni. Her website shows cloth pads hanging on the clothes line, soaking up the sun. How natural and beautiful, shifting the paradigm for all women! (http://www.moontimes.co.uk/)

6   Women are so often pulled between being and doing, the feminine and the masculine. Helen M. Luke's *The Way of Woman: Awakening the Perennial Feminine* (1995), guides women to a deeper contemplation of our feminine nature by celebrating our worth.

7   Riane Eisler the writer who, through *The Chalice and the Blade: Our History, Our Future* (1987) brought women powerful images of Paleolithic and Neolithic times before women were so widely oppressed, also wrote *The Power of Partnership: Seven Relationships that Will Change Your Life*, (2002). Partnership is portrayed as the alternative to domination, which leads to oppression. She has turned the relationship power game inside out so conversations of healing can begin.

8   Groundbreaking then and now, Jean Baker Miller wrote for the hearts of women about our delicate relationships, how to deepen connection and how to weather storms of emotional trauma to remain connected, and what to lookout for that may yield disconnection and engage in repairs. All of this is unraveled in *Toward a New Psychology of Women* (1976). For hours of exploration about women-centered research, http://www.jbmti.org/

9   I mention Clarissa Pinkola Estés again because I cannot resist the delightful way her teachings

appear. Find all of her books and audios at your library or at www.soundstrue.com

10 Mary Oliver is one of many poets who interpret the language of Nature, women love that she speaks into our hearts through the familiar second person, and cheers us on at the end. This is an excerpt from Wild Geese found in *Dream Work*, her 1986 collection of poems.

11 Brené Brown, a graduate professor in Social Work from the University of Houston, has changed the face of shame, vulnerability, worthiness, courage, and showing yourself to your community. Backed by amazing research, she continues to publish her discoveries in consumable form. *The Gifts of Imperfection* (2010); Daring Greatly (2015) both meant for self-discovery and *Rising Strong* (2015) brings the conversation into the wider spheres where life revolves around others—home, work, church, and community service.

12 Anne Lamott is a writer's dream coach. *Bird by Bird: Some Instructions on Writing and Life* has been a classic since it was published in 1995. When I read *Help, Thanks, Wow: The Three Essential Prayers* (2012) I realized how these prayers connect all women, to ourselves and our Mothers, and everywhere, all around the world, to one other.

13 I felt *resistance* for years and only began to recognize it as procrastination, then as hesitation, as fear, and as avoidance of my life's joy. Then I read Stephen Pressfield's *The War of Art: Winning the Inner Creative Battle* (2002). My love affair with resistance had already begun and I found ecstasy in this easy solution: See, embrace, and vanquish resistance.

14 We are all trackers through our Ancestral lineage. Since one of my main influences in developmental thought and human ecology was Paul Shepard, I have kept track of his wife. Florence Krall Shepard introduced me to *Ecotone: Wayfaring on the Edges* (1994) when I was lost in grief and needed to know that I was investigating an edge ecosystem. Grief and Earth offered me a doorway. Walking in silence has become a deep practice. Her newest book, *Sometimes Creek: A Wyoming Memoir* (2012) is written in the genre of a Spiritual Elder's legacy.

ELDER ENCORE

THE INTENTION:
UNDERSTANDING PERSONAL WISDOM TRADITION

Life has trained you well, my friends; the juicy-saucy Threshold I call Elder En-core is far ahead, the first of your two Elder Thresholds. You have only entered the training ground and do not yet need to think of Elder except to wrap your arms around one of us. We probably have a gift for you. In this lovely space just across the Threshold of middle adulthood, your ambitions have been filled and redefined, children are still growing, often ready to leave home, or long gone. The force of women who never had children has grown in power over the past decades and all women agree, women's experience is complete without children. Do not buy into negative stereotypes for another minute: Those sayings—over the hill or on the downhill slide—are passé. Do not worry about getting older. No woman is truly old until her last 13 Moons.

I want to believe you took that mighty big leap of faith across the Deepening Womanhood Threshold and celebrated with a quietly raucous affair. Eddy up, find the still waters where no river current or fast waters can reach you. Remain quiet enough to allow your sleep-time to integrate all the changes you have invited. This will take a year of Moons, a time for exhaling and for reflecting. Those twenty years of adulthood held all of life and delivered so many opportunities to grow: Desire and motivation, accomplishment, adventure, children, crisis, sex, love, birth, death, and rebirth. What could possibly be ahead? The answers are as varied as women, completely individuated, and gorgeously evolved: Spiritual practices, revolution, peacemaking and forgiveness, food, movement and body work, spirit and consciousness, peace and justice, and cultivating your inner Divine Feminine.

THE EAGLE'S VIEW

Throughout all of life, your evolutionary journey towards destiny has blended your heart's desires—intentions, luck, and synchronicity—with determination including sweat and clairvoyance. Maybe your Soul planned all the events of your life to happen the way they did. Your accumulated experience of the earthly and celestial realms has developed your beliefs. You know with some certainty which parts of new age and old age philosophy belong in your worldview. Isn't it sweet that everyone's viewpoint is unique?

If we could shatter a point of light into its energy parts, the Divine or Source connection would be obvious, all light leads to and from the center. Human creativity would also be illuminated. Every earthly thing, material and spiritual, relational and emotional, has intricately woven into your energetic and evolutionary process and shaped you. Your relationships, your family, your home and décor, everything on your resumé and all of your adventures combine to weave your desire and determination into something. Please look around you, look within too. Now is the time to take stock.

Your middle years, the decade of your 50's, may be capped by a croning because these ceremonies, celebratory women's gatherings, are fun. Like a birthday, you can accept the spotlight for one day and night to feel the power of the Maiden-Mother-Crone archetypal energies and how those appeared for you. Stretch your croning to a weeklong celebration if that feels right.

Include Flowers for Points of View, Points of Light

Reminiscing is nostalgic. These energies are real. When you look within and without, see that you and all women are more differentiated than similar. How will you mark your place in time?

Consider this coincidence: Our medical advantage predicts decades of health and vitality will elongate both life stages ahead, Elder Encore and Spiritual Elder. I believe the elongation affects both stages of adulthood also. We simply live in a time unlike any other. To be born into this time and with such possibilities has layers of potentiality.

Half way to anywhere is a belief. Let's make an agreement with the Universe that the best of life is ahead. Life is about beliefs and how your emotions show up in your body. Are you learning how your heart guides your mind? Each thought is powerful. You are a supreme and evolutionary distiller of knowledge and experience. So much has been discovered about the brain's capacity, all of us absorb much more than we can use. I am really talking about Soul capacity. When I wrote *Soul Stories: Nine Passages of Initiation*, I adapted a concept that rose from my Women's Circle called double-tracking.[1] I have learned that this has scientific merit. We know this spiritually, but now the concept of time-binding has offered validation.

The theory of time-binding goes in simultaneous directions through time. The entire life-work of Alfred Korzybsky[2] weaves science in and through the semantics of time to demystify how knowledge accumulates and is passed along from one generation to the next. Relationally, you with your Soul-self have an innate capacity unique to the triune brain of humans. This gift of evolution means people learn from experience, especially mistakes.

Triune Brain Theory

Lizard Brain	Mammal Brain	Human Brain
Brain stem & cerebelum	Limbic System	Neocortex
Fight or flight	Emotions, memories, habits	Language, abstract thought, imagination, consciousness
Autopilot	Decisions	Reasons, rationalizes

The Triune Brain in Evolution, Paul MacLean, 1960

One Tiny Glimpse is Enough

With your miraculous brain,[3] and across the timeline of your days, you were born with the ability to grasp the past, present, and peer into the future nearly simultaneously. You are the recipient of parental influences and ancestral traits. Your Ancestors have gifted knowledge, mannerisms, and wisdom directly to you from their life experiences. Generously, if they applied the Golden Rule to all relationships, it will seem most natural to you. Other habits you may have to work through since you will be Ancestor one day, passing along traits bound in time.

Watch this compounding: Throughout our lives we learn from everyone we come in contact with and we learn from everyone who shares their special knowledge and wisdom, as in literature, music, and specialized crafts. Much more complex than all this first appears, each person inherits all of the knowledge that has gone before, recorded as well as cultural. An expansive worldview surely, it is still much larger. Each Soul has the capacity to bring influences of past lives into the present and influence the future. When you understand your timeline for gathering your legacy, somewhere along the accumulation of days you will wonder truly, how you know all that you do know.

I invite you to consider your Soul as the next great teacher in your life! How do you harvest your Soul's gemstones? Gathering your stories, intentionally drawing in learning, will prepare you for the Threshold ahead. Now you understand why silence is so important.

REST ON YOUR LAURELS

Perhaps this is the year to "rest on your laurels," as my Mother used to say. Even the most brilliant mind and body needs rest to locate the spiritual side of living. Locate your Soul in the midst of this swirl. Dive deep into inquiry, give yourself this extraordinary gift. Then take time to *integrate*, a holy transformation of Mind-Body-Soul connecting the past to the future.

Before you receive the call to initiate as an Elder, careful navigation of the years ahead will prepare you to embrace your Elder Encore. This is the time, while you are still a baby Elder, to recognize your mortality and take the blinders off denial. As surely as we are born to this world we will pass from this world. Death is ahead as surely as it walks with each one of us through every day of our lives. You were born with a purpose, maybe a different energy for each Passage. Search for still hidden gifts, you have something more to offer, something great. What is it you must do and only you can do? This is the time to set yourself up for that one big thing you came to do or say, write or paint, build or develop, while your burning desire still radiates heat.

What could this mean, set yourself up? In preparation for the next giant Threshold, each woman takes a personal inventory. This means, harvest your personal sparks of joy from the story of your life. Like almost every woman, you have had peak moments, lofty memory places where you touched the Divine. What energy still lives in you to share with others? This is called Encore for a reason you have yet to discover.

Carefully inspect life-lessons unique to you; each offered something in contrast to your joy-filled peaks. I often refer to the contrasts as troughs. Find your gratitude for these times of trial, moments of loss and grief, and times when you have spun your spiral of life down to learn from your shadow side. We all learn so much during a lifetime, in the light or through shadow. I find my deepest gratitude in the contrast. Can you truly know one without the other?

Looking Back to Womanhood Bloom and Ahead to Spiritual Elder

Women who are Mothers often will begin reflections through their womb creations. What did your children teach you? All women agree that the ecstasy of birthing another human being goes beyond imagination and into the realm of miraculous. Think of all the Passages that have come along as change agents for yourself and your children: Weddings, births, divorces, graduations, these are the mini-Passages and unique to each woman's story. Nine life-stage Passages including this 7th one, your Elder Threshold create the common threads that connect all women.

After deep introspection, I see how the initiations that I have experienced combine with those I have led; both bring me to a broad consciousness about the Village. The original fracturing of the Village concept happened when people gained mobility to move long distances. In 1878, my own Great Grandparents spanned oceans and continents.

When we adopt Rites of Passage as a life affirming system to see one another, then we will reclaim the adhesion to form our Villages with strength enough that they will retain their shape. Rituals are that powerful and when they are personal, and inclusive of every person all around the Life Spiral, then true connection will begin to repair the culture.

I have become an adopting Grandmother which compliments my Elder years. My arms spread wide like wings for children of every age to fly under for a time. I understand the future of the dream we all call tribe or Village includes and extends beyond our families. Our collective future depends on Elders helping to hold it all together for the Mothers who want our help. This is the time when your Encore may touch many lives.

Because I am without children, I embrace a large number of dear women friends who have also had no children. Perhaps you are one of us. We love the capacity of mothering; it just was not our path. Without children, we may have missed the ecstatic experience of birthing and the joy of raising a child or several, but there are always children to care for when we find our capacities to help Mothers. Every Mother appreciates help!

Weaving these pieces together, Elders who know themselves through initiation will become the whispering ones. We are the ones who see the Eagle's View first because we have finished with careers and intense domestic duties that consumed so much time. We begin with ourselves, then our closest family members, whispering how memories are formed, how imprints matter, indeed how personal stories matter. We understand, even if vaguely, how the Ancestors influenced our path. This, naturally, includes relations and teachers who have shaped us so that we may see to be useful to others. Our whispering includes practicing and sharing our rituals, this is where Elders will have so much impact for the future of the Village. We may even find our way into Circles of Clan Mothers.

Metaphorical Heart of the Village

Including both vantage points, bearing and non-child bearing, women create the heart of the Village around the children. If we are out in the workplace, improving our life and others', the youngest generation is often at the heart of our work or in our thoughts, benefiting from our actions. At every edge of our society, the concepts of patriarchy, which has kept women bound, are beginning to crumble like a cookie without enough binder. This is thanks to every woman for her daily efforts.

YOUR GREATEST GIFT

When women reach a certain age, time becomes demystified, it simply moves at lightning speed. Since I have lived about 24,000 days, I have come to see time as the gift of an Earth walk. Every day that same gift is repeated, exactly and precisely the same. I have learned that there are two times of day, the filling times and the emptying times. To be effective, you honor your special rhythm. Even without the language of biorhythms, you know when you are able to operate at optimum. Those are filling times. The emptying times include sleep, but may also include reading and journaling, and all of your story-time.

In this wonderful blend of rhythms, live morning-doves and night-owls. You have come to know your Moon rhythms and how you feel in the cycles of New Moon and Full Moon and back. You also know your most and least favorite season. Rhythm is your personal instinct for survival; we cannot all be the same. As a youth or even as an adult, rhythms and their boundaries could be pushed around. Now, approaching this Threshold, when you look inside to understand your rhythms, this deeper knowing will be personally enlightening. Honor the one you are without apology, find balance with your own bio-system.

One of the old Greeks said, "Know thyself," and this becomes more essential with each passing year. The depths of your Soul are vast, exquisitely cavernous, holding capacity, potential, and your promise. Soul secretly holds unimaginable complexities. Humble earthlings, you and everyone you know, strive to unpack these mysteries. Knowing yourself in the noise of modern life requires quiet time. I am not saying silence, because even deep in the wilderness, Nature is noisy. Your Soul thrives on the unique ways you have learned to wrap yourself in quiet. Your Soul essence will communicate what is left for you to explore if you attend to your rhythms and find quiet enough to listen. Dare to ask.

All Passages lead up to this Elder Encore Threshold. Every day of childhood, adolescence, and adulthood have been the training ground for your

Elderhood. The delight-filled experiences of all of your 50's, maybe even half a decade into your 60's, are the developmental capsule for creating meaningful experiences, stretching your capacity and living in wholeness at full potential. Every emotion filled day has helped you get ready for your Shawl Ceremony.

La Luna is always with you, through all your seasons

MOONPAUSE

If you grew up through an expanding consciousness while you were a bleeding woman, you have nearly completed a long series of Vision Quests for yourself. You are the first since ancient times to step inside your womb-body for this honoring. When you began this practice, forty some years ago, you held the idea of 400 eggs. That seemed like so many Moons. You only have a few eggs remaining now because time has a way of passing—the Earth rotates and the Moon turns the opposite direction on her axis following the Sun. The exact number of your Moontimes is a mystery.

Moonpause is coming, the gateway to your Elder years. Don't worry, it's the new in-thing. Everyone you know is on this wave of becoming her Elder-self with no blood left to release. Please, take a journey to yourself, for one year. By remembering, you will practice extreme self-care and open your neuropathways in memorium. Crossing five or six Passage Thresholds with a ceremony for each has helped you find honor in your position and honor for all of your days lived.

Soon you will know the bundle for Deepening Womanhood is well wrapped and can be put away. You will know when the time is right—the Elder Encore Threshold will appear out of the mist, but you must be watchful. Only you know how Moonpause—the arrival of your beautiful Crone years—relates to the Threshold ahead. Does one herald the other? Women without all their womb parts still have a womb-space and a 2nd chakra. These Sisters are often quiet about their experience because it's fashionable to share experiences about Moonpause. Please stop judging and denouncing women! Celebrate uniqueness and womanhood. The Elder Passage comes, unique to each woman, with or without Blood.

A little story: Becky was a beautiful woman who challenged me to think outside the box. During an early ceremony with these Nine Passages, she felt inner conflict. She faced this Elder Threshold with certain courage. Knowing and feeling that Elder Encore was her true place on the Spiral, she accepted her Elder Shawl in ceremony, in celebration, and with personal protest. She was still bleeding. Just over a year later, Becky died but she was thrilled to be an Initiated Elder.

WOMEN OF THE RED BLOOD

Young and old connect heart to heart
Womb-to-womb through Blood …
Like sleeping and dreaming,
Mystery is born of Creation
Pumping through wombs, releasing
Red Blood to a woman's Soul …
Each Moon offers
Life and Death as familiar gifts.

© Gail Burkett

If you have danced, really danced in the last month, then you are in your body; if you walked, been outside to wander around, then you are in your body. If you floated in the hot tub or a hot bath with candles lit and music playing, then you are in your body. Your body is a tool and a temple, a source of delight and a source of pain. By the time we reach a certain age, bodies hold memory and capacity that few have written about. Christiane Northrup[4] has several large reference books that explore the intersections of body with emotions, with spirit, and with actual physical responses. Your body holds more information than anyone can put into books. Spend time to focus on your inner self; take this opportunity to harvest your own personal wisdom. Everything you need is inside; answers are more abundant than you might think.

When you truly separated from your Mother, maybe you were nearly 30. You fell into the loving arms of your Earth Mother and began to enjoy the fruits of her labors. Now we call in the Indigenous relation, Father Sun, for the image of wholeness and harmony. Fuel, food, energy—throughout your life's days, every single thing comes from Mother Earth. A brilliant synergy of life between the Sun and the Earth, made whole with air and water, and for that synergy we are here because nowhere else sustains life. These ingredients combine for ceremony: Earth, Air, Fire, and Water, this you know already.

A Gift of Serenity from an Elder Sister

This difficult time in collective human evolution calls for daily ceremony. Ceremony infuses your day with gifts from your emotional body through your energy centers and into your daily record. Personal ceremonies of gratitude and observation will reveal what you are all about, why your life is this way. Deep listening, through playful questioning in the Cosmos, may give rise to a plea for action. Some have begun Moon Lodges and Red Tents for all women in their Village but these are only two examples to fill the voids of women's collective needs.

Reflect how Moon teachings and observations around your menopause, your Moonpause, have shaped you, even prepared you for this time between Thresholds. You have traveled far; consider this an invitation to share all you have accumulated about the Earth and la Luna, the Moon. Being culture-makers, perhaps an earthy tradition will rise from our collective blood. Madre Grande is the only home we have, the home of our children and grandchildren. Contemplate, in your journal and in silence, the legacy all women are weaving for future generations.

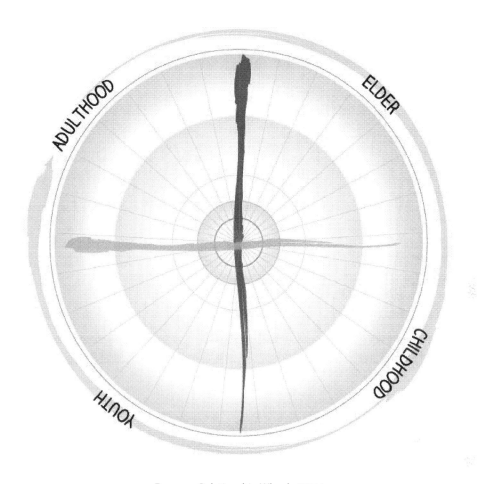

Focus on Relationship Wheel ©2016

This is a good place to introduce a little exercise that was shared with me by Janis Monaco Clark. When she journeyed through *Soul Stories*, she used this Four-Season mandala to remember all the people who held her, loved her and taught her something. Of course, some of those people in your relationship Wheel are blood relations and extended family from your personal origin story. Every one of those names radiate out of the quadrant of your child-self. This is the circle you were born into.

RELATIONSHIPS: CURRENT AND PAST, CHARGED WITH ENERGY

Over the years, Youth became Adult and your relationships proved themselves: Some were deep and some shallow, and a few other precious relationships started as intentional, like a chosen teacher and a chosen subject. Women enter Elder Encore with friends who originated from three prior stages of life: Child, Youth, and Adult. This begins to create an image for the concept of *tribe*. We are lucky to bring one or two from childhood and we feel joyful for teen friends who have been tribal since forever. Diving into the stories beyond your Deepening Womanhood Threshold, we each feel deeply privileged for friends who navigated the emotions and stresses of adulthood and stayed strong.

You know by now who is in your tribe. So many people have been called in by your Soul or by other means, to fill a contract in karmic lessons or offer a gift. The others, the tribe members, came along from stardust with you and will return. If this concept, which points to eternity, stretches your comfort zone, look deeply into your relationships.

Who has been in your life, in deep or shallow relationships and what gifts have they brought to you, consciously or unconsciously? This question gives me pause. The answers are legion and could take some time, but that is the gift of days, we have time.

I have released a few relationships that still cause a little twang in my heart. In my immediate family, two siblings released the whole rest of the family so I have released them as well. Both of my parents have slipped through my arms and crossed over. I will say this, all four of these relations are still my teachers.

On this frontier of human consciousness, these relational connections that serve your heart and Soul are rather Divine. Reflections from my Sisters, real and adopted are a reflection from Source, the Great Mystery. You may call this God or Goddess. I use all terms interchangeably. I am wildly fond of my family members and sweet friends who wish to be in relationship with me.

What and who serves your heart and Soul and what does not? You know.

You see how sticky this is, not just for me but for all of us. Relationships are current works, charged with energy. You use analysis, emotion, understanding, sympathy, empathy, forgiveness, mostly love and constant communication to understand and nurture them. There is the excitement and titillation of new relationships, your wide circles of friendships are always fluid and growing, especially if you give spontaneity a twirl once in a while. Beloved people who hold all of my history in the depths of their heart, those are my keepers. They return nothing but love, occasionally a question, rarely a challenge, and the complexity and richness of mutuality feels wonderful.

Light a candle and spend time with your relationships on paper. See where and to whom you have given and still want to give your attention. Remember what the toddler taught us: We all thrive on *focused attention*. This is the opposite of distracted attention, what it is not, may help clarify.

Why would I send you looking for the intersection between time and relationships? You've been practicing this for years. Because we are human, we can be wounded and we can do the wounding. People hurt people. This is a fact of living, we either go unconscious or discover a limitation or set a boundary that hurts feelings. I once lost a friend, an exciting new friend, because I asked her to stop bombarding me with questions. Zip that was it, all she wrote. Now she waves but that is as close as she will get.

When you give the subject of relationships this extra attention, someone who needs your love and attention will probably rise to the surface. It may be someone with whom you want or need to make amends, to apply glue enough to super-hold that relationship like new. Someone you wish to thank will also rise. Appreciation is infectious. Maybe you need to make a few biographical journal entries to understand relationships of this age or another. Touchstones that include love and forgiveness are valuable and will keep your heart open.

CIRCLING

I speak of Circle because of community
I speak of community because of Mother Earth
Women's Circle gives from heart directly to Earth
Your friends reflect the Divine Feminine you have been looking for

© Gail Burkett

At every age I highlight body-mind and spirit-mind because of personal evolution, we are all constantly changing. In the exciting field of neuroscience, researchers are revealing the interconnectedness of feelings.[5] Your emotions matter! Doctors like Daniel Siegel who love the body's mystery have unlocked the secret of integration. His name for this is interpersonal neurobiology, an umbrella term covering all sciences and spirituality, to discover the vast connections between thinking, feeling, beliefs, stress, and wellness: These all hang on the same web. Neuroscience and spiritual explorations have developed a large body of literature which Siegel and many others are now weaving together. Your personal validation is available through silent observation, by looking inside. People who meditate have firsthand knowledge of this web of connection, Mind to Body to Spirit.

When you scan your inner terrain, you can be intentional and actually notice neuropathways forming. Thoughts travel along the expansive transmission system of the body. When I write, it seems my fingers are thinking. Can you take a long view of the past and examine how your body has changed as your thoughts about your body have changed? How have your spiritual beliefs changed as you crossed over each Threshold?

Women need women to share, understand, and witness one another's crossroads. We need to talk about the personal evolution of body-mind and spirit-mind. A Women's Circle allows you to take your friends along on your sacred journey. The original few groups of women I circled with helped shape me by listening. Often what I said surprised me, but that is the nature of a safe and sacred space. Every single woman has concentric rings, always moving out. My concentric ring has moved as I have moved. Change in me has been punctuated by geographic change. Only a few people in my inner ring hold my whole story.

Each of the Women's Circles in different places has brought new friends. To make new friends requires focus and bonding: So many of your facets are polished that it's hard to share all of them at once. You have lived through joy and pain. All of your journey has been yours to feel and to claim, the highs and the lows always feel very personal. Sometimes it seems that to have one you must have the other, low is followed by a gradual rise back to a peak, a different high. To know suffering causes a deeper appreciation for joy. Joy is something you want to share with friends. Sharing the good times refreshes those neuropathways.

Entering a sacred portal, women experience one another in a Council way. This type of Circle uses ritual and confidentiality and passes a talking stick around. Women have much to learn about our inner workings—what we think about growing in this Elder quadrant, and how we feel about our bodies, about our minds and spirits. How will we know these things if we do not hear those words fall from our hearts?

Passing a talking piece in a sacred sister's Circle will bring up everything: Change, grief, relations, activism, joy and celebration, even dysfunction and mental illness from family of origin. Circles practice folk psychology, this is true. Practice kindness and seek help outside of your Circle if something big rises to the surface.

Women in Ceremony

After circling together, beneath the Sun and the Moon and watching the cycles of Nature move, your catalysts of change will become apparent. Around the Circle, you will know instinctively if one of you or all of you feel the calling of an initiation Threshold. Allow this feeling of Rites of Passage to come into the heart of the group. Ceremonies that celebrate personal evolution demonstrate a love for capacity, for honoring life, for stepping into your Genius, for giving yourselves this opportunity to elaborate on your life.

Perhaps you will find your path as a way-finder needing to lead a strong group of women. Initiated Elders can do the most good in mixed-generational Circles. The collective wisdom of women, supporting one another through stories, will show younger women how to locate their higher calling. Women who share good food as nurturance and deep listening as receptivity are practicing what the Divine Feminine teaches. Choose the smartest women you know and commit to one another: First Monday, second Saturday, you will decide together. These will become holy, visionary days. Find ways your core circle overlaps others' core circles.

Mary Catherine Bateson[6] describes the urgent need for women's vision as Earth dwellers to extend far into the future. Unlike any other time in history, women now approaching this Elder Encore Threshold are energetic, vital, and natural visionaries for the future. Gather with your women friends, listen for the ring of truth in Mary Catherine's call to action: We are brilliant women who possess the creative womb energy of second chakras; we can see far enough into the future with our fourth and sixth chakras to imagine great-great-great grand-children. Allow yourself full expression from your third and fifth chakras. Using your personal power to peer into the collective future Seven Generations ahead will create *cultural guides* of Initiated women Elders for the first time in dozens of generations. Your time and your wisdom are extremely valuable for this century. Circle and find out what you have to say! You may be surprised.

Through these Wisdom Councils, where women may discover the Clan Mother archetype long hidden from our view, we will all learn what our personal power is yearning for by hearing what we each have to say. Our collective legacy will influence the children of the future because we can imagine ahead that far.

Everything that needs attention or needs fixing is truly overwhelming, but we could form concentric circles to talk through our most pressing concerns. The only charge inside our Women's Circles is to pass the talking piece and be heard. Carrying emotional baggage is stressful and aging. Outside of the Circle, women will find ways to take care of our place on Earth. Inside of Circle is for *being*; outside the Circle is for *doing*. All of us can do more for our particular place on the planet. Let's do it with our girlfriends!

Take my caution here. I once lost a fabulous Circle of women to the divide between *being* and *doing*. We claimed cultural repair as a purpose, watch out for this vast ambition. Even though my Circle banded together over initiation, and really felt well bonded, we fell apart over the gigantic ambition of cultural repair. Women's Circles have a simple, sacred purpose: Being together to give our stories space to breathe.

I advocate for a Woman's Circle for every woman. I also warn about mixing *doing* into the delightful heart of *being* together. Playfully, joyfully, sharing stories, and sharing teachings and learnings, this is enough for any Woman's Circle. If passion meets with a call to action, find your partners and take the *doing* part outside of your Circle.

The Elder's journey ahead defines the entire quadrant of life which may be the longest by total days. It's very hard to imagine life without Grandmothers, especially now that we have that privilege. When we Grandmothers step into our place as Elders, all younger women have a model and a clearer idea where they are going on their journey. We walk in beauty our entire lives. When you reach for Elderhood, you will have spring, bounce, and beauty in great abundance. Do not worry about it; prepare now to embrace the power and glory of these last two stages, for they last a very long time indeed!

ORACLES FOR AWAKENING AND DEEPENING

An important planet in everyone's birth chart is Saturn. I refer you to Astrology occasionally for its uncanny accuracy. Like any symbolic language, this is a study and discernment. Seeing deeply is not always easy or possible, and interpretation is potentially powerful. How the sky full of planets interacts with you is *personal science*, only you know. Be perceptive about who you allow to influence your study of planetary positions and interactions with the Moon and how you might be affected. I read five or six astrologers in a Moon cycle, but I am a beginner. Your personal astrological chart aligns with the Universe. We can thank the digital world for a wide variety of astro-voices available through newsletters; talk about alignment!

The visible sky tells the story of the moment and cosmic energies change constantly, kind of like humans. Learn about the specific ruler of your chart, the interactions of the Moon with each planet. This will teach you why, for example, your day may start full of vigor, seemingly in optimistic control, then, an edginess appears out of nowhere. The explanation, at least for me and millions of other people, depends on how these celestial bodies interact with each other and how that network of influences affects my body-mind.

Women in Council Unifying the Past and the Present

Each one of us is seeking wholeness. I recommend using many avenues for personal explorations; epiphanies and openings happen often with oracles. Astrology offers a language of belonging. I understand my place on Earth by paying attention to the sky. The information, both spiritual and psychic in content, is quite revealing.

What does this cosmic language offer you? Are you operating with all the information at your disposal? You heart's desire may cycle with the zodiac. One of my wise teachers is Teri Parsley Starnes[7] and she recently wrote, "Our desires may shine like the stars but we have to accept that we are human and fallible. ... Honor the tide of feelings. They are important too." At the very least, this is a little practice, opening to personal consciousness, where we learn to be reflective and quiet enough to hear our feminine intuition. At best, we can align with the secret power of intention where the creation energy of the Cosmos waits to be summoned.

Saturn returns to its place in your birth chart at the beginning of your Womanhood Bloom and again just before your Elder Encore Threshold appears on the horizon. After your second Saturn return, you will feel the call to change, you will feel another transforming experience is unavoidable. The energy of Elder will rise up to meet you where you are and invite a look. The cosmic energy of Saturn announces your Elder Encore with this legacy question: Are you prepared to give the gifts of your Soul? As an indicator of the Threshold's presence, you do not necessarily need to step across until it can no longer be avoided.

The Relentless Question as a Gift from Saturn: Who were you Born to Be?

Watch for coincidences and synchronicities through your interior lens; Saturn helps realign your priorities and supports your own inner task master. Other oracles may feel increasingly profound because Soul needs answers to certain questions. You have something to gift the world that is of true and lasting significance. What is the meaning of life, your life? How has your life experience led to this very time? What golden nuggets might be assembled into a "bundle," a gathering of all of your stories? Saturn is like the pestering Coyote who asks, how are you progressing on the deliberate aim of your life? Who were you born to be?

I found this for myself: I was born to be an Elder. Crossing my Threshold in February 2015, I quickened and further awakened to my purpose. To prepare for this Threshold, I had returned to school and wrapped myself around the wonderful world of Women and Nature Studies. At 50 I received my PhD and began sharing life with my future husband.

The experiences from those watery depths are maturing just now because I took such a deep and questioning dive: As Nature beings, how do we locate the important intersections of personal searching, worldly experience, and human development? I felt like an Elder in training, but my Elder Threshold did not appear until all those years of research and synchronicities were completely composted. I had been in a receptive mode while in school, the degree placed a spin on things. My Father died just then. All of patriarchy seemed to flow out of me. I didn't know so much was in me. In this river of life, I see that my Soul was being prepared by Source energy. Saturn helped a great deal by serving to focus on the question, I was born to be, period. Other oracles not clearly seen in the academic realm were also leading me to the receptive, nurturing, warm side of my life.

I offer you the secret that worked for me: Use sacred inquiry to reflect back over the Moon cycles as they draw you into rhythm and dare to dream. Set clear intentions for one Moon cycle ahead, New Moon to New Moon. You will see that this creates a remarkable year.

A time warp of twenty years flowed out of my Deepening Womanhood initiation and the same will be true for you. No complete vision appeared in front of me, I was simply guided to put one foot in front of the other. Co-creation works like this. What my Soul dished up for me is so clear in reflection, but it was not always clear each day. I am a women's advocate; I have done many ceremonies for women and for girls. Each of these experiences has taught me something more about myself. There is always more.

Saturn represents only one energy from all the planets in orbit around our Sun. What I love most about Astrology is the real intrigue and mysterious energy of relationships and archetypes. As the orbiting relationships are constantly in flux, watch and wonder: How do those interactions affect me, my emotions, and my psychic inner world? The answers are rather astonishing.

I have learned a little about Tarot because it always raises an eyebrow and makes me laugh. A new deck, *Nature Spirit Tarot,* came into my hands in 2015 and I treasure the messages from the book. There is no coincidence that this new deck was made by Jean Herzel, creator of my logo.[8] Also synchronistic, Jean uses Nature for her sacred inquiry, what could be more Divine? When I draw a card, somewhere deep inside of my body-mind, the message resonates. Then, when I raise my question, I come to know something new.

As a gift to myself, my newest inquiry is reading the hexagrams of the I-Ching. I was taught many things by a beautiful old Mentor, Dolores LaChapelle.[9] I am now studying the I-Ching with her son. Both crossed around the time, a very deep mystery, but fortunately their earthy wisdom was left to us in their books.[10]

Three Parts Merge at Birth: Feminine, Masculine, and Soul

I have always loved oracles: Tarot and I-Ching are both revealers. Astrology predicts relationship interactions, generally between me and the Cosmos, occasionally between me and another. Every thread, from the Cosmos or from the pages of ancient wisdom, leads to the core of you, to the touchstone which is your Soul. Something resonates in your energy field, it's that simple, really.

I spend enormous blocks of time alone, in contemplation, walking, studying and writing. In all this listening—to the quiet, to others, to myself—I have continually responded to the call of my Soul. I didn't fully comprehend that it was all Soul until my year of initiation as an Elder, my joyous, edgy, penetrating year of rituals to honor the core of me. I grew in touch and conversant with the Soul I travel with in life and beyond. Now I can speak about the previous lives of my Soul and the future lives in much the same way. This is because I use the rhythm of one Moon for a Vision Quest. What began with the journey I took through *Soul Stories* laid down practices for my inner work; the practice and I have become good friends. I believe the same can be true for you. Because we are energy beings, we actually feel resonance and tingle as that juicy charge rushes through our cells. This is Soul, make yours a conscious companion.

In reflection, patterns will appear through a most enjoyable review of opportunities and synchronicities. I call this my rear-view mirror. Many of your days will appear as whole poems. Living to the fullest that life has to offer, without regret, with courage, and with a strong connection to Soul, this is women's manifesto. Gathering the lessons and wisdom of your stories, the patterns found in relationships, in review of the light and delight of your life, you will summon the honor your life needs to regenerate your whole self. When I moved across that Threshold as an Elder, I felt whole-hearted and ready for the responsibility of modeling and teaching about intergenerational connections.

Wrapping myself around an archetypal persona as the contemplative Elder in the culture, especially initiating other women, offers an edge that I want to explore. I want to know when Elder women were last revered by the entire culture; I want a tribe of Initiated Elders.

I would like to offer strong women who have modeled the matriarchal archetype an Elder's Shawl for keeping the archetype alive. Families have scattered and shattered before our very eyes and often in our personal experience. Think about what you want to model for your family. The Threshold for you to receive your Shawl is coming up your timeline.

While your Soul is preparing you for this future, you will continue to blossom; your Soul is quietly busy with you. Use your time wisely; an ecstatic and peak experience is coming to you. What have you been training for your whole life? How can you best deliver on the gifts you were so generously given? Maybe an oracle will come to your aid as a perennial questioner. Maybe your girl-gang, your Women's Circle, will serve as oracle in their reflection back to you. If we do just one thing together, let's hold the image of 10,000 Boomers reaching 65 every single day, all looking into the same future, at the same time. If we all gathered up our Soul's creative juice, understanding that we came to Earth all at the same time, what were we all born to do?

PRACTICES: SPIRIT AND CONSCIOUSNESS, MOVEMENT AND FOOD

In this lived reality we must constantly choose, refine, and winnow our playing field. Your world and worldviews continue to expand. We constantly learn even when we fail to realize that. Each one of us, living now, has a shared experience far too large to story; *exponential personal evolution* has become this reincarnation. Use inner quiet to recover from the culture's noise or to preserve your sanity. At any time you can step out of your comfort zone and do something daring with your resources.

You have infinite subtle inner worlds, worlds to explore through practices. Your chakras, those personal and Divine energy centers, will continue to invite you inside for some measure of each day. I locate the invitation by closing my eyes, but I also have practiced for years. These inner energy fields spinning on gossamer threads reveal how you are holding space for yourself and others. Rebalancing and realigning deepen this practice for me. There are always questions. What answers do you receive in your sacred inquiry?

A Cultural Challenge: To Harmonize Masculine and Feminine as well as a Flower

Women are enjoying the rise of the Divine Feminine into our consciousness. Like every other layer, once you perceive how this energy presence wraps the Earth, she floods your perceptual field and connects you into the shimmer. You will feel expansion and connection to all other women. The energy of the Divine Feminine cannot be explained easily, but women are opening the oppressive cracks in patriarchy in refreshing, delightful, and healing ways. Collectively, energy is flooding through the cracks. The reception we feel in return, utterly new, opens to the esoteric and to the deepest aspects of inner beliefs. We receive inspiration to meditate, to research the Goddess in archetypal form and cross cultural names, symbols come to mind, we light candles and say our prayers of gratitude. The Divine Feminine will continue to offer balance. Through your radiant smile, this energy reveals an inner divinity to you and others.

Consider how important the strength of your connection when the drums of war beat in various parts of the world. Your perception and connection are vitally important. Curiously observing the culture, you have learned a little something about how patriarchy and the Divine Masculine has a deep dark side. What you discover in your global inquiries seem so distant, waring men, oppressed women. Will the world ever change? Women have opportunity now, as we become clear vessels, to model something the world desperately needs: Peace lovers, light workers, Initiated women will help Earth come into balance. It's only a big job if we feel alone.

Through your rituals and symbolic images, you will find the Divine Feminine and Divine Masculine relationship within yourself which connects to the cosmic consciousness. A whole throng of people are finding this connection as the basis for faith in the future. Hopefully, through the longevity of these wisdom years, you have begun to accept the revelations of your private inquiries. Powerful forces are working with you.

You begin to know your true self in this stage. It does take thousands of days, perhaps 20,000 before the answers align and the world begins to make sense. Amidst layers of complexities, you will find peace in the little auric bubble of your inner world. The outer world needs to continue shattering into zillions of fragments. The shattering and apparent disintegration of culture will coalesce into acceptance and regeneration; this is an eventuality.

About spirituality: Find yours and go as deep as you can; welcome the next teacher. My collection of Mentors have taught me this continual and gradual reach for consciousness is what earthlings are supposed to do and continue to do right up to our final Threshold. All kinds of wonderful teachers are appearing on the world stage making growth of the sacred aspects—Mind, Body, and Soul rather easy and quite thrilling. We each have the far dimension to receive us; until then, find your spiritual practices and investigate profoundly. Deepen your well every season. Others will notice and bring their inquiries to you making you a Mentor. This is the highest calling of all.

Your 50s is the best decade to fulfill the desires of your body-mind. Find your tools for balance. Be very clear with your practices so that all you do to take care of your body pays dividends. This includes being in the best shape of your life and discovering all that gives you pleasure, sexual and physical. Your practices are meant to take you deeper into the trifecta that makes you, you: The Mind-Body-Soul connections, intersections, and potential transformations.

At some time along your spirit trail, accidents or illnesses may have derailed you. Ask why and set intentions to be the best in your body you can be. I am physically more challenged because of my history so I have struggled with this mind-body connection. Far too many serious accidents have derailed me but I experienced spiritual awakenings from each one, like the Divine gift of guidance. My sweet Womb-mate says my spirit likes to *just go up and have tea*. Sometimes, it is simply better to go out of my body.

When I look at my fellow travelers, I know I am not alone with the body challenge. Yet we are all perfect trifectas. Your body, like my body, makes the heart-mind and spirit-soul complete. I rebirth a new intention every day to befriend my body as I sit on my yoga mat and breathe and stretch. One of my most profound experiences is following the breath of life, in and out, it moves my diaphragm up and down. Conscious breathing is a spiritual practice for me and it oxygenates my blood. By this time you will have discovered, there is always more, the unfolding of life simply means, opening to more. Reach for the gap where busy-mind stops and peace floods in.

Approaching the decades ahead, through your 60s, let's explore what is meant by practices. By now you likely know, but this is for your sisters who do not. I include yoga as a practice, in all its lovely, lively forms. Meditation is a practice, sitting quietly or walking quietly. Chanting and visualization are practices. You may be a runner, that is a practice. Hiking to the top of a mountain may be a practice. Standing before an easel, writing song-lines, studying stream flow, silently watching birds, listening to music, these are all practices. Sorting and releasing my over-abundance, this is a practice. What consistently brings you joy?

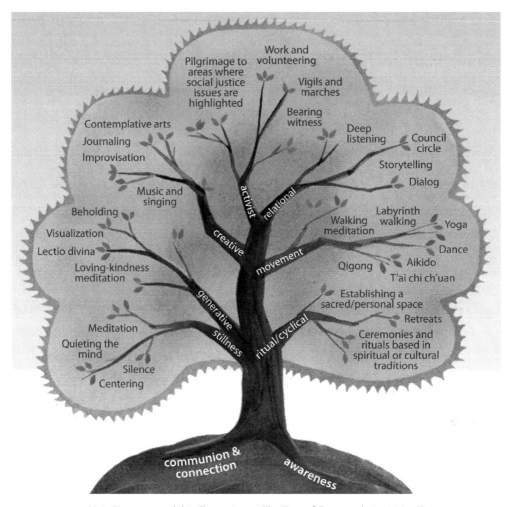

Maia Duerr created this Illustration as The Tree of Contemplative Living[12]

Personally, my practice is diverse. I meditate every day in a different way. Some mornings I sit in silence, other mornings I chant to the Goddesses, tantric style with Sally Kempton, and most days I walk as Thich Naht Hanh has taught, with my feet kissing the Earth and a quiet-mind for walking.[11] You are still the actress on the stage of your life. How do you connect to the places you dwell, both your inner and outer places?

Amazing as this sounds, we think of food at least three times a day, and no wonder, it's our fuel. Along the way, I have learned only a couple of things about growing food, it's a practice and a hard one at that. Those who devote their Soul energy to growing fuel for others' bodies, have earned my deepest respect. Before I turned 60, part of my Saturn return was to question the origins of food, how to grow it, and all that is involved. This deep inquiry has provided delicious dividends. Medicinal herbs became my second true love. I know you have loves in the plant kingdom. Take a moment to name yours and send little blessings. Yes, you can send blessings!

Hot Food Grown by Children from the School Garden

Consider the entire food distribution system. Can you believe, asparagus in October and February? Well, those far-away farmers cannot be hugged as can our locals who grow for the Farmers' Markets. I love the experience of peeking into the hard-working lives of those who grow food for a living. Do you know that 100,000 different products might be offered in the largest supermarkets? Can you believe this crazy abundance, all coming from Mother Earth? Obviously there is more to this story. Know your food sources so that you can know yourself better. Food is spirit and body medicine. But you already know this from all of your lived days.

As you have claimed a place on Earth for yourself and your family, have you become a stakeholder, part of the grassroots to make your place better? Show your young people—grandchildren, nieces, nephews, cousins and all your adopted/extended family—that they can count on your wisdom. Bring back letter writing both for the connection and to deliver a little keepsake for sweet ones far away. I still have my Grandmother's letters from decades past. Be as grounded and dependably available as possible. This rootedness offers a practice of being present to yourself and your relations.

I have filled a beautiful cookie jar with Almond Sesame Crackers as part of my practice, it feeds my giving side. They are made with a rolling pin and when I offer the jar, I say to visitors of all ages, "Take one for each hand." I adore practices, they are earthy, healthy, and steadfast. Can you name your top three relationship practices?[13]

If you agree that this is an age to be open to more, what is on your list? Recently, joy has risen to the top of my list as a measurement. What truly gives you joy? Do you read voluminously? Who do you share those good reads with? When someone loans a book, do you take time to talk about it later? Do you have a flair for something domestic? Are you teaching anyone to help you? Do you love international travel? How do you share your adventures with others?

YOUR PLAYFUL WISDOM TRADITION

Consider all that you have experienced in your spiritual life. Acknowledge the many ways you have received Divine guidance. Maybe you didn't ask, but you did receive. Tosha Silver calls this her Divine guidance spirit trail.[14] She tracked back through her life and discovered stories of where Divine guidance had intervened. This recognition caused her heart to leap with joy and recognition. She also gathered stories from her friends so, *Outrageous Openness: Letting the Divine Take the Lead* is more than observation, it is truth and wisdom for our time.

I loved this book because it reminded me of what I have ascribed to the mythic Coyote character in my own life. This rear-view inspection of where miracles have occurred returns me to a mindful practice of observation and wonder; Guides and Angels are always here. Every Soul comes in with a Guardian and more energies come as needed. See how this concept of Divine guidance has worked in your life and notice how remembering feeds your Soul.

Free Form Child-play is the Best for all Ages

I have mentioned this before but when my old Mentor, Joe Meeker, asked me to write my play history, I was astonished at my lack. He talked a lot about play, but always ended his thoughts saying, "Poor play." I wanted to know why so I studied play. Like any awakening, in my heart I discovered play had been waiting patiently for decades. To me, play means being lost along the creek, inspecting the nature of stones; it means not thinking, just wandering. In solitary play, I relish the company of spiders, butterflies, rabbit tracks in the snow, while I dance with my Soul. One-on-one with all of Nature, I belong to the planet and this recognition has had a deep healing effect on me. Through play I have found joy again.

Thank you Joe, I am able to give my granddaughter 100% attention while she draws me into her play, I feel newly teachable through her child-eyes. I have found a practice, a meditation through play that I couldn't have imagined earlier in my life. If I had just one wisdom tradition to pass onto her and to you, one legacy, that would be play. All of my cells are happier when I take time to play with myself, with the planet, with my dog, and with one or ten children at a time.

Muse of Inspiration

In this sweetness, play has a diffuse focus, a relaxed and non-demanding air. Play has no agenda and if you try, in your highly skilled way to play with an agenda, then play will vanish for another day. With the great awakening that begins around nine months old, play offers to human animals what it offers to all beating hearts: We each are given the opportunity to become wholly true to the design intended by Great Mystery. Even though I lived for years on the 19th floor, I have learned that I am most human in the natural world with pure play surrounding me. This core philosophy was born out of working for corporations. The transformed me who walked through fire to invite change, insists that playing for myself, being playful with others, discovers a spiritual experience through play which infuses energy into my creativity. Pure play has the ability to reset every cell in my being.

I use my brain for its distillation capacity and its ability to receive transmissions of inspiration. I laugh out loud when I am visited by the muse of intuition; messages of Divine guidance are joyously abundant out in Nature. I have been walking for a few years to directly connect with the Divine Feminine energy of inspiration. You can too.

Stone Invites Playfulness

To create your own storyline of Divine guidance or minor miracles, you may need to track your beliefs through the filter of your life's events. Be sure to include your history of play and magical time in Nature. When I created an events timeline, a simple exercise of "this happened, then this happened," I was able to visually *see* how my beliefs developed and all the ways my life has been guided.

Dispel any downhill slide metaphor with your witchy-wand; exchange all such metaphors for one long peak ascent, getting better, wiser, and personally more powerful each day. Embrace all your friends who are growing older with you and often, lovingly, joyfully and definitely playfully. Probably you will nourish one another's legacy story. Be playful in your assessment: What do you long for before you cross the Elder Encore Threshold? How do you need to prepare yourself to continue building on your wisdom tradition?

You know much more than you think. One sign of wellness is the thirst for knowledge, clearer understandings, and ease in creative explorations. Another sign is light and joy in your being. You have healthy relationships if you realize unlimited opportunities for growth are alive in every opportunity and people around you mutually support growth.

Become friends with Energy workers: Herbalists, Reiki Masters, Seers, Shamanic Practitioners, and Doulas. These people are Medicine for our culture. If you are stuck or stumped, energy workers women and men will help you unblock to understand the pathways your Soul longs for and your spiritual life needs to take. Follow your intuitive messages and your growth will accelerate.

A FIRE CEREMONY

Please gift yourself a ritual created with folklore and inheritance. Some catalyst of change, perhaps offered by your Soul brought you this moment of maturity. Probably only you know. Summon a ritual for yourself, candles, silence, good Earth and Sky, use a drum to return a fire ceremony to its place in your bones which remembers the need for a celebration. I imagine for you an honoring event to acknowledge change as part of your life's wholeheartedness.

Call on the Ancestors who hold the symbols of the 4 Sacred Directions. See how the Above and Below and Center energies of Earth and Sky quicken your Soul. Symbols blend with the rising and setting of the Sun and the Earth moving through her seasons. Reach into the sacred toolkit held by your adult self and find your symbols for Earth, Air, Fire and Water to help you.

Your substrate may be both solid and needy, you have smiles and tears, and so much water has flowed beneath the bridge you are building. May I suggest this cleansing ritual to release your pain? Smoke cleanses, salt cleanses, water cleanses, what do you choose to help you stow your healed memories safely away into your heart pocket?

You cannot really be mindful and present with joy until you burn through or release the painful hooks of the past. Transformation is an action verb and an alchemical process. Many never heal their pain. This sad truth has a bright side. The wounded can become wounded healers. All of us who walk this path have used diligence and intention to transform our worldview and personally evolve.

When I finished my graduate work, I could only exhale. Right then, a year apart, I buried both of my parents. My mourning felt intense, overwhelming sometimes, the tears were automatic and flowed privately. Then I would "buck up," something else my Mother used to say. At age 50, I had gifted my Mind-Body-Soul with questions so large I was stumped and engulfed in grief. Integration took quite some time.

This is the question I held: I had something to do, what? I was essentially on a sabbatical without awareness. Claim your rest, see if you can do nothing. All Thresholds are agents of change. If you need rest more than anything else, you are not reaching for a change. Not yet. You are still integrating, be patient with yourself. Surrender to play.

RELEASING AND FINDING LOVING INFLUENCES

The great space of years ahead is where simplicity reigns. So many women now practice simplifying, de-cluttering, and downsizing, it has become contagious. This may be the time for you to find that balance for yourself. We must all come to resolution with our possessions. Along with the material challenges–ahead, there will be spiritual challenges. So often the choice to simplify includes a geographic move. If you are one who loves deep roots and you decide to move, you will step out onto a wide emotional-spiritual wave. Detachment will become your spiritual focus, but keep standing up on the wave and you will eventually reach the shore and solid ground again.

When I look at my Grandmother's old rocking chair, sitting alone in a corner holding a basket of maps, I think of the poetry of that. Maybe I could plan a trip with the maps or sit and hold the basket on my lap to imagine spaciousness enough to stop and write poetry. Will I give myself permission? What does your stuff inspire? Does it hold a silent call to action for you?

GRANDMOTHER'S ROCKER

She comes to my thoughts unbidden but welcome
I feel grateful for her intrusion enough to stop.
Gamie's softness and her laughter come back easily
The feel of her, the sound of her causes a giddy up
In my heart, fluttering in love with her jerky or biscuits.
I pine for a woods walk with her looking for morels
If I ask her nice we could make donuts this morning.
Instead, I lift the basket of maps and sit down to rock
Asking, where could we go if only in our imaginations
Me with my Grandmother who's gone but very present.

© Gail Burkett

With maturity comes a natural ability to ease your grasp and release. I want you (and every woman) to appreciate how big your *influence* is and continues to be, in ever-wider circles. You are the ripple on the pond. I invite you to think of influence as a spiritual concept. From the womb, you have been influenced, guided, taught, and indoctrinated. You have learned to unlearn or dispatch some of what has stuck to you. Now is the time to use great curiosity to peer into all of those influences radiating inward and outward. One way to understand all that has shaped you, consider your big choices and their consequences on you. This is an inside-out view of influence. Compassion without judgment, please; life is wholly a Soul experience.

Influence is power and strength, it is the ultimate connecting thread to your past. As you follow this thread of inquiry, you will naturally turn the influence around to see your spirit trail of influences on others. Own this. Examine it for its gems and nuggets. Can you see your ripple? This is self-esteem building; mature women need this as much as teen girls. Tend to your needs by giving yourself acknowledgments. Of course, recognition of your influence on others is wonderful, however, recognition of yourself to yourself, that is of a much higher order. Surely in the years ahead, absorbing the holiness you discover, you will be that Divine woman who listens and influences many others by your model of living.

Once you understand how this concept of *influence* has shaped you, offer yourself a releasing ritual. As one who has walked through fire to release the influences of addictions, abuse, suppression, and oppression, I believe in this personal work. Release is incredibly potent with a personal ceremony. Retain those influences that belong and release all those that have hooks. I hold all of my own answers inside, so do you.

Moon Sculpture: Work with Silence to Find Guidance

Very carefully and deliberately release the emotional charge that some influences still hold. Move aloft with your spirit, pour a cup of tea, view your stories and their patterns as the great teachers they have been. When you can realign with gratitude over all that has influenced you, the dim and the bright, release them all. Become an empty vessel who lives in the present moment, the one who understands her wisdom is coalescing with each passing season. Be the one who offers guidance as influence to all those coming up, all the Youngers who need your wise woman's council. You have remembered how life moves, always in a flow, sometimes as a quiet eddy and sometimes falling over a waterfall. This is true for everyone.

I have been fortunate enough to see and feel this Divine guidance of influence work through me. Your life stories also offer this lens. If you begin the list of interventions of Divine guidance in your life, you will understand how those holy influences shine through the decades. You will feel less alone as your path unfolds. Review your stories, share with your friends as a way of releasing painful ones. Hold the joy to your heart and allow it to expand. This is an act of gratitude.

Goddess as Model for Divine Feminine

If you are in the wide concentric circles of my tribe, Nature calls to you. I take my influence from Nature. Mother Earth is our home away from home. I feel my intuition is ignited by wild Nature and her critters, those sentient beings who share this planet with us. Outside, moving across the landscape with an empty mind, I often receive exquisite messages. Certainly my relationship with Nature spills over to my relationship with all other beings, all my loves, and returns me to peace. What do you do to ignite your intuition?

I am a behind-the-scenes activist, watching everything and contributing to many good causes. This is my legacy from early Women's Circles. Thousands of women also carry this legacy, probably millions. Do you touch enough wildness? Have you worked to protect the wild? In a groundswell that begins local for each one of us, I urge you to become a stakeholder for your place on Earth. This is our collective legacy, the united wisdom tradition we hold together as a force of Initiated women. We understand influence.

MODELING

You need to be a rock for others, so who is your rock? Think of a woman in the stage or two stages ahead who will hold a space for you to grow. Describe your life to this holy woman. This relationship has the potential to grow into a deep spiritual experience. Give it time and focused attention. You will both feel lighter from this telling of your life story and inspired by all that you have done. Each woman benefits from deep listening, but what you will find fascinating is what you have to learn by sharing your spiritual heart with another. You will probably find direction by listening to your own words.

I go beyond the traditional view of modeling to include more than role modeling. Women have one another for this, the role model of every archetype, the Mother, the Grandmother, and all the Goddess archetypes. We even have a variety of witchy archetypes: Good Witch, Green Witch, Kitchen Witch, Bad Witch and Magic Witch. Within our Souls, we each have touched down into and experienced a wide array of these human templates. What are we going to do with all that makes us smile?

A great deal of research is available on archetypes or template personaes, and terrifically good reading.[15] I suggest Carolyn Myss online and her book *Sacred Contracts*. Jean Bolen's books *Goddesses in Everywoman* and *Goddesses for Older Women* explores the true natures of your practical intellect, how to view yourself as a mystic, spiritualist, or Nature intuitive through the lens of the Greek Goddesses. Another favorite teacher of archetypes, explored through the cross cultural lens of Hindu Goddesses, is Sally Kempton, a prolific author and workshop leader. I have used these wise women to develop my heart and inner world. There are others, ask around your circles. Helen Luke will lead you to the Divine Feminine. Helen calls this the tender new growth of consciousness. This energy inside of you is part of your unconscious until you begin to know her.

Whether you use this language or not, your inner Divine Feminine is your psyche's source of female presence and energy, receptive and nurturing. Much like patriarchy has been a global meme, the collective power of the masculine has been dominant for centuries. Inside of women, the Divine Feminine is awakening in women's psyches to restore the future with balance and healing. As the Earth turns and seasons change, the mystery and primal power of our Madre Grande, our Great Mother has modeled this feminine power multiple times in your lifetime. Remember the Divine Feminine is the unconscious in us until she becomes known through intentional practices and reading. Ultimately, we have been taught how to hold quite different perspectives such as wild and nurturing, destructive and creative. When I think of the energy potential inside of you, the Divine Feminine, I imagine a starburst, a sparkling ray of aspects and potentials. By this time in your life, age 60 and onward, all of these shining facets combine into your Elder wisdom. Claim the Divine Feminine in yourself, allow her images to swim to the surface of your consciousness.

I finally understood how the many sides of womanhood have influenced me. The search for the truth in my feminine nature took years of dismantling my masculine nature and more work to deconstruct my armor. The modeling you reveal to your different circles, your family and friends, includes your personality and psychic imprints from all that have shaped you. When events call on your nurturing side, for example, your Soul as Divine Feminine, knows what to offer another through your practices of cultivating and cherishing relationships. This modeling is now a result of you making conscious, deliberate and creative choices. First we please ourselves, then we show to others what we have chosen. This gets much easier over time. Finally, we might grow in agreement, modeling the feminine reveals that our practice is our way of being.

When I think of my portrait in the culture, the image I am modeling is Elder, receiving inspiration through deep listening, and planting seeds in the moist soil of women. I have made this my practice now. This is the spiritual experience you are preparing for also, nurturing and patiently waiting to receive inspirations. To be part of Earth's recovery, women must recover our symbolic life and begin dreaming the Cosmos. In *The Way of Woman: Awakening the Perennial Feminine,* Helen Luke elucidates these thoughts.[16]

"Yet, the instinct of the feminine is precisely to use nothing, but simply to give and to receive. This is the nature of the earth—to receive the seed and to nourish the roots—to foster growth in the dark so that it may reach up to the light. ... If we can rediscover in ourselves the hidden beauty of this receptive devotion; if we can learn how to be still without inaction, how to "further life" without willed purpose, how to serve without demanding prestige, and how to nourish without domination, then we shall be women again out of whose earth the light may shine."

A pinnacle, this is the magical peak of all of your life experiences. For my heart connection, I look to other Elders to see how they wear their mantle. Those in my purview are cloaked as intelligent, judicious, and sagacious beauties. We live for ourselves first. This has been our hardest lesson, how to end both the narcissism and slavery of our younger years. Stand in your power first, allow it to overflow naturally to serve others.

Certainly your experiential beauty and wisdom combine in unique and glorious ways to be shared. Please understand how the culture has dismissed the Elders in the generations immediately older and still connected to the Millennial Elders. Our Mothers and Grandmothers in their old age may have been waiting for permission to be rather glorious and visible. Some of these magnificent old women barely connected to their Divine Feminine. They grew old and older and were devoured by the patriarchy.

Women Making Ceremony

Next Generation of Initiated Elders

We, you and I, are going to be the first Initiated generation of Elders in centuries. We have had our labors and they have shaped us. Through recovery of your Moon visions, your relationship with Mother Earth, you understand the difference between doing and being; you feel serenity and security in a balance between self-care and service. You have found your practices, what returns you to balance, what feeds your Soul. When you are spiritually satiated and the Divine Feminine is alive in your consciousness, you can model this for other younger women.

INITIATED ELDERS

In my book, *Soul Stories: Nine Passages of Initiation,* I offer a guided journey of self-reflection for a year as a pathway to honor and find the epiphanies in the stories of your life. When you journey with other women, our collective blend of spiritual practices will grow exponentially beyond my suggestions. Let's foster this idea of a generation of Initiated Elders.

In our shared her-story, we have knowledge of the Goddess cultures of old Europe from 30,000 years ago. Marija Gimbutas'[17] very courageous and edgy work

Goddess Symbolizing the Divine Feminine

brought the figurines from the culture of peaceable women into our collective consciousness. Women of long ago inform the culture of women today because they left us clues about peace and devotion. Women also have knowledge of the Burning Times. Even though we have this knowledge and these evolutionary genes in us, maybe in our Soul- selves, we each need to find our way to creation energy to express all that is uniquely ours. Expression of my Soul-self is my purpose and probably yours as well. I use these ancient threads of connection, the symbols of women's collective her-stories to remember how our gender has been brainwashed, crushed, and hushed.

Now we are living in the midst of great changes, a time called the Great Turning where the edge of the industrial age meets the era of life-sustaining and Earth-loving awakening. It is our time, a moment when we can claim what is ours to give the world. What gifts do you receive from your Soul to nurture?

Where does your Genius lie? These questions can only be answered in silence, in walking, in art, in journaling, and finally in sharing the images of your deepest passion with your most intimate friends.

Let us take a moment here, together. This is the stuff of imagination Dearhearts. We can only write a new story. Nowhere in any of the references or literature is there a mention of a culture of Initiated Elders. Nowhere have these words been put together for women to rise up through our life stories and claim our Elder Shawls. The essence of the oldest generations, finding our internal power and standing together, this is an imaginative, fictional thought unless we choose to make it real.

Of course all things begin with thought. If you hear only two things, I say go on a pilgrimage to recover your wandering Soul parts, come back to wholeness through the deep harvest and healing of your stories. Close with this commitment to yourself: Receive all that belongs to you and give what you are meant to give. Nothing more. Heal those rough edges wherever they jab you. This journey will produce an essence of yourself you have been looking forward to but didn't quite know how or where to find it. Go ahead, this is why Encore is the Passage title, become someone you barely dream to be. When Initiated Elders model this for the culture, everything will change.

STEP INTO YOUR PLACE

For every person in the culture to receive their gifts of maturity, older women need to step up, initiate as Elders and begin to blend our ideas in Wisdom Councils. When women step into this naturally powerful stage of life, men will heal also. It's not a matter of question and certainly not coercion; it's a modeling that women have always done.

The Seventh Generation is Here, the Time for Elders has Returned

Elder is the age that all others look up to for leadership, wisdom and guidance. Reaching down the generations, you will feel the power of pure love when a granddaughter or a grandson comes with a desire for connection. You can share just the right story to help untie a knot; you can offer solace and a listening ear in a way that no parent can. This is true for all children who cross your path. I didn't understand Elder role until I adopted an elementary school and started receiving hugs from little ones. It is possible to overcome all barriers to discover relationships of the heart variety. When a year old child, just taking her first excursions, toddles toward me across the barnyard, my heart opens wide. Innate and instinctual for connection, the only response I have needed is kindness and devotion. When I give a child attention, she gives me attention, so I lean in. All women of a certain age become Grandmother to all children.

When we were 10 and 11, we learned a skill that has never left us: We learned to observe and compare. Beginning around nine months old, this skill blended six senses and grew into your personal sensory antennae, which you perfected before puberty. We become great watchers, filters, and interpreters of culture. Every woman must be watchful for imbalance and offer help there. Then we become makers of culture.

Standing as an Elder, especially beside other initiating Elders, our collective purpose floats over us like an umbrella, challenging, inviting, and daring *us to be* what the world needs. The culture is dependent on how the Elders are portrayed and valued. As our families contribute to regenerating the culture, it's up to each woman individually to practice the modeling of an Elder.

Closing with the concepts of influence and modeling, ask when the young girls throw their scrutinizing antennae toward you, will they see the model of a woman in grace who also feels whole in herself? Will they hear clarity and feel your nurturance? Will they feel gifted by your presence? As you ponder the long road ahead, Elder women with gorgeous wrinkles and stunning grey locks will populate the top tier of the Life Spiral. Are you preparing to consciously model what it means to be an Elder? Has your Women's Circle considered this enormous cultural change, where you live long—time-binding the past and present into collective Elder wisdom—preserving the future?

A Beautiful Circle of Initiating Elders

AN ELDER ENCORE STORY

What I learned by offering Rites of Passage ceremonies to women and girls aroused a wake-up call within me. I began to ask, what about initiation for all of us, myself included? We have all missed ceremonies because our culture lacks these traditions.

I feel gratitude for several dozen women who gathered around a fire altar with me to call forth ceremonies for First Blood, First Flight, and Womanhood Bloom. Leading this recovery effort, many somberly walked a Medicine Wheel. That ceremony captured our imaginations and that is what I continue to celebrate. We remembered how much change happens to women through decades of living. The change from Birth to Bloom takes 30 years, which is no less dramatic than all the changes from 30 to 80 or 100. Dear Souls walked the Wheel of Life with me to bring life to the Nine Passages Spiral; we knew silence would reveal, so we spent five months reviewing our lives, collectively and silently, before we came back together.

I offer a deep and humble bow to my friends. These women honored me because I stepped up. My scholarly search into our life cycles emerged as pivot points for initiation ceremonies for every woman who finds herself in the grasp of an agent of change.

From that first circle of Elders who helped conceive *Nine Passages*, an outpouring of Divine Feminine flows from each one of these extraordinarily beautiful women. Five years have passed now and the witness in my heart who watches is using my gift as Storyteller to move things along. I want to understand what the far side of our Elder Threshold holds. A culmination of this and many other ceremonies went into *Soul Stories*, a life review manual to initiate women and Elders.

A Winter Flower Ceremony for Grief

Women of this Elder Circle have pledged to grow old together. From my inner view, I watch my circle of friends with great love and interest. We will always be sisters of initiation. All of our stories hold that particular shimmer that contains delight, truth, and love. Just imagine how deeply rich and meaningful their symbols have become, after these years of modeling Elderhood.

At that final ceremony for initiating women, I found the grief in me to be bottomless. For the deeply spiritual process of honoring one's Soul and listening for Divine inspiration to awaken those gifts, only a very few women have received this blessing, an initiation to awaken their gifts. Most miss out and often never heal. I know this by listening to the complaints in the wind.

During my first Elder initiation, I spent five months writing a story about a self-initiation that happened as a sudden spiritual awakening. This was preliminary and personal, I had walked the Earth with the Grandmother Spirits and shed past influences. Both actions, the walking and the writing, were release ceremonies. I remember the dynamic opening which caused me to examine my life. It was the beginning, the validation of me, I began to listen for the messages from my Soul. I learned a lot by writing and reflecting on that story because fifteen years had passed. Those five months were just the next opening to my Soul-self. I learned to stand under my questions for understanding.

Something was lacking. I was not following a pilgrimage to become more acquainted with my Soul, I was not digging into my current or past pathology to find its source: I needed structure and guidance to make the initiation meaningful.

To link an intention to my purpose, the grief I felt lingered for a year or two; the language, the model, the philosophy, and the structure and purpose of Rites of Passage deserves an entire library of collected efforts as large as the body of publications for flowers and gardening. I have one voice, but I want company.

One who Knows her Soul is One with Earth

The desire for Rites of Passage is becoming a cultural meme. It is working! The pond has begun rippling with women's stories of initiation.

NOW HER STORY: JANIS MONACO CLARK

Meeting Janis Took a Couple of Years

When I ask for guidance about whose story to tell for this chapter, one story emerges particularly filled with delight; she calls it soaring. This is the story of Janis, the model of an Initiated Elder whom I deeply admire. I hope to tag along with Janis for all the rest of my days.

Janis said she remembers first seeing me at the local elementary school where, as a Master Gardener volunteer, she offered to help me in the children's vegetable garden. We talked on the phone about an article she was writing, praising our Edible Schoolyard; I mentioned the school was holding a Harvest dinner: The PTO feeds dinner to the whole, rural community for a very small sum.

"This will be the 58th consecutive year for this Harvest dinner, please come." Janis is a yes person; she said, "I think we might come."

Thus, our first brief encounter was in a noisy cafeteria filled with joyful people. She and I sat back to back, but she was shiny and I could see her essence: Wise, mischievous, wild, and loving.

When she was diagnosed with breast cancer, I told her my cancer story and how fear turned into empowerment. We both felt glad to share. Her life got rather small and focused intensely on surgery, radiation, and a heroic healing. We continued to slightly connect, but not quite. Timing had to be just right. Chemistry, magic, some combination of mystery delivered Janis to me when I most needed her juice. Our friendship has blossomed into truth-telling and compassionate understanding.

Grandmother Margaret Behan

We found another tiny opening, a way to connect, through the Council of Thirteen Indigenous Grandmothers. Janis called and explained that she and a couple of friends had seen Global Grandmother Margaret Behan[18] speak in Sandpoint, Idaho about the 13 Grandmothers, and knew of their upcoming gathering at Grandmother Margaret's reservation in Lame Deer, Montana in 2013. She asked if I knew how she might deliver 13 pairs of slippers that she and two friends had knit for the Grandmothers. What a wonderful and generous offering of heart and Soul. Suddenly, Janis and I were becoming friends. I invited her to the tipi pole peeling party, quite a little enterprise in my circle of women; 13 tipis were handcrafted[19] to be assembled at the Lame Deer Council, one tipi for each of the Grandmothers. Our bond was sealed. Then came the slippers, they were part of the handoff to Grandmother Margaret, that she would have another Pacific Northwest gift for the Global Grandmothers.

Slippers fit into Bags Painted by Children; and Slipper Knitters, from left, Charles, Janis, Michelle

As soon as I heard the keywords, editor and writing teacher, I asked Janis to read a draft of *Soul Stories*; I am so glad she said, "Yes." I learned she had taught creative writing in workshops and adult education and helped people write their life stories, so I thought, yes, she would be a good reader and critic for me. Without a single bit of hesitation, Janis signed up to go on the journey through all of the Passages with me; she had heard the call of initiation. She knew now was the time to honor her own inner Elder.

I put Janis' editorial background to the test and asked her to be my Editor as well as my journeying sister. She said, "Yes," and "yes." We have collaborated closely through Divine inspiration and very hard work for two years. Somehow and absolutely together, we birthed the first book, *Soul Stories*. Through the sheer miracle of grace and ease, we initiated one another as Elders.

Janis dug way down deep to create a space in her life to do these two things while I plugged into my own creative outlet. We chose Summer Solstice 2014 to be our Womb Threshold. That was bold, so bold, we could hardly stop and think. We just took the leap in great faith and inspiration that such an auspicious journey would fulfill our heart's desire for Rites of Passage. On this pilgrimage to the Soul of ourselves, five other women came along in their own fashion. We all had the same rough draft of the *Soul Stories* manuscript to guide us along.

The Threshold Became a Guiding Force for Relationship

Wait, the liminal ground rushed up to meet us. *Soul Stories* said to mark our calendars with the Sun and the Moon, align with these cosmic energies and begin in a good, ceremonial way. Quite suddenly, we were, metaphorically and spiritually, in the wombs of our Mothers. The images are very rich. In our storylines, we followed a thread and imagined being back in the womb-space after more than six decades on Earth. Although this requires an active imagination and is purely illusory, the origin story of a Soul's life in a body serves as a unique way to remember the journey through time. Women know one thing unanimously, we all come from the stars; we are made of stardust and receive our inspirations from Source. Throughout life, creative energy continues to beam into our womb-space.

Janis with her Mom, 2015

Janis asked her Mother, "When did you first know you were pregnant with me?"

"At the opera, Aida." As a lover of music, Janis jumped for joy.

Hers was a close Italian immigrant family, intergenerational and fascinating. All gathered around the table at huge celebratory meal times, laughing, telling stories. Before this initiation journey, Janis had spent years excavating her family tree like a professional anthropologist. She had all of her Ancestor stories to support this inner journey. While she was in that womb-space, hearing the stories for the first time with her adult brain and body, those Ancestors came in close and became even more dear to her heart. Her Mother at 95 is still vital, the Mother-Daughter piece remains precious and palpable. As with many relationships, the clearing of sticky energies has freed Janis' continuing Soul journey. Her birth and childhood setting is storybook, she was raised in Hollywood, CA; I can barely imagine such an imprint.

We had notes to compare and processes to improve, so my journey included a daily visit out on my land and the quiet space of my candle-light journaling. Janis had her garden, a brand new Boxer puppy, and out her front door, the mighty Clark Fork River; we moved through the Passages alone and together. We talked weekly, often for an hour or more. My greatest joy throughout our parallel journeying together was an occasional visit across the state line to Janis' cabin. I always arrived completely filled with joyful anticipation. Comfortable in her body, she bounds down the Nature stairs of her front yard like a sprightly young woman.

For this pilgrimage we visited the days of our lives, more than 24,000 days. Never quite linear, our introspection felt circular, around to then and back to now. Deeply immersed, we walked in two worlds. We found our stories interesting, boring, and full of surprises only because the adult brain was reviewing. Janis is proficient in Tarot reading and Astrology. She worked with the I-Ching for many years, beginning right after her divorce took her away from her native Catholicism. Her ability to language this spiritual journey derives from deep explorations throughout her life.

From birth and before childhood unfolded completely, Janis' story was filled with joy and grief, with the angst and wonder of growing up. She was raised devoutly Catholic and educated throughout elementary and high school by sweetly passionate nuns. Janis remembered her childhood and wrote about each relationship as the people re-appeared in her life. This may be the finest and most evolved way to initiation, and especially to catch up our early Passages: People shape us more than time and more than self. Being thorough in this review, Janis remembered her first encounter with death, at eleven years old. That tender time was when her Grandfather died and she heard her Grandmother and Aunties wailing, so utterly grief stricken.

Janis (r) on the Beach with Ilse

Because she had such a vivid imagination, naturally there was a first time when trouble rained heavily down. That was a story of running away with a classmate. "I know where we can get some horses and ride to Montana" Janis fibbed. She and her accomplice were 12. Even though they didn't succeed, and they did get in a heap of trouble, the possibilities of the story still fill a young girl's heart with joy.

Her First Blood Passage is vivid, as are most of the times she shed her blood. Unlike so many women in the same era, no shame or disguise was present in Janis' story of her Moon cycles. She simply loved her periods!

Janis told me she and her friends could be excused from class by asserting a so-called "menstruation emergency." Then they sat giggling in the lavatory and thought how clever they were. Her early menses were her freedom. Quite honestly, the trials of living informed Janis' best stories, as every good story holds conflict needing to be resolved.

Janis shared about leaving home; she remembers this moment very well. Her First Flight Passage was early marriage when she was nineteen. Contrast that to how the culture feels about teen marriages today. All of the hardship and heartaches have been gathered together in the bundle of stories which produce a Threshold of change; she resolved the pain of living without a trace of shadow carrying over. While she harvested stories between each of her Passages, I watched the cocoon of transformation spin threads of golden silk around her.

The personal spirituality that Janis had advanced through her life was well-formed before this Rites of Passage journey sparked something new, an opening that will continue to expand. When she says she is soaring, I know it and feel it. Even though her story includes many different jobs in many different places, Janis has gleaned the best from those experiences, especially the lessons, and views the shadows with a wise smile. Janis' long journey through life has navigated many deaths, three marriages before thirty, children and very hard work, every single day. Her Soul-mate came later and they have been married 30 years.

I have been witness to Janis' process that honored her Ancestors, those she knew and those she did not know. This has been a defining spiritual awakening. At the root of belonging, Janis discovered the legacy stories of her Ancestors, from 1605, births and baptisms, marriages and deaths, recorded in Italy in Latin. Hearing a few of those stories has caused me to look at belonging from that angle, we all come from a gene pool more varied than we can imagine. Peering into those Ancestors lives, going back to Italy to visit their homeland, meeting family, learning about the times they lived through, these brightly colored threads have been a defining way that Janis has come to know herself, deeply. When she accepted the *Soul Stories* journey, she was ready to peer into her peaks and troughs, the light and dark of her glorious life, and find her Elder Encore.

Rarely have I met a friend so balanced that I feel better just being in her company. Let's look at how she got that way: Raised in West Hollywood, and nested in a multigenerational Italian family, Janis found her ways to see through life; she was gifted with an inborn sense for delight and joy. Did she turn sideways with the trials of life? Not Janis. At a young age she found her loves: horses and music. I remember her describing the stationary Palomino pony across the big street; she would take her dime and ride with the wildest imagination of a country kid. She found solace for her wild imagination at other times, too.

Janis' love of music drew her all the way into the world of concerts and musicians. "It was a great time for music in Los Angeles: the Ash Grove, the Troubadour, the Hollywood Bowl. I heard as much music as I could and wanted to meet everybody, and I did." Yes, that glittery world shaped Janis, it gave her the unending connection to the joyous sound of life, the dancing quality that her life has now, even the special lilt in her step. Throughout the highs and lows of sex, drugs and rock n' roll, she forged her philosophy about spirituality; it is delicate, deeply engrained, and easily damaged if not tended.

Through this guided journey of remembering, Janis realized that all these times of her life were real and fun, even though she did encounter trials and error like anyone. Yet, delight wins and commands her attention more. She has taught me to appreciate wherever you put your heart and mind, that is what becomes bigger. As the old story is told, which wolf do you feed?

Initiated Elder Beauty

When I asked the legacy question, Janis offered a juicy tidbit about mentoring that I cannot resist: This is the legacy to which all women could rise. She said, "I find that as an Initiated Elder, I want to share what I have learned along the way, help women into their power wherever I can. I want to be a Mentor, to share stories and define my Spiritual Elder time that way. The beauty of looking back now is that the pain is gone, only the dazzling memories remain."

In this snapshot I realize how much there is to know about a long-lived and well-lived life. Our time together is organic, what rises is miraculous because it feeds us. I am not writing a biography, I am sharing about an initiation Sister who dazzles me with her brightness, intrigues me with stories beautifully told, and honors me with her curiosity. We have experienced the opening of our Souls, we have found the patterns that serve us and how marvelous it feels to release the energetic hooks of stories that once held pain and anguish. Joy is the option we choose because in our rear-view mirrors, Janis has helped me see that all of living is about how to choose well and choose again.

We continually touched in and shared stories. By walking with the Moon and following the seasons of the Sun, Winter Solstice marked the place on our timeline where we came face to face with the present moment. As a natural progression, Janis felt ready to complete the pilgrimage, but I needed to hold back a Sun sign. My marriage at the age 52 marked a transition if not a transformation and needed an extra month of appreciation.

By the middle of February, three in our group had completed our journey and four had not. We set a date to celebrate the end of our journey and close the portal, far enough ahead that the others might want to join in ceremony.

The story of our journey together has two threads, the part we shared with only our Soul and the part we shared with one another. The day was May 9th, 2015, a day to remember for the Divine energy that held us in a bubble and a day to treasure in photos. Janis arrived at Grouse Creek, a special place north of Sandpoint, all decked out as usual, 'dressed to the nines' we have said in our generation. One of the things I truly love is how she plays dress-up with me. It's fun and so youthful. She brought her Goddess which set the stage for the day. I wanted to introduce her Goddess to my Goddess. We reflect on this now as inner and outer.

Two Goddesses Meet

As a gift from the world of stones, my Goddess washed up on the banks of Grouse Creek on Christmas Eve. Janis' Goddess statue came as a gift from a dear and spiritual friend. The positive recognition of the Goddess presence in our lives, inner and outer, may be the special mark of Elder. We walked the trail to the creek; Janis so reverently kneeled before the water's edge and washed her Goddess as in a baptism to mark the day as holy. The energy of initiation captured us and sent us into rapture together. When I introduced my stone Goddess to Janis, she placed hers beside mine so they could commune. I told the story of the stone's arrival and how, through floods and the hardship of winter, this stone Goddess had insisted on staying with me through the initiation year.

We must have been complete after the Goddesses met because we wanted to simply sit and be. Their aura infused our hearts with togetherness, celebratory and initiatory oneness. We left the creek to greet our special younger sister, Laura, who joined the ceremony because she had been along on her own journey and was ready to greet her Deepening Womanhood Threshold.

To be in the midst of the wild woods in ceremony, I had put up a large tent at The Crossroads. This place was so named for the girls of summer who had their Rites of Passage at the same location. Our hearts were one with those girls as we were once girls and our journey through stories brought our inner girls back to life. It was lilac season, two weeks early as everything this spring. At the entrance to the tent, I placed the same smooth hide those girls had stepped across, some exquisite Nature creature gave her life for our Threshold. Another feminine spirit worked that hide with her own hands, we relished the gift. Sitting together in this tent, the three Goddesses of initiation smudged one another, prepared an altar to hold our stories, and made flower crowns for our heads and beaver-chewed Elder staffs to move us forward. Until we were complete, we shared about our long pilgrimage through the days of our lives.

When we left The Crossroads, radiant beneath our flower crowns, holding our staffs gifted by the beavers and wearing our Elder Shawls, I laid down my staff and invited my sisters in initiation to step across with intention. Our liminal portal closed then, nearly one year after we crossed the opening Threshold. We each felt complete at the end. Complete was a state of mind that lasted a few days. Another full year was required to integrate all of the change that comes on the far side of a Threshold. We have allowed that process to work on us in dream-time and when we were not looking. Stories make a life, and we got busy making more stories. We learned and truly, our stories matter.

Looking back, we have been pleasantly surprised by the shining that we feel radiating from our Souls. Whether it's soaring or shining, we feel different each day, more enthusiastic about life, ready for the challenges of our Elder years ahead. We rise each morning full of energy, in loving devotion, we cultivate receptivity and reach for JOY. Thank you, dear Janis, for traveling with me into the future.

Emerging From a Long Journey

GIFTS FROM THE ELDERS: ELDER ENCORE

Maybe your Soul planned all the events of your life to happen the way they did. Consider your Soul as the finest teacher in your life. Embrace the journey ahead as a Soul journey! With maturity comes a natural ability to ease your grasp and release.

* How can you possibly release all that has come in but no longer serves? Very carefully and deliberately release the emotional charge that some influences still hold.

When you look within and without, do you see that you and all women are more differentiated than similar?

* From the place of wholeness at Birth to now, what do you believe and what more do you want?

* Who has been in your life, in deep or shallow relationships and what gifts have they brought to you, consciously or unconsciously? Light a candle, refer to the relationship wheel at the back and spend time with your relations on paper.

You took that mighty big leap of faith across the Deepening Womanhood Threshold: Those twenty years of adulthood held all of life and delivered so many opportunities to grow.

* What could possibly be ahead?

* You were born with a purpose. Search out your hidden gifts, you have something more to offer, something great. This is the time to set yourself up for that one big thing you came to do.

* What is it you must do and only you can do?

* How can you best deliver on the gifts you were so generously given?

With your miraculous brain, and across the timeline of your days, you were born with the ability to grasp the past, present, and peer into the future nearly simultaneously.

* How will you mark your place in time?

* Are you learning how your heart guides your mind?

* Are you operating with all the information at your disposal?

* What consistently brings you joy?

Harvest personal and special sparks of joy from the story of your life. Look for your gratitude for times of trial from your shadow side. Crossing five, six, or seven Passage Thresholds with a ceremony for each has helped you find honor in your position, honor for all of your days lived.

* Can you take a long view of the past and examine how your body has changed as your thoughts about your body have changed?

* To create your own storyline of Divine guidance or minor miracles, be sure to include your history of play and magical time in Nature. Embrace all your friends who are growing older with you lovingly, joyfully and definitely playfully.

Are you becoming more intimate with your cosmic relations, Mother Earth and her elder sister, Grandmother Moon?

* How have your spiritual beliefs changed as you crossed over each Threshold?

* Astrology offers a language of belonging. I understand my place on Earth by paying attention to the sky. The information, both spiritual and psychic in content, is quite revealing. What does this cosmic language offer you?

* The cosmic energy of Saturn announces your Elder Encore Threshold is near with the second Saturn return: Are you prepared to give the gifts of your Soul?

* Saturn is like the pestering Coyote who asks, how are you progressing

on the deliberate aim of your life? Who were you born to be?

What do you long for before you cross the Elder Encore Threshold?

What would you love more of?

* When I speak of legacy, of purpose, I wrap one thread around the Earth and another thread around the Moon to help you find your Gift for Gaia.

* Reflect on how your Moonpause is shaping you. How has it prepared you for this time.

* Have you claimed a place on Earth for yourself and your family?

* Have you become a stakeholder, part of the grassroots to make your place better?

* If you agree that this is an age to be open to more, what is on your list?

* How do you need to prepare yourself to continue building on your wisdom tradition?

Elder is the age that all others look up to for leadership, wisdom and guidance. The culture is dependent on how the Elders are portrayed and valued. Are you preparing to consciously model what it means to be an Elder?

* Contemplate, in your journal and in silence, the legacy all women are weaving for future generations.

* Gather the lessons and wisdom of your stories; see the patterns found in your relationships. Review of the delights of your life and you will find the honoring that your life needs to regenerate your whole self. What have you been training for your whole life?

CLOSING BLESSING

This is only the seventh Threshold, your time ahead is long and lovely. Of all the threads to carry you forward, find the ones which satiate, follow those. To feel satisfied, a number of natural forces must blend harmoniously. The mind has wants, the heart has desires, and the body has needs. Humans are emotional beings; an intricate and wide range of emotions propel this ride through life, creating ups and downs. Elder is the age to see all these forces as loves. Seeing the dichotomy of joy and bitterness, choose joy for this half of your life.

* As always, listen to your Soul-self

* Walk in nature

* Spend time creating, perhaps with one or two other women

* Find babies to cuddle, little ones to play with, and teens to listen to

* Practice love, stroke yourself, stroke your partner, share hugs

* Spend time every single day doing things that satiate (gratify, satisfy, quench)

* Do your body scans, seek the help you need, seek pleasure as a healer

* Harvest your stories, because your life matters, your stories matter

* Share all of this with another woman who needs mentoring, this is our legacy.

NOTES ON ELDER ENCORE PASSAGE

1   How can women of 40 or 50 or 60 experience something they missed at 12 or 14, at 18 or 29? My Women's Circle decided on an experiment we called double-tracking. By living fully in the present, we believed we could take a long life review and bring ourselves across all the early Thresholds. This made a beautiful story for two dozen women, and I share its basis in *Soul Stories: Nine Passages of Initiation* (2015). The story is posted on my website www.ninepassages.com entitled *The Great Catch-up Ceremony*.

2   Alfred Korzybsky (1879-1950) was the first to describe the two filters through which the world is experienced, the first is one's grasp of language and the second is the inherited structure of the nervous system. *Filters* means that the world is not experienced directly, but shaped, inherited from Ancestors, what they knew and taught through interaction with the environment. Nature and nurture are both components of time-binding. A good example is how often I use my Mother's colloquiums, such as "rest on your laurels."

3   Fascinated by brain, by how these two ideas wind around each other, time-binding and the triune brain, I introduce Paul D. MacLean (1913-2007) as the original scientist who explained the triune brain. As these notes illustrate, I appreciate the complexity of your life.

4   Christiane Northrup promotes women's health and well-being. By delivering one book after another to women, all that we need to understand our bodies better is here, in wisdom generously offered. These books were written for all of us: *Mother-Daughter Wisdom* (2006); *Women's Bodies, Women's Wisdom* (2010); *The Wisdom of Menopause* (2012); and *Goddesses Never Age* (2015).

5   I especially love the book, *Brainstorm* (2013) wherein Daniel Siegel highlights the teen-age brain, and the book that introduced me to the further work of Siegel and colleagues. *Mindsight: The New Science of Personal Transformation* is the integrative master work that hangs so many disciplines on the same web and illustrates how science and spirituality are woven together.

6   I have followed anthropologist Mary Catherine Bateson since I read the major works of her parents, Margaret Meade and Gregory Bateson. Two books, *Composing a Life* (1989) and *Composing a Further Life: The Age of Active Wisdom* (2010), have help deepen my thoughts about the life cycle.

7   I name and include one of my favorite astrologers, Teri Parsley Starnes, because I never fail to learn something remarkable from her newsletter: Starsdance Astrology is profound every week. Her website www.starsdanceastrology.com, may also be a teacher for you.

8   Long before I had my hands on this amazing *Nature Spirit Tarot* deck, I often visited Jean Herzel and she would reveal her progress. Her deck is stunning and poignantly insightful and I draw a card every single day as one of my practices. Who can resist the title of this reference that Jean gave me as a guide into the spirit of Tarot: *Spiritual Tarot: Seventy-Eight Paths to Personal Development* (1996) by Echols, Mueller, and Thomson. Jean Herzel's website: wwwnaturespirittarot.com

9   Dolores LaChapelle, one of the Ancestors now, was gifted as an interdisciplinarian and teacher of human ecology and deep ecology. She walked with me up the slopes of Mount Wilson in Colorado and helped me see what I might do with an advanced degree in Women's Studies. By her ex-

ample, I added Nature Studies to weave disciplines together because she demonstrated that new knowledge is found at the intersection of disciplines. With Dolores' help, I found old knowledge in Rites of Passage that insisted on a new life.

10   Raised as an only child, Dolores' son, David LaChapelle found his wisdom early in life. David wrote beautiful parables: In 1993, *Mountains of Light and Pathways of Love;* in 1995, *A Voice on the Wind: A Fable about Coming of Age.* Many other books can be found at the website set up after David crossed in 2009: http://www.lachapellelegacy.org/Bookstore.html. I love his final work, published posthumously, *A Hymn of Changes: Contemplations of The I Ching* (2009).

11   Meditation has come to the West from the East but perhaps it was here all along. All peoples who revere the Earth feel awe, often by walking in Nature. Now we revere teachers such as Sally Kempton, Pema Chodron, Thich Naht Hanh, and many others who remind us what some of our esteemed Ancestors knew: We must find our way to quiet mind for the great gifts that are waiting.

12   Created in 2015 by Maia Duerr; I love this illustration and asked permission to post this into *Nine Passages.* Crediting this illustration found on her website http://maiaduerr.com/

13   Sesame Almond Crackers are made with almond-flour and eggs, yummy and healthy. Ask me for the recipe: gail@ninepassages.com.

14   When I read this book, *Outrageous Openness: Letting the Divine Take the Lead* (2014), I cried over this simple validation. Divine guidance is the way people experience the miracles of life and now I know I am not alone in this worldview. Tosha Silver offers videos and workshops at http://toshasilver.com/books/.

15   Unlocking most of my secrets, which is the reason for writing, Here I share my learned teachers. Carolyn Myss, online and in her book *Sacred Contracts* (2001); also every one of Jean Bolen's books especially—*Goddesses in Everywoman* (1984) and *Goddesses for Older Women: Archetypes in Women over Fifty* (2001). Other favorite teachers of archetypes, Sally Kempton explores the cross cultural lens of Hindu Goddesses and for the Divine Feminine archetype, Helen M. Luke is unsurpassed. Joan Borysenko is such a prolific writer, but I loved *Woman's Book of Life* (1996).

16   Helen M. Luke has come to me as a gift from an initiating woman. Thank you Laurie Evans for your generosity, I hope we can continue mentoring one another through our Elder years.

17   News often travels underground like mycelium; so it was that I heard many women speak fluently about the work of Marija Gimbutas (1921-1994). In her long career as a professor of archeology at UCLA, she excavated evidence of the Civilization of the Goddess of 30,000 years ago. Most women find hope in the fact that matrilineal cultures have existed before. Her three major works are *The Goddesses and Gods of Old Europe* (1974); *The Language of the Goddess* (1989); and *The Civilization of the Goddess* (1991). Her life was put in a documentary by Starhawk and Donna Read, *Signs Out of Time: The Story of Archaeologist Marija Gimbutas* (2003).

18   Global Grandmother Margaret Behan was once a member of the 13 Indigenous Grandmothers. In 2014, she told her story of hosting 12 other Grandmothers at Lame Deer while she taught her special sculpting techniques for making dolls of clay to a group of post-modern Elders. She is a strong woman leader of her tribe and a teacher of Cheyenne culture.

19 A little historical footnote, now, the gathering hosted by Grandmother Margaret in 2013 at Lame Deer, Montana gave my Women's Circle lots to do for a couple of years. One woman, Debra Williams, handmade 13 tipis (see www.sagebrushtipiworks.com) while the rest of us peeled tipi poles, hundreds of poles, and my editor, Janis Monaco Clark knitted slippers with her friends, the Slipper Knitters.

SPIRITUAL ELDER

~~~~~~

THE INTENTION:
ENJOYING THE LONGEVITY OF THE LIFE SPIRAL

A prayer for you: I bow to all your days lived, Elder Sister. Each name we use for the Great Mystery beyond—the One who astonishes, the Source—has been drawn into this prayer for the events and blessings of your life. God and Goddess, Divine Love and Womb of the Universe, I ask to share this embrace of you, my dear woman. I revere the walk of your life, dear Spiritual Elder. You are so God-like and so Goddess-like, we are all blessed to be in your company. Nested within your journey, we find hope for our own. We want to give you what babies need very much: They, like you, need quiet presence and focused attention.

Dearheart, I feel only reverence when I think of this pinnacle place on the Life Spiral. Most often, one image rises: You are a powerful, whole being between 65 and 100; you are a walking, breathing mystic who has found a zillion solutions to life's puzzles. You carry marvelous gems from your adventures with Nature and family. The deep repository of your stories gives the rest of us great pause.

EAGLE'S VIEW

Life peaks here: An evolutionary miracle has made the glory of each life stage possible, Spiritual Elder is the eighth stage, the one before Death. Once you've decided to move from Elder to Spiritual Elder, or some catalyst of change has pushed you, you might easily find yourself in a kind of limbo space. Such transitions are truly deep initiations and require nothing from you, only savoring and not rushing.

Before you step across the next Threshold, consider which parts of your life need to be released. Only you know the threads you want to carry forward to place in your final bundle, your Spiritual Elder bundle. Release is a big part of this ceremony.

Like a long runway, your approach to this Spiritual Elder Threshold is mental, psychological and spiritual. Preparing for this tender time, you will clearly see the contents of your Elder Encore bundle representing all your early elder years. You are still savoring this recent storyline as the cobblestones that bracket both sides of the Encore Threshold: Review your Life Spiral and begin to recognize personas. When you are ready to release your many trials and joys along with habits that no longer serve your higher purpose, all these belong in your bundle. Begin to work with forgiveness to invite change which is outside of ordinary time; this will be a deliberation of your deeds, your needs and your wants. Surrender to the pure joy of being.

You hold an intention to have life your way: Just enough of the busy life, maybe less all the time; just enough of the Grandkids, just enough of your family. What other aspects do you choose? If you revere community, you will want the perfect blend of Youngers and Olders and you will want your girl-gang to flock around once in awhile. Design these years ahead with intention from years of practice.

How do you nourish Mind-Body-Soul? You know all about good food and sunshine, and have learned about exercise and life-long learning. You have learned something more: Twisting the threads in your classic way with equal focus on Mind-Body-Soul has actually been the creative force leading to your longevity. Weaving your days with all of these colorful threads, you have been among the lucky ones to enjoy a miraculous elongation of this life stage before the debilitation of old age. Because you have focused on body-mind, you have learned about the neurological elasticity of your spirit. You have learned about the value and potential of your breath in meditation and you have connected with your Soul Guardians. In a regal but humble manner, you acknowledge, "if not me," who will step up to be the Sage of your community?

When sleep leaves you in the morning, you spend moments with God and in gratitude. Your dreams are cinematic wonders that linger throughout the day. A well-captured dream gives you hours of pleasure while you puzzle the symbols. This practice before rising is the mystical essence and spiritual connection that brings excitement for each new day. You are a modern mystic and I am pleased to help you reveal the Threshold for your Spiritual Elder time.

YOU NOW OWN THIS LIFE SPIRAL

Look again to the Life Spiral so we both understand this conversation. Peer into the cobblestones. There are many more ahead. After you cross your butterfly Threshold, an integration occurs. The cobblestones that bracket this butterfly represent your Encore time. I hope you dreamed big enough! Now you are preparing for the heart of your life. The great bundling of your life still lays ahead, the making of your legacy story.

I find that I can no longer Mentor, I can only speak as your friend also on the journey myself. We have been on a very long adventure together. I cannot let you go, I cannot let me go—we are Evolutionaries ™ using grace to model a good life all the way to Death.

The Life Spiral

An Intentional Study of Your Whole Life

You have crossed the Seventh Threshold, your time ahead is long and lovely. When you step across and put the Elder Encore at your back, feel the brush of those butterfly wings. This altered place just after your ceremony requires nothing of you except a rest.

Of all the shimmering threads to carry you forward, find the ones which satiate, deeply satisfy you and play with those. To feel satisfied, a number of forces naturally must blend harmoniously. The mind has wants, the heart has desires, and the body has needs. You want adventures, you desire precious moments and, oy vey, your body always needs attention. Humans are emotional beings; an intricate and wide range of emotions propel this ride through life, creating ups and downs. Elder is the age to see all these forces clearly as loves and to finally find peace with the internal flame, the water works, and the biology of your nature.

In the first Elder stage, an Encore came alive in you. Sometimes you were overwhelmed by the spin of your mind and the desires of your heart. You may have been evolutionary, revolutionary, entrepreneurial, or all three. Spend time with your Soul; walk in Nature; wander around. Tend your little garden and feed your body with the finest molecules of the spirit of breath and whole food. This spiritual place, knowing a full life is in you and Death is in suspension, infuses you with grace-filled enthusiasm for each day. Your knowing, your story, your contract with life emphasizes the mystery of life. As a modern mystic, staying as teachable as you have always been, will bring younger women knocking on your door seeking your wisdom.

Many more stories, in fact, many more years yet remain in your long-life contract. We represent a unique generation, a first ever time in human history, when five generations are living and feeling amazing vitality. This conscious perspective has never been seen or experienced before on this planet Earth. Let's make certain the Earth benefits from our joyous long lives.

We are working together now –you reading and me writing– to define this evolutionary gift. I will make a giant leap to my faith place and claim that we were born for this gift, you and I.

As our guide through this journey, the Life Spiral has elongated into this Spiritual Elder life stage, which may be the longest by year count. It may be the most glorious as well because of your wisdom, distilled from your accumulated knowledge and experiences. This is serious news, this is a game changer for everyone. I am celebratory and watchful: At 65, I am a late bloomer; I would like to be an Elder Mentor for two more decades. I have just learned what I need to know. Maybe the gift of collaboration with younger talents will provide the energy to become more philanthropic, a treasured volunteer in a school, a high flying adventurer. We can all make plans, we must continue to make a life.

LONGEVITY, A GIFT OF EVOLUTION

Since each decade has been different from the last, this rapid advancement of longevity has changed the culture from within, where it's difficult to see these changes. Mothers and Grandmothers of the early 20th century enjoyed an average age for their life span of 70. In *Composing a Further Life*, anthropologist Mary Catherine Bateson[1] reminds us that 30 years have been added to our life span in the last century and 20 of those years have been added since World War II. Seemingly when scientists weren't watching, women especially, began living longer, more vital and healthy lives through their 80's and 90's. In 2016, the second decade of the 21st century, long lives are no longer a phenomenon. Looking forward to 100 is becoming the norm. In ways mostly invisible, the culture is celebrating and adapting.

Can we truly delineate between Elder and Spiritual Elder? Elder certainly has her eyes on a prize, something more needs doing and she has the resources and energy to be doing the one thing that can only be done by her. Although she makes time for her inner world and cultivates a conscious relationship with the Goddess who constantly expands her Divine Feminine inside, she still feels ambition and drive as an Initiated Elder. This remarkable woman who flourished all through her Encore years is you. Through Elder Encore, you filled a niche in the culture because so much needed to be done. Maybe you traveled the world part of the time, and you learned that connecting to the youngest generation has been food for your Soul.

Ceremony for Releasing

Dearheart, the ritual of releasing, of finding your balance again, brings you down to the Earth, into the arms of Great Mother. The elements begin their work on you in this chaotic place between heaven and sky. Invite the transformative energy to hollow you out, to take you into an altered state. Here you will find the stillness between Heaven and Earth known as Peace in the I Ching.[2] Linger here for moments every day.

A change occurs, perhaps a crisis of some kind: The catalyst for change may come from the death of a beloved relation or a health challenge; divorce after 40 years of marriage is not uncommon. Waves of down-sizing and simplifying have deeply altered many lives. You may be your own agent of change. Once you feel loss and grief as your Soul directs, like a Phoenix, you will rise again and flourish. Any number of life-changing events will create an opportunity to rethink all your *doing* out in the world.

You embraced this change and stepped across the Elder Encore Threshold. You accepted being an Elder in your heart and the Spiritual Elder Threshold beckons, but not so fast. First, define and design this space for yourself, this space between Thresholds, you may be here for a few years.

CASTING OFF A SPELL

Old age, perhaps caused by hard work and many babies, by unhealthy habits and little inner focus, threads through our memories as a cultural meme, an archetype. We remember our old Grandmothers, we watched our Mothers grow old. Many of those experiences left a hollow feeling in our power centers, our time will come but old age will not define us. You and I will help create the model for this gift of longevity.

As your life span continues to roll out in front of you, the paradigm continues to shift. Consider all of your body parts for a moment. Within this longevity you are enjoying, many things have already gone wrong with parts of your body. You can easily look back over the decades, do a mental body scan, and tell your body's story through its trials, ills, repairs, and challenges. You will agree, what goes on and even wrong with the body does not necessarily disable or debilitate. The body recovers!

Each time you suffered a crisis—something big or something little— you learned how your body has its own memory and its own mind. It knows how to heal, it knows what harmony and balance feel like. With this body-mind, you have been led to Medicine Women with healing hands. You have healed yourself. This is the evolutionary miracle of you, wise old you.

Many have found a niche in the practice of geriatrics, old age medicine for the elderly. I would like to point out the difference between an honored and Initiated Elder and an old, elderly person. Your attitude and your personal practices have shifted the paradigm: Your inner life and how you feel your spirituality daily, these combine to make all the difference. This spell about old age and ageism will be cast off by you and your friends. Set the burden of that label aside, it no longer serves the collective consciousness.

With the coaxing of integrative medicine and functional medicine, the

M.D.'s have advanced their practices; they have evolved with the times and with your needs. They were helpful to make those past ills of your body-story as good as new. Along with this experience of combining healing methods, many alternative healers evolved which led you to self-healing practices. Alternative modalities are numerous. Perhaps you dive into a self-care practice using plant medicines in oil. You might begin with basic massage by your own hands to help you connect into how your body feels. Many of us have learned to give self-message to our body parts. Our own hands are well informed and skilled to detect changes. This is personal integration.

If you are able to cast off *old age* as a spell, consider casting off, at least in metaphor form, *retirement* as another spell. If you knew for sure you would live three decades after your career, would you retire that whole time? Perhaps instead you might engage your imagination to understand more about the art of living. Add what juice or spice is needed to launch you into new stories. Surely you deserve to play, but I am one who prescribes that for every day. Carefully consider your needs, you have learned some of what it takes to be whole and happy with yourself. What else can you contribute to the world at this peak of your life? More than any other time in life, your word, your vote, and your voice carries considerable influence. Knowing how different you are from your grandparents, the tone of challenging yourself will not surprise you. In *Composing a Further Life* Mary Catherine Bateson asks, "How, in growing older do I become more truly myself, and how does that spell out in what I do or say or contribute?"

The great suffering caused by the idea of growing increasingly worthless and disabled has lasted decades too long already. That suffering has been a weighty mantle crushing attitudes and dampening the spirit of gorgeous old women. Only the women with strong family support or Women's Circle support have survived cultural stereotypes.

Here is their secret: Discover how the culture operates through interdependence and collaboration. In little bands of women, little tribes and circles, swirls a magic juice for thriving. Your opinion, your passion, your favorite cause may only need support, perhaps you will be a direct match with one or two others. When darling old women share from our hearts, the culture will follow. Youngers are always attracted to Elders. Begin an intergenerational circle. You and your friends create deep culture while the Youngers create pop culture. Both are mutually curious and attractive. I have witnessed life in adoptive families; they are wonderfully interdependent and collaborative without any hooks or barbs. You might adopt whole families for the exchange of gifts.

You have everything you need to slip out from beneath the old cloak of ageism. Purely a mantel of disguise, the culture has used marketing very well to obscure the vitality and wisdom of your peak decades. When you see how wide this divide is, you will want to join this silent revolution.

We have all suffered through the urgent demand to look and feel younger than what is absolutely beautiful and natural for our bodies. Inside the cultural niche of the old and infirm, marketing through the Internet has caused waves of sensation: Trainers and body workers promising eternal youth with their methods; peddlers of vitamin supplements are predators in this niche so our elegant age has become its prey. The vulnerability that goes along with this life stage is still wrapped around old age beliefs, surviving beliefs work through the cultural consciousness. You no longer need to seek what does not belong to you, that you know. Look inside your vulnerability for its hidden gifts. Long ago you learned to trust yourself and your body.

The seed question for your legacy is, "Do you have another chapter?" In your creative imagination, what will it be like? In your lifetime, the Women's Movement and feminism have given way to the Divine Feminine. Even if you have been on the edges of this cultural meme, allow me to pull you into the middle now. I have offered mentoring rather lavishly. This continues to be the Divine Feminine spirit within me. As she awakens in me, I have felt the wind of patriarchy, of domination and control, simply blow around and past me. She has taught me kindness and vision. I still see patriarchy but with my heart open to Divine Feminine; I no longer suffer domination or oppression of the unconscious variety. See if this is true for you.

This ability to *see* came as the great gift of early circles of women, a pool of energy now for all women to draw from as our heritage. A long time ago, in the 1960s and 1970s, women gathered in consciousness raising groups. This was the seed of activism continuing from the 1910's and Women's Right to Vote in 1920. Remember to hold the sacred practice and rituals of your Women's Circle inside the circle. You and a few others may work *outside* the circle for a grassroots effort to change the culture. No matter how much we have already done, there is always something more that needs done.

YOUR RITUALS

This is another training ground: You have navigated so many already. Be in your silence with Source energy. Before you are called home, can you imagine this space filled with beauty? Can you offer your tranquility to a harried Mother? How do you hold your Soul Sisters when they reach out for help?

Elder's Hands Observing Silence

Allow Earth's elements to help you: Watch emotional attachments melt away like falling water; let fire illuminate the value of your days--maybe you need to remain quiet for a while longer; invite air to radiate light, send a rainbow of chakra energy shooting out of your crown. Allow time for your own energy to mingle with Divine Love. As you breathe, feel the shower of kundalini stardust return you to wholeness and back to the Earth. The Threshold for Spiritual Elder rises when your heart and eyes turn their focus inward for longer periods of the day. You will always love to do, but a catalyst of change such as this one is rare and worth the notice.

Much about life needs processing again, the story of your life waits to be gathered into one elegant bundle. If you have not yet completed the healing of your emotional and psychic self, raise your consciousness to do this quiet review with grace and ease along a timeline of comfort. Summon your Eagle's view and your spirit self to help you with any remaining emotional knots. Linger with the edgy places until you can smooth them over. Use what you already know—perhaps you will write to process, or talk or weave or paint. The physical part, your body, is an equal partner in your wholeness, and must feel completely ready for your Soul to move you forward.

Plans need to be made to organize your life and at a time of your choosing, you will know when to make a ceremonial presentment of your spiritual memoir. You know you have time, perhaps you know exactly how much time. Perhaps you are beginning or you are in the middle of your Spiritual Elder years, you will have many years before you cross into the last 13 Moon stage of life. I have referred to the Death Threshold as the last 13 Moons because every single human experiences this; it is the final thing we all have in common. During the 13 Moons before we cross over, our differences melt back together, unity actually arrives and we release ego, preparing to return as One to the Source of all, home, God, heaven, known by these and other names. This final year or perhaps two years while the body releases, that is when *old age* finally arrives.

Until that time, as a new culture of wise and Initiated Elders, we can harvest the riches of our future place together on the Spiral with our Elder Sisters. Elders are the ones to bring honor to those who cross over the Spiritual Elder Threshold. Women together are the ones who are going to change the world. We need one another through all the easy times of joy and laughter, through all the times of tears and despair. No one escapes from these realities.

There is much more to life yet to come. Your life will be defined by you all through your 80s and 90s. This is a new phenomenon, this Spiritual Elder time. It's new in the culture because of the longevity of so many Elders. The longevity of thousands and millions will cause a revolution in everything the culture itself knows and does. You live among a generation of game changers, on an evolutionary edge right now. History is being made by you. You were born for this.

Imagine the crossing of this Threshold for yourself: Is your ceremony with your kindred spirits at a garden party, a tea party, or gathered in a tipi or a meadow? Circles of Elders can simply gather in a living room. This generational phenomenon of initiation and honoring may seem much like a dream, but in the Eagle's view, women are the ones who see, we are the ones who know. For the culture to understand what we are about, for the culture to bring ceremony and ritual into everyone's lives, our family, friends and adopted relations look to us for how we hold this pinnacle of our lives well lived. To shift the paradigm of the culture, each woman must step more into her story.

Life is an art form, not a linear, predictable process. We live to the hilt and then we rest. Each woman does the best she can at each potential turning point, given the information and the self-knowledge she possesses.

SPIRITUAL ELDER NOTES

We are the imagination of ourselves,
Someone said this.
I ask: Who am I born to be? What do I know?
I know I'm lucky to be alive! My Guardian Angels worked overtime.
Some friends passed on, through no fault of their own, while others finished
    early
Their work done, and others just in the wrong place.
What I do know is immediate: Reframe current and past Thresholds
And pay good fortune forward.
It is time to tell a different story, rewrite the script

What I know as absolute may not...
Be present to what is actually happening, ditch illusion
Get ready to be Spiritual Elder, the deepest work yet!
Why am I still here when brighter stars have fallen?
Let me show gratitude to Madre Grande for leaving me standing.
Time is a Great Beauty.
I fill the corridors of my life with mirrors and view
Opposite sides.
Where is the comedy in my tragedy?
Where is the joy in my sorrow?
Meanwhile, I will share my lifetime's harvest
Before dancing and singing my heart to heaven.

©Janis Monaco Clark

A LIFETIME OF HABITS

Longevity is a fact of your life now, so look closely at your personal formula for success. Certainly your interior life feeds your exterior demeanor. They both work together. The more you integrate all of your good habits, the more you raise your awareness about their spiritual power.

When your practices become sacred, your personal secret becomes obvious to you. Your daily practices and how you break routine with a surprise for yourself, how you move your body, how you feed your body, these all combine into a self-care secret because you practice integration. How these practices have become interconnected deserves your mental awareness. They have become your secret to peace and happiness. One of the Laws of Nature: You grow your own seed, you are what you think and eat, your body speaks of care and love. All of this you share with your girlfriends, invite them to talk about their secrets.

Boomers turned 30 before the personal computer hit the marketplace. You have driven the information age. Think of all you've learned through this spread of information. You and most of your beautiful friends 70 to 100 and beyond have practiced some form of meditation. The miraculous spread of silence and meditation may be because the Internet has become one of our tools for raising consciousness. Do you walk alone, garden alone, sit in silence with an empty mind? Do you meditate with your friends? These practices have evolved your spiritual life. You have caught the meme in the culture about brain intelligences and have learned that meditative practices of all varieties expand your inner life, manage stress, and help you to hear from the entities that surround you who help you on this Earth walk. You have introduced your gift into the culture and have demonstrated an awareness of how everything works together. Celebrate what has been offered you, an integrated life.

One of the great lessons of all, humble and true, is this one: There is more to learn, there is more to experience, even on the days when you say "no more," you know there is more. Living life perpetuates a hunger to live life. If only because you can name the peak experiences of your well lived life, you know there are peak experiences to look forward to in the days ahead. You know the increments of time well and treat yourself to joy and adventure each season. This anticipation is part of your secret. Like a string of pearls, the ventures you look forward to are precious and have kept you involved in your life.

Now you have time to read, so make it a practice. Give reading as a gift to yourself, it's the truest form of leisure. You might like to go for a walk listening to a book. One of my wise Spiritual Elders sparkled when she shared with me her favorite author and story teller, Jean Kirkpatrick.[3] After listening to three books of the dozens that Jean has authored, I want to share the spark. These many stories are about the pioneering life of the mid-1800s. How marvelous that Jean has recreated these stories so the time comes alive. Then-to-now reveals the great change in women and the places where we melt back into one another.

This can be the highest form of sharing with your friends, what has inspired you and why? Perhaps you do not need a book club because your reading rate and diversity are different from the group. Still your friends want to hear the good juicy tidbits of what you are reading. Obtaining digital is freely available from your local library. I add this reminder only to keep your neurological pathways elastic. The easiest exercise for your mind is imagination. Do you have a fictional story in you? Do you dream in stories?

One of my favorites and possibly yours is the spiritual practice of relationship building. I have learned for a fact, that everyone I meet has a chemistry that matches mine, or not. Those that do have the magic juice deserve nurturing. For my beloveds, I remain open to receive what they offer me. They remain open to what I offer them. You remember this Law of Human Nature: Balance comes through giving and receiving. Women especially, have given, given, given until it has become an expectation and another cultural curse. Not you. In your longevity, you have learned about receiving, you have remained spiritually open to gifts that simply come as love. It's the love you thrive on and have put into your spiritual practice.

Women have this deep knowing in common. Others have stated this as one of the exclusive nuggets for how the Universe operates: What goes around comes around; what you put out comes back ten-fold. In our stories, each of us holds many examples of this spiritual truth. You practice this balance in your relationships—you open to receive equal to your version of giving. How does this great pearl of wisdom express through you?

WELCOME YOUR SPIRITUAL ELDER THRESHOLD

When you feel the Threshold coming, when the call arrives for you to give your legacy gifts preparing to return to your star, invite your beloveds to gather around you more often. This Spiritual Elder Threshold follows the Encore performance and signifies a time for reflection, for harvesting the pearls of your life and for sharing intimately with your beloveds.

If you gaze into the Life Spiral you will begin to understand the significance of this stage. Do not hesitate to create a ceremony for yourself when you feel you are nearing the end of your Encore projects. Many adventures lie ahead as you can see by the largest number of cobblestones of any stage. Very likely this could also be the longest in number of years and in spiritual experiences. By adventures, I do mean great fun; I also mean introspection and collaboration. This is the time of life when Youngers seek you out because your wisdom has unlocked so many of life's closely held secrets. For the sake of evolution of the future human beings, the ones just coming to Earth, find the encouragement here to be open, to share your magnificent stories. The children of the Earth will benefit by your sharing. This includes your relations, your tribe, your Village and all stages younger than you, now.

Take great care, moving from Moon-to-Moon, to continue your practices as an ultimate modeling for others in your Village. This is how people in the culture benefit. We all look to you for clues about the trajectory and shape of our own lives. You have already helped to cast off a spell that has haunted all women of a certain age: This spell diminished the experiences of the old. Focus only on your fullest expression of the interior you, your mind and body and spirit. Do not for one minute entertain the myth of becoming less when you feel such fullness for your holy story. You want more life out of life, not less.

Elder in Three Parts: Encore, Spiritual, and 13 Moons of Death

When change can be fully embraced, your Soul dances with joy. Change little things first like rearranging your kitchen drawers, then change bigger things. If you are still working, know that people of all ages are watching you. You are a miracle because you have a certain glow, a certain magnetic aliveness. This is your ultimate modeling shining through. Your attitude toward change as creation will be made visible.

As an Elder for so long, probably since you were 60 or 65, you have re-invented yourself at least once, perhaps twice through the remarkable pinnacle of your Encore. You have been practicing rituals and doing ceremonies all your life. I am happy to surprise you, another is coming.

I am honoring you with this special life stage review. As a perennial researcher and culture watcher, my eyes can see this evolutionary moment. Academics have written about it: All the other stages, the other generations have recently elongated. Acknowledge these evolving dynamics and become the first generation to create a legacy out of your life story.

STORY AS LEGACY

You have learned what every Elder learns, it is lonely on this Elder pinnacle and it is sweet. All that life has offered you, all your peak experiences coalesce into each sunrise. Those dear ones who come around, younger by generations, cannot appreciate all that you know. All of your peers, like you, are vast storehouses of experience and wisdom. This is the nature of long life: Your knowledge and experience has accumulated into greatness. You may know this already, I say yes, it's true, your Genius is showing.

I suggest expression. Your stories are so sacred as to be God-like and they need something from you: Honor and respect. This is a form of the bal-ance equation, you receive respect when you give it. Give your stories respect. All that lives inside of you is needed by the rest of us. Make time to speak or write your stories down.

Remember what lives inside of your holy bundles from each of the Life Spiral Thresholds—she who was you, in her many former versions. She was you as little child, big girl and the darling who learned about Moontime and survived the hard school of the 20s. She has been your champion who stepped up bravely and learned how to do everything. Through every peak and every trough, she was your companion who presided over family traditions. Now it's your turn to shine the light on these former selves. They created you. They are all inside of you, cheering for your victory lap. Please tell the whole story of how you became the woman you are today.[4]

Women in circles and sharing tea at your kitchen table will help you strengthen the new genre of writing called spiritual memoir. Remember Alfred Korzybsky[5] and how time-binding works? Do not leave your marvelous stories locked inside your heart. Tell us about your memories and we will give you the gift of delight for all that you share. Your relations will return your gift with one of their own—time-binding will carry your stories forward.

Chronology is only one key to this holy exercise. Your story holds the magic of your life, the miracles, all the Divine Guidance. You might work from an outline that follows the Life Spiral or you can chose to delineate by decade. Within each decade, look for how change worked with you, in you, through you; these are a few of the stories to tell.

One of your personal secrets lies in creativity: How have you created this life filled with stories? It's personal, juicy, and took decades to evolve. How has the act of creating many things of beauty, your precious family and so many other things that please you, how has all of this evolved into the breathless piece that awakened your spirituality, your beliefs, and made sense of your foundation stones? Creativity surged through your blood, in your unique way, will you tell us how? Some call this your juice, your magic juice: Follow a thread back to Birth; your creativity lives within the stardust you brought from your star. You live in a generation that has given itself permission to be wildly creative. Be a pioneer who breaks out of the mold that the culture believes about the infirm elderly. Cast off wrong messages like, "You can't, you no longer have what it takes." I say, "You can!" Until your last 13 Moons you have more than enough to live your wildest creative life. Express! Your story needs to be boldly told.

If this suggestion feels vulnerable, that's very good. If it feels like too much shame will come, then that is where your focus needs to be for a while. Read the series of books by Brené Brown.[6] We all feel shame, our lives have been warped by it. So many masks were created for hiding what we believed others would judge. This is the time to reveal those masks to yourself.

There are masks waiting for me to reveal to myself, this is the essence of initiation. I do this to honor the time I lived, what that cultural story had to offer me and my generation. I am honoring the scared and lonely little pubescent girl who woke up her inner judge and critic as guides for her life. I have placed the light and dark events on a timeline so that shadow has equal opportunity to be present in my story. I am interested in the dance of my inner Animus because for too long, masculine energy and patriarchy were the driving force I felt from my Aries Moon. How my inner Divine Masculine dances with the awakened Divine Feminine, this is like a crack in the world.

Women are rapidly evolving. Working, even playing with our interior lives, I am one of many women who see how patriarchal energies, so present and obvious, have seeped into thoughts and deeds. Seeing is the key to dissolving the power of domination that secretly lurks everywhere. Now old women's stories will expose the truth about how the evolved and balanced inner masculine and inner feminine are going to be the driving force of awareness and change on our dear planet. We are of the Earth, we are of the stars, we are celestial beings. What legacy, what story might we leave for the Seventh Generation to discover? What is obvious and present in your interior life?

With integrity, I will share my story: First I am writing for myself to honor my life as a legacy for those who have loved me. Perhaps I am also writing for Mothers who have daughters, perhaps I am writing for my peers. That love is precious, I feel it. Writing is my way to return respect.

An Elder Crossing called herself a Single Drop of Dew

RESPECT AND REVERENCE

Respect is an energy that first we give to ourselves and then to others. As a form of love, out of respect, we open to receive love and return it like a boomerang. This is mutuality. An early Mentor of mine, Sara Lawrence-Lightfoot,[7] used Indigenous ways to reclaim respect. She teaches that our differences make us equal. Sara helped me understand, by close observation, that women and men have misused the power and meaning of such a sacred word like respect. Can you see how different a respect-filled worldview differs from darker times when power over respect formed the hierarchical triangle? In the former way of perceiving, respect was paid because of some assumed and lofty position of power. Now I see women's collective works in the world are causing a major change in thinking, the beginnings of a paradigm shift returning respect to its sacred place in relationships. Out of respect, which translates into love and mutuality, all peoples can elevate respect for one another into reverence for Mother Earth.

Slowly, women are reclaiming this mutuality from our deepest emotions. Rather than seeking power over, I respect you because I feel you respect me. Feeling your respect is such a different perspective, but we can place our awareness to helping this paradigm shift and we can claim it and love it for its Divinely Feminine quality. Respect is energy common among friends.

When we are able to see and practice respect as a Divinely Feminine quality, it becomes larger. In its exponential form, respect becomes awe which becomes reverence. This is a thread the world needs us to weave. Now that many have left domination and oppression somewhere in our back stories, women naturally lead the way for respect to return to the culture in its bigger forms.

Reverence is the quality that shows deep respect for someone or something; it is completely missing when troops go to war. Reverence for the gifts of Mother Earth is completely missing in the extraction businesses. Women can slowly turn this around because we feel deeply about the Earth and her innocents. By speaking more clearly about respect and reverence, we will be able to cause the pendulum to swing back to more Indigenous worldview where we are one with Nature because we are from the Earth.

As a journey, your spiritual memoir can offer endless hours of enjoyment. You will learn about your evolution and discover new information about yourself. Perhaps one reason to write is to see and respect the patterns along your memoir journey. The keepsake of your life's adventures, your hardships, and your spectacular joys will teach the generations to come—relations and others—all will delight in sharing many of your secrets. These stories should not die with you. I love what Wayne Dyer said and practiced, "Do not die with your music still inside."[8] I am suggesting, one of your great giveaways at this pinnacle of your life is your very spectacular storyline that includes your treasured photos inserted into your story.

Sara Lawrence-Lightfoot responded to her own Mother's age in a holy way. For two years the two women sat together telling and hearing stories and a biography was produced. Daughter tells Mother's story in Balm in Gilead:

Journey of a Healer.[9] This treasure of a story came early in the Elder's years when Margaret Morgan Lawrence was 74. There are few finer ways to honor the Mother/Daughter relationship than sharing biographies, where stories of mutual respect touch. As is the case for many of us, this was only the beginning of the Elder's journey; in 2016 she is 102 years old!

In June 2002, Margaret said this in a commencement address, an Elder speaking to the heart of Youngers:[10]

> *Identifying one's own gifts means that you are able to use them for your own growth and enhancement. And in addition you may use them in the world, in your relationship with others, both personal and work-life. There will be myriad opportunities to assist others in calling forth their gifts. You can easily see how this process of identifying gifts builds on itself. At your graduation, I now charge you to have a major concern for your own gifts, from this day forward. I refer to gifts, which I might speak of as ego strengths ...*

Now that your reflection has begun, harvest your life-long gifts. The memory of you is your legacy gift, like this amazing centurion, Dr. Margaret Lawrence. May I say, if you diminish your life story, you diminish the gift of your memory when you are gone. Self-respect is ongoing all through life, and will be greatly enhanced by this whole look back into your life.

Keep the spirit that lives within you moving, one of the best ways is to share your story with your peers, do this for each other. Share your story with your heirs, this is your personal legacy and will live far longer than anything else inheritable. In addition to raising your self-regard, story teaches awe, wonder, and joy. These are the riches of life. Naturally, no life has all light, and some of the greatest teaching moments travel along a darker thread. Still your story is yours and will be told through your generosity. I promise you will learn something, maybe quite a lot, when you write your spiritual memoir.

How you have come to your own consciousness about your spirit life and your relationship to the planet Earth, this is the radical difference between you now and other generations of women who formerly occupied this pinnacle place on the Life Spiral. You caused this shift by casting off stereotypes and discovering your ability to see. Your involvement with the new level of consciousness was needed to make radical changes in all other stereotypes and assumptions. We are intrinsically connected because sometimes we can see and feel the Spirit that moves through all things. As often as Great Mother Earth demonstrates this, you have been reminding us that every living thing is connected as one thing—we are a living, throbbing ecosystem.

SPIRITUAL CRISES

I would like to acknowledge one of the more difficult paths for coming to consciousness occurs in a crisis known as the dark night of the Soul or the Phoenix Process.[11] Your stories need to be told, for within them lives an alignment with the greater flow of life from Nature. The connecting thread between women is very powerful because we survive such Soul challenges. Perhaps you would not call yourself a mystic, but I will because the forces at work invited by your Soul came from the Universe and gifted you with a deep spiritual experience. If you go into this story, now that you are out of the crisis, you will see how your consciousness shifted. You will learn that all of Nature worked with your Ancestors to gift you with expanded consciousness.

A crisis state is never fun or funny. When it's completely past, an opportunity will arise to search out the answer and understand why this happened to you. I speak from experience.

Several times in my life a crisis rocked my world, tossing me out to sea. Now safely encapsulated in a story with almost no connecting threads to pull me back under, I am able to find the gifts inside the experiences. Only Divine Guidance pulled me through and the same grand energy delivered the real gifts: Expanded consciousness, true fellowship with others in crisis, compassion for human suffering, and a deep, loving kindness without boundaries. I feel so blessed by all those trying experiences.

Women who survive suffering can personally benefit from this Soul-cleansing journey. Write to learn more, write to help others through their own dark nights and deep oceanic journeys. People hold remarkable stories of kinship that will benefit us all.

So you see these two paths—the first is a slow and steady opening, the second is an opening by crisis—essentially gifting all of us; we are a generation of living mystics. When you see this path of Creation, how your Soul travelled from a star, experienced life and prepares to return as Soul to that same home star, you have the vision of a mystic. Because there can be mistaken interpretations, we probably will not say this aloud to many, perhaps only to each other. Your spiritual knowledge about Oneness, this is what will heal the planet. Put that in your story. Your story will help others evolve and open their consciousness.

You can make your memoir small and modest if you wish, if that is your way. You can make it poetic and picturesque. You can co-create with one of your children or grandchildren. I am in the habit of saying, "Do this, please leave us your story that we may learn about you, that we may remember your life, that we may be filled with wonder about your longevity." You will cross the Threshold for this Spiritual Elder stage and find great freedom for more living and more joy and adventure. Use some of that time to become a story-teller, your beloveds will feel cared for if you leave your life story as your legacy.

YOUR LEGACY GIFT

Each woman will offer her legacy gift in a unique way. These suggestions may only plant a new seed in the beautiful clamshell that has held your life stories, certainly they are fluid and flexible. You know yourself and you know how to accept help. For all your loves, and there are many, you want to leave behind something of yourself when you cross. If you sweetly lift off the planet without this final giving ceremony, then that is your way.

Being ever more conscious women, we learn that those lessons experienced are one of the reasons for this Earth walk. In your young pre-pubescent bundle, you practiced judging and critiquing. These are two of the most common discernments from your large brain capacity. In your First Flight bundle, you learned to compare, then you put people, things, even yourself in categories. The usual dualities—good or bad, fun or boring, happy or sad—entered into your thoughts and your language. For your Legacy story, this is the time to unwrap all your Spiral bundles, those sacred packages you assembled when you journeyed through early Life Stages and crossed many Thresholds of your child-self, your youth and adult-self. This easy summary will follow your life chronologically until the sacred place when your consciousness opened. When you discovered the secrets of the Universe within you, you learned you are the Universe and we are One. This worldview inspires you to share how the stages of life opened you, invited you and finally revealed your inner divinity.

Your Beautiful and Blessed Lessons

May we say, every lesson is a pearl? Your lessons found their natural place in your story. When you string these lessons together, when you highlight the events of your life, you will see in all new ways how your Soul has been with you all along. You will also see the trajectory of your journey from the beginning to the end. This is the time to string all your pearls.

APPROACHING THE LAST 13 MOONS

As we have shared all along this journey, embracing change is a high calling, sometimes more than a challenge, and the only way to find grace. Remember how, from the Bloom of our womanhood through our timeline, we have each become radically different in our orientation and our world-views. This is the Threshold when all of that merges into wholeness and finally into Oneness. You have always been One with Source. When you crossed this Spiritual Elder Threshold, you rejoiced in acceptance. Life has been glorious, it has been a struggle filled with suffering, but more than any description I could choose, you know best, your life has been all yours.

You can see ahead, only one Threshold remains and at some point, you will need to consciously begin detaching from the earthly pleasures and possessions. Naturally, the loves who remain behind after you cross over, these tender hearts are the hardest to release. This is the holiest of all your earthly experiences. My dear friend and Mentor, Shirley's story follows as the one who taught this by example. Her words about detachment, as an action verb, taught me how to approach the last 13 Moons.

To enter the realm of conscious dying in this century, change is coming rapidly; your beliefs are as sacred as ever, but the language is evolving. Measure what you believe against what Elizabeth Kubler-Ross[12] found in her 1965 research. She presented the 5 stages of dying and went into great detail to explain how, in the last century, this was the model: Denial, anger, bargaining, depression, and then ultimately acceptance.

Eastern thought has influenced a new way of thinking in the West, helped by the Midwives or Doulas of the hospice movement who offer an evolved service of care and devotion for those who wish for a conscious death. Learn how Death may be only a doorway, talk about how it has been revealed in your life, how Death has influenced your spiritual maturity. Find a Doula to talk to about how to evolve your own thinking. You might even ask her to attend your Threshold ceremony and come for a Moontime visit that will begin your personal vigil and ceremony for your crossing.

You will remember the particular catalyst of change which waltzed you across your Spiritual Elder Threshold. I have shared many cups of tea with you and you have taught me acceptance and joy and wild diversity of character. I say this knowing we are Source energy, you and I, we are of one Source.

A Ritual for 13 Moons

SHIRLEY HARDY'S STORY

I first met Shirley in 2007 when I was a newcomer in town. For more than 20 years Shirley had been the behind-the-scenes coordinator for the Gardenia Center in Sandpoint, Idaho. I am sad that I write in past tense, for Shirley's time on Earth ended in 2015.

With an unmistakable radiating energy, the Gardenia Center became a spiritual hub for our little town. Shirley barely had a title although she had a long list of little jobs. To post on the announcement board or into an email newsletter, everyone worked with Shirley. Every time I did, she explained it was not supposed to be her job, but it was.

My second winter in Idaho's Panhandle, a weather anomaly happened. Before New Year's Day, the snow piled high along every country road and by the first of February 2009, the Panhandle had received 6 feet of snow on the level, and snow-blowers had created 8 foot tunnels. In the midst of these continuous weather events, I had lined up activities, which included weekly lunchtime talks at the Gardenia Center, called the Brown Bag series. Shirley was out with the weather, too, much more than she wanted to be. While I was dipping my toe into the community, all that weather gave her the catalyst she was looking for to pull her whole self out of responsibility and involvement. This is the paradox of age, as I learned from Shirley. She and I talked about this: We are given the dual gifts of capacity and days; we do what others call us to do until the number of days require us to do for ourselves. As Shirley demonstrated so beautifully, something else called her to be a quiet presence before she was called across her Spiritual Elder Threshold.

Shirley and I became friends in the springtime when she invited me over to her little garden plot. I began to see her story as a picture. Once married and Mother of two children, Shirley loved to go way back in time and tell her little child stories. I loved that her inner child was always present. She marveled at her early beginnings, how idyllic the farm life had been for her and her sisters. Her parents were gigantic influences. She loved to reminisce and she loved to spin her memories into snippets, little stories.

Both of us were busier that we wanted to be, but I could see that I was gathering some of those little stories about Shirley. Before she moved to Idaho's Panhandle, she was the driving force and organizer for the Siddachalam Ashram in New Jersey. She had decided to follow a Jane Monk, Guruji. His name was Acharya Sri Sushil Kumarji Maharaj and he refined, some would say perfected, the science of sound behind the Namokar Mantra. This part of her story is for others to tell, as I lack enough details to relate how deeply this shaped Shirley's life. She talked about it more as a container for spiritual development and practice than in the story form of her young adulthood. I do know that she was the worker bee behind the scenes.

The suffering caused by divorcing and separating from her beloved family soon dissolved into a need and a special ability Shirley found inside of herself, to help build a new ashram, from the ground up, into a spiritual center. Practicing and teaching yoga were supportive roles for her, and she met a woman who continues to anchor for both of us. That is Maria. After Maria left the ashram and moved to the Panhandle, so did Marilyn Chambers and so did Shirley and so did I. Soon I found my yoga-swami, Maria, by neighborly geographics at the same time as I found Shirley. The two have been essential for my feeling of belonging and sense of awakening to my higher self, my inner mystic.

Shirley gave some of my questions of attachments a wave of her hand. We had reached her age of detachment and she really heard God's message. Now I know that she had completely processed each part of her life and left it to rest. What a grand teaching, being with our Elders as they release. This is an ultimate demonstration of mindfulness and how we can stay present with one another and in the moment.

Sometimes I like to take an Eagle's view and see the patterns. Much more is at work than we can understand, our Soul's orchestrate far beyond what our imaginations are capable of doing. Isn't it a marvel that I moved to the Panhandle to find Shirley, after she had been here with her friends for so many years? Not lost in the pattern of this orchestration, I say, isn't it a marvel that Shirley and Maria are such long-time friends? My connection is just as my Soul intended this to play out for me.

An Old Stack of Stones as Vigil for Becky

There are more layers: Becky Kemery was another one. Shirley and I also had Becky in common as friends although we never formed a tight triangle; that is, I was never in their company at the same time. When Becky crossed early, Shirley pulled me in closer. We both needed each other to grieve but Shirley wanted me to finish Becky's work. I love Becky's work with the feminine and masculine coming into balance with Earth energies, but my work is separate. It connects I agree, but while Shirley was still living here in Idaho, I found it difficult to talk about my work. My thoughts had not yet fully formed and I was just coming into alignment with the gifts I had to offer.

ELDER ENCORE

Shirley had an encore in her early Elder years that was deeply satisfying for her. She had acquired a computer program and machine that would recreate the frequencies of most earthly blends of plant medicines and minerals. She would charge distilled water with these frequencies, making homeopathic remedies. I completely believe in homeopathic medicine, less is more and intention to heal is the power behind the belief. I had personal experience with homeopathic medicine and remedies before I met Shirley.

To gather more of her stories, a while after Shirley left the Gardenia Center for her Elder Encore, I quit much of my busy-ness in our little town, 15 miles away. I found time for many lovely visits to her little rural cottage and a couple of homeopathic cures. Through many common threads, Shirley and I became fast friends. On one of her excursions to visit a friend in Washington state, she took me with her. I have never felt so thrilled to peek a little further into the lives of two old friends. Friendship is a marvelous adventure of the heart. I see how it nurtures spirits of women and I always want more of that juicy and deep connection.

Shirley held my own journey up for me to see, she even talked about it with others. More than anything, I was clearing the way for a future version of myself as Elder Guide where I would show women how to see their Soul more clearly. She sat and listened to me when I told the story of the *Great Catch-up Ceremony*. Twenty-five women, including Maria, stepped across a Threshold to spend the winter of 2010-11 with our stories, in liminal space and time. This initiation was co-led by our mutual friend, Becky. It was spiritual because we had carefully set the stage by storying the major change events of our lives, it was liminal because we entered a metaphoric bubble with a beginning and an end. Becky reluctantly took her Elder Shawl in ceremony because her Soul guided her to before she crossed. Shirley and I talked long about how Soul surrounded each person and received reminders to guide our earthly adventures. I see now that Shirley mentored me through story and by example, by presence, and through great love that grew between us.

Shirley's Departure

SPIRITUAL ELDER

You could say I was shocked when I dropped by and Shirley was packing. She had visited her family in Massachusetts the season before, she had a great granddaughter climb up on her knee and say, "I miss you Grandma." A more powerful change agent cannot be found, those words worked on Shirley until she spun into action. The Threshold of her Spiritual Elder appeared before her, she did not hesitate to step into the action of liminal space, although she probably did cogitate a fair amount. What I saw was the most graceful move I could ever imagine.

When that Threshold appeared she merely floated over it. For one long season of 90 days, she packed and snipped all her ties with people in the Panhandle. Those days were liminal for her as she described them. She was

Divinely led to each step through each day and found the golden wonder in her experience. Everything was Divinely directed, God-guided, from listing and selling her little house, to releasing her land and her much loved possessions. She kept only what would set up a little apartment in Massachusetts, she sold her car to the woman who took her to the airport and she was gone. Her possessions went by container and were waiting for her when she arrived. Swoosh. The magic of transformation wrapped around her and everything changed.

I tell this story because of her example of the God wrapped grace she felt. She used intention and courage, tightly woven. She used every skill she had accumulated in her years of living. Her Soul needed the experience of being near her family and relocated her one last time. We shared many phone calls, sometimes for two hours at a time. Telling our stories takes time.

I asked her to be my Elder Mentor while I journeyed through a year long initiation and she was glad to be a part of that process. She always wanted to feed me information, she wished I was part of the Gaia network, but I saw Shirley clearly. She was plugged in and absorbing all of the old material being presented in new ways and delighted with every single day. Our last communique, she sent me the YouTube for Gregg Braden, telling me that he is part of everyone's Soul cluster, one of our Masters. When I was with Shirley, I felt that she was a Master!

During the summer of 2015, Shirley's body began its release from the Earth plane. She had a stroke that would fill her with emotions she had not felt for decades, if ever. Under the care of good medicine, prayerful friends, and her very capable daughter, Shirley suffered her release until she could suffer no more. She passed on Saturday, September 19.

I will mostly miss her excited storytelling and her radiant smile. All of her wisdom crossed with her and reminds me that our stories matter. If I can glean what her example taught me, it is to live all-out every single day that we have, to share our stories because they do matter. Someone will remember that we were here, that we polished the gifts we had to give the world, and when we complete that task, we released to cross in peace. As I write I find so much more to share, as with all of us, there is always more to share. Shirley shared her inner light freely; hers was a life well-lived.

Shirley had the deep love of family, hundreds of friends, thousands of acquaintances. Each one of us holds and tells a little piece of her story in our own way. She will be remembered long and now will guide from the other dimension when we need her. As her daughter said in the quiet announcement of crossing, may Shirley rest in peace.

To this I add, may we feel love and give it as freely as Shirley did.

Reverently, respectfully, and in my own joy filled grief, I bid you adieu again my friend. We will talk often. You have my great heart of love, Gail

She carried Buddha's smile

FAVORITE SHIRLEY HARDY QUOTES FROM HER GARDENIA TALK IN JUNE 2014:

"We are all light beings sharing a similar vision and together we are part of a growing bubble of a living, loving consciousness that is touching everything existing around us as it continues to express itself."

"Each and every one of us are to be commended for our individual role in carrying our torch and holding to our beliefs of a dream being created. We have joined many other communities around the world and the momentum of the worldwide communities continues to grow. Our individual light of consciousness has connected to all the others and we gather together in the loving acceptance of all who are participating in this wondrous movement as it continues to spread around this earth and far beyond into the future."

"There is a higher order running this show and the vision becomes much clearer when we look down at the larger and greater picture. That is when the clarity presents a clearer view. Worry and confusion blur our view and diminish the perfection that is being presented. I accept the possibility that there is no limit to how far this can be directed as we put the limitations on ourselves."

LITTLE BLESSINGS FROM THE OTHER ELDERS: GIFTS FOR THE SPIRITUAL ELDER

After you cross your butterfly Threshold, an integration occurs.

✳ Preparing for this tender time, use forgiveness to invite change, which is outside of ordinary time.

See how you are one of many Evolutionaries™ using grace to model a good life all the way to Death.

✳ Mind-Body-Soul has actually been the creative force leading to your longevity.

✳ You may be your own agent of change.

As a modern mystic, staying as teachable as you have always been, will bring younger women knocking on your door seeking your wisdom.

✳ Spend time with your Soul; walk in Nature; wander around.

✳ Invite the transformative energy to hollow you out and to take you into an altered state.

Longevity is a fact of your life now.

✳ If you are able to cast off *old age* as a spell, consider casting off, at least in metaphor form, *retirement* as another spell.

✳ Youngers are always attracted to Elders. Begin an intergenerational circle. You and your friends create deep culture while the Youngers create pop culture.

✳ Discover how the culture operates through interdependence and collaboration. In little bands of women, little tribes and circles, swirls a magic juice for thriving.

Please tell the whole story of how you became the woman you are today.

* Much about life needs processing again, the story of your life waits to be gathered into one elegant bundle.

* How have you created this life filled with stories?

As a journey, your spiritual memoir offers endless hours of enjoyment.

* Tell us about your memories and we will give you the gift of delight for all that you share.

* Your stories are so sacred as to be God-like and they need something from you: Honor and respect.

Continue your practices as an ultimate modeling for others in your Village.

* There is more to learn, there is more to experience, even on the days when you say "no more," you know there is more.

* You grow your own seed, you are what you think and eat, your body speaks of care and love.

Shirley asks us to remember, "We are all light beings sharing a similar vision ... There is a higher order running this show ..."

NOTES FROM THE SPIRITUAL ELDER PASSAGE

1   By writing *Composing a Further Life*, anthropologist Mary Catherine Bateson reminds us, so well, that times have changed. Now the life cycle is different from 100 years ago. The magic number seems to be 100, the new age we all want before we cross. We do live in a miraculous time and we can hold the archetype of old age off for as long as we are able; we will know.

2   David LaChapelle produced such a lovely volume of the I Ching, *A Hymn of Changes: Contemplations of the I Ching* (2009). The place between Heaven and Earth is known as Peace, the 11th hexagram.

3   One of my wise Spiritual Elders, Loie DeLaVergne, sparkled when she shared with me her favorite author and storyteller, Jean Kirkpatrick. I love a good story, so I have devoured 3 of these marvelous historic novels and will read all of Jean's work, woven in with my favorite non-fictions.

4   May I recommend a work of fiction that illustrates the idea of a spiritual memoir. In *The Boston Girl,* Anita Diamant's lead character is asked this question, "How did you get to be the woman you are today?" I consider this book a superb template for women of a certain age to tell our life stories. Sharing our stories will cause our traumas to lessen and our authentic identities to step forth. Life events may seem ordinary to us, but to the next generation, our daughters and our granddaughters, stories that shape us will be historical references and important models; our girls will experience challenges we cannot imagine.

5   *Science and Sanity: An Introduction to Non-Aristotelian Systems and General Semantics* was originally published in 1933. In it, Alfred Korzybsky (1879-1950) was the first to describe the two filters through which the world is experienced, the first is one's grasp of language and the second is the inherited structure of the nervous system. Filters means that the world is not experienced directly, but shaped, inherited from Ancestors, what they knew and taught influenced by the environment. Nature and nurture are both components of Korzybsky's time-binding theory.

6   Master sociologist, Brené Brown from the University of Houston, has changed the face of shame, vulnerability, worthiness, courage, and intimacy. She continues to publish her research for readers: *The Gifts of Imperfection* (2010); *Daring Greatly* (2015) both meant for self-discovery and *Rising Strong* (2015) brings the conversation about shame and worthiness into the wider spheres where life revolves around others—home, work, church, and community service.

7   *Respect: An Exploration* (1998) was written by Sara Lawrence-Lightfoot, a much more comprehensive examination of respect than I'd bargained for, but it stands the test of time. Brilliant.

8   I began asking, "Who were you born to be?" in your teen years, and repeated this as the message from Saturn at age 29 and 59. In 2001, Wayne Dyer wrote *10 Secrets for Success and Inner Peace* (2001) based on the most important principles he wanted his children to live by. The one that replicates my question and rolls off one's tongue easily is, "Do not die with your music still inside."

9   Sara Lawrence-Lightfoot uses the voice of Daughter telling her Mother's story in *Balm in Gilead: Journey of a Healer* (1995). Margaret Morgan Lawrence was 74 at this telling, but is 102 at this writing. Women needed the barriers cracked; Dr. Margaret was the first African-American woman to achieve degrees from both Cornell and The School of Medicine at Columbia to become a physician in 1933 when most white women and all black women were turned away.

10 This irresistible quote was found by searching Margaret Morgan Lawrence, a wonderful example of a Spiritual Elder. These words are found in the middle of a short commencement speech given on June 1, 2003. http://www.swarthmore.edu/news/commencement/2003/lawrence.html

11 In author Elizabeth Lesser's book, *Broken Open: How Difficult Times Can Help Us Grow* (2004), she weaves her own spiritual crises around others' stories she has labeled the Phoenix Process, as the mythological bird who rises from the ashes. Many, if not most people experience a darkening event linked to the Soul. With raised awareness, we can find the message from Soul buried in the ashes.

12 Elizabeth Kubler-Ross wrote her seminal book *On Death and Dying* in 1969 and the conversation began. Over the past 40 years the paradigm has finally begun to shift toward consciousness and dying as a natural combination.

DEATH PASSAGE

THE INTENTION:
FINDING CONSCIOUSNESS IN LIFE AND IN DEATH

If you have arrived or are nearing this final Threshold, I offer you my 13 Moons Blessing. You are a Daughter of the Earth and Sky, you have been Sister and Mother to yourself, you have loved the Moon as your Ally. Remember my beloved friend, you have held your gift of life with respect, and you have touched so many. Your legacy is rich and will live on long after you cross this Threshold. You will remain vivid and alive in our hearts. Let's work together for this time remaining to design a conscious experience for you to open the doorway and to cross over into the heavenly dimension beyond.

You are rare and precious, one among us is so revered and indeed so exquisite, we feel inspired to express how you are the one we love truly and will deeply long for after you are no longer in your physical body. We feel privileged to call you Great Grandmother. When you separate Soul from body then we will love you more tenderly, sweetly, and longingly because we feel the loss of you: You are our Spiritual Elder facing your last 13 Moons.

The treasure trove of your wisdom belongs to all of us. We have been gifted by your stories. You are the amazing one who has seen extra decades none of the rest of us can even imagine, you have seen another world and touched another time. Holding all the changes one life can hold, you have crossed all of your Thresholds except the one ahead, Death.

Your journey has been long enough to know Death already, perhaps intimately. At the beginning of this long Earth walk, I promised that Death is friendly and walks along with you through all of life. For a quiet moment, think of all the big "D" and little "d" Death encounters your Soul revealed to you. Without apology, you have learned enough about Death to know all those characters—family, friends, and sweet pets you have loved—now wait to welcome you home.

For me to be writing about Death and for you to be reading about Death, we must smile at the agreement that we made coming to this earthly experience: No one gets out alive. And still, Death is nothing at all. Soul is the essence of your being, when it slips across the veil into the other dimension, naturally it leaves behind your body, the vessel you have loved. That precious vessel is now worn-out. At Birth, this became the motion of life: Live fully to learn all the lessons your Soul asked to learn and find ways to dissolve judgments about them. By that time your body will be tired. Each human comes with this same contract with Death.

DEATH IS NOTHING AT ALL

Death is nothing at all.
I have only slipped away to the next room.
I am I and you are you.
Whatever we were to each other,
That, we still are.

Call me by my old familiar name.
Speak to me in the easy way
which you always used.
Put no difference into your tone.
Wear no forced air of solemnity or sorrow.

Laugh as we always laughed
at the little jokes we enjoyed together.
Play, smile, think of me. Pray for me.
Let my name be ever the household word
that it always was.
Let it be spoken without effect.
Without the trace of a shadow on it.

Life means all that it ever meant.
It is the same that it ever was.
There is absolute unbroken continuity.
Why should I be out of mind
because I am out of sight?

I am but waiting for you.
For an interval.
Somewhere. Very near.
Just around the corner.

All is well.
Nothing is hurt;
nothing is lost.
One brief moment and all will be as it was before only better.

©Henry Scott Holland

This piece is shared at many funerals.[1]

BELIEFS AND REALITY

Every single human, billions strong, who walks on this great Earth holds a different view about Death. While the result is precisely the same, the beliefs about that result are widely variable. Some think "Blessed Death," and thrill with the idea of afterlife, some will consciously anticipate the relief, and others are less enthusiastic, still hoping they will recover from their illnesses. The entire spectrum is represented, individually colored by each day of life lived.

I am no different than you. When my first clear consciousness happened, I was 44 and ripe for my *shaktipat*, a deep awakening to my spiritual life. Mine is not what you think, yours is not what I think. We each must take time to be with our thoughts, our beliefs, including the big topics: Source energy, God, Birth, Death, Goddess, Afterlife, Dante's Inferno, Angels, Satan, the Bible, the Koran, Bhagavad Gita, Mother, Father? We have practiced who, what, where, when, and why on these along with other key words. By deciphering these mysteries for ourselves, we have released fear by deciding among our choices and pulling the threads of belief into a weave that belongs to us. We are not rigid and we are ultimately flexible; events have change and shaped our beliefs. I love what I believe and so do you, with all our hearts.

Death was the one concept that I could find peace with, probably it was the first concept. I found the peace and understanding, even the necessity of Death before I found peace with life. When I didn't die, in several of my close encounters, I found the holiness in life, my gifts had yet to be delivered here on Earth. When those gifts have been completed, accepted as gifts by others, then perhaps my Soul will be more useful on the other side of the veil between the dimensions.

CONSCIOUSNESS AND CONSCIOUS DYING

I have enlisted several friends into this conversation about conscious dying and about consciousness itself. Long ago I found my way to be with Death through a near death experience, but opening to converse about it, that is stimulating my own consciousness. My esteemed editor, Janis Monaco Clark, has listened to my views and shared her own excitement about a book, *The Fun of Dying*. This book demonstrates how our minds open to consciousness without actually knowing that is what we do, or without using that label.

"Before Death, what is Life? Life is consciousness and consciousness is all that exits. Each of us is part of consciousness: Matter is composed of consciousness: dog, cat, tree, rock. The start of conscious thought is the Birth of the Universe, the Big Bang.

"Consciousness is a kind of energy not like material energy. It does not obey material laws, there is no time or space. The laws of physics only exist in the material universe, a small part of the greater whole. You never began and you never end. The minds of every living human being and everyone who ever lived are part of one continuous thread.

"There is no "I." Consider, there is no such thing as private thought: Your consciousness is open to all consciousness and all who have come before; privacy is a human concept and it is an illusion.

"The basic force of consciousness, God, is unconditional love beyond all understanding. Whatever you have asked for, believe you have received it and it is yours. In Death we remain connected to this consciousness we've always known."

Janis included this very sweet note: Thank you, Roberta Grimes, author of *The Fun of Dying*, for these insights.[2] Linger on these words, read them in observation of the many little deaths that surround daily living. We could not possibly live without Death.

EVERY DAY DEATH

I embrace openness about Death and dying as a tender way to relieve all the fear still flowing from previous centuries. I feel supported in my views with the teachings of Ram Dass.[3] As a teacher, he has brought many Eastern philosophies to our Western minds, but he has specialized in Death instructions for the past decades. I can be overwhelmed in the Autumn with the Death of everything around me. It's a perfect time for this ritual meditation: Death is coming to greet me, Death is coming to take me, I am ready to go home. When a loved one crosses, they wait for us on the other side.

Bubba's Last Walk

One by one, over my years of conscious awakening, I have been curious about many other concepts and found peace with my own spirituality, and my own daily practices of renewal. Perhaps you remember reviewing your spiritual beliefs in the Womanhood Bloom stage of your life. They were fluid and flexible then; they can remain that way until your dying day. Now you know more from decades of deep inquiries. Have you found peace? Do you want something more? Can you name that and ask for what you need and want now?

Because I have encouraged you to bring your beliefs to the surface, I want to imagine that the despair held by past generations will be transformed into peace inside of you. This sense of peace has the capacity to prepare you for the time of your Death. Preferable to unprepared, you feel ready to surrender to cross this next Threshold, free of anger or fear; you arrive feeling prepared. This is not an ending and that concept needs some emphasis. This is the next stage of your Soul's journey. There are more choices ahead.

Being forthright and open, I have deeply considered this tender place, facing Death. I support conscious dying, at home if at all possible, with a Death Doula who supports your ceremonial crossing. All through the 20th century, many of our parents and our grandparents modeled something different. By not speaking and not sharing, their deepest feelings and their bravest thoughts were buried in fear and denial. I felt the high privilege to witness the baptism of my 80 year old Dad one Sunday. He trembled in fear but all he would say was, "Just in case."

Conscious dying creates spaciousness for the sweet presence of your Soul. You have an opportunity for healing, yes, healing your fear by speaking your truth. Always a mystery, exactly what happens at Death? Our age of information has slowly begun to change the fear of dying into more of a final, earthy, spiritual experience. Many books and sites tell about near-death experiences. Perhaps you have had close encounters with Death. For the final story, I am going to share my own.

In their seminal book, *Who Dies?* Stephen and Ondrea Levine[4] write of the 200,000 deaths on each day in 2012, "Some died in surrender with their hearts open and their minds at peace."

As a biological and spiritual being, your final transformation will be wholly biological and miraculous. Lewis Thomas[5] in the *Lives of a Cell*, said it in this forthright way:

"We will have to give up the notion that death is a catastrophe, or detestable, or avoidable, or even strange. We will need to learn more about the cycling of life in the rest of the system, and about our connection to the process. Everything that comes alive seems to be in trade for something that dies, cell for cell."

Each time we have been ill, we had an opportunity to contemplate our impermanence. Illness is a grand opportunity, often wasted, to explore the way we are living life and to explore how we view Death. A crisis of illness often reveals what we are most afraid of in living and in dying.

You have opened your mind to meet the unknown with openheartedness; all your lifelong practice with courage now allows life its deserved fullness. Whether in the newspaper headlines or obituaries, reading about others' deaths reinforces your survivorship. Your depth of experience with Death has prepared you for this final gesture of life. When you realize the many incarnations of your Soul without your body you will recognize the false logic in the debate between mortality and immortality. During your quiet moments, reading, walking, meditating, you sensed the presence of your Soul. You have long known your Soul is a timeless being, part of you but able to separate from your body in flying dreams, in near-death experiences and other altered states of being.

TO ACKNOWLEDGE IMPERMANENCE

Acknowledgment of impermanence holds within it the key to life itself: Your body is impermanent but your Soul is eternal. What is the truth of the presence we experience as that timeless being who has been our constant companion? The essential and eternal essence I call Soul with no hesitation is a force which seems to have no beginning in which we sense no end. Since early in your conscious life, you have walked hand in hand with your Soul as a daily practice.

An Elaborate Ceremony for Death

One whose wisdom I carry with me as a small and secure knowing is Crazy Horse. He reportedly said, "Today is a good day to die for all the things of my life are present."[6] Since my near death experience in 2000, clearly an initiatory and spiritual event, I have walked with these words on the surface of my heart. That experience showed me how Death has always walked with me. The presence of Death has helped me know my Soul and led me through spiritual experiences, witnessing many Deaths and just as many Births. I have learned about my attachments, how material things are sticky. My teacher, Shirley Hardy, showed me her process of detachment and how it became the source of her great peace.

Each of us who step onto the Life Spiral discovers how mortality is the certainty of biology— that we all do die. We learn about immortality because our Souls, the essence of our being, cross over into another realm. Do we dare say that Soul survives? Search through your beliefs and how they were formed; this truth you need to discover for yourself.

Just as you have moved through all the Passages, learned to live in the wholeness you have found at each Threshold, this final Passage is designed for an elaborate celebration of your imagination. You have lived life fully and well. Your dreams will all be released into holy completion. This is the moment to come to peace with your mind that insists on more. You have had more, now is the time to release even that attachment.

Notice how fear, guilt, anger, confusion, and self-pity can be left at the Passage doorway where each of those feelings arose. At each Passage Threshold, you assembled a bundle as a sacred part of your life. Those many parts were real; they lived in your mind and body. And then you released them in exchange for living into the next Passage. Notice too, how much fuller your life has been by doing your rituals on a daily basis. You have learned to recognize the many ways Death has walked with you through each moment of your life. You are wholeness, ready to release the breath keeping your body alive.

EACH THRESHOLD NOW HOLDS A BUNDLE OF STORIES

By consciously bundling your ego-self and securing your stories, you have found the purpose of consecutive Thresholds: A gentle detachment, a small "d" death, for all that went before—stories, loves, births and deaths—allows them to die away to greet each new Passage. In discovering more of your humanness, you have learned detachment; you have practiced death rituals at each of the Threshold doorways to advance into more consciousness. Now you deeply understand the great gift of these consecutive Threshold ceremonies. Your expertise with death rituals, has prepared you for Death, you have had practice with enough other moments, and you are prepared for this moment.

Remember all of your ceremonial rituals. When you reached the Womanhood Bloom Threshold around 30, you did a Death ritual for your first 29 years as a recognition that all of Childhood and all of Adolescence had passed. You have been practicing mindfulness for years already, you fully understand the past is no longer part of this moment of living.

There is no perfection, there is only embracing the wholeness of your Soul, acceptance of the agreement between life and death and now the final detachment is possible because you have grown your Soul, you have added to her overall experience as an immortal being. She wants to release the body of you and travel on.

In finding peace enough to allow your Soul to travel on, you realize that Soul has been the watcher all through your life. She is the being-ness of you who now rejoices and longs for freedom. I believe your heart is your Soul, through your work on this Earth walk you have enlarged your Soul by enlarging your heart.

These 13 Moons are here for you to say goodbye and see you later. By working with ritual your whole life through, you have broken through the conditioning of the culture. Your Death will be a celebration of wholeness that you have embraced through life. Notice how inadequacies like shame and guilt are in your past, they left when you began your love affair with resistance and stopped resisting your life in all it messiness. When you learned to see and to love resistance, you also learned to see and love denial. You know how these are cut from the same cultural cloth as fear and anger.

Your woman-self was privileged to have so many opportunities to experience the Death of each egg that once had the capacity for life and for Birth. Then your Moontime became both a meditation for Death and a preparation, using intention, for a bigger life experience.

Long ago, you discovered the answer to this simple question, what is your relationship to Death? You release more than 400 eggs, one at a time. By doing ritual with the Moon, you sat with little "d" death and you sat with your menstrual pain until both dissolved into memory. When Moonpause came, an entirely different transformation was required. From hot flashes to weight gain, this was a wholly new Threshold for growth. Moonpause ushered you across the Deepening Womanhood Threshold and became the Divine opening for your Elder years. Once again, transformation became an energy driving new ways of being with life and death.

As an Elder, you felt the poignancy of each passing year. Your bundle of memories include so many Deaths: As you face this final Threshold, these images may be helpful … Grandparents, parents, children, pets, seasons, trees, plants, little road kills, and too many cat-killed birds. Be with the images that arise. Feel the hooks of emotions that come.

ENTER THE POSSIBLE

I love the very practice of reviewing my illnesses and injuries. When I put my mind on them, they seem so clear, so real. They are now an illusion, plain and simple. Each one of your past illnesses and the imminent frailty of the immediate future, offer you an opportunity to be with your Death. These experiences will help you find the essential nature of yourself as more than your body.

In my early years of studying Rites of Passage, I was interested in past lives because my friends were talking about Raymond Moody's first book, *Life after Life,* and quickly we all found the Brian Weiss' book, *Many Lives Many Masters.*[7] Both doctors are Ivy League trained psychiatrists who have investigated many angles of death experiences through case studies. Their books, the early ones and those more recent, follow the journey of Soul; a fascinating way to open up your thoughts and open up your heart to the inevitable that is about to happen.

Just like the choices that were made before you were born, your Soul is the instigator of an agreement with the terms and conditions of your Death. Life is lived for those lessons which have increased your Soul. All along your life journey, every kind of help has always been available to you. Let us call on those Divine Angels and Guardians now. You may be like me, an interesting menagerie of critters have also helped me through many lessons.

You are always the model for your relations. All that you do with your time remaining, if it is an actual 13 Moons, one year plus or minus, will teach all those who follow you how it might be when their time comes. If you followed the suggestions in the previous Passages of your life, all that came before the Spiritual Elder Threshold, you have probably finished your legacy stories. You have put your photos in order. Together these form the legacy, the only part of you that can be left behind in this life. These are more precious than money or possessions because they are you.

Prepare your own list of things to do, so this transition will be quiet and filled with well earned respect. I suggest this sequence only to inspire your imagination. How it looks is wholly up to you. You are the mystic now.

As my Spiritual Elder friend taught me, Shirley worked through her *attachments* to release them. She knew her transition was imminent when she talked to me about *detachment*. Touching in with Death for you, I remember this now, the detachment process that Shirley was working through. She prepared a final list of gratitudes for her life, she accepted and detached from her hard lessons, her most wonderful memories, and finally she spoke of her treasured relations.

These are lofty concepts and deserve a few days of your prayers—attachment-detachment, gratitude and acceptance. This is how you come to peace within yourself and this is how you share the grace of that peace with your loved ones.

GIFTING OF YOURSELF

You created your spiritual memoir for yourself, but if you feel your time is near you may want to create a presentation ceremony. This is the keepsake of your life, the compilation of your stories. Someone needs to be the keeper of your stories, your daughters and your sons, this seems natural. They will feel inspired to begin the gathering of their stories. Your grandchildren and great grandchildren will be participants and recipients as well.

Talk to your beloveds what you believe about Death so they can find the same peace as you. This has been a thread of your life; you have worked on beliefs for five or six decades. Do not hold back now. Let your people know you must leave them but you will be nearby. Tell them you know this because of who waits for you on the other side. A few people have been waiting for you, watching over you, soothing your ruffled feathers for some time, many of them for a long time.

Please share what you wish for your parting ceremony when you do cross the Death Threshold. You deserve your final wishes and ritual is your model. People will talk, they will grieve, you need to help them do this one thing for you. The most important part of conscious dying is talking with your beloveds. This is the one step most of the last generation did not always complete before they crossed.

I once knew a woman known as the Grand Dame of Pahrump in Nevada. All her life she had been a journalist so she worked long and lovingly on her legacy story before she gathered her family around her. She was 100 years old and felt quite ready to cross. Her gift day was also her ascension day, and quite a party was underway. Her children, grandchildren, and her closest friends were on a treasure hunt to locate their special gift hidden in her drawing room. They would know it when they found it because they were connected to it their whole lives. Concealed somewhere for each relation was a tiny digital drive with their name and her gift of story.[8]

Beloved Great Grandmother and Spiritual Elder, standing at Death's door, you have been teaching us life and its expansive capacity beyond all the stirring and the busyness of adult life. As surely as Elder is the Threshold beyond Adult, you stepped across your Spiritual Elder Threshold to move into a place of ease and quiet watching. Like the baby you were when you learned things, you watch. Now your capacity to see further weaves with your deep inner world. You watch like the teen you were when you mimicked other women, oh that was fun. As a dear old woman and our Spiritual Elder, you can see the necessity of this watching; you absorb life for weaving and to offer back your wisdom.

Finding one's true self has always been the task of the youth. It was never easy to stay on the course trajectory with your gifts, being true to your one authentic self. This was the task of the Adult. As Spiritual Elder your eyes watch your daughter, now a Grandmother. You are the beloved place holder at the pinnacle of the Spiral. You moved gracefully into this honored position to make room for maturity and increased capacity so your progeny may grow through their adult and elder years. Your graceful acceptance of Spiritual Elder made room for the Mothers and Grandmothers of all the little children.

OLD AGE FINALLY DELIVERS GRIEF

Decide what your level of security is for the days of your dying. To be fully conscious, morphine must be limited. Can you be with pain to be conscious? Do you choose a conscious Death for yourself and your beloveds?

You have given your all to this lifetime; your heart is full of love. Long ago you made amends because you need to enter this sacred time free of angst. Now make amends to yourself. Put your lists away for another life or give them to your beloveds. Speak your final regrets. Move past those emotions with grace to bring yourself ease. Take your sweet time. Invite your Death Doula to help you and when you're ready she will close your chakras and through this Divinely Feminine heart practice, you will leave through the top of your head. You will feel your last act of courage in this body knowing this is a safe journey. A knowing enters the sacred air you breathe. Mull this over in your mind.

> *dying is like being born | an invitation to open your heart |*
> *be with your heart | invite a sense of completion |*
> *release expectations which cause suffering | die your own simple death*

Teach your Family to Prepare Quiet Rituals

The day arrives for your holy crossing. You have a Doula present with you who is also ready to help your loved ones grieve. In the 20th century, history changed Death and dying, large numbers lost in wars erased old rituals. Pain and grief over your body coming loose of your Soul-spirit can be so very real that forgetfulness overpowers the peace of preparations. Death will be sad, even messy, possibly painful and likely absurdly hard at time. You know this. You've talked about it, your generation has brought back lovely rituals to accompany you across this Death Threshold. Remember to trust your preparations.

Even though you decided 13 Moons ago, your time approaches. No one can ever be entirely prepared. Yet Death happens, to every person. Like the glorious moment of your Birth, this moment is just as inevitable. Surrender, Darling, your Doula will help your family grieve. Reach out to all those hands waiting for you.

GRIEF

Grief brings tears, wailing even, it brings flowers and candles. Grief inspires everyone to tell their version of your stories. You had a little idea how to cross over your Threshold, you have no real control over how your loved ones will grieve. You could ask for a wake, a community gathering out in a meadow, you could ask for the spontaneous sharing of love. After you have asked for these little details, you will have to make this part of your surrender.

If this is your Threshold, worry not about the consequences. Grief offers lessons to those who are left behind. When you are on the other side, rather occupied with your next stage of being as a Soul, a traveler between lives, you will have many opportunities to be a thought floating through their hearts.

Trust your great nature and all the light will call to you and sing to you. Go to the light. Be with your body for completion, send loads of love. Sing your song with the light. If you are left behind, tell the person who crosses, they've only died.

TRANSFORMATION

Like the melting of an ice cube
Earth dissolves into Water
At Death's early appearance
The edges of your body begin melting
You may call out when you can no longer move
Then water dissolves into fire
Fluids stop moving through the body
Transformation is as lovely as it is inevitable
As the fire element encounters those fluids
Your body begins to cool
Solidity decreases, fluidity increases

From solid to fluid to air
Through each stage more ease comes.
You begin to feel light
And you become pure light
The feeling of Death
Exactly the opposite of Birth
Is such a pleasant experience.

© Gail Burkett

A Stone Vigil for Friends

A FEW DEATH STORIES

First though, a prayer for Souls to whom I formed special attachments while they were on the Earth, beautiful relations and dear friends. To Fern and Leo, my parents and to five wonderful grandparents who made everything seem so fairy-like for those 17 years when I was inside the bell jar of my early development: I will be with you again, soon enough. I often think of other relations I have loved who are no longer in this dimension, and too many friends to name. I could tell a few more stories but I will let them rest in peace. In my inner circle, here in Sandpoint, Idaho where I have felt so loved by community, I treasured my long visits with Lois and with Becky. They both died when they would have much preferred living on.

When researching dying, as in what had happened in the most recent of my three near-death experiences, my visual-perceptual-spiritual understanding expanded. I immediately saw the many intersections in my life where Death has been present. I was seconds from being pronounced dead, when a surgeon decided to slice me open from my pelvic bone to my breast bone to repair internal damage. That was 2000 with my dear husband-to-be, Kenny, by my side. It was a rather interesting time to be 50 and begin the new century.

As I pull in God's sweet air and push it through my body, oxygenating my blood and my brain, my fingers and toes, I know how miraculous my life is, and your life is, and all of life. My diaphragm moves up and down, with or without my conscious mind, and that is a miracle worth noticing. Before the rare surgical repair, it was ruptured and sucking the life out of me.

Strange as it may sound, it was so much like the song-chant, *Opening,* I continued to encounter my fully consciousness heart about Death. From that car accident which also broke the Atlas bone on top of my spine, a memorable encounter with Death began to unfold only nine months later.

It was Summer Solstice, 2001, a ceremony and celebration of my doctoral work began next door to where my dear old Dad lay in semi-consciousness. So the story unfolds—the same week that I received my PhD and became a doctor in academia's eyes, my Father, a marvelous family doctor, crossed over his Death Threshold. I felt I knew nothing about Death and needed to learn about consciousness—life and death, living and dying, grief and loss. Everything knotted into a tangle and I walked every day for a year to untangle the knot.

Walking with my dogs to grieve my newly departed Dad, I learned about grief. Happy to know about honoring his memory in this way, I found this Father Daughter story poignant, as one might think. I also discovered deep regret, celebration, shame, and joy. Look at all there was in the tangle. As the months moved along, my walks became deliciously longer and longer, this was such a luxurious way to discover mindfulness. The ecosystem was very rare, a healthy edge of mountain and desert, a true ecotone. Blending these two languages of discovery, the ecotone and expanding consciousness, brought an unusual harmony to my deep well of grief. Close to the end of a year of walks, I felt like a blessing had been bestowed from the Ancestors. My own Father was long gone, he had become an Ancestor standing with those on the other side who had welcomed him home. Some of them I know about, his parents and grandparents, but knowing names and a few sketchy details of their lives, is hardly *knowing* them. I think this is why we are born with imaginations.

It was Mother who taught me about 13 Moons, that was what she wanted for herself. She really wanted solitude. My Father had crossed one year before and I didn't want her to be alone on that anniversary. Mother told me when the house was in moments of deep silence, she saw the Red Fox come to the glass of the double French doors and peer in. Because he came around a few times and lingered so peacefully, Mother decided that was Dad, offering her a hand to ease her across the Death Threshold.

She accepted and the next thing I knew, I was on vigil at her bedside. I watched very carefully as my Mother crossed over. Her passing was quite unexpected; just the week before, Kenny and I had visited her and she seemed fine. Mom and Dad were married 56 years, only they could appreciate that high level of intimacy. She had spent her time mourning, remembering, releasing and was ready to go. I thought standing by her bedside, she was once solid, now she's becoming fluid. As the hospital staff informed us that her organs were shutting down, I imagined that the fire was going out of her, the chakras that once spun with energy and often in pure alignment, were becoming still like air.

Mother lingered for 5 days, enough time for the whole family to gather around. I walked my dogs, felt the stress of the family, and my thoughts swirled around this Death Threshold. Vigil at Mother's deathbed felt doubly powerful because waves of grief over Dad's loss seemed to return. Although I had mourned deeply and grieved intentionally, Mother lying there seemed to double my loss. Regrets flooded me around my parent's fear of dying. I could never break through it, they would not discuss this Threshold with any of their children.

When she did become one last thread, a whisper of radiant air, she breathed her last breath into my ear. She had opened her blue eyes after five days of being comatose, I leaned over to say my goodbyes and wish her a good journey. I was assuring her that Dad was reaching out and her exhale came into my body. At first I was afraid of this omen. Then as time passed, I learned that her last breath insured our continued connection.

I walked with her in silence for another year, wondering about our strange and often estranged relationship. Now, almost 15 years later, she comes into my thoughts less often, but her phrases still fall from my heart onto the page I am writing. Love is very present in these years after unlike before, when I felt unsure about the emotional field that often felt energized between us. I have not forgotten her gifts to me. Because I received this double Death story without their conscious participation, I began to consider how I want my story to go.

LINGERING LONG ENOUGH TO LET GO

Take a breath with me. When I consider Soul as the bringer of lessons, even I cannot fully appreciate the dimensions of that deep knowing. Each one of us, living through seven or eight decades, can review lessons brought by our Soul. With each review, we can discover new understanding.

We have the rare opportunity to change culture. Because we can we must. When you imagine the Death ceremony you wish to have for yourself, do you wish to remain conscious? Many of us are called across the Death Threshold to be of more service as a Soul from the other side. This is perhaps the highest form of service. Attending to one's crossing in a conscious way, and giving the heart and mind attention to the subject erases much of the fear of dying. There is nothing to fear, it's an energy exchange. Your Soul chose your body for this one incarnation, one of many before and one of many to come.

Be very deliberate in your planning, you literally can have your celebration any way you want. Often to bring your family to such an agreement, you may have to talk it through long before. Ask them to give thought to their celebration, this will make it a much bigger conversation.

Together, in these pages we are beginning to understand how Soul works with Death to encourage appreciation of our sacred vessels, our bodies. Over the year of journeying with my stories, 2014, I placed each Passage, each little part of my life review, into sacred bundles which wrapped each Threshold in forgiveness and highlighted my teaching stories. So much trauma has penetrated my body and your body, we have been influenced by our emotional and spiritual intelligences.

Some of my life stories have revealed impermanence and immortality to me. Soul works with the body to harmonize all incoming influences and to have growth experiences. I am deeply grateful that my many encounters with Death have taught me the guidance of the holy breath, the present moment, and storytelling with my sacred sisterhood. I would like to hear your story now.

We have these big subjects to talk about, until our dying days. Our experiences will teach us so we may share our teachings, we will learn from Death. As in life, Death offers teaching on detachment, legacy stories, and how to hold a much longer vision for the Seventh Generation.

Dearhearts, carry lightly your stories about Death, the doorway is only a moment, a sacred, holy moment and transformation will be complete. I am about transformation rather than endings, so allow me to honor you with this Namasté and a wholehearted bow: See you later.

Death's Doorway: Walk on Through

GIFTS FROM THE OTHER ELDERS BEFORE YOUR DEATH

* Surrender, Darling, your Doula will help your family grieve.

* For the last hooray, do not be too sad, Dearheart, be glad your body served as well as it did, be glad for all the love you received. We have prepared carefully and together every step of the way. If you feel you still need something more, contact a Death Doula and read this little checklist together. I wish you only peace.

* You are always the model for your relations. All that you do with your time remaining, if it is an actual 13 Moons, one year plus or minus, will teach all those who follow you how it might be when their time comes.

* As in life, Death offers teaching on detachment, legacy stories, and how to hold a much longer vision for the Seventh Generation.

* As a complete being, your final transformation will be wholly biological and miraculous.

* Conscious dying creates spaciousness for the sweet presence of your Soul.

* We smile at the agreement that we made coming to this earthly experience: No one gets out alive.

* The treasure trove of your wisdom belongs to all of us.

I abbreviated this checklist from Ram Dass; I cannot resist sharing. From his book, *Polishing the Mirror: How to Live from your Spiritual Heart* : [3]

"If you are to die consciously, there's no time like the present to prepare. Here is a brief checklist of some of the ways to approach your own Death:

• Live your life consciously and fully. Learn to be present in your soul, not your ego.

• Fill your heart with love. Turn your mind toward God, guru, Truth.

• Continue with all of your spiritual practices: meditation, mantra, kirtan, all forms of devotion.

• Be there for the death of your parents, loved ones, or beloved animals. Know that the presence of your loved ones will remain when you are quiet and bring them into your consciousness.

So long.

Totsiens.

Goodbye.

Adieu.

Au revoir.

Tschüss.

¡Adiós!

Arrivederci.

Shalom.

Allah hafiz.

Sala kahle.

Toksa.

See you later.

NOTES FROM THE DEATH PASSAGE

1   Including a funeral poem feels odd, but perhaps it's comforting to know that *Death is Nothing at All* (1987), book and poem with the same title by Henry Scott Holland. Even the conversation about consciousness, limited or expanding is personal, although the family would love to be included. In fact, we could help our friends and beloved relations if we included consciousness in our conversations.

2   Almost tongue in cheek, Roberta Grimes, author of *The Fun of Dying* (2010), releases all the drama of Death and inserts a dry humor. She calls herself the Afterlife Expert, and I have met several other women who are specialists in this afterlife vocation, so I know her claim to be serious in spite of the genuine light lilt in her writing.

3   Ram Dass offers his teachings freely in many books and endless videos. Perhaps, in the last 13 Moons, taking in more information will offer ways to release. Perhaps no more is needed. We are all so different in our needs. For podcasts, videos, blogs, and books—many to support the bereaved as well as those departing Souls, comfort can be found on this cross-cultural and interfaith website: www.ramdass.org

4   For decades, Stephen and Ondrea Levine have been on the lips of many who speak of Death or bereavement. Together they have written a dozen major books about Death. I was moved deeply, when I was drafting this Passage to discover that Stephen passed on the very day I typed his name into an Internet search, January 17, 2016 at age 78. I feel indebted to this couple for their fearless devoted vigils and offering a bit of solace for thousands of Souls who crossed. Like their friend Ram Dass, there are many hours of CDs available at www.levinetalks.com/

5   Lewis Thomas, in the *Lives of a Cell: Notes of a Biology Watcher* (1974), gently reminds us thinking animals that we are biological, like all of Nature.

6   Win Blevin wrote of the life of Chief Crazy Horse in a rather magnificent biography called *Stone Song* (1995). I have personally been guided by these words since I read them, "This is a good day to die ..."

7   My curiosity is insatiable, but I am not alone. Raymond Moody's first book, *Life after Life* (1975) began the string of experiments into the phenomenon of past lives and regression hypnosis. Brian Weiss' book, *Many Lives Many Masters* (1988) kept the conversation going so strong that the reading list now includes more than 50 authors and that, as they say, is just the tip of the iceberg. www.brianweiss.com/reading-list/

8   At the very end, do I dare tell you this is fantasy? This is how I want my last day on Earth. I have worked hard on this manuscript, *The Grand Dame of Pahrump*, part three of a trilogy, but I have not finished yet. Maybe I will work on that next.

EPILOG

I advocate creating a more conscious and peaceful world by reintroducing an intergenerational practice of community initiations, Rites of Passage ceremonies for all ages and stages. I offer this book as an opening to the larger conversation we need to hold in our communities. In old initiation stories, rituals included death and rebirth; this may be why the long threads from our Ancestors' ceremonies were laid down on the ground.

Most people call the change which is so complete that the old self and the new self barely recognize one another, a transformation. Every person has this reflection, transformations happen to everyone living. Our culture could grow up considerably if we learned to simply celebrate the natural growth we see in all our relatives, adopted and related.

Ceremonial Life Spiral

At this planetary time, we are meant to call forth ancestral and blended traditions from several cultures and immerse ourselves back in nature to find our metaphors for change. I am only one among many helping to bring Rites of Passage and rituals of maturity celebrations back into our lives because it is necessary to be seen and necessary to feel developmentally mature and whole. When a person is visible to family and Elders, our world is a much safer place than otherwise. It feels wonderful to be in a conscious community.

CEREMONIAL SPIRAL

Everyone can learn to see. Seeing into this Spiral of Life with my Elder eyes, I see nine distinct stages marked by biological development. More markers may be discovered, but I suggest we start where it makes most sense for everyone. The nine stages around the Life Spiral are biologically timed. Teaching awareness and ceremony for these stages of development feels urgent: The old self must give way to the new self with a small "d" death ritual.

Within extended families—aunts, uncles, parents and grandparents, nieces, nephews and all of our adopted relations—enough adult-power exists to get this started for the youngest ones coming up in your community. Babies must have a ritual that becomes part of their own mythology. Those who are seven will soon be eight, they are the ones we offer a Rites of Passage to next. There are many compelling reasons to welcome initiations for every biological and spiritual life Passage.

The Life Spiral

© 2016

I always ask, "Where am I and where are you?" Each of the in-between spaces represents experience, teachings, and skills building. With a practiced eye, I can help you find yourself. This is known as the Life Spiral because Earth's four seasons and their half steps, the cross-quarter days, spiral each one of us through our years.

Seeing yourself and your loved ones around the Life Spiral brings a new understanding of how change comes in increments. Time stretches between each portal of change, enough for trainings to build a life. We can each relax in considerable comfort between the edgy times. To see and be seen on a level of one Soul appreciating another, that requires a bit of practice. No one is an expert. These ceremonies are for all of us. They may be especially valuable to witnesses standing on the sideline, considering their own quest for personal evolution and answers.

One of my favorite elders, Clarissa Pinkola Estés (Dr. E to her students), says we all know how to do initiation; it's an instinctual and ancestral birthright, it's in our blood. Lack of experience may be our only excuse and I hope and pray to fill that void with stories of Passage rituals. No one requires complicated instructions to gather up family and community and acknowledge a change is eminent or already happened, especially change that can be seen in our biology or behavior.

The wholeness I wish to see is a Village of people, a community in cooperation, tied together by geography and heart—communities networked and intertwined—to witness and celebrate initiations for the ages and stages of each individual. In the last century alone, the life stages in the Spiral have been elongated, literally changing how we live. Seeing through developmental eyes, two stages of each clearly appear—two child, two youth, two adult, and two elder stages.

If not now, then when? If not you, then who? Let's work to make this the great Evolutionary leap of the 21st century. I feel the Mentor's Spirit all around me; if you would like to contact me about Mentoring, about Passages for women and girls, please do not hesitate. gail@ninepassages.com.

AUTHOR'S BIOGRAPHY

Gail Burkett guides initiation journeys for women and girls through all their life stages, teaching about these developmental changes through ceremony and ritual. At the heart of this work, one's own personal story grows through time with the Moon and the Sun providing the framework to continually evolve.

As an Elder initiated by her peers, Gail knew that with guidance, greater depths of the Soul could be reached. Watching the culture, seeing

Gail Burkett, Author

that Rites of Passage for youth were being birthed all over the world, Gail wrote *Soul Stories: Nine Passages of Initiation* for all women from 30 to 100. This guidebook answers the need for women to be initiated, to feel initiation in their bones, before passing it along to their families.

For a decade, Gail gathered her life's masterwork. She offered initiatory ceremonies and wrote *Nine Passages for Women and Girls: Ceremonies and Stories of Transformation*. Once initiated into their own lives, women can bring Rites of Passage to their families and the whole Village. Everyone leaves home, for adventure, for education, and to find their calling; most build a new home, a Village, so their growth and transformation may be acknowledged.

Watching the culture for decades before and after her doctoral studies, Gail finally assessed her own hertory; this introspection was the key to unlock her inner mystery. She grew up in rural Idaho on a cattle ranch, descended from a strong line of pioneers. Fond of all she learned as a child and adolescent, she knew there was still more. Gail was actually shocked to find the wild and free 1960's in full swing when she went off to college. Coming to the party with an unconscious work ethic, she always worked at something. Her life purpose was very slow in dawning, but Gail discovered that life review work combines with ceremony to bring purpose to consciousness rather easily. She feels compelled to share the secret of transformation through ceremony. This is how Rites of Passage became one of the answers; remembering to play to balance work serves both Spirit and Soul.

The whole Village, honoring young and old alike, holds the future of Rites of Passage ceremonies. Imagine the potential of personal transformation, evolving the deepest sense of belonging to one's self. The markers for maturity follow a natural continuum from Birth to Death. Moving through life with these rituals is Evolutionary™. Join the movement and offer ceremonies to your relations. Gail invites you to become an evolutionary.

EDITOR'S BIOGRAPHY

Janis Monaco Clark grew up in West Hollywood, CA in a Jewish-Italian neighborhood at a time when Los Angeles was a beautiful mecca. She lived in a four-unit Spanish stucco apartment building where Andre Previn was once a tenant. Each of the four units was occupied by members of her father's family, who bought the building in 1946. In this intergenerational environment, ritual and celebration were the cornerstones of her life.

Janis Monaco Clark, Editor

Janis has worked for social change throughout her life. Her passion for tilting at life and ideas, like a feminist Doña Quixote, has led her to editorial collaboration with Elders and spiritual teachers. When she read Gail Burkett's first drafts of *Soul Stories: Nine Passages of Initiation,* she recognized the relevance of Rites of Passage to women as culture-makers.

Janis lives with her husband and dogs along the lower Clark Fork River. From her loft windows, she traces the cycles of the Moon across Montana's Big Sky. She is a Mother, Grandmother, Great Grandmother, Auntie, Mentor, and initiated Elder.

DESIGNER'S BIOGRAPHY

Laura Lee Wahl was born to a world of expectation, an upper middle class that provided a full education "ride" with strings attached. Strings that got cut, time after time. Comprehending the "folly" was a lifetime of work. It took her from the suburbs of Detroit, through rehab, decades of recovery, travel, a career start in New York City, and an escape to the west, finally landing in Sandpoint Idaho raising two beautiful girls as a single mom. Trying to make sense of it all, at her half way mark (50), she embraced the process of "Nine Passages of Initiation". There she discovered, there was no "folly" involved. She had done exactly what she was supposed to, exactly when she was supposed to, but had just done it with no guidance, no elders, no ceremony, no ritual and no tribe. As a middle child, she had walked the woods in magical awe, she entered her First Blood in secrecy, rebelled in anger through her adolescence then took flight and saw the world. Turning 30 brought her out west to start a family... all the passages at the right time.

For her own girls she wants a tribe around them to acknowledge and guide the process. No one need do it alone and that's what she has found; a tribe of women. "When I grow up I want to be an old woman" a line from Michelle Shocked has gained new depth, now what she wants is to be an Elder with something to offer the next generations of women. We can do better; we can teach and we can guide, but first we must understand our own journey. It's a beautiful, powerful gift.

Laura Wahl with daughter Sage

And she just happens to be a book/magazine designer with 25 years in the field of graphic design.

MY GRATITUDES

You, Dear Reader, top my list of gratitudes, your curiosity meets with the offering of this gift. How magnificent. I look out to the concentric circles of relationships that have shaped me and find many shining Spirits. These include family and helpers, my delightful council of Elders filled with Sister-love, and the gorgeous women I call Initiates.

Feeling the reflection of these beautiful people, I feel enormously thankful that everyone named here has stood in ceremony with me. My dear and darling husband, Kenny Olson, has sparked an eternal flame in me and held me through all times of sickness and health. Together we feel the comfort of knowing we are bound until the last Passage. We truly believe in the power of prayerful ceremony: Four times a year we stand side by side with our flower ceremony and speak our grateful prayers to the guardians of the Directions. Thank you, sweet man.

I feel deep gratitude for my family; we are characters, feeling and showing love in all ways. Each of the days of my life I have been shaped by my parents and grandparents, now on the far side. My siblings are geographically dispersed but spiritually connected and I feel immense gratitude for their good teachings.

I must mention my dogs (2 horses and 2 cats before them) to feel complete. As with all my other relations, I have been positively shaped by my four-legged companions. For their time on Earth, I have been monogamously related to these charmers, Ginger One and Two, Tiaga, Midnight, Bear, Kinau, Kioki, Sierra, Bubba, and Rosie. The gaps in my life, without a 4-legged present, well, those are darker days without the light of love keeping two eyes on me.

I have felt Sisterhood from two special women: Kathleen Bjorkman Wilson and Diana Eldridge. Tears leap to my eyes whenever Kath calls me Womb-mate, for we have truly known each other all our lives. That spiritual connection must be eons old. Our Mothers were friends and pregnant with us; from the womb-time, when they hugged, we hugged. Diana became the sweet light lifting my wings, first to heal my brokenness and hold me while my consciousness opened, then she stood beside me as a Sister. Each time I think of either of these gorgeous and loyal women, my hands clap together in the prayer mudra and I send them a kiss.

My beloved helpers have put arms around me and this project: Janis Monaco Clark is doula, midwife, Soul Sister, and extraordinary Editor for all of the Passage books, including *Soul Stories: Nine Passages of Initiation*. We have merged our energies to become Elder Mentors together, offering the profound joy of recognition to women we hold dear. Before Janis came Arianna Husband and Lorene Wapotich who spent hours talking about the Life Spiral with me. Laura Wahl is a shining wise spirit who pours her artistry into bookmaking. All four, in fact, have taken the Soul Stories journey with me. I honor you as Divine helpers, you will always have my deep love and gratitude.

Feel my arms around you beauties in my Elder's Circle, remarkable and loving women who share Fire and Water, Earth and Air. I didn't know you all until Becky Kemery, rest in peace, invited me to talk to you. When we met around a Fire Circle, I recognized at least half of the shining faces. All those beautiful women of the Inland Northwest Women's Council shared a grand celebration of the Life Spiral and clearly launched me onto this path. I feel your love, your devotion, and your Sisterhood. Thank you Maria Albergato, Gail Daehlin, Jane Sloan, Debra Duwe-Eagle Woman, Debra Williams, Hattie Goodman, Kay Walker, Kit Kincaid, Sandee Meade, Janet Daehnens, Brenda Roberts, Jennifer Ball, Dieka Gericke, Kara Sweeney, Sadie Johnston, Natasha Stone, Liz Manthei, Lisa Cirac-Krause, and yes, Becky Kemery. To complete my Circle of Elders, I offer recognition and gratitude to Nancy Smith, Chris Woods, Jo Davidson, Gayle Anderson, Nancy Schmidt, Karen Lanphear, Nancy Gilliam, Linda Navarre, Martha Hoxley, Marilyn McIntyre, Belle Starr, Diane Green, Paula Johnson and Janet Simmons. The Circle continues to grow! For the high privilege of witnessing one superb Native Sundance Women's Ceremony, I thank Claire Walpole, Karie Knoke, and Colleen Mooney.

For this journey to even begin, my sweet husband arranged for the first initiate to come out to the Wilderness. In 2000, Geri Brennan, sweet Mother now Grandmother, brought her beautiful 12 year-old bud of a girl Lauren Aunschusteghi, now Mother of two babies, for one week of womanhood training and Passage rituals. My helpers for that first ceremony, I give thanks to my darling womb-mate Kathleen Bjorkman Wilson, our beloved friend Diana Eldridge. We had such daring, grand fun.

Since that first Rites of Passage ceremony, recorded in *Gifts from the Elders: Girls' Path to Womanhood* (2004), a few more sweet Mothers and daughters have stood in initiation ceremonies with me: Accalia Carter and Anathea Woods, Kelley and Alethea Ward, Heather and Aresa Berry, Kara Oliver and Lena McCollum, Michelle Brown-Koval and Summer Koval, Aubrey and her grandma Debra Williams, Laura Wahl and Sage White and Mason White, Christine Corcoran, and Simone Poulin, Heidi Stewart and Emma Hogan, Jennifer Ball and Maya Goldblum, Jani and Sloan Davis, Cassie Faggion and Kestrel McLaren, Kathryn and Amelena Eagen.

I send blessings now to Sisters of my heart, daring and darling adult and Elder initiates: Rachel Rauch, Karen Porgozelski, Accalia Carter, and the three I call my Beauties, Kim Gridley, Julia Zalesak, and Sophia Rubedo. I learned so much from the first group of Soul Sisters, thank you Janis Monaco Clark, Arianna Husband, Judy Lay, Laura Wahl, Kit Kincaid, and Kay Walker.

One beautiful journey for initiating Women and Elders connects deep longing and many diverse ages. I am grateful for the opportunity to lead a group of initiates from Winter Solstice 2015 across consecutive Thresholds recovering Soul Stories together. Within the larger circle held by Elders, two smaller circles led by, Becky Jaine and Wren Wolf, thank you dear women. Together we all created a conscious collective, a magical and amazing group of women initiates who traversed stories and crossed Threshold well into 2016. The Elders will continue to hold for their long integration of 13 Moons which follows deep immersion and consecutive Passage ceremonies. Our guide was *Soul Stories: Nine Passages of Initiation*, I place my hands over my heart to thank you for you: Annah Sophia, Denise Dombrowski, Linda Northrup, Michele Burkett, Mila Mockoba, Sharon River Burdick, Natalie Bryant-Rizzieri, Deborah Hart Gift, Kanga Katrin, Accalia Carter, Rachel Hertogs, Iris Kelly Candea, Lorene Wapotich, Laurie Evans, Kelley Ward, Kimberlie Marshall, Sue Faggion, Lara Rosenberg, Rachel Baez, Betsy Dickes, Lisa Trevena Kruger, Alissa Eckstein, Christine Gerker Lennon, Adrienne Crum-Fincher, Jeanie Coen, Barb Longstreet, Terri Hull, and anonymous women who kept rather quiet, although they were watching and enjoying their own journeys.

I must remember all that nourishes me. For an elementary school gang of gardeners known as the Northside Edible Schoolyard in Sandpoint, Idaho, these mentors helped me while I have had the most fun of my life: Jill Edmondson, Michele Murphree, Janet Clark, Carleen Pratt, Gray Henderson, Deborah Hart Gift, and Perky Hagadon-Smith. Our joy is visible in good food and happy kids.

Journeys with all of these Dearhearts through the past 20 years kept my fire burning to complete *Nine Passages for Women and Girls: Ceremonies and Stories of Transformation*. Now I look to you, dear Mother and Grandmother, sweet Auntie and Mentor. You may have many women standing in ceremony with you, hopefully Mothers with daughters, Grandmothers with granddaughters. Let's bring Rites of Passage to our feminine selves, until we no longer feel parched. Then we can translate this material for the men and boys in our lives.

We have good mentoring to give one another, as a deeper sense of belonging and Sisterhood make us into stronger, more resilient, thriving women. The tools to begin the evolutionary journey in this Mentors' Guide are offered with endless love. We are **Evolutionaries**.™ Pass it forward until we touch the Seventh Generation. Then Rites of Passage ceremonies will be in the fabric of our culture once again. You know women we do not, share with your friends and family.

Thank you. Blessings from the Elders.

Om design by Laura Wahl.

MOON PHASE

EMOTIONAL BEING

PHYSICAL BEING

DATE

DAY

MOONTIME
WORKSHEET

Download color worksheets online www.ninepassages.com

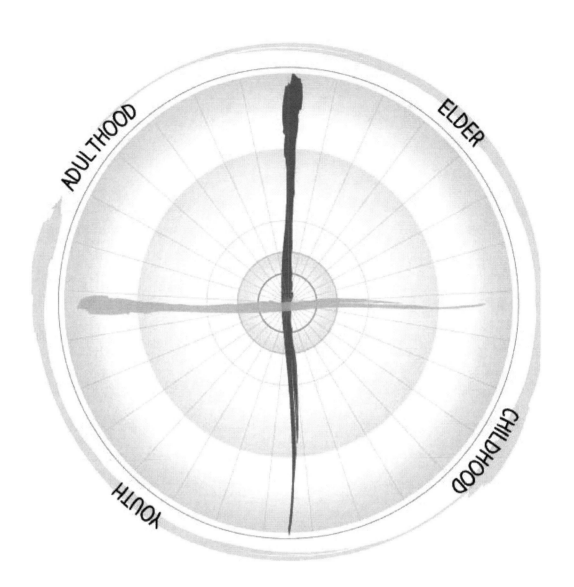

RELATIONSHIP
WHEEL

Download color worksheets online www.ninepassages.com

Made in the USA
San Bernardino, CA
28 June 2016